American Businesses in China

# American Businesses in China

## Balancing Culture and Communication

NANCY LYNCH STREET AND
MARILYN J. MATELSKI

*Foreword by* Albert Cohen

McFarland & Company, Inc., Publishers
*Jefferson, North Carolina, and London*

The Holiday Inn story appears courtesy of Six
Continents Hotels, Inc. (successor of Holiday Inns, Inc.).
Material on the Foxboro Company appears courtesy
of Invensys Product Management (The Foxboro Company).

Library of Congress Cataloguing-in-Publication Data

Street, Nancy Lynch.
   American businesses in China : balancing culture and
   communication / Nancy Lynch Street and Marilyn J. Matelski.
   Foreword by Albert Cohen.
      p.      cm.
   Includes bibliographical references and index.

   ISBN 0-7864-1544-4 (softcover : 50# alkaline paper) ∞

   1. Corporations, American — China.   2. Corporate culture —
China.   3. China — Economic conditions — 2000–.   4. National
characteristics, Chinese.   I. Matelski, Marilyn J., 1950–   II. Title.
   HD2910.S74   2003
   338.8'8973051— dc21                                            2002152807

British Library cataloguing data are available

*On the front cover:* The red and gold medallion is a traditional Chinese
good luck charm. People often give such "knotted art" to friends at
the Chinese New Year. The red symbolizes good luck and happiness;
the gold coin in the center symbolizes wealth. *Background:* ©2000
Artville, LLC.

Manufactured in the United States of America

*McFarland & Company, Inc., Publishers*
  *Box 611, Jefferson, North Carolina 28640*
    *www.mcfarlandpub.com*

To our families and friends—
you know who you are

# Acknowledgments

This book is a culmination of several journeys, actual and metaphorical, to understand intercultural relations between China and the United States. Without the candid insights of professionals on each side of the Pacific, we would have accomplished very little. We'd like to thank them all for their wisdom and their frankness. We would especially like to acknowledge the following for their insightful case material and conceptual development: Ravi Saligram, Carol O'Keefe, Vicki Gordon, Franklin Moore, Mahmoud Masood, Grace Lau (all from Six Continents Hotels); Paul Miller, Dan Carrie, Mike Godek, Ron Pariseau, Ed Westhaver, John Sun, Chris Du, Lu Yun (from Foxboro/Invensys); Shane Frecklington, Amy Gu (from AmCham Shanghai); and Shi Mingzheng and Yang Lihong (from CIEE).

For aiding and abetting our cause: Carolyn Matelski (proofreader *extraordinaire*), Wang Keqiang (interpreter and friend), Gu Hang, the CART Center at Bridgewater State College (BSC), the BSC Class of 1950 (for its generous alumni research award), the ORA at Boston College, Laurence Richards and Mary Saunders.

Finally, for graciously enduring our endless preparations for trips and interviews, as well as understanding our frustrations with computer crashes, missed dates and a general glaze over our eyes for the past five years, we thank our families and friends.

# Contents

# Foreword

## by Albert Cohen

This remarkable book was made possible by the unquenchable spirit and resolute perseverance of two dedicated and gifted academics, Nancy Lynch Street and Marilyn J. Matelski. Their mission: to offer fresh insight into the historic events of the distant past, culminating in the miraculous development and global stature of the world's oldest and most populous country. In the process, they have created an historic mosaic. They guide us on a memorable journey through centuries of cosmic changes from ancient times to modernity. Moreover, they have accomplished this Herculean task with a crisp narrative style, liberally flavored with anecdotal tidbits. This makes the journey not only more insightful, but a good read, encapsulating the cataclysmic social, political, economic and technological upheavals that engulf humankind to this day. Their revelations run the gamut from Confucian wisdom, to the cultural sea change created by globalization, to the irresistible and universal charm of *Sesame Street*.

Nancy Lynch Street's first book, *In Search of Red Buddha* (published in 1992), encompassed the experiences of two student-faculty exchanges sponsored by Bridgewater State College in the mid– to late 1980s, and included dozens of interviews with Communist Party members as well as Nancy's day-to-day experiences as the first American faculty member to live in mainland China under Bridgewater State's exchange agreement. Since returning from the People's Republic of China, Nancy has continued her dedication to countless students who have come to Bridgewater from mainland China for master's degrees. She has advised or served on numerous thesis committees, trained many students as teaching assistants or research assistants, and has made sure that everyone she "adopts" has living quarters that are safe, clean and affordable. (Often times, this devotion leads to one of Nancy's famous "charity drives," where everyone she knows is expected to donate blankets, kitchenware, clothing, canned goods, etc., to help a newly arrived Chinese student get settled.) She also invites them for Thanksgiving and Christmas dinners as well as her annual Chinese New Year parties.

Marilyn Matelski has long been fascinated by the Chinese culture as well, as evidenced by some of her more recent publications and presentations. Many years ago, I described to her the details of an important business transaction involving a high-ranking Chinese government official. When the pace of our negotiations seemed unnecessarily protracted (from my standpoint), my body language gave me away, whereupon this elegant gentleman responded with exquisite tact: "Mr. Cohen, in China, we *first* become friends; *then* we do business." I raise this story at this point because I still recall the unusual impact this incident had on this bright college student. She later told me that this episode provided valuable insight into the most efficacious approach in future negotiations with the Chinese.

The timing of *American Businesses in China* could hardly be more felicitous. China stands today on the cusp of sweeping change. A dynamic new leader will soon mount the world's stage. And China's recent membership in the World Trade Organization is yet another seminal event. The appeal of this book should be widespread. It should evoke great interest in the educational community as well as among business leaders, politicians and government officials.

For the co-authors, it represents the apex of their distinguished careers. Their challenging task became a labor of love. Fittingly, they were inspired by an ancient Chinese proverb: "The journey of a thousand miles begins with a single step."

*Mr. Cohen is a retired senior vice president of publicity and marketing at Winkelman's and Adjunct Professor of Marketing at Lawrence Technological University, Southfield, Michigan.*

# Introduction

    This book is an outgrowth of issues that have arisen during our years of experience teaching intercultural communication to university students in both the People's Republic of China and the United States. Over time, one's teaching style, content, and lines of argument are often modified as world events change existing contexts. This is especially true in the case of understanding, interpreting and acting upon intercultural communication principles. It also relates directly to American business negotiations in China.

    Since the 1980s, China has undergone significant changes in its social and institutional infrastructure (political, legal and economic), its transportation, and its communications networks — a veritable sea change — at least on the surface of things. This is particularly true in coastal cities, as opposed to China's rural areas (where some 800 million people live). Roughly 100 million Chinese now belong to China's "floating population," or *min gong* (migrant workers). With China's induction into the World Trade Organization (WTO), the *hukou* (system of permits to live in the cities) has been eliminated. Under this "progressive" and democratic surface, however, China is faced with mounting trials and tribulations, as state industries are dismantled, millions lose their livelihood and the "iron rice bowl, and protests abound."[1]

    The Chinese are not alone in their apprehension about the future.

Observers from abroad (including an often-critical United States) may wonder if China is progressing quickly enough, and how far it can progress without abandoning communism. But must China become a mirror image of Western style democracy and capitalism? Finally, what are the consequences of too rapid a conversion from a centrally planned, socialist economy (with its attendant social services such as health care, jobs for life, free education and care for the elderly) to a free market? Had this type of conversion occurred, as it did in Russia, without the requisite institutional and physical infrastructure, the results might have been catastrophic for the Chinese.

In fact, as we write, China's economic goal of a 7 percent growth rate each year from 2001 to 2005 is causing considerable unrest. The requirements of participation in the WTO (and "globalization" in general) necessitate far more than the reform of ailing state-run industries. They require a near–Copernican revolution in the thought patterns of Chinese workers— and not necessarily just the older generation of workers. As we indicate throughout this book, one must always be cognizant of the growing inequities in many areas— education, health care, economics, access to technology and infrastructure — between city dwellers and people in the countryside or interior provinces of China.

In the Western cultural context of communism and the Cold War, an assumption was often made that with the end of communism, the entire world would embrace capitalism. One need only visit Russia and several other Central and Eastern European countries to understand that this is not the case. We in the West have become even more aware of this fact after the tragic events of September 11, 2001. Recent protests and warnings from the Middle East suggest that some cultures may be resisting the globalization process and its ramifications. The Chinese, on the other hand, chose to embark on a path to join the world on its way to globalization directly after the end of the Cultural Revolution, which is to our benefit. And this decision may not be (and we can hasten to assert, will not be) to the benefit of — at least in the short run — most of the Chinese people. There will most certainly be repercussions and leadership challenges, which may, in turn, eventually evolve into a more repressive regime than the current one.

Within this prevailing climate, communication between East and West does not, and cannot, blossom. Each side sees the other through the prism of its belief system. Communication scholars and others have noted that we see what we want to see or what we are trained to see. If we in the West insist on seeing only red and evil intent in every action taken by the Chinese, we miss what is fundamental to China — a way of life created several thousand years ago. The current lifestyle is an evolving one, but one with roots in Confucianism, Taoism, Buddhism, communism and, more recently, developing roots in modernity and globalization. Thus, the "face" of China now reflected to the world cannot be a mirror image of the "face" of the West, but an integrated "face" with "Chinese characteristics."

Despite the impatience of the West, rapid changes have occurred in China, including the overthrow of the Qing Dynasty and the Emperor Puyi in 1911, the rise of Chairman Mao, and Deng Xiaoping's "open door" policy in 1978. More recently, Jiang Zemin paved the way for China's entry into the WTO in 2001. These extensive changes have tilted the Chinese worldview in the past hundred years. However, the Chinese refuse to surrender the 21st century to the West. Proponents of a "wait and see" or even a punitive attitude (like past Congressional battles with the executive branch of government to withhold most favored nation status toward China) may have to wait a very long time for communism to be overthrown in China. For, should the Chinese people (however unlikely this scenario might seem in 2002) decide to do away with the communist leadership and ideology, the political and social structure is not likely to be altered significantly. What may occur is social and political chaos, an end to growth, and an invitation to outsiders to once again plunder China as they did in the 19th century and the early 20th century. That the Chinese government and people resist such a scenario is scarcely novel.

In short, while Western political officials might appreciate the Chinese using some other designation for their form of government, this "new" government would function (in all dimensions) very like the existing government. The reason for this is because fundamentally, Chinese governments (on Taiwan or the mainland), regardless of professed ideology, tend to function out of their shared traditional and Confucian context. Further, while Chinese may emigrate to other lands, they remain Chinese. No better example of this exists than in the contemporary joint ventures with overseas Chinese.

Despite the lingering Cold War mentality, the anticommunist hostility and paranoia, China is not, as some have suggested, "the new Evil Empire." Understanding China requires much more of us than the scintillating trivial designations assigned during the Reagan and early Bush eras of diplomacy.

## RAPPROCHEMENT

China's post–World War II persona began with the restoration of its seat on the United Nations Security Council. After its reinstatement to its place in the world power structure, Chairman Mao and Premier Zhou Enlai then sought rapprochement with the United States. The resulting 1971 visit to China by then United States president Richard M. Nixon (masterfully orchestrated by then secretary of state Henry Kissinger) formed the spark that ignited the prodigious changes which began in China, following the deaths of Chairman Mao, Marshal Zhu de and Premier Zhou Enlai in 1976. This episode in U.S.–China relations is still viewed as one of the most significant events in modern Chinese history, paving the way for Premier Deng Xiaoping's new socioeconomic policies.

From 1976 until his death in February 1997, Deng Xiaoping opened China up as it rarely, if ever, had been opened before his leadership. By the mid–1980s, China had begun a series of plans designed to gradually alter the economic, social and political posture of China. Prior to Deng's leadership, China had followed the communist model of planned economy, communes and egalitarianism. When China "came out" under Deng, however, there was a great necessity to move a nation of more than one billion, two hundred million people in new directions. This called for new "carrots" and "sticks." The proposed changes also had to be made with several important elements in mind: the existing hierarchical structure, ideology, education, natural resources and cultural context. As a sign of the changes to come, in 1978 China adopted a second constitution granting rights to education and freedom of speech; the right to demonstrate (with approval); and "women's equal rights with men in all spheres of political, economic, cultural, social and family life."

## THE FOUR MODERNIZATIONS

China launched its drive to modernity in the early 1980s with the Four Modernizations— the development of industry, of science and technology, of agriculture and of national defense. Much of the public political rhetoric of the 1980s focused on these Four Modernizations, as the government concentrated its energies on development of the internal and external networks, relationships and facilities necessary for yet another Asian "miracle." In 1985–1986, the Chinese media, including the ubiquitous loudspeaker system found in every Chinese work unit across the land, reiterated — morning, noon and night, and in Chinese rhetorical fashion — Deng Xiaoping's call to arms: "Education must face (serve) the four modernizations, the world and the future!"

Chinese intellectuals, still wary after having been only recently restored to their former place in the hierarchy, responded with the intense effort needed to teach the still-growing populace to use the necessary tools for effecting change. Amongst other efforts, the Chinese set about acquiring the necessary language skills— English, Japanese and other relevant languages, as well as the language and skills of technology. At the same time, they sought to restructure and downsize state-owned enterprises while seeking joint venture capital and establishing external relationships strategically targeted to achieve their goals in industry and defense.

# EAST AND WEST—THE FOREIGNERS ARRIVE IN CHINA

Foreigners *in situ* were needed to achieve China's new goals; it was within this context that foreigners from East and West were drawn to China. Many Westerners became sojourners (or "English missionaries") in the 1980s, quite innocent and unaware of the developing drama in which they were to play their parts, according to the norms of Chinese culture. Their motivations were mixed, often generated by the lure of the exotic lands of Kubla Khan, tales of the Silk Road, the writings of Jesuit Matteo Ricci or the novels of Pearl Buck. Others— entrepreneurs— saw China as a kind of last frontier for capitalism. Still others came to teach … and while teaching, spread the gospel of Christianity. Few of them, even the "overseas" Chinese, were prepared for the China they envisioned prior to landing in Beijing, Shanghai or Guangzhou to begin their adventure. In addition, there was the forbidden lure and malevolent lore of Red China. Often, they might be asked, "Aren't you afraid? What if you are imprisoned — how will you get out?" Clearly, many globetrotters from the United States carried with them myths and assumptions— most of which they would not recognize until they experienced severe culture shock.

The Chinese, on the other hand, were operating under yet another version of myth. Its Cold War characterizations of the United States as warmongering and capitalistic, intent on global hegemony —cultural, military and economic — still lingered in Chinese attitudes, as did the parallel American version of the Cold War mythology. At the level of macroanalysis (cultural) and microanalysis (interpersonal interactions), even the Chinese "intellectuals," recently oppressed and exiled by the Chinese government, sometimes viewed the Western itinerant scholars with suspicion. Meanwhile the peasants, many of whom had never seen a foreigner *(waiguoren)* before, were much more empirical in their investigation of these "round eyed, big noses," and would crowd around Westerners in the marketplace and in the streets, touching their clothing, hair and face, laughing and pointing. To them, Westerners were such very odd creatures, but not at all threatening. The Chinese were the Han, "the people." Westerners were (they may have felt) sub-human or "the others."

As Westerners we (the authors of this book) were often puzzled, as they came to know the "intellectuals" (not the peasants), as to what the Chinese believed in; for we felt that one must believe in something. Pushing Chinese colleagues to answer, we only became more puzzled. Laughter or no response was a common answer. The preoccupation of our Chinese colleagues over dictionary definitions and the desire to know in endless detail the syntax of the English language, combined with the lack of privacy as we understood it and the lack of control over our daily teaching schedules and free time, was devastating to our psyches. We were not permitted to participate in decision-making and we were virtually incapacitated by the incredible amount of time, once a request was made in writing, for the answer to come back. Neither our Chinese friends and *confidantes* nor we Westerners knew it at the time, but we were on the cutting edge of cultural context — and we had little leverage and few tools for discovery.

The nature of our relationship, however, was that of an educational exchange program. It was a "win-win" situation, and ultimately trust began to develop. Trust is a necessary condition for interpersonal and intercultural communication. Our Chinese colleagues began to help us understand the culture; we began to help them to better understand Western culture; we shared perspectives. In sharing, we each came to know not only the culture of the other, but our own — both for the first time. Eventually, we *min gong* returned home — and over the years, many students from our Chinese university came to study in America, while other colleagues and American students went to China. Without these relationships, it would be difficult, if not impossible, to understand this nation's whirlwind development within the last two decades.

## China Today

The China of the early 1980s, when Deng Xiaoping introduced his policy of the Four Modernizations, had little to offer in the way of good roads and modern amenities like refrigeration, indoor plumbing, telephones, or kitchen appliances. Water for human consumption had to be boiled, and women cooked on coal stoves. Today's China reflects the years of intensive work to improve living conditions. It has more good roads, some plumbing and refrigeration, and many consumer electronics like televisions and computers. Videos, including new releases, are available. International hotels even provide air conditioning. On the other hand, the changes in ideology and policy have brought poverty to many. In addition, the privatization of industries—along with technological development—throughout the world has changed the political and economic landscape considerably (see Chronology). This is proving to be both advantageous and disadvantageous as we collectively enter the new millennium.

## THE IMPACT OF GLOBALIZATION

As multinational corporations sprawl across the map, the globalization of corporations no longer needs governments or citizen-workers—only cheaper labor. More and more, these corporations influence national and international policies as they gain access to cultural and physical resources—including raw materials, labor, underlying necessities such as roads and utilities, and financial, legal and political systems. These are all factors one must consider in the study of globalization and developing nations such as post–Cold War China.

Developing countries sometimes appear to want to "develop" according to Western dictates, as well as to allow Western popular culture to obliterate national historical culture. If this is the case, we are well on the way, as a world of nation-states, to even further dominance of the West over the East. However, many factors pose threats to the onward and upward progress of globalization. One major threat is that of terrorism. As we now know, terrorists (who often perceive themselves to be disenfranchised) exist worldwide; Al Qaeda and other terrorist groups span the globe, from Palestine to the Philippines. It may then be the case that the worst off today may, in the final analysis, not be the worst off in the future. It may be the case that each country involved may select not to play according to the rules established by the dominant West.

Interestingly, it is our observation that China may be a case in point. China may illustrate that the path of globalization yet to come is a thorny one, but worth the effort of traveling, with patience, diligence, and an appreciation for different customs, perspectives and worldviews. To this end, we have constructed this book accordingly: Chapter 1 attempts to provide some insight into the Chinese worldview—a fusion of Confucianism, Taoism, Buddhism and communism; Chapter 2 addresses the impact of globalization on all business ventures (and especially China); Chapter 3 discusses changing Chinese consumerism, highlighting large differences between urban and rural populations as well as a distinctive generational divide. Six case studies follow, dealing with specific organizational and corporate challenges in cultural and academic exchanges, co-productions, joint ventures and foreign investment. Chapter 10, "Final Thoughts," offers some general conclusions as well as suggestions to those interested in doing business in China. Appendices follow, with sources for updating statistical data about China for those interested, as well as a glossary of terms and extensive bibliography.

One last note: The "American businesses" referred to in the book's title are now multinational conglomerates. None started out this way — they were all American companies that have grown far beyond their wildest initial expectations. We have grown as well, in our understanding of the Chinese worldview, the Chinese consumer and working within a *yin-yang* environment.

# Chronology

## SIGNIFICANT DATES IN CHINESE-AMERICAN TRADE HISTORY: 1786–2002[1]

*Entries in bold are addressed at length in the chapters.*

1786    The Massachusetts Bank finances the first American ship, *The Columbia*, for the burgeoning China trade

1883–1885    China loses some of its colonies to France and Great Britain

1895    Japan forces China out of Korea and takes possession of Taiwan

1898    The United States proposes an "open-door" policy for China to trade freely with all foreign powers, despite China's loss in colonial territories

1900    The Boxer Rebellion erupts and is put down by the allied forces of Great Britain, the United States, France, Japan and Russia

1911    Revolution: The Emperor Puyi is deposed and a republican government is formed under the leadership of Dr. Sun Yatsen

**1915    The American Chamber of Commerce in Shanghai (AmCham) is founded — only three years after establishment of the American Chamber of Commerce (See Chapter 10)**

1916   The Republic of China falls

1919–1920   May 4th Movement period

1921   The Chinese Communist Party (CCP)/Communist Party of China (CPC) is founded

1925   Dr. Sun Yatsen, father of the Republic of China, dies, creating a power struggle between capitalist and communist partisans

1921–1927   China enters its first civil war period

1928   Chiang Kaishek becomes head of the capitalist Nationalist Party (Kuomintang)

1927–1937   China enters its second civil war period

1934   Mao Zedong begins his Long March from Jiangxi Province to Shaanxi Province

1937–1945   World War II

1946–1949   China's War for Liberation takes place, culminating in Chiang Kaishek's exile to Taiwan and the founding of the People's Republic of China (1949)

**1949   AmCham is discontinued in China (See Chapter 10)**

1950   The United Nations formally recognizes the Republic of China (ROC); it does not recognize the People's Republic of China (PRC)

1957   Mao's Great Leap Forward — a five-year plan to improve Chinese infrastructure — is affirmed

1957   First semiannual Canton Trade Fair opens to Westerners (except Americans)

1958   China's first television stations begin operating in Beijing and Shanghai

1960   The USSR removes all financial aid to China as well as the foreign experts who worked there

1966–1976   Another Great Leap Forward — the Cultural Revolution (CR) — takes place, with Mao and his "Gang of Four" (including Mao's third wife, Jiang Qing, along with three low-ranking political officials — Wang Hongwen, Zhang Chunqiao, and Yao Wen-yuan)

1967   All Chinese television stations suspend broadcasting due to the Cultural Revolution

1968–1970   Chinese television stations resume broadcasting, but under a new structure

1968–1970   A more moderate politician, Zhou Enlai, takes over the daily governing duties, and begins to restore China's diplomatic relations and trade agreements with other countries

1971   US table tennis team accepts an invitation to visit China; Richard Nixon reverses his position on diplomatic relations, lifts trade embargo

1971   US Secretary of State Henry Kissinger makes a "secret" visit to mainland China

1971   The People's Republic of China is recognized by the United Nations

1971–1978   Small, restricted groups of US citizens—"radical tourists" (including doctors, educators, scholars and union members)—allowed to travel to the People's Republic of China in small "study groups"

1972   US President Richard Nixon and Secretary of State Henry Kissinger visit China; the first American company representatives attend the semiannual Canton Trade Fair

1972   China contracts RCA to install a $3 million satellite communications earth station—the first formal contract between the PRC and a large American corporation

1972   The National Council for US-China Trade is established in Washington, DC

1972   Deng Xiaoping, vilified for his capitalist philosophy during the Cultural Revolution, returns to active politics

1973–1977   Over 400 Chinese technicians come to the US for training

1973   Chairman Deng Xiaoping speaks to the United Nations

1973   US business leaders create a new organization, the National Council for US-China Trade

1973   Boeing opens its Beijing office

1974–1978   Pullman-Kellogg builds eight ammonia fertilizer plants in China

1975   Trade negotiations between US and Chinese businesses enters a new phase, introducing more formal procedures by Chinese graduates of foreign language institutes

1976   Mao Zedong and Zhou Enlai die; Mao is succeeded by his protegé, Hua Guofeng

1976   Zhou Enlai's death and Hua Guofeng's subsequent rise to power create turmoil through China, leading to a demonstration at Tiananmen Square

1976   Deng Xiaoping is held responsible for the Tiananmen Square protest, and disappears from public life

1977   Deng Xiaoping returns to power and ousts Hua Guofeng

1978   The semiannual Canton Fair opens with the theme, "New Flexibility, New Era?"

1978   China grants many visas to large numbers of American tourists

1978   Coca-Cola signs a distribution agreement with the PRC

1978   US President Jimmy Carter encourages the National Governor's Association to "bond" with the Chinese

1978–1984   Governors in twelve states declare "sister" provinces in China; numerous cities set up similar arrangements as well

1979   Deng Xiaoping visits the United States; the US and China renew diplomatic relations; Deng asks for American technology and investment in the reconstruction of his country

1979   Chinese bureaucrats approve over 800 joint venture proposals; but in 1980, only 13 are activated

1979   China's Institute of World Politics is founded

1979   Bob Hope brings an entertainment tour to Beijing; the entourage includes Big Bird from *Sesame Street*, vocalists Peaches and Herb, and Mikhail Baryshnikov

1979   China Central Television (CCTV) agrees to its first program exchange relationship with an American TV news service (UPITN)

1979   China inaugurates its one-child policy to control its population

1979   The first four "special economic zones" (SEZs) are declared in China, providing tax incentives and private enterprise for foreign investors

1979–1981   China accorded "Y" status, giving it the same trade restrictions as the Warsaw Pact countries of the Soviet Union and Eastern Europe

1979–1985   American oil companies spend about $1.7 billion on petroleum exploration in China; the investment proves to be a great disappointment to all concerned

1979   Prices begin to rise exorbitantly for foreigners doing business in China, including a new 45% income tax on their salaries as well as 100-200% increases on customs duties for office equipment, etc.

1980   Bloomingdale's creates an "exhibition" of the sights and sounds of the PRC in New York

1980   CCTV airs its first imported American TV series, *The Atlantics*

1980   CCTV begins to include foreign commercials on a regular basis

1980   The Gang of Four is put on trial –Jiang Qing and Zhang Chunqiao receive suspended death sentences; Wang Hongwen is sentenced to life imprisonment and Yao Wen-yuan receives a 20-year jail term

**1980   Council for International Educational Exchange (CIEE) sets up its first overseas program in Beijing (see Chapter 4)**

1981   China removed from its "Y" trade status and placed in a special, less-restricted category (although not equal to the NATO nations)

**1981** *Sesame Street* first dubbed in Mandarin, and distributed through CCTV (See Chapter 6)

**1982** The Shanghai-Foxboro Company Limited is created — the first joint venture in China established by an American manufacturer (See Chapter 9)

**1983** Beijing Jeep becomes a joint venture with American Motors in China ( the origins of Chrysler Corporation — See Chapter 8)

1984 China creates 14 "open cities," with incentives similar to the SEZs of 1979

1984 Great Britain's Prime Minister Margaret Thatcher signs an agreement to return Hong Kong to China in 1997

1984 US President Ronald Reagan makes his first (and only) trip to China

1984 The Central Committee of the CCP begins to lift price controls and limits the role of centralized planning in the country; as a result, China's consumers begin an unprecedented spending spree

1984 A black market emerges, as "money changers" trade Foreign Exchange Currency (FEC) for Chinese *reminbi*; they also smuggle goods to their Chinese friends from the newly-established SEZs

**1984** **Holiday Inn Hospitality ventures into China with its flagship hotel, the Beijing Lido (See Chapter 7)**

1985 Deng Xiaoping inaugurates an urban redevelopment plan for China

1986 CCTV begins its first foreign-language channel — in English

1986 China limits the use of FECs

1986 Foreign investment begins to decline for the first time since China opened trade to foreigners in 1979; as a result, Deng Xiaoping invites a delegation of bankers, financiers and lawyers to visit his country

1986 China inaugurates new incentives for foreign investors, including lower taxes and land-use fees; but they do little to change the downward trend

1986 Students start demonstrating for democratic freedom at China's universities

1987 CCTV contracts with CNN for program exchanges

1987 Despite Deng's efforts to encourage foreign investment, Westerners in China find their jobs in jeopardy

1987 Chinese university students, ignoring an official ban, march on Tiananmen Square

1987 Chrysler buys American Motors Corporation, and assumes ownership of Beijing Jeep

**1987**   **AmCham is re-established in Shanghai (See Chapter 10)**

1988   Hainan Island is designated as a separate province, as well as a SEZ

1989   The Tiananmen Square crisis erupts over high inflation and government corruption (among other things); many American businesses either re-structure or abandon China

1990   China opens a TV programming export office in Los Angeles

1990   Shanghai is declared a SEZ

1992   CCTV creates an overseas correspondents' office in Washington, DC

1996   China changes its policy of *hukuo*, allowing people more freedom of professional choice as well as where they might want to live

1997   The first "bullet" train comes to mainland China (PRC)

1999   The Monetary Policy Committee of the People's Bank of China creates guidelines for commercial lending

2001   China joins the World Trade Organization (WTO)

2002   The Chinese government establishes new guidelines for foreign investment and joint ventures

# 1

# The Chinese Worldview

In carrying out our modernization programme we must proceed from Chinese realities. Both in revolution and in construction we should also learn from foreign countries and draw on their experience, but mechanical copying and application of foreign experience and models will get us nowhere. We have had many lessons in this respect. We must integrate the universal truth of Marxism with the concrete realities of China, blaze a path of our own and build a socialism with Chinese characteristics—that is the basic conclusion we have reached after reviewing our long historical experience.

*—Deng Xiaoping*[1]

Deng Xiaoping's comments during the Twelfth National Congress of the Communist Party of China both illustrate and illuminate some of the issues in discussing the contemporary Chinese mind. The Western idea that the Chinese mind is "inscrutable" and based upon primarily Confucian principles provides only limited access to understanding its complexities. While the authors do not pretend to know the Chinese mind (and hence how to best negotiate with the Chinese), the concept of mind and the "evolution" of mind may prove to be beneficial in this discussion. In analyzing the inputs into the contemporary Janus—faces of China itself—one might profitably take into account the numerous philosophical and religious contributions derived from its distant past. There were and are numerous schools of thought in Chinese culture; among them are Buddhism, Taoism, Confucianism, and more recently, communism. Two of these belief systems traveled to China from another land (Buddhism and communism); two are indigenous (Confucianism and Taoism). Nevertheless, all but one originated in the East.

Moreover, other comparatively recent events (such as the humiliating Opium Wars, the loss of Hong Kong and Macao to the British, the foreign "concessions" in Shanghai and elsewhere, World War I, World War II and the Cold War) have come to China from an oftentimes unwilling association with the West. These associations also influence the contemporary "Chinese mind."

# HISTORICAL OVERVIEW

The overthrow of the Qing dynasty and the last Emperor Puyi in 1911 by Dr. Sun Yatsen and the Nationalist Party (Kuomintang — KMT) can be seen as the first merge between Eastern and Western traditions in modern history. (Despite China's long history of peasant revolts, no history of a republic can be found before 1911.) This change in political philosophy was due, for the most part, to Chinese scholars who went abroad to Japan, France and elsewhere and brought home to China new ideas, among them the ideas of Karl Marx, and the concepts of a republic.

In addition to implementing the ideas of Dr. Sun Yatsen, Chinese reformers also implemented the ideas of Karl Marx when, in 1921, the Communist Party was founded in Shanghai. Here, the impetus and teachings came from the newly revolutionary country of Russia, influenced by leaders such as Zhou Enlai and Deng Xiaoping, who had met and studied with other Communist party members in Europe. The Russians had obtained communism from the writings of Karl Marx, Lenin and others, and had overthrown the Tsar. The ensuing revolutionary path taken by both the Chinese and the Russians was aimed, in part, at overcoming the feudal system still intact in each country at the turn of the 20th century. Until evolving into power hungry, totalitarian and sometimes brutal regimes, both Communist parties sought equitable land reform and a better life for both peoples.

After the Third Civil War and the defeat and exile of the Kuomintang in 1949, China entered into a close relationship with Russia. This lasted until the late fifties and early sixties. Ironically, the People's Republic of China (PRC) was denied membership in the United Nations to punish its leaders for "going communist" just at the very time it was shutting down diplomatic relationships with Russia. In response to Russia's coldness, the denial of membership as "China" in the United Nations (UN) and the McCarthy-era Communist witchhunts in America, China slammed its door on the world. What happened during these years—known to most as the Cultural Revolution—yields other contributions to the Chinese perspective.

Mao Zedong, wanting to obliterate the past, encouraged children to inform on their parents. In 1966, Mao called the Red Guard (made up of students from the middle schools and universities) to Tiananmen Square and exhorted them to revolutionary action. Citing the "four olds" (old thought, old culture, old customs, old habits) as destructive to the ongoing revolutionary nature of modern China, Red Guards were urged to destroy the remaining vestiges of the old culture.[2] This included closing all schools and the prohibition of Western influences (including books) from 1966 to 1976. In this, the Great Cultural Revolution, students were to learn from peasants, not intellectuals contaminated by the West.

In the seventies, after twenty years of virtual isolation from the West (and the West from China), the People's Republic of China was admitted back into the UN, the Cultural Revolution ended, Chairman Mao died and Deng Xiaoping took control of China. Since then, China has been developing a market economy "with Chinese characteristics" and the concept of "one country, two systems" within the framework of experience described above. As one can well imagine, the upheavals and societal evolution in the 20th century have chipped away at the foundational beliefs of 19th century China.

## CULTURAL DYNAMICS

The following discussion surrounds intercultural communication, language and perception, and what we call "cultural dynamics," illustrating some of the contributing dynamics to the Chinese mind over the distant past, as well as the past two centuries. Of necessity, given China's long and complex history, we can only highlight certain selected periods here. **Cultural Dynamic I** focuses on the merge of the Chinese language, perception and worldview. **Cultural Dynamic II** explores the interaction of Taoism, Buddhism and Confucianism and that worldview. **Cultural Dynamic III** centers on the incursions of the foreigners (Westerners) into the ruling hierarchies of China following the Opium Wars. Of particular concern are the aftermath of that period and the persistent (until 1997) humiliation felt by the Chinese people and inflicted by the West, especially Great Britain. **Cultural Dynamic IV** traces the evolution of the revolutionary worldview upon Chinese life and thought during the period from 1900 to 1950. **Cultural Dynamic V** discusses communism as practiced in the People's Republic of China and the death, displacement and despair created through the implementation of the Great Cultural Revolution by Chairman Mao Zedong and other leaders. **Cultural Dynamic VI** explores the impact of the "new China" inaugurated under the leadership of Deng Xiaoping and the quest for a better life for China's people, while maintaining "Chinese characteristics." Finally, we draw these perspectives together, illustrating the complexities in knowing and understanding the multi-faceted Chinese worldview.

But before discussing each cultural dynamic, it is important to look at the evolution of culture and communication as scholarly disciplines and contextual necessities.

# INTERCULTURAL COMMUNICATION

The study of intercultural communication was originally seen as an anthropological locus. Since the work of Edward T. Hall and others in the forties and fifties at the Foreign Service Institute in Washington, D.C., it has moved into the communication discipline. In part, this shift in emphasis emanated from the particular focus which Hall's work took as he, Ray Birdwhistell, and others sought ways of improving the curriculum of Foreign Service personnel in training to go abroad.[3] Foreign Service personnel did not want abstract formulations of culture or cultural artifacts, or stories about living with the Navajo Indians or Samoans. Instead, they insisted on learning the practical dimensions of living abroad, how to interact with the specific opposite hierarchy and conduct everyday life in a specific country, with minimum discomfort, civility, and maximum results professionally.

Out of this need, new directions in the study of intercultural communication were conceived. Edward T. Hall began to focus on "what he termed microcultural analysis: on tone of voice, gestures, time, and spatial relationships as aspects of communication."[4] These were considered to be the "out of awareness aspects of communication." Out of awareness aspects were designated as "informal" communication, while more traditional aspects of culture were considered "formal" communication.[5]

Hall's work, *The Silent Language*, offered "the complete theory of culture as communication."[6] He published his first book on intercultural communication, *The Anthropology of Manners*, in 1955.[7] In Hall's era, Americans were just beginning to travel abroad, multinationals were relatively scarce, and the world was quite a different place. But Hall and other anthropologists such as Margaret Mead saw early on that "The whole mesh of human social life might logically, and perhaps in other contexts, fruitfully, be treated as a system of human communications."[8]

## THE COLD WAR

Unfortunately, the understanding of a system of human communications fell afoul with the Cold War that emerged following WWII, and the clash of ideologies espoused by the two victorious superpowers— Russia and the United States. The rhetoric of communism versus capitalism dominated the world stage. Though the two superpowers did not wage war, their proxies did; so Korea, Vietnam, Cuba and a host of other "small" wars dominated the world's agenda for nearly fifty years, precluding and preempting an incipient logic of intercultural communication.

Almost unnoticed (and certainly not immediately and widely understood as universally significant), several other major developments occurred prior to the end of the Cold War. The first was the advent of hyper-technology. Though the United States government and multinational corporations had access to computers, these were intended principally for the military until quite recently (within the past 15 years). Second, though many people wondered why many "foreigners" were "buying up America," few citizens understood this development initially. Third, due to Cold War prohibitions (e.g., difficulties in obtaining visas to certain countries), many countries were "quarantined" until the Fall of the Wall in 1989 and the breakup of the Soviet Union in 1991 and the official end of the Cold War.

What has become apparent (at least to these authors) is that with the cordoning off of half the world from the United States, Americans were cordoned off and isolated as well. They also apparently assumed that, when the Cold War ended, mirror images of the American self would emerge in all parts of the world. As "victors" and "liberators," we would naturally be loved.

Because of this misguided assumption, Americans have made significant errors in diplomatic relations and in business negotiations, not only with China and Russia, but also, as we see from the September 11, 2001[9] attack, and its aftermath, in the Middle East. American errors have become compounded by the tendency not to listen well, the lack of desire and perceived need to understand "the other," and American isolation as a people (not a country) from the newly redefined world, i.e., globalization. While still a work in progress, globalization (made possible through the incredible growth of computer technology, the internet, e-mail, the wired infrastructure of global banking and international business, the creation of the World Trade Organization, the development of the European Union, the development of ASEAN and a host of other organizations) dominates the American workplace. And it happened without the essential awareness of the American people.

What can we do to understand where and who we are in the 21st century? The task is enormous, as it involves getting to know the other players. One can't negotiate well if one doesn't know what prompts a smile or a nod or if one has just outraged the local population by defiling the Buddha in some way at the local temple. Or if one is ignorant of the "rape of Nanjing," the "Long March," the Chinese fight to drive the Japanese out of Manchuria, or the large numbers of people who suffered and died during the "Great Cultural Revolution." In fact, the past century saw numerous wars on the same territory and the horror of war was shared by all, especially in Russia, Eastern Europe, Western Europe, Vietnam, Cambodia, all of Africa, all of South America, all of the Middle East and Asia. Russia lost 23 million citizens; China lost 21 million citizens. Most of the world's peoples have been subjected to true horror many times over. To them, respect for their history, wars and unending struggle is imperative, even in the relatively anonymous era of globalization.

Until September 11, 2001, unlike the rest of the world, the continental United States had not been attacked by outside forces. Our homes had not been destroyed, our museums looted, our women raped, our people, the old and the children, gutted by foreign soldiers swarming across the continent. Perhaps a newfound empathy can be viewed as one positive outcome to the horrific terrorist attacks on the U.S. in 2001— empathy tends to breed better relationships. And relationships are best forged by shared language and perception.

# CULTURAL DYNAMIC I— LANGUAGE AND PERCEPTION

In virtually all of human history, the "language-in-use" in the world belongs to the victors. Thus, one is not surprised that English is the "first" language in much of today's world, complete with the idiosyncrasies and nuances unfamiliar to non-native speakers. For example, everyone in the United States understands that Saturday and Sunday are "the weekend." We know this so clearly that we are not conscious of it, nor do we tend to reflect upon it. Yet, until quite recently, the concept of the "weekend" was unknown in most of China. One of the authors (Nancy Street), asking for the weekend off at her work unit in 1985 (and refusing to teach on Sunday in China), was told that there is "no weekend in China." When one stops to think about this, of course this is true: "weekend" is a concept derived from the culture and language in the United States.

"Weekend" is like "gravity"—one sees the effect of it all around, but one does not "see" weekend. A thing exists because we say it exists. If one does not call a thing into existence through language because it is a part of the culture, then it does not exist, for one does not experience it. Initially, the Chinese did not observe the Western weekend. Nor was Saturday or Sunday a "holy day." These are Western designations, made real through belief in certain religious concepts, which in turn, are based upon beliefs or "things not seen." Axiomatic communication theory asserts that "we see what we are trained to see, we do not see that which we are not trained to see." If we don't see it—if it is not a precondition of our culture—it *isn't*. Similarly, time is a concept and a convenient fiction developed through participation in the culture.

Perusing time, one sees that time also differs from culture to culture—as well as what time means within the culture. In the eighties, our Chinese friends working in the same unit were constantly puzzled by the Western saying "time is money." If "time" is "time," how could it also be "money?" If one says of an event such as 11 September 2001 that "it occurred at approximately 9:00 a.m.," is that an equally truthful statement in China, where the time of the event was 9:00 p.m.? Or, if an event happens at 2:00 p.m. in America and 2:00 a.m. in China, did it occur "today" in both countries or "tomorrow" in China? In 1986, daylight savings time was inaugurated for the first time in Shanxi Province. For weeks, people went around saying, "The leaders tell us it is 9:00 a.m., but it is really 8:00 a.m."

Again, focusing on time, many cultures follow different calendars. In the United States, we follow the solar calendar, which, incidentally, has been altered on several occasions. The Chinese and others, however, follow the lunar calendar. This means (among other things) that the New Year is celebrated on two quite different days—January 1 in the West, and sometime in January or February in the East, according to the lunar calendar (see Appendix B for PRC holidays). Further, the year 2003 on the Gregorian (Western) calendar is actually the year 4701 in Chinese culture;

in Jewish culture, the year is 5763–5764; and, in Islamic culture, the year is 1423–1424. Given the influence of the West, people in these cultures (Chinese, Jewish, Muslim) must maintain two calendars all the time. Thus, this is the year 2003 because the West says it is. In short, time is arbitrary, emerging from the culture. Like language, time is also subject to the vagaries of the victor.

But time is also relative, depending upon who thinks what is relevant. In 2002, the world was transfixed on the Israeli-Palestinian standoff between Ariel Sharon and Yasir Arafat and the Israeli army and the Palestinian terrorists. When trying to decipher the origin of the crisis, who can tell which came first — the incursions of the Israelis on the West Bank and surrounding Yasir Arafat, or the terrorist attacks by Palestinian persons on Israeli citizens? Each side "punctuates" the sequence differently.

In China, one remembers the spy plane incident of May 2001. An American spy plane, engaged in some kind of scuffle with a Chinese fighter pilot, made an emergency landing on Hainan Island without permission from the Chinese government. This caused great consternation worldwide — American president George W. Bush, clearly drawing a line in the sand, accused the Chinese of refusing to give back the airplane. The authors suggest a more simple explanation: that the Chinese may not have known how to go about giving it back.

In most incidents of this kind, it is quite common to inspect the aircraft for national security and intelligence information, no matter what nation is involved (e.g., the Soviet spy plane forced to land in California in the 1970s). As to the removal of the aircraft from the island, even American engineers and pilots needed several weeks to figure it out. Given that China is so far away and Hainan Island is nearly primitive (having begun the process of modernization only in the late 1980s), the Chinese may have had little clue as to how to offload that plane. In short, they may not have been recalcitrant; they may have simply lacked the knowledge and necessary infrastructure to get the plane off the island. Rather than an aggressive affront, this episode may have been more an issue of "face" for all concerned, with no reasonable solution.

Which leads to our next point. The Chinese are given much credit for many "things" that they do not have or even know about. In the more remote areas of China, for example, physical infrastructure is not up to code. Updated versions of Chinese economic advancement make it very clear that the economic and physical infrastructure regeneration is to be found primarily within the coastal cities. The many port cities in China benefit greatly from the new China's market outlook. They include (in rank order): Shanghai, Ningbo, Guangzhou, Qinhuangdao, Tianjin, Dalian,

Qingdao, Shenzhen, Zhoushan and Lianyungang. According to *AmChat*, "these top ten ports' total amount of throughput was 917 million tons of cargo in 2000, representing an increase of 18.2 percent over the previous year."[10] Those in the countryside do not have the same economic advantages as the Chinese coastal cities. Because of this inequity, Eastern cities are expected to help their poorer western brothers; they are doing so as the older technology is transferred to the inland cities and towns to make way for newer technology and production in the eastern coastal cities.

In addition, the further one goes inland, the less likely the inhabitants are to speak English. If they are less likely to speak English, they are also less able to obtain the best trade arrangements, and to fund schools and universities with English-speaking programs at the same rate as in the coastal cities. This, in turn, makes it difficult for students in these areas to learn English so that they might work in joint ventures, go overseas to graduate schools, work in tourism or teach English.

The language barrier is a seriously divisive one. If one lives in the provinces, opportunities to speak English are limited. Further, the English spoken in the classroom may be taught by someone from Great Britain, Canada, the U.S. or Australia, in which case one acquires a different accent, words and meanings. More than that, the Chinese language, while having some tenses, is far less "time" bound than many other languages. Many sentences are stated in the present; one is expected to understand time and gender from the context. This clearly shapes language and perception.

Likewise, there are no gender endings in Chinese as there are in Spanish, or gender pronouns or articles as in both Spanish and English. Thus, Chinese is contextually situated in a grammatically gender less present. This makes translations from Chinese into English and back difficult. It also suggests a different "take" on reality.

This "take" on reality requires an understanding of: (1) the Western either-or dichotomy; and (2) the Chinese both-and fusion. As we see from the Taoist yin-yang symbol, Chinese look at life as neither "good" nor "bad," "this" nor "that"; it partakes of both. The Western view is that things are either this or that, good or bad. The English language — not surprisingly, with its genesis within the Catholic church during the early and middle ages in England — is similar to an absolutist morality play in which events, things, dogs and people are either good or bad and there are no shades of gray. This has significant consequences when dealing with cultures whose favorite mode of response may be a relativistic "maybe" or "perhaps," instead of "yes" or "no."

Similarly, the infusion of Christian thought in the West posits "God" or "the Devil," "right" or "wrong," "black" or "white." Most Chinese do not see the world this way — they do not, traditionally, anticipate the future or an immediate heavenly afterlife. Belief in reincarnation is not similar to the Christian afterlife. If one believes in a heavenly afterlife, then what one does here decides that future life. If there is no future life, what one does here is all-important and may, for some, impinge on the next life, which may be, once again, earthbound. One way to look at this conundrum may be that the American need for instant gratification takes place not only in the world of the stock market and earnings, but also in the belief of some in the instantaneous afterlife. Chinese, on the other hand, with their longer earthbound history, have greater patience than Americans. They can save and wait and move more slowly and carefully to their goals.

As to the gender issue, the Chinese view of the world construction obviously alludes to the male hierarchy (women are attached to that hierarchy by being attached to the male), thus, *ta* can mean "he," "she" or "it," depending on the context. This introduces yet another firmly held concept in intercultural communication. China is a high context culture, whereas Americans live in a low context culture. Everything must be spelled out for Americans, as for example in the negotiation of contracts. Americans tend to think that when the contract is signed, the deal is done and the arrangements made. For the Chinese, this dimension of negotiations is simply a step in the process. For Chinese, things do not begin and end so definitively as for Americans. They interrelate with many other elements, and most often within the context of Confucianism, Taoism and Buddhism.

# Cultural Dynamic II — Confucianism, Taoism and Buddhism

## Confucianism

Confucianism, the moral and religious system based on the teachings of Confucius, began with the family and an ideal model of relations between family members. It then generalized this family model to the state, and to an international system (the Chinese world order).[11]

Communication literature abounds with useful articles centering on Confucianism and the concept of face or *mien tze*,[12] focusing on the impact of these concepts on intercultural and interpersonal relationships. For instance, June Ock Yum, in "The Impact of Confucianism on Interpersonal Relationships and Communication Patterns in East Asia," discusses, among other concepts, the "four principles from which right conduct arises; *jen* (humanism), *i* (faithfulness), *li* (propriety), and *chih* (wisdom or a liberal education) ... practicing *jen* implies the practice of *shu* ... to empathize with others."[13] Others writing on interpersonal relationships, such as Myung-seok Park and Moon-soo Kim, identify Confucianism as controlling "interpersonal relationships," while Oded Shenkar and Simcha Ronen focus on comparing the Chinese negotiator with the American negotiator. In their discussion, Shenkar and Ronen discuss "the [Confucian] tenets of harmony, hierarchy, developing one's moral potential, and kinship affiliation having relevance for interpersonal behavior." The analysis is extended to include "recommendations for preparing, conducting, and concluding negotiations with one's Chinese counterparts."[14] Yet another article by Ringo Ma, entitled "The Role of Unofficial Intermediaries in Interpersonal Conflicts in the Chinese," is useful in this context as Ma discusses the inconsistent meanings of "interpersonal conflict" and the use of intermediaries to manage conflict. Ma makes the point that Chinese intermediaries tend to be "unofficial," while Western intermediaries tend to be "official" third parties such as lawyers.[15] Ma's work is important to the arguments in this book because it both directly and indirectly brings together a network of assumptions fundamental to Chinese society — the concept of face, the value of the elders, the lack of direct confrontation, indeed, the avoidance of confrontation in Chinese society, and the use of intermediaries in negotiation to aid in the building of relationships through *guanxi*.

In their article, "More Than Relationship: Chinese Interaction and the Principle of *Kuan-Hsi [Guanxi]*," Hui-Ching Chang and G. Richard Holt (while interviewing Chinese on Taiwan) found that

> the principle of *kuan-hsi* (relations) undergirds the functional aspects of Chinese interpersonal relationships ... [and] has evolved into a social resource in a sense somewhat at odds with the Confucian ideal, that is, more as an interpersonal resource in Chinese society.[16]

Chang and Holt ask their Western readers to reconsider their idea of an either-or dichotomy between East and West and "dig" to determine if these dichotomies hold in today's Chinese societies. For example, are Chinese societies really "collective" with no regard for the individual? Are Western societies, particularly the American, really only concerned with gratification of the individual? Chang and Holt go on to extend the relevant concepts of Confucianism in their discussion of the "Family Relations as the Basis of Society." The five relationships basic to a stable society are:

(1)  father-son (the relation of love);
(2)  emperor-subject (the relation of righteousness);
(3)  husband-wife (the relation of chaste conduct);
(4)  elder-younger (the relation of order); and
(5)  friend-friend (the relation of faithfulness).[17]

These five relationships are the foundation of the state — the linchpin of the Confucian-Chinese worldview. Coupled with the concept of *guanxi* (relations), the two concepts have been taken for granted by Western scholars and thus the either-or dichotomy continues, perpetuating the myth that the Chinese have no sense of self. This, in turn, fosters beliefs about the nature of the Chinese person as individual and Chinese society as a viable entity. Chang and Holt suggest (and the authors of this book concur) that these Confucian ideals may not, in fact, always exist. Further, we suggest that relatively few (and none of the above) interpersonal relationship and or negotiation studies have been done in mainland China. While it's true that basic Confucian values have been intrinsic to Chinese society on Taiwan and in South Korean society, there are two significant differences between people living in these countries and those from the PRC. First, both Taiwan and South Korea are small countries with populations in the few millions — they do not approach China's 1.3 billion population.

More importantly, unlike the mainlanders, South Koreans and Taiwanese (for good or ill, willingly or unwillingly) assumed many Western values and accepted the protection of the West, and in particular, that of the United States. Mainland China, however, especially under Chairman Mao Zedong, did not embrace Western ideology. While Confucianism remains at the roots of these three societies, world events in 1949 set them on very different paths. Although Confucian-style government was in vogue until the late eighties in Taiwan under the rule of the Kuomintang, the significant economic development of Taiwan is largely the result of its close ties to the United States, as is that of South Korea.

By contrast, the research for *American Businesses in China* has been done primarily in the PRC. All of our interviews are with students and colleagues from the PRC, conducted and recorded either on the mainland or in the United States, between 1985 and 2001. Travel, historical and critical research, and field work have enabled us to see the fundamental differences in the 20th century development of Confucian-based cultures such as Hong Kong, Taiwan, Korea and the PRC. In her book, *In Search of Red Buddha*, Street questioned a student in Shanxi Province (a former Red Guard named Xiao Shi) on the issue of Confucianism and relationships. He replied:

> My family is very traditional, in other words, is very Confucian to a large extent. All the children obey the parents, and I listen to my elder brother and elder sisters as well. I was trained to know some necessary etiquette like to always offer the first bowl of food to the eldest, to never argue back with the old, to always obey the parents and teachers, to always be modest and never be arrogant, to love the country and listen to the leaders, and to know one's perimeter to always keep a harmonious relationship with everyone.[18]

While Xiao Shi's answer corresponds to the five points of Confucian relationships described above, the actions of Chinese students from the mainland while in the States and in the PRC might be described as "confused Confucianism." Perhaps under the influence of a century of war, and the adoption of communism and the lessons of the Cultural Revolution combined with exposure to Western lifestyles, these students (young to middle-aged) began to think, a little, in terms of "I" and to conduct an altered version of traditional Confucian "relationships" or *guanxi*. As Chang and Holt note in their study, "The term *Kuan-hsi* [*guanxi*] has taken on an additional semantic dimension through its usage in Chinese life. At a deeper and more subtle level, *Kuan-hsi* refers to the manner in which Chinese strategically employ relations as a social resource."[19]

*Guanxi* is clearly a complicated — and to Westerners, misundersood — concept. It also centers on the idea of insiders and outsiders, which is not necessarily a Confucian ideal. In part, this may be due to the fact that few foreigners visited the "Middle Kingdom" until the past two centuries. Nonetheless, in today's society, in both Taiwan and on the mainland, *guanxi* has taken on a meaning that is at odds with the Western perception of the Chinese psyche.

In 1989, author Nancy Street asked Shi Hong (a student of hers from the north of China and living within her work unit at Shanxi Teacher's University in Linfen, Shanxi province) to explain *guanxi*. As Shi Hong explained,

> Relationships have advantages. We often try to form the relationships. We can get a better job or get a larger house or be sent to study abroad if we have good relationships.[20]

At the same time, he confided that he rarely asked (or told) his parents about his life, rather, he sought answers from friends, down to the selection of his girlfriend. In regard to being an outsider, he had this comment regarding his fellow students, to him foreigners (*waiguoren*):

> I was very moved when I went to Mary's (a foreign expert) class last year. She treated me like an ordinary student. She took care of me. If Chinese students find a student who does not belong to their class, they ignore him, don't want to talk with him, may mistreat him, maybe don't want him to listen to the class.... Westerners are treated well, perhaps because they (the Chinese) may get some advantages from them, like changing Renminbi to FEC.[21]

He might well have added that in addition to running the black market in currency, the Chinese in a university work unit often relentlessly pursued the foreigners to be sponsored to come abroad to study. As late as 1997, Chinese students were visiting us with gifts of three-foot-tall Tang horses or bags of Chinese candy, mushrooms or powdered tiger bones.

As the above discussion indicates, Confucianism, the Chinese concept of relationships (and the meaning of *guanxi*) and the notion of "the collective" and "the individual" are far more complex than one initially realizes—and complicate negotiations with Confucian-based cultures. Other work has been done in the People's Republic of China, however, which is of use to anyone attempting the negotiation process with persons from a Confucian-based culture. What follows is a summary of results of a study conducted in Shanghai in 1983 by Edwin C. Nevis, an American management scholar. Nevis and his associates have summarized eleven major cultural assumptions underlying Chinese management:

1. The nation has priority over everything; loyalty to the country is of the utmost importance.
2. Consideration for the family is very important.
3. Personnel selection (leadership) is based upon exploits or ideological contribution.
4. One should have great respect for age.
5. Equity is more important than wealth.
6. Saving and conserving (money, resources, etc.) is to be valued, as is high respect for traditional ways.
7. It is considered unhealthy for individuals to stand out or to take personal credit for their accomplishments.
8. Every decision must take ideology into account.
9. Communal property is more important than private possessions; collectivism is the best economic mechanism.
10. Emphasis focuses upon group forces for motivational purposes.
11. Emphasis focuses on central planning and the powerful state.[22]

As the reader has doubtless heard about mainland China, things change very quickly. While the above concepts were articulated in 1988, other factors, such as the growing alliance of capitalism with socialism through joint ventures, coupled with inflation, have seemingly eroded some of the findings of Nevis, at least on the surface of the society. Further, what can it mean to say that "communal property is more important than private possessions; collectivism is the best economic mechanism" in a country in which the meaning of collectivism has subtly begun to change in the past fifteen years?

In the 21st century, government policy no longer upholds the standard of the "iron rice bowl." Students will not necessarily return from an international exchange program to the original work unit as they may have in the past, but may go out to seek their own positions, as now happens. These and multitudinous other factors will influence the viability of some of Nevis' observations if the current trends in China continue.

From our observations, there is strong evidence that personnel selection (leadership) is not solely based upon exploits or ideological contribution, but also upon one's relationships and skills in the polite forms— Western and Eastern. One further observation is worth noting here. From conversations with students in the late eighties, we learned that (for them) joining the Chinese Communist Party (CCP) was not the way to get ahead. Lately, there may be a reversal in this view as more and more joint ventures come into play on the mainland. Anyone who has ever wandered the back streets and byways of Seoul, Taipei or Beijing knows that ordinary folk in those cities can be every bit as loud, rude, pushing and shoving as ordinary folk in New York, Paris or London. Yet there are norms of behavior in all of these cities that can help to make or break ventures. The Chinese know both the Eastern and Western norms, even if they don't overtly practice the latter. It would be helpful for Western negotiators to learn to become masters of illusion and purveyors of the endless negotiation, just as the Chinese are.

## Taoism

Lao Tzu, traditionally the father of Taoism, was born around 600 BCE, or some 50 years prior to Confucius, who lived from 551 BCE to 479 BCE.[23] David Hall and Roger T. Ames, in *Anticipating China*, describe through Taoist thought what some of us have begun to understand experientially about the Chinese perspective. They illuminate why some things, to those of us enculturated into the Western world, do not make logical sense (which is, after all, our model), yet contain an internal logic. One may also have difficulty because, having read or listened to the *Tao*, one cannot generate the Eureka response, but rather, "yes, of course, and?" And this does not seem to be like argument nor a form of argument, but obvious— so obvious one doesn't speak it. This illuminates a crucial point which we make in this book regarding the differences in Chinese and American thinking patterns: perception, language and culture promote a particular perspective on reality.

The *Tao* reads:

> A path becomes a path by walking it.
> A thing is made a thing by being so-called
> Why are things so?
> They are so because they are so
> Why are they not something other than what they are?
> They are not something else because they are not.

The concept of the *Tao* is, as George A. Kennedy says in *Comparative Rhetoric: An Historical and Cross-Cultural Introduction*, "common to most Chinese philosophy, but the term 'Taoists' is specifically applied to the followers of Lao-Tzu." The teachings of Lao Tzu included:

> passive nonaction, identification of the individual with nature, and spontaneous righteousness; it rejected verbal distinctions, categorizations, and logical argument and suggested that what seems real is often an illusion and what seems a dream may be real.[24]

Kennedy makes the point that in Taoism, there is a reliance, not on the audience, but on the rhetor. The *Tao* is concerned with *ethos*. We shall also discuss this further in Chapter 10 in regard to Chinese communication-negotiation style and the lack of pervasive importance of the contract to the Chinese. Kennedy also demonstrates that transcendence is not a meaningful category for understanding Chinese traditional thought, as the focus is on the now, or what we in the West might call the existential. This is often confused with their "mandate of heaven." However, "the mandate of heaven" is not the equivalent of God's will, nor is heaven envisaged as the Christian heaven, and few aspire to it. It has a place in the Chinese hierarchy, but that place cannot be understood while remaining within the Western Christian context.

Following Hall and Ames, as well as Kennedy, the authors of this book agree that values in classical China provide a foundation for morals and ethics in contemporary China and are oftentimes counter-intuitive to Western thought. Beginning with the pre–Socratics, Hall and Ames argue that the transcendent assumption of truth (salvation), rather than the imminent assumption, took the two cultures in different directions. Calling Eastern thought "recessive" in Western thought, and Western thought "recessive" in Eastern thought, the authors put forth the proposition in yin-yang form.

For example, unlike Christianity, where one cannot be both a Protestant and a Catholic at once, the Chinese can (and often do) practice Taoism, Buddhism and Confucianism without feeling at cross purposes. In 2002, they may also practice these three, along with capitalism, communism and free trade. The subsequent impact upon the culture, and hence, communication, is an important concept in this book, as is Buddhism — another contributing factor to the Chinese mind.

## Buddhism

While Confucianism and Taoism "grew up" in China, Buddhism came to China from India. Siddhartha Gautama lived from 563 to 483 BCE. Saying, "Let my skin wither, my hands grow numb, my bones dissolve; until I have attained understanding I will not rise from here," Siddhartha began his journey to enlightenment. When he finished, he was the Buddha — the "Enlightened One."[25] In a sermon near Banaras, he revealed the four "Noble Truths" to his followers:

> First, "Birth is sorrow, age is sorrow ... death is sorrow." The second Noble Truth holds that all suffering stems from craving the pleasures of life. Thirdly, only by ending craving can one achieve an end to suffering. The fourth Noble Truth then reveals the eightfold path to achieve this end: "Right Views, Right Resolve, Right Speech, Right Conduct, Right Livelihood, Right Effort, Right Mindfulness, and Right Concentration."[26]

Analyzing the third and fourth truths and comparing them with the principles of both Confucianism and Taoism, one sees little contradiction and the convergence of compatible ideas.

Sites to visit to experience the Chinese adaptation of Confucianism, Taoism, Buddhism (and the modern era as well) are everywhere one looks. Consider the holy mountain TaiShan in northwest China; the sacred peaks of HuaShan in Shaanxi Province; the Temple of Confucius at Qufu in Shandong Province; the Kong Miao and Guozijian (Confucian Temple and Imperial College) in Beijing; or the Yonghe Gong or Lama temple in Beijing. One of our favorites is the Daming Si (Great Brightness Temple) in Yangzhou, not far from Nanjing in Jiangsu Province. Founded more than 1000 years ago by the Tang dynasty monk Jianzhen (the monk who went to Japan to take the words and worldview of the Buddha), one becomes aware that the Chinese have created a worldview of philosophy and religion and life which is uniquely their own and which is also not incompatible with socialism.

Confucianism and Taoism were already in place when Buddhism arrived in China in 100 BCE and it spread quickly. According to Wing-tsit Chan, in "The Orderly Realm of the Chinese Sages,"

> When the scholar Chang Jung died in A. D. 497, he was holding in his right hand a copy of Buddhism's *Lotus Scripture*; in his left, two books, the *Confucian Classic of Filial Piety* and Lao Tzu's *Classic of the Way and Virtue*.[27]

In Buddhist temples throughout China, the iconography of the temples is quite similar. In addition to the male manifestations, according to Joseph M. Kitagawa in "The Eightfold Path to Nirvana," the "Mahayana Buddhist pantheon grew — saints, deities, compassionate beings. Among the most revered: Avalokiteshvara, merciful redeemer who is in China as Kuan-yin[28] and in Japan as Kannon — took feminine form; Maitreya, a Buddha-to-be who in China became the round-bellied Laughing Buddha; Amitaba, who rules an Eden attained by faith and good works."[29]

If Americans claim a Judeo-Christian foundation as their guide to politics, business and personal relationships, it seems equally understandable that a core element of the Chinese worldview incorporates a spiritual dimension as well. The difference is in the focus of that dimension, not the dimension itself.

# CULTURAL DYNAMIC III—THE OPIUM WARS AND THE GREAT HUMILIATION

With the exception of the extensive commerce along the Silk Road (linking Asia to Europe, running from Canton (now Guangzhon) through Xi'an, Anxi, the Taklamakan Desert, Samarkand, Bagdad, Alexandria and Antioch), there was little communication between Asia and Europe in the First Millennium. The visits of Jesuits such as Matteo Ricci, or other foreigners, made little lasting impact upon China (or the "Middle Kingdom" to which many countries brought tribute). In those days, few Chinese left home. Even now, the Chinese prefer to remain at home, despite circumstances, e.g., the Cultural Revolution and China's engagement with the world through globalization, that have brought about an exodus. The Chinese may discuss leaving their motherland, but usually discuss, if at all possible, a return someday. If they leave, they send money home and heavily invest in China today.

Despite the Silk Road culture (from approximately 1500 BCE to 200 BCE) there was little communication between ordinary people in the East and West. Certainly the Emperor never went to the Court at Versailles, nor the King of France to China. East and West traded, but there was little significant communicative interaction. The difficulties of proselytizing must have been immense for those Jesuits who came to China. Learning the language and customs, setting up housekeeping, doing translations and working with interpreters, meeting with the hierarchy, obtaining permissions, all these activities, simple and complex, were fraught with difficulties, just as they were in 1985 in China, and to a lesser degree in 2002.[30]

As luck would have it, both authors were in China in 1997 when Hong Kong was returned to China. Included among our many adventures was judging the first public speaking contest ever held (in any language) in the ancient city of Nanjing (about 5 million people) in Jiangsu Province ... the only *waiguoren* amidst a sea of Chinese military uniforms. Nanjing is located not far from Shanghai and Pudong — hubs of Chinese industry, shipping and financial growth and mainland China's proud answer to the challenges and opportunities of globalization. Nanjing benefits from proximity to Shanghai and is connected to that city by impressive transportation infrastructure. Inhabited for the past 5,000 years, Nanjing has been the capital of various dynasties and governments, including that of the Kuomintang,[31] which is why it was spotlighted in the many national celebrations honoring the 1997 Hong Kong handover.

As communication professors, we were fortunate enough to be asked to judge this very first public speaking contest in the city's history. The topic was "The Return of Hong Kong to the Motherland." Earnest young men and women recounted for us the terrible humiliation suffered by the Chinese people as a result of the Opium Wars and the unequal treaties of 1842, 1860 and 1898. How did these treaties come about? The story was repeated over and over by our speakers.

Among the many issues in the first Opium War was whether the Chinese had the right to object to the British illegally importing opium into China. As Yoko Mizui says in "Looking Back on the Historically Inevitable," "The British won the conflict, then forced a number of trading concessions and won the use of several ports, including Hong Kong, from the Chinese."[32] The lesson was an important one for the Japanese — one could fall behind if one closed the door to the world. Unfortunately, as the film "The Opium War" depicted, the sea battle between the Chinese and the British was truly terrible. One realizes in this film (directed by Xie Jin and produced in China) that the Chinese, under the Qing dynasty in the 19th century, had virtually no technology. Worse, they had no idea they would be so badly unprepared to face down the British attempt to dominate China. In his review of the film, Yoko Mizui says,

> The 2½ hour film is like a good history book, with an in-depth analysis of each country's political and social situation at the time. The story is told objectively, portraying the war without treating one side favorably. The war itself has a strong political significance, but Xie Jin successfully refrains from making political statements. Instead, he presents historical facts with an emphasis on the events that caused the war.[33]

One of the authors of this book (Nancy Street) saw this film and it was truly overwhelming — the Chinese had virtually no fire power, no technology or range which could even reach the British ships. The sea battle between the British and the Chinese was a rout. For too long, the Chinese had cut themselves off from the world. The Chinese, early inventors of gunpowder, faced advanced technology with which they could not compete, nor hope to overcome. Worse, they were so out of touch, so isolated from the rest of the world, that they did not know this prior to going into battle with the British. The Chinese felt no need to explore and conquer the Western world, they felt themselves self-sufficient and powerful enough within the Asian world. Approached by the Western predators, they were defeated and suffered the humiliation of losing Hong Kong and Macao to the British. They also, as time went on, essentially lost Shanghai to the West through the foreign "concessions." In Cultural Dynamic IV, however, we see how the CCP sought revenge in Shanghai and other cities for this humiliation at the beginning of the People's Republic of China. At the time, there was nothing they could do about Hong Kong and Macao. However, the British were scheduled to turn Hong Kong back in 1997 and author Street observed the year-long event. The Chinese have long memories and the need for "face" was amongst those attributes of the televised (and much maligned in the West while wildly appreciated in China) British handover of Hong Kong in 1997. This event was carefully planned and became a benchmark date for all Chinese.

The issue was also covered in the Western press, with dire predictions of "Red China's" destruction of the economy and democracy in Hong Kong. Much was made of the fact that the Chinese Red Army crossed over into Hong Kong at midnight on June 30, 1997 (after 156 years of British rule), as though it would then become a military state. It is as though Americans do not know that all countries have the military move in, with the flag, when they enter a new territory. In the years since, Hong Kong appears to be surviving well. During the recent Asian economic crisis, Hong Kong mustered through with infusions of capital from the government in Beijing. This was in keeping with Deng Xiaoping's theory of "one country, two systems." During that difficult time, the Chinese government went through great pain to keep its promise to the world.

Prior to the event, a great electronic board soared high over Tiananmen Square in Beijing, monitoring the countdown of days until the handover. At the university where Street taught (see Chapter 4 for a more detailed description of her academic exchange experience), time was measured by the days remaining until the handover. In addition, students were required to watch historical videos featuring and praising Deng Xiaoping, as well as other leaders instrumental in the smooth return of Hong Kong. History lessons centered on China during the Opium Wars, the decadence of the Qing Dynasty and the repeated ignominious defeats of China in the 19th and 20th centuries at the hands of primarily the British and the Japanese.

For the Chinese people and the Chinese government, the handover had to go smoothly, "face" had to be regained, even though in the years immediately preceding the handover, every effort was made by the West to taint and subvert the process, even perhaps attempting to forestall the return of Hong Kong through fortuitous creation of another incident such as Tiananmen.[34] As Frank Welsh has noted, "The history of the colony is indissolubly linked with that of China's relations with the West, and the development of the West's attitudes towards China."[35]

China's position vis-à-vis the handover was that Governor Patten's efforts to democratize Hong Kong — beginning the process just five years prior to the handover (after 150 years of British rule) — was in violation of the Joint Declaration as well as a deliberate attempt on the part of the West to resurrect the pro-democracy movement, not only in Hong Kong and China, but around the world. In turn, this would create chaos, perhaps preventing the return of Hong Kong or marring the handover, should such subversive efforts actually work. It is difficult to imagine that the Chinese were wrong on this point. Indeed, the actions of Governor Patten, backed by Great Britain and developed in the American press, were to many observers transparently a continuation of the "Cold War" mentality. This Western weltanschauung forged the alliance between British Prime Minister Margaret Thatcher and President Reagan in the eighties. Those involved in that alliance could only pray for another Tiananmen Square situation to evolve from the actions of Governor Patten, in order to forestall the handover of Hong Kong to China. During this era, of course, China did not have most favored nation (MDN) status, nor had she yet been admitted to the World Trade Organization.

The issue also clearly involves power — and who shall have it. It appears that China may have reason to maintain fairly tight control over her enterprises, as well as her modernization strategies. Her 100-year association with the British and other Western countries, and disputes over the importation of opium and control of her own port cities such as Shanghai, have left her with a bitter taste and the resolution to determine her own future, with minimal interference from the helpful West.

# CULTURAL DYNAMIC IV— REVOLUTIONARY CHINA—1900–1949

Like the Russian Revolution of 1917 that overthrew the Tsar Nicholas II and Russia's feudal society, the Chinese, in time-honored fashion, overthrew the Qing dynasty in 1911, ousting the Emperor Puyi (1906–1967) and installing a republic, led by Dr. Sun Yatsen (1866–1925). Sun Yatsen had been educated abroad and was the provisional head of the new Republic of China. He was ousted by the warlord and first president of the Republic Yuan Shikai (1859–1916), who was ousted in turn in 1916 amidst the chaos of revolutionary China. China was then a battleground of competing ideologies, competing warlords, and competing foreign invaders, either economic or military or both, including, but not limited to: the United States, Germany, France, Russia, England and Japan (all, once again, in business in China). The original revolution was spearheaded by those who wanted China rid of its feudal past, as well as rid of foreign intervention and "concessions." But Sun Yatsen's party, the Nationalists (founded in 1912 and in Chinese known as the Kuomintang or KMT), was not strong enough to forge a new and lasting government, nor to rid China of foreigners. This was a major issue.

Others, more radical and following the Russian model, adopted communism as their dominant ideology and on July 1, 1921, the Chinese Communist Party (CCP) was born in Shanghai. From the beginning, there was conflict between the "right" and the "left" in the CCP. Those cadres on the right (such as Deng Xiaoping) often had been in touch with the West and wanted to invite the Russians into China as advisors. Those on the left opposed any outside intervention or help. Among those who opposed foreign aid and intervention was Mao Zedong, a middle peasant from Hunan who had attended Peking University in Beijing and who had never been abroad. In 1922, "the revolutionary principle" of fighting against imperialism and feudalism was formulated; at the third meeting, the CCP agreed to the united front (the coalition of the KMT and the CCP) proposed by Dr. Sun Yatsen, who died in 1925.

For a brief time the coalition held (from 1923 to 1927), but the successor to Dr. Sun Yatsen, Chiang Kaishek (1887–1975) attempted "to take control of China by purging the CCP" from the united front. In this effort, "Chinese and Western scholars agree that Chiang Kaishek had the support of the Western powers, including the United States, as well as the military (from the Qing dynasty structure)."[36] What seemed to be the central issue (other than at base "who shall have power?")? This was class war, not unlike many of the conflicts around the world in 2002.[37] Chiang Kaishek (from a wealthy family and indoctrinated into Western ideas, as well as supported by the United States) was perceived by the CCP as an elitist. Educators, by virtue of their knowledge of the Western worldview, also tended to follow the KMT (which would come back to haunt them following the founding of the People's Republic of China under Chairman Mao). Additionally, the CCP favored a more egalitarian worldview and sought land reform and other entitlements for the peasants. Some members of the CCP wanted Western (and Russian) help and influence; others did not.

## Winning the Hearts and Minds of the Chinese

And what of the beleaguered Chinese peasants? They wanted relief from the feudal system with its warlords and landlords. They wanted relief from countless invasions, looting, raping and burning. The question was how to achieve this. At the outset, it was Mao Zedong who developed the formula that would bring the peasants to the CCP and initiate their subsequent revolution and ultimate victory over the KMT in 1949. During the second and third civil wars, however, Mao was a thorn in the side of the CCP. Hoping to rid themselves of Mao, the Chinese Communist leaders sent him on a mission to Hunan to organize the peasants.[38] In his report, Mao said,

> The armed forces of the landlord class were smaller in central Hunan than in the western and southern parts of the province.... Taking over these old armed forces is one way in which the peasants are building up their own armed forces. A new way is through the setting up of spear corps under the peasant associations. The spears have point, double-edged blades mounted on long shafts.... [39]

How could one fight a revolution with spears against planes and tanks and modern equipment? Wherever they turned, the Chinese CCP revolutionaries met the armies of the West, of Japan and of the Chinese warlords, as well as the military material of Japan and the West. Nonetheless, Mao and his armies recruited more and more peasants nearly everywhere they went. Mao also saw to it that the peasants learned basic reading and writing to ensure national unity, using his Little Red Book as a major guide. In his Hunan report, Mao emphasizes the need of another text:

> Some of the peasants can also recite Dr. Sun Yatsen's Testament. They pick out the terms "freedom," equality," the "Three People's Principles" and "unequal treaties" and apply them, if rather crudely, in their daily life.... From now on, care should be taken to use every opportunity gradually to enrich the content and clarify the meaning of those simple slogans.[40]

Later, Mao went on to create the "Red Army Schools" as he and his armies made their way through the interior provinces during the Third Civil War and other campaigns. He also made a practice of treating the local people with respect and insisted on this behavior with his army also, most of whom where peasants which he collected on his march to take Beijing. Following his principle of "taking the countryside," the CCP revolution was ultimately victorious and became the stuff not only of history, but of myth. To this day, the peasants think well of him. Conversely, the strategy pursued by his CCP comrades—that of taking the cities— was ultimately a failure.

One celebrated story from these revolutionary times is the story of the "Long March." Besieged in the south of China, Mao led his army under the most primitive conditions for a 9500-kilometer march in 1934 from Jiangxi Province to Shanxi Province. Guo Pu, Party Secretary at Shanxi Teacher's University in 1986 (a former Red Army teacher and Long March participant), told author Nancy Street in an interview:

> At twenty-one I joined the Party. To tell the truth, I joined only after learning the theories of Marx and observing Party practice. With revolutionary practice I came to believe in the Party fundamentally. I believe that without the leadership of the CCP there would have been:
>
> 1. No anti–Japanese party;
> 2. No victory over the KMT;
> 3. No new China;
> 4. No modernizations; and,
> 5. No Guo (me) in such a position.[41]

## The Second and Third Civil War Periods

During the Second Civil War period (1927–1937), the struggles between the KMT and the CCP were interrupted by the Japanese attack and subsequent occupation of the northern provinces, installing the deposed emperor Puyi as a puppet emperor in Manchuria. The KMT and the CCP realized that they would once again have to unite to drive the Japanese from China. At the end of World War II, "the KMT occupied Changchun, the former capital of Manchuko. On April 14, 1946, The Communist forces attacked; the War for Liberation had begun."[42] After losses at Changchun and elsewhere, Mao Zedong and the CCP proclaimed the People's Republic of China in Beijing at Tiananmen Square on October 1, 1949.

Retreating to Taiwan, the KMT took with them much of China's ancient treasures. The communist era thus began inauspiciously, with a war-ravaged countryside, a starving populace, and an economy in ruins after nearly thirty years of war. The West, however (especially the United States), was appalled at the victory of the CCP. In retaliation, the United Nations refused to seat Red China (as it was then called), and instead seated the exiled Generalissimo Chiang Kaishek's Republic of China. In reality, the Taiwanese government, until the late eighties, closely resembled the government on the mainland. Both were authoritarian and based on the traditional system. But Chiang Kaishek was backed by the United States, and thus declared a "democracy." Over the years Taiwan became, like Korea, an "economic miracle."[43]

Mainland China, having had the door to participation in world affairs slammed shut, and being subjected to economic siege (as was Cuba), decided to turn her back to the West. Instead, she embraced the Russians (at least initially) and began her odyssey to redress the grievances and wrongs of the past for all her people. However, under the "Great Helmsman," revolutionary-turned-ruler Mao Zedong, there were more wrongs to come. In Cultural Dynamic V, we discuss the Cultural Revolution and its devastation.

# CULTURAL DYNAMIC V

With the end of World War II and the Civil Wars, China was in ruins. Most of her cultural artifacts had been removed to Taiwan as the Kuomingtang (KMT) prepared for exile on Taiwan. (Those artifacts can be found in the National Museum in Taipei.) After 50 years of war, it was clear that

China had to rebuild. The CCP also had to learn to govern. Growing angry with the Russian advisors, Mao decided to break off relations with the Soviets. As Street says in "The Great Proletarian Revolution,"[44]

> The revisionist movements of the fifties were followed in the early sixties by a terrible drought in China; simultaneously, the Russians demanded repayment of the loans made to China during the conduct of the Korean War. Struggling under this burden and the need to modernize education, technology, agriculture and science, the Chinese, against all odds, were recovering.[45]

With no help imminent from either East or West, China was isolated from those who could (or would) help her. By 1966, Mao Zedong became restless. A poet and a revolutionary, he surveyed the physical and mental landscape and found it wanting. In 1966, he called for the "Great Cultural Revolution," one of the greatest disasters in Chinese history, which turned child against parent, student against teacher, employee against employer, citizens against leaders, reversing all the Confucian precepts of hierarchy and behavior in Chinese society (see **Cultural Dynamic II** above). In so doing, Mao also erased his achievements during the Civil War Periods, at least for critics in the West and for intellectuals, the primary victims of the Cultural Revolution in China.

When Mao and the CCP moved through China like a gathering storm in the thirties and forties, the people were taught to read and write. Mao also taught respect for the peasants who were bearing the brunt of the many incursions from various warring factions. Rules were adopted in this battle to "take the countryside." Author Jean Chesneaux says the rules promulgated to win the hearts and minds of the peasants included these instructions:

(1)  Replace all doors when you leave a house;
(2)  Return and roll up the straw matting on which you sleep;
(3)  Be courteous and polite to the people and help them when you can;
(4)  Return all borrowed articles;
(5)  Replace all damaged articles;
(6)  Be honest in all transactions with the peasants;
(7)  Be sanitary and, above all establish latrines a safe distance from people's houses.[46]

From the above, one can see the preoccupation with behaving in a way which would encourage the peasants to believe in what would be a new dynasty. It also reveals the living conditions of the Chinese people and where they were in a "modernization" process that we take so for granted in the United States. American students often ask, "Why would people want to live like that?" The response is, of course, that they do not, but have no choices readily available, since they are "Third World" countries and have had, until recently, very little physical infrastructure to work with — as was true in the United States during the 1930s and 1940s.

During the Cultural Revolution (CR, 1966–1967), the schools were closed and children (and adults) ran wild. Teachers were tortured. Temples were destroyed or damaged. Lives were arrested at 15 or 16 years of age. Sometimes they made it out of exile (students were sent from middle schools and universities to the countryside to "learn from the peasants"). From 1966 to 1976, Red Guards ran the Chinese work units. Families were pulled apart; teachers, intellectuals and others were killed. Books and paintings were burned. The people turned on one another, with directions to:

(1) put the power holders who are in favor of the capitalist road to rout;

(2) criticize those bourgeois reactionary academic "authorities," to criticize the ideology of the bourgeoisie and of all other exploitation-classes; and,

(3) reform education, to reform literature and art, to reform all the superstructure which are not fit for the socialist economic base.[47]

Despite the realities surrounding him, Mao was determined to proceed with his original ideology. To be fair, the Chinese people were living better than they had for many centuries. However, they lacked the modern infrastructure enjoyed in the West. Peasants often crowded around the single television set in their villages. One man interviewed by Nancy Street described how films were brought to his village during this time — on rutted unpaved roads in a cart pulled by a donkey, and then shown on a sheet in the middle of the village square. Families slept together (and still do) on a single *kang*. Indoor plumbing was scarce (and, in rural areas, still is), books were scarce (and in universities all over China, still are) — there were too many people, too far behind the developed world to partake of total modernization.

Without the implementation in the 1980s of the one-child policy, the problem would not have been even remotely solvable. Even with single child restrictions, the goal of socioeconomic equity is daunting, if not impossible. Today, China's population exceeds one billion, three hundred million people. With 800 million people in 2002 living in the countryside, only those in the coastal cities can catch up in a meaningful way. In addition, the move from state-owned enterprises (and lifetime employment in the "work unit" way of life) has disintegrated, leaving hundreds of millions of Chinese peasants without a "social safety net."[48]

It may be too soon to fully assess the shattering impact of the Great Proletarian Revolution upon the culture, given the current move to a partial market economy "with Chinese characteristics." For all practical purposes, the Cultural Revolution ended in 1976. Deng Xiaoping became the leader in 1979 and China opened up. As we indicated at the beginning of this chapter, Deng Xiaoping addressed the Twelfth National Congress of the Chinese Communist Party in 1982, laying out the new program. Since that time (except perhaps during the Tiananmen Crisis in 1989), the Chinese have scarcely had time to assess the last half of the 20th century. They are much too busy making money and creating physical infrastructure for reflection on the impact of the ideological whiplash of the past fifty years.

# CULTURAL DYNAMIC VI

Following the deaths of Mao Zedong, Marshal Zhu De and Zhou Enlai in 1976, events took another turn in China. The Gang of Four was arrested and tried for the crimes and horrors of the Cultural Revolution, and Deng Xiaoping re-emerged, becoming the leader of the CCP. Upon his return, the Chinese people began the arduous restructuring of the entire society — the infrastructure (physical and mental).

From the seventies until 2002, China has been guided by very different goals than those provided by Chairman Mao when he called for the Cultural Revolution. Early on, these goals (first articulated by Premier Zhou Enlai) were incorporated into the "Four Modernizations": the development of industry, of science and technology, agriculture, and national defense.

Given the dearth of educational opportunities in China during the CR, the education system had to be recharged. Teachers and professors schooled in the Russian language and culture had to retool and learn English and Japanese — this, after a long ten years of the CR when one could not read or study anything. At mid-life, professors and teachers were all expected to acquire new skills and perspectives. They, along with their students, had not gone to school in years. It was a stunning reality. Children born in 1960 may not have attended school but for one year (and often less) until they were 16 years old.

Since the Chinese school system is, in many structural ways, similar to that of the United States, the question arises: if one did not go to school until age 16, what background could one have for college? This was a startling dilemma — rarely talked about — of the Cultural Revolution. Teachers became teachers without a high school education. Professors in universities became professors without a college education. In addition, the absence of an academic system meant that many millions of Chinese lost out altogether on the education lottery, due to its many restrictions (as the CCP sought to modernize, develop trade, law schools, shipping berths, media, banks, transportation and communication infrastructure). The task of development during the 1980s was almost impossible. However, the CCP, in defiance of the wishes of the West, tried to take things slowly, knowing that the civil society could not withstand the stress and strain of modernization and of globalization taken too rapidly.

As author Street experienced just 15 years ago in Shanxi Province, communication, transportation and the sanitation infrastructure was virtually non-existent. Yet in the late nineties, the communication, transportation and sanitation infrastructure helped make possible the double-digit growth in GNP in the nineties. A CCP Party Secretary in 1989 explained:

> In 1978, at the Third Plenary Session, we came to realize the appropriate road is Chinese-type socialism. Under the guidance of this principle, production in agriculture and industry has been developed and people's lives have been improved and things are politically stable.[49]

Now things are not always stable, as the country struggles to grow and modernize in the coastal cities, while also enabling those who cannot fully participate in this great experiment — the 800 million Chinese peasants living in the countryside. As their city cousins espouse the slogan "to get rich is wonderful," many Chinese have yet to be affected in a positive way by the growth and participation in world commerce, as have those in the coastal cities.

Only time will tell the results of this internal strife and turmoil. To this point, the vast majority of Chinese people have enjoyed the same lifestyle, same transportation, same food, same benefits, similar clothing. Now, a coastal "elite" of sorts seems imminent. Will the Chinese tolerate this situation — or will the Chinese peasants arise, as they have so often in the past, and bring an end of the current holders of the "mandate of heaven," only to replace them with more of the same? Or, in this era of globalization, can they afford the luxury of overthrowing the current government?

## CONCLUSION

The tumultuous history of modern China blends with the history of ancient China, creating six identifiable cultural dynamics to provide us with a template for understanding the Chinese as they are today. They are people, who (like everyone else) have been affected profoundly by religion, politics and power. These circumstances, in turn, create a very unique "worldview." This worldview becomes essential in understanding the contemporary Chinese life. It also addresses the inherent mistrust of current globalization economic policies (through the World Bank and the International Monetary Fund). These entities, along with myriad other considerations, affect the Chinese and other developing nations (the poor or the "have nots") in their relationships with the Western industrialized nations (the rich or the "haves") that control the new world order.

# 2

# Issues in Globalization

The Chinese people are not the only citizens who currently protest the concepts and consequences of globalization and membership in the World Trade Organization (WTO). In the past few years we have seen massive demonstrations in the United States, in Canada and in Europe protesting the WTO, which developed through the advent of technology.

Until the late 1980s, most of the world's citizens were blissfully unaware of this "new world order." From the ordinary citizen's point of view, the coming of Automatic Teller Machines (ATMs) also heralded the dawning of a new age. Manufacturing and trade became globalized soon afterward, with interconnections between banks, corporations and labor amongst the countries of the world. At that point, Third World or developing nations, through their labor forces, assumed much of the manufacturing of clothing and electronics for the First World. For the most part, laborers in these impoverished lands were happy to have the work. And governments (whatever the ideology), entrepreneurs and the manufacturing industries profited hugely as well. In fact, some countries, like India, bet and won on technology, computers and education. India's computer industry now services businesses around the world on a 24 hour shift, seven days a week — the computers are never "down" — in India.

But there are several objections to globalization. The first is that it

45

does not, in its current form, promote democracy. Second, although First World countries (such as the U.S.) demand that developing countries open their markets and not subsidize their laborers, in fact, the United States in 2002 increased its subsidies to farmers. The increase was not to small farmers, but to United States agricultural conglomerates. This spells out a non-egalitarian approach to globalization. Third, the fact that the International Monetary Fund (IMF) can tell various countries, such as South Korea, what they must have in place to receive aid curtails democracy and the potency of nation-state governments. Finally, globalization (and the media) make terrorism possible. We need not look to hijacking planes in the United States to shut down the economy. All that is necessary is for terrorists to infiltrate our manufacturing facilities abroad and just one of the companies that supply them to cause a meltdown in America.

In "Unmade in America: The True Cost of a Global Assembly Line," Barry Lynn asserts,

> The global assembly lines that manufacturers such as Dell, Ford, Motorola, and Intel have so expertly engineered these past few years— in which, say, a single semi-conductor might be cut from a wafer in Taiwan, assembled in the Philippines, tested in China, fit into a subcomponent in Malaysia, plugged into a component in Brazil, and loaded with a pro-gram designed in India — are just as audaciously complicated as any of Enron's financial schemes. Yet because manufactured goods are so much less fungible than money, these systems are vastly more vulnerable to the mysterious mutterings of God or the deliberate hand of man and state. We now live in a world where a single earthquake, or terrorist attack, or embargo, could in a moment bring our economy to a halt.[1]

Lynn insists that we have not given adequate thought to our own national security, as we outsource our products around the globe. The United States has used both China and Taiwan for production, never dreaming that we might become dependent on them. In this regard, Lynn says:

> A decade ago, no large U.S. company was dependent on China or Taiwan as either a market or a place for production. Today, hundreds are. When he took office early last year, George W. Bush inherited from his predecessor and from his own father perhaps the greatest failure in the history of American geopolitical thought.[2]

## HISTORICAL OVERVIEW

According to Gordon L. Walker and Mark A. Fox, "The macroeconomic and technological preconditions for globalization were not in place until the late–1970s and early–1980s."[3] Until that time, computers were not widely available outside of the business arena. However, the privatization of industries throughout the world has changed the technological, economic, and political landscape considerably. This is proving to be both advantageous and disadvantageous as we collectively enter the new millennium.

As the world is beginning to notice through the many protest marches accompanying WTO conferences around the globe, globalization no longer needs the consent of governments. This is especially true if the process is in the hands of multinational corporations which can move from country to country, when one indigenous labor population becomes too expensive to produce their wares. Examples of this include South Korea and the People's Republic of China. Back in the late '80s, the Korean GNP was much lower than it is today. Once it approached $4,000 (U.S.) a year, however, industries were moved to other areas of Asia, which might only pay 60 cents per day to their laborers. China was a leading "recipient" of foreign investors at that time. In 1985 in China, the Chinese laborer made approximately $20 each year. Today, the average worker in China makes $100 a year.[4] As the Chinese economy continues to grow, its labor market will soon price itself out of outside investors, giving way to newer, more labor-intensive and "exploitable" countries. Africa may be next — but only if they can bring the various wars and HIV-AIDS epidemic under control. John le Carré, in *The Nation*, writes,

> The Cold War provided the perfect excuse for Western governments to plunder and exploit the Third World in the name of freedom; to rig its elections, bribe its politicians, appoint its tyrants and, by every sophisticated means of persuasion and interference, stunt the emergence of young democracies in the name of democracy.[5]

What is the motivation for this course of action in the Third World? And what cultures and countries make up the Third World? The Third World is largely African, Asian, South American and Middle-Eastern, as well as much of Eastern Europe or the former Soviet Union — in fact, most of the earth. Having barely emerged from colonialism, many of these nations, such as Algeria or Vietnam, were, in their post-colonial incarnation, ripe for the next stage in trade and market expansion. As to motivation, as always, money and power go hand in hand.

This new era, begun some time before the end of the Cold War and the "fall" of the Wall, is known as "globalization." Following the established world trade routes controlled by such forces as the Roman, Ottoman and Mongol empires and later by Spain, Portugal and England in their quest for the New World, today's corporate entities are the new imperialists—adjudicating trade policies and "New Millennium World" trade routes.

Author John le Carré focuses on the mega-pharmaceutical companies in particular. According to him, "Big Pharma"

> offer[s] everything: the hopes and dreams we have of it; its vast, partly realized potential for good; and its pitch-dark underside, sustained by huge wealth, pathological secrecy, corruption and greed.[6]

Down the line, the Asian market may no longer provide the cheapest labor. Having depleted or despoiled (physically or morally) the remaining resources of the Asian countries, the mega-companies will want to capture the African and South American labor markets, as well as what might remain of their natural resources.[7]

In the American labor market, jobs have been lost to the free trade rules of NAFTA, creating horrific labor and living conditions along the Mexico–U.S. border. In addition, the population of the American labor market has increased in its diversity — and lowered its pay scale in many industries— by the influx of documented and undocumented labor forces from around the world. In the past twenty years alone, 30 million people have emigrated to the U.S. Currently, the government is considering amnesty for undocumented immigrants, primarily Mexican, to utilize them for the "bottom of the rung" labor. Sadly, the "bottom rung" in America is, in any case, better paying than a similar job in Mexico, yet another graft-ridden, poverty-stricken country, despite its many years of cooperation with the United States.

## GLOBALIZATION DEFINED

The concept of globalization (and the belief that it cannot be reversed) makes all this possible: an exchange of so-called "big government" for "big business" (multinational corporations) which guide both national and international policies.[8] Multinationals have the advantage of surveying the entire world for location, natural resources, labor resources, existing physical infrastructure (roads, power plants, electricity, communications). They also have the requisite resources to gain access to (or aid the developing nations to put in place) governmental institutions, legal systems, social and political systems and the requisite financial institutions. Multinationals also have access to exploring and promoting historical beliefs, attitudes and values. In short, multinationals have intimate knowledge of (and access to) the physical, cultural and financial infrastructure of the developing country of their choice — for the express purpose of profiting from the labor of others without giving back.

What is globalization? According to Walker, there are many facets to globalization. "The modern meaning of globalization implies a global perspective of the particular area of study, a perspective which arises from the increased interdependence of national institutions and national economies."[9] Perhaps more to the point, financial institutions are now so globalized that, in this area (and short of unthinkable devastation, despite the protests at the WTO in Seattle and the G-6 plus Russia in Genoa), there will be no retreat. As Walker notes (confining his observation to the developed nations), "Economic activities are stretched across the world as geographical constraints recede and deepen in the sense of interconnectedness."[10] However, once again, the bonding occurs amongst the Western developed countries with similar history, culture and economic systems. Conversely, the so-called Eastern countries may also seek to bond together, citing strength in numbers. Once again, this scenario, orchestrated by the advancing West, pits East against West.[11]

Factors which feed into any focus on globalization include: "new technology, ... macroeconomic change, global culture ... global threats to peace and security, problems of global underdevelopment and poverty, threats to the global environment, and mass migration."[12] In the case of China, the rapidly growing problems of underdevelopment (or infrastructure) and poverty are often ignored.[13] In the cases under consideration in this book, this multifaceted focus provides a kaleidoscope of China's belated entry into the globalized post–Cold War world. The Philippines share similar concerns with China as they pursue globalization, hoping that it will result in the materialistic blessings prevalent in the West. Within this context, it is useful to discuss their circumstances.

## THE PHILIPPINES AND AGENDA 21

In discussing globalization and the Philippine Agenda 21, the Center for Alternative Development Initiatives (CADI) suggests that there are five types of unsustainable development in the wake of globalization, particularly in Third World development[14] (although we think that the case can be made in a Western country such as America for several forms of unsustainable development). CADI lists and describes five types of unsustainable development:

1. *Jobless growth* results when economic output increases amidst high unemployment and underemployment.

2. *Ruthless growth* is forcing millions of Filipinos to live in poverty; a few individual billionaires and millionaires enjoy an income level equivalent to the combined income of the millions in poverty. Globally, for example, the 1999 UNDP Human Development Report estimated that the $140 billion combined assets of Bill Gates and the two other top owners of Microsoft are more than the combined gross national product (GNP) of the 43 least economically developed countries and their 600 million people.

3. *Futureless growth* results from the destruction of nature through improper mining practices, use of pesticides, insufficient and improper environmental planning for the construction of dams and a range of other ecologically unsound development projects.

4. *Rootless growth* refers to the cultural decay and loss of meaning and identity which often accompany economic growth fueled by globalization and the entrance of materialistic lifestyles in industrialized countries.

5. *Voiceless growth* is economic growth racing ahead of direct human rights and democratic processes and participatory governance essential to modern societies.

To the aforementioned, CADI adds a sixth concern: "meaningless growth," or growth which results in "loss in creativity, perspective, meaning, hope, and morality [that] necessarily expresses itself in suicide, violence, drug addiction, crime, corruption and other social ills."[15] In this book, we refer to these concepts of growth from time to time as we discuss the globalization of the Chinese economy and its culture.

As discussed above, the split between East and West is an important one to understand as "developing" and "developed." Further, it is important to acknowledge that the rules of the globalized world have been laid out by the dominant and "developed" Western countries. We have learned that to many, the current economic and eroding nation-state infrastructure fuel globalization — and that there is no retreat from this situation.

For these reasons, developing countries sometimes appear to want to "develop" according to Western dictates, as well as to allow Western popular culture to obliterate national historical culture. If this is the case, we are well on the way (as a world of nation states) to even further dominance of the West over the East. However, many factors impede the onward and upward progress of globalization, as we have seen in the case of the

Philippine Agenda and the patterns of "unsustainable growth." It may then be the case, that the worst off today may, in the final analysis, be the worst off in the future. It may also be the case that each country involved may select not to play according to the rules established by the dominant West, as confirmed by the 2001 World Trade Center attacks. China may also be a case in point. She may best illustrate the thorny path of globalization yet to come, as the most populous country to undergo globalization.

China embarked upon "the Four Modernizations" in the 1980s under Deng Xiaoping, following the end of the Cultural Revolution and the death of Chairman Mao and Zhou Enlai in 1976. In the years that followed, the Chinese government took "baby steps" toward globalization, as it opened the doors that had been closed for nearly thirty years. The impact of globalization on Chinese society, its workers and their attitudes and beliefs can be illustrated through examples of the Liaoyang and Daqing oilfield crisis in March of 2002, China's recent entry in the WTO while celebrating its MFN (U.S. trade — most favored nation) status, and winning its bid to host the Olympics in 2008. Perhaps the preparation for the Olympics will prove a fortuitous advantage for China as it moves its economy to globalization, opening up jobs for the jobless and enhancing physical infrastructure for use beyond 2008. The benefits could produce much more than a fervent nationalism; indeed, the preparations and the Olympic Games may provide the impetus China needs to forge a viable bridge between the "haves" and the "have nots."

# TUESDAY 9/11

Two days after the authors wrote the first draft of this chapter, the United States was brought to its knees by a terrorist attack on two of its major (if not *the* two major) symbols of American prosperity and might. On the morning of September 11, 2001, terrorists attacked the twin towers of the World Trade Center and one "wedge" of the Pentagon. The terrorists, thought to be disciples of the Saudi Osama bin Laden, accomplished their mission through dive-bombing into the structures in *kamakazi* style. No one on board the four hijacked planes involved in this mission lived. Two planes that took off from Logan Airport in Boston took out the twin towers of the World Trade Center in New York City, that city's signature skyline. A third plane, taking off from New Jersey, took out a newly renovated "wedge" of the Pentagon in Washington, D.C. A fourth plane, assumed to be heading for the White House or other monument in Washington,

D.C., crashed in a field in Pennsylvania. The nation has been in chaos since that infamous Tuesday in September, asking, "Why?"

Both the World Trade Center and the Pentagon are symbols to much of the rest of the world of America's privilege and might. The *Boston Globe* "Focus" section on Sunday, September 16, featured a headline that read, "Why Do They Hate Us?"[16] Under that banner, numerous experts wrote their responses. In some instances, these responses had to do with globalization. There may be, or so it seems, some good reasons for others to hate us, particularly in the Middle East, as well as other Third World or developing nations.

At any level, the age-old divide between the "haves" and the "have nots" generates hatred, jealousy and envy on the part of the "have nots"— those with nothing left to lose. We do not know the feelings of the "haves," insofar as they have feelings about the "have nots" (or even take notice of them). In the American belief system, these people need to put their shoulders to the wheel—as Americans have done so successfully—to "earn" their prosperity as Americans have done. These people are simply lazy and uncreative. And, as Americans, we tend to disdain the people who haven't the sense to copy the "American Way"—clean drinking water, good sanitation, cutting-edge technology and transparent institutions. In short, the poverty and lack of amenities in the Third World is seen by Western "others" as due to a lack of initiative — not as the result of many complex factors.

If we have the identities of the terrorists who guided the hijacked planes into two of America's iconic institutions, for example, we might learn that the terrorists' lives had been lived in countries with far different opportunities and values than those found in the United States. Not, however, with differing basic concepts such as family and basic physical necessities. People everywhere value life, family and living a good life. But not all people have access to these basic needs. Holocausts, wars, famine and disease ravage peoples of the Third World. And the rest of the world stands by and watches, occasionally lending a helping hand. Often, however, we reach out to these peoples, pretending to help; but in reality, exploiting them, in collusion with corporations and governments.

After more than fifty years of warfare in the Middle East between Israel and the Palestinians (between a state and a non-state group) the events of Tuesday, 9/11, should not have been a surprise to the world — or to Americans. We have, after all, witnessed on a daily basis the enmity between the two groups of people. Choosing, as we did — to ignore the ongoing struggle — only made the "have nots" angrier and stronger in their commitment to take revenge on those, including the United States, who have deprived them of nation-state status, of a place to be. (Or, in the case of the Saudi Osama bin Laden, infiltrated and corrupted legitimate government.) What followed was a horrific attack on the United States — the first on U.S. soil in modern history.[17] In contrast, China has adopted a more constructive stance (over time) in its attitudes toward the "haves."

## THE STRUCTURE OF GLOBALIZATION IN CHINA

In 1980s China, there was great resistance to allowing foreigners as equals in Chinese enterprises. Moreover, while living in Chinese society during this relatively early formative period, one of the authors (Nancy Street) experienced directly the lack of awareness of the coming globalization opportunities for China by the average person either in China or the United States. A short example will suffice.

For several decades, China had two forms of currency: *renminbi* (RMB) and Foreign Exchange Currency (FEC). At that time, the rate of exchange was roughly 1 FEC to 3 RMB. Foreigners were forbidden to use RMB. The problem was that in 1985, outside of Beijing, Guangzhou and Shanghai, most Chinese did not recognize FEC, but demanded payment in RMB. Further, outside of the central bank in Beijing, banks knew little or nothing about traveler's checks. When Street arrived in Linfen in Shanxi Province in 1985 to teach at Shanxi Teacher's University, she could buy nothing. She had no RMB and the bank did not recognize FEC, traveler's checks, credit cards or American dollars. So, despite having all the above, with the exception of the RMB, she could purchase nothing. Without RMB, she was penniless.

The only way to obtain useable money was to take the train back to Beijing (18 hours one-way), get a room at the Friendship Hotel (built with the help of the Russians back in the heyday of the Chinese-Russian friendship in the fifties), then take a bus or a cab to the one bank in Beijing which could cash a traveler's check. Next, she had to obtain FEC and exchange money with a Chinese person for RMB, so that she could buy food in the free market, stamps for milk and stamps for letters in Linfen.

Linfen at the time had some 300,000 residents in the city and the surrounding countryside. In the free market in this small city, where the peasants brought their produce, many of the vendors had never seen foreigners before. When Street and her students stopped to buy eggs or rice, the Chinese would circle them, eager to touch their hair and clothes, often laughing at some absurdity of their outfits. The locals, on the other hand, were dressed quite similarly in blue, black or green Mao jackets and matching pants. In the winter, they looked chubbier than in the summer. (The Chinese wore the same clothes much of the year, but in winter they wore layers of clothing, discarded in the spring and early summer, when their clothes hung on them.)

On the Shanxi Teacher's University campus, there were several televisions, a few phones and by 1988, two computers which were under armed guard day and night. The campus also had several cars for administrative use, and occasionally for the foreign teachers and students. As for postal facilities, if the one person at the downtown postal office who sent international mail was out of town, the mail could not leave Linfen until his or her return. The same situation existed if someone wanted to make a phone call, send a telegram or take a train.

Since Linfen was a "closed" city, getting tickets for the train was a nightmare of obstacles. First, one had to have a document with the "red seal" on it to order tickets. Second, there was the ongoing confusion of FEC versus RMB. Third (although Street and her students did not at first understand this), there arose the delicate decision of whom to select to go with the Westerners on such a trip. This latter enterprise involved selecting a Chinese travel companion, deciding in which class they should travel, and paying for all their expenses—otherwise, one could not leave the city. Clearly, this was not a world preparing for globalization.

By 1988–89, the rules had relaxed on the money issues and the black market was rampant in China (in both the cities and the countryside). Ironically, despite the change, train tickets were no easier to obtain and there were no more private cars for hire (except, perhaps, in the various work units). Roads were still poor to nonexistent, especially during the rainy season. But one thing was clearly improved — mail efficiency. To her surprise, Street discovered the post office at the Beijing Lido Hotel. This discovery saved countless hours (and trees). In Beijing, one was also able to ship things in cardboard boxes instead of custom made wooden boxes.

In 1990, following the Tiananmen Square tragedy, life in China looked much as it had in 1985. As a member of a Fulbright Study Group in China, Street was able to once again travel the route from Beijing to Xi'an to Shanghai by both train and plane. She observed only small changes to China's landscape — noting that not much was different in the countryside (although from the train it appeared from the size of the houses, that many of the farmers had been doing quite well). Millions of Chinese peasants still lived in "caves." In the fields, one could still see a lone farmer pulling the plow. On the roads, horse-drawn carts and three-wheeled vehicles dominated the highways.

Just twenty years ago, the Chinese worker or peasant could expect a job, a house, a work unit or plot of ground, health care and a relatively free education. Bicycles were not taken for granted. Everyone (young or old) dressed in gray, black, blue or green Mao suits or padded cotton jackets and pants. For winter, one knitted and wore long underwear. Everyone wanted the best bicycle — the "Flying Pigeon." Workers had a job for life. State-run industries were often poorly run and not profitable; nonetheless, people grew used to the "iron rice bowl" life. A BBC report from China on March 11, 2001, indicates that the new social security system for China

> will involve people making contributions to pension or unemployment insurance schemes, unlike the current system in which state-owned enterprises (SOEs) are responsible for their workers for life. Officials say that as the number of elderly people in China grows, the old system is unsustainable in the long term, and stifles the ability of state-owned companies to compete ... the new programme is expected to cover about 200 million people, but not the majority of the population — more than 800 million rural-based peasants.[18]

One of the many problems associated with globalization in the recently modern China is that of the literacy and skills of the worker population, due to the effects of the Cultural Revolution (1966–1976). As Professor Lian Hong of Shanghai's Fudan University points out,

> These people, who grew up during China's political movements of 1960s are a lost generation ... they were assigned jobs in factories so they didn't have a chance to study more. There are new jobs in Shanghai now — but they're usually for technically skilled workers, and the competition is very intense.[19]

These are some of the realities of today's China — important cultural dynamics that are necessary to know for successful corporate ventures. But how can American business executives be made aware of all the necessary data needed for negotiating a mutually beneficial agreement?

AmCham, the American Chamber of Commerce in Shanghai, has become a key source of information on China for many multinational corporations (and will be discussed in greater detail later in Chapter 10). For more than two decades, this nonprofit organization has provided essential insights for those interested in pursuing business interests in China. In a 2001 position paper, for example, AmCham put the current Chinese socioeconomic situation into an understandable perspective:

> China is 65 percent agrarian, but only 30% of the population is involved directly in farming. There are about 300 million people on farms, and

many of those are moving out, or are about to move out, of food production. This compares closely to the United States in the 1930s, when 30% of the population was still involved in food production. Now in the U.S.A, however, the figure is less than 2 percent. Chinese government forecasts predict this same trend for China's employment makeup over the coming century, a massive, complex social change that will uproot as well as strengthen the Chinese economy and society.[20]

The comparison of China in 2001 with the United States in the thirties is well taken, particularly in agriculture and infrastructure. However, as discussed here, there are also many social problems associated with the upheaval thus far. The task of the Chinese government is to move from a socialist, state-run economy to a capitalist, market economy and still emerge as the government. The social and political fallout can only become more intense in the short term.

## CHINA, MODERNITY AND GLOBALIZATION

With China's entry into the World Trade Organization (WTO) in 2002, it began a radically new phase of development. One must keep in mind, however, that as a developing country, China began to enter the modern world in terms of physical infrastructure just 20 years ago. When Deng Xiaoping inaugurated the Four Modernizations[21] as Chinese policy in the early eighties, there were few good roads, virtually no refrigeration, little indoor plumbing, few telephones, televisions and (at least those common in the Western world), few kitchen appliances in China. Most Chinese women cooked on coal stoves, walked or rode their bicycles to the free market, where mountains of vegetables could be had. People had to boil all drinking water or risk severe illness (which is still true today).

After years of intensive work in all areas of the economy and newly-induced poverty for many, China has some good, key roads, some working indoor plumbing for cooking and bathing, some refrigeration (and, in international hotels and first class Chinese hotels, air-conditioning). As recently as 1997, persons living below the Yangtze River were not able to have electric heat in their homes. As a result, most citizens (at least in Nancy Street's university work unit in Shanxi), tended to have small heaters where everyone huddled around, teeth chattering, wearing all the outer clothing they owned. North of the Yangtze — known home to China's "three ovens,"[22] citizens could not have air conditioning. Multitudinous electric fans in some homes were the only means to lessen the ferocious heat in summer. While the heating and air conditioning situation may not have improved significantly in the past five years in China, today its citizens do enjoy many televisions, telephones and other consumer electronics, including computers. Department stores bulge with household items. Many women have electric or gas stoves and refrigerators. It's really a different world. Video stores are full of films from around the world, including newly released films.[23] In short, China has already come a very long way in entering modern times, primarily in its cities—those which have strong ties to the West, to trade, to shipping, to industry of all kinds, as well as consumer goods.

While China's physical infrastructure burgeons in the coastal cities, its institutional infrastructure lags behind that of many other nations. By "institutional infrastructure," we mean legal, social, political, economic (banking), health care, education and the honing of the relationship between government and labor. The recent unrest in northeastern China in Liaoyang is a clear example of this latter issue. According to the on-line BBC news:

> Several thousand Chinese workers have been protesting in the northeastern city of Lioayang over unpaid wages, pensions and alleged corruption.... The demonstration comes in the wake of two weeks of huge protests by sacked workers at the northeastern Daqing oil field.... China's state-controlled press has not reported the protests.[24]

Social unrest is a fact of life in China, as the state-controlled industries give way to privatization (deemed necessary to China's economic success). On 19 March 2002, this headline captured the plight of disenfranchised workers: "Thousands of Workers Protest in Chinese City." According to the report,

> Thousands of laid-off workers from six factories surrounded government and police headquarters today ... to demand the release of their missing leader, a corruption investigation and back pay from the government.... Protesters and witnesses contacted by telephone from Beijing said workers from six factories in Liaoyang, a gritty city 350 miles northeast of the capital, have been protesting layoffs and government corruption since March 1.... Protests by workers and farmers are becoming increasingly common in China as the gap between rich and poor widens. For the past five years, the incomes of factory workers and farmers have been basically flat while those of white-collar workers and government employees have increased substantially.[25]

The ideology of the protests may be viewed as a "mixed bag." On the one hand, all Chinese would like to be rich; on the other hand, the recent rich in China are perceived to have acquired their riches on the "backs" of the poor. Nearly 100 years ago, the Chinese rose up to rid themselves of serfdom. Under Mao's rule, one of the guiding principles was "class struggle." As terrible as the civil wars were (along with the tremendous toll which all the wars combined in the first half of the 20th century imposed on China during the period from 1950 to 1980), people articulated the egalitarian vision. This vision meant vigilance and continuous revolution — not to do away with communism, but to enhance and spread communism as the ultimate egalitarian goal.

People do not easily discard basic beliefs and values once inculcated. To lose one's safety net (health, education, welfare, to say nothing of houses, work and salary) at mid-life may, in the long run, be best for the country, perhaps even for the worker lucky enough to live in one of the coastal, shipping, trading or industrial cities in contemporary China. But, as we have learned, most Chinese (roughly 800 million) do not live in those cities. Rather, like the workers described above, they live in what is called "the rust belt." Not benefiting (indeed, actually losing) from globalization and modernity with their attendant opportunities and riches, these citizens may feel bereft and betrayed. Further, a new form of government cannot hasten improvement in their living conditions, and they are often told that some must wait for their turn to come. Like most people everywhere, these betrayed workers want to eat and live in the here and now. As an angry worker in Liaoyang said, "We're not benefiting from any of this…. Everybody talks about China's miracle. Well, there are no miracles here."[26] The article further illuminates the increasingly dire situation in northeast China which echoes the grievances of the Chinese peasants at the overthrow of the Emperor Puyi in 1911:

> Moreover, millions of urban workers have lost their jobs the government has attempted to reform state-owned industries, often by selling them at bargain prices to local Communist Party officials. Farmers, meanwhile, have been impoverished by high taxes imposed by local governments that have all but stopped receiving funds from Beijing. The demonstrations in Liaoyang have underscored the presence of a time bomb ticking alongside China's breakneck economic reforms.[27]

Pausing here for a moment to reflect upon some of the difficulties which China has encountered with the United States and the strong criticism of China by government and media sources, a note regarding the nature of that criticism is in order. Now — twenty years later — after critiquing China for not moving fast enough in its economic and political reforms,[28] we begin to see the tip of the iceberg in the nature and magnitude of the endeavor to bring China to modernity. China's "breakneck economic reforms," its foray into developing laws, rules and regulations regarding trade, as well as labor issues to meet requirements of membership in the WTO, are consuming much of its energy and sapping many of its people of their joy in life. The price may be huge.

In addition to the massive layoffs and lack of a real safety net for workers, there are other problems associated with the collapse and bankruptcy of the state-owned industries. These problems include rising worker grievances "because workers believe that many factory managers and government officials, in privatizing the factories, are stripping off their assets and selling them for vast profits."[29] While this may or may not be the case, one can be certain that if there is money to be made in this dissolution of the state-owned industries, someone other than the ordinary worker (who, after all, used to own the means of production, in concert with his/her follow workers) is on the receiving end.

As usual, when oil is involved, as it is in the Daqing worker protest, there are profits to be made — at the expense of the citizens. As one newspaper editor in China put it, "They are the forgotten people of China. These workers are waste paper. There isn't anything that anyone could do to save them."[30] Some 60 percent of workers in Liaoyang are unemployed as "tens of thousands of workers have protested in Daqing and Liaoyang. In Daqing, workers are angry at PetroChina Co., one of China's biggest oil companies, which has laid off tens of thousands of workers in a bid to transform itself into a competitive firm. China's entry into the World Trade Organization and PetroChina's listing on the New York and Hong Kong stock exchanges have added urgency to that task."[31]

In this one example, we see the specter of what is to come for the Chinese as gradually all state enterprises are sold off, their workers dismissed, the safety net of the past 50 years in tatters, lives shattered. Yet the way "forward" is led from within the CCP.

The truth is, the Chinese government cannot please everyone and also that the unrest in China may be fundamentally fueled by the loss of the promises of socialism for the promises of globalization, coupled with anger that most (initially at least) cannot benefit from globalization. Given the size and population of China, one can safely assume that this will not happen under any form of government. Examples of the "miracles" of Korea and Taiwan ignore the vast differences in size and population amongst these three countries. One cannot compare these three Confucian-based countries or suggest similar remedies to the social, legal and political problems which China now faces as a result of modernization, globalization and its entry into the WTO.

# A POSTSCRIPT

One cannot predict the outcome for China in the globalization scenario. At the moment, with the protests in northeast China, the outcome is not certain. However, we have yet to factor the impact of the 2008 Olympic Games, not only on China's economy, but its physical and mental infrastructure. This intervention may prove extremely beneficial to China, its people and its government. As we have discussed elsewhere, the authors of this book were in China during the handover of Hong Kong in 1997. As a visiting professor at that time, Nancy Street witnessed the intense six-month preparation for the Hong Kong celebration in July of 1997, in Nanjing and throughout the country. The people of China are not easily discouraged, as we have seen from their long history, as well as the history of the 20th century.

Though it may appear at the moment that the Philippine Agenda 21 may in part apply to China's situation today, i.e., jobless growth, ruthless growth and voiceless growth, that is the perception of the moment. As the Tao says, "The path that is marked is not the way." China will find its way.

This period of globalization with its attendant discontents is but a comma in China's history. The Chinese solicit outside investment and joint ventures. They want to belong, in part, to the world. Deep down, they know that it will cost and hurt. Participating in globalization and the WTO is the goal of both the people and of the government. Despite the problems and pain, there will be change in the existing system. And the Chinese will accommodate that change through perseverance and with grace, as exemplified in their evolving consumer behavior.

Referring to the efforts of the United States to support democracy in China, Barry Lynn, in "Unmade in America: The True Cost of a Global Assembly Line," muses on the irony of it all:

> The greatest danger of all may not be that Beijing one day dares try to coerce the West but that the plan to undermine Beijing actually works, that the massive movement of money, goods, and ideas will lure freedom-seeking citizens back to Tiananmen. Revolutions, as we sometimes forget, can turn violent. How long, if violence strikes China, will we have to wait for our shipments of semiconductors and alternators and gaskets to arrive? Might we not find ourselves obliged one day, by the selfsame economic interdependence that was supposed to undermine Beijing, to prop up that regime in order to ensure the proper functioning of our own economy?[32]

# 3

# The Changing Chinese Consumer

According to Conghua Li in *China: The Consumer Revolution*, China's gross domestic product (GDP) should exceed that of the United States by 2015, with a continued increase in future decades, making it "the fastest growing consumer society" in the world.[1] As in most developing countries, China's greatest expansion will be concentrated in retail sales (including fast food, clothing, cars, cellular phones and DVDs), agriculture, financial services, telecommunications and construction. However, the way in which the Chinese will adapt to this trend is different from most Western societies. They will achieve their "new identity" based on a systematic series of cultural adoption and revision. They will then invent a "new culture," based on ancestral tradition as well as technological innovation. Author Jianying Zha refers to this vacillating condition as "'the third way' or 'the Chinese way,'" in contrast to the Soviet model ... ridden with contradictions, ambiguities, and often impossible dilemmas."[2] The path to China's new culture may take various turns, but must always blend old ways with current realities. And when looking at changing consumer behaviors, two major factors must be considered: (1) the rise of a market economy and all its implications; and (2) clear generational differences. This chapter will address each.

## MARKET ECONOMY

Most financial analysts would agree that much has been accomplished in a very short time as China moves toward a consumer-based financial system. For the most part, this progress has been due to foreign investment and joint business ventures, which have provided greater per capita earnings in most segments of the Chinese population. *China: The Consumer Revolution* notes that more than 20,000 international businesses have come to China each year since 1991. Along with these businesses come increased pay and benefits for employees—sometimes 2 to 4 times more than for similar jobs run by state enterprises.[3] These pay increases have allowed for more disposable income, to be spent on such (former) luxuries as air conditioners, video and DVD cameras and recorders, color televisions and washing machines.[4]

But why did this change come about, and how did it happen so quickly? China experts might credit the late nineteenth century famine as much as anything else for the move toward market economics. The resulting poverty, disease and general hardship drove many Chinese overseas; they, in turn, sent money back for their families. As times changed and Chinese life improved, the expatriates were able to turn toward a longer-term goal—investments in foreign ventures—to create national stability and international recognition.

At the same time, government policymakers under Deng Xiaoping worked toward changes in the nation's infrastructure and future growth. Clearly the first step in managing the development of the country was the single-child policy, put into practice in 1979 and administered to all regions within two years of its legislation.[5] This policy did not prohibit couples from having more than one child; it simply removed the government's responsibility from supporting more than one. However, population reduction was not the only necessary change in government policy—state ownership of corporate enterprises was another issue at hand. According to the Janet Matthews Information Services (Quest Economics Database):

> Since the revolution in 1949, the Chinese economy has been largely centrally managed, so much so that despite recent economic improvements, "privatization" remains an unpopular word. In recent years, however, momentum for change has grown. Economic decisions have been decentralized closer to production and significant numbers of small and medium enterprises have been returned to the private sector, under the auspices of local authorities.[6]

In addition, the government undertook several measures to redefine itself, including:

> The transferal of state-owned enterprises to joint-stock companies listed on the stock exchange, the attraction of foreign capital for the restructuring of companies, the reallocation of capital within enterprises, a change in employment policy (for example, the introduction of labour contracts), the regulation of bankruptcies of loss-making small and medium-sized enterprises, and the development of the private sector.[7]

These policies have impacted Chinese citizens in several ways. On the negative side, increases in privatization have, in turn, brought about reductions in state subsidies, especially in retirement pensions and housing benefits. Relatedly, the "iron rice bowl" (or guarantee of life-long employment commonly found in communist societies) has begun to disappear. No longer can one expect to be in the same job forever. And higher pay does not necessarily compensate for the potential lack of security, especially in one's older years.

Overall, China's more relaxed government policies have allowed its people more "choice" and "quality" in their daily lives. Until 1996, for example, residents lived under a registration system called *Hukou*. Its purpose was to classify citizens as either urban or rural; agricultural or nonagricultural. Once classified, workers could not change either their professions or locale. Similarly, young Chinese might be "assigned" to a particular school or university, whether if they wanted to pursue a certain profession or not. Today, Chinese can move more freely to different areas of the country. They can also apply to any institution they choose (although it may cost more). This was due to a revision in the old *Hukou*, allowing many the ability to migrate to different work units (farmers to cities, etc.), and perhaps seek new professions or entrepreneurial ventures. The revised *Hukou* is not without its drawbacks, however. As in any change, market-based economies carry with them both freedoms and constraints.

On the one hand, citizens of the "new" China may choose where to live, establish residency, and gain whatever benefits they can from living in a particular work environment or locale. They also permitted job choice, rather than assignment to a particular work unit, thus allowing people to change professions if they are not happy in them and creating a potential for social mobility never before seen in China.

Conversely, freedom to move to another part of the country also means the "freedom" to starve, because relocation to a new area no longer necessarily implies that one can find work there. In the old *Hukou*, assignments to particular work units were given to ensure that there would be as many positions as needed for any given project. Under the new system, a person can move from the countryside to the city or from city to city, but the move doesn't necessarily mean guaranteed employment. Moreover, since there is no more guarantee of life employment, all the benefits previously allowed by the government (such as housing subsidies) are gradually disappearing — hence, a fear of financial instability heretofore unknown to the Chinese.

To address these new concerns, business ventures are emerging, especially in the areas of home construction, life and health insurance, savings and investment plans, elder care and pharmaceuticals. The most dramatic changes to meet these needs have been in three areas of China's infrastructure: communication and technology; business ventures and investments; and transportation.

## COMMUNICATION AND TECHNOLOGY

*Telephones.* Both mobile phones and fixed telephone lines have increased exponentially in the last fifteen years. According to the 2001 Janet Matthews World of Information Report, more than 102 million main phone lines can be found throughout the country (including both private and public pay phones), in addition to a growing cellular market of more than $7.2 billion USD.[8] And both continue to expand. The Matthews Report counts one Chinese among every seven new mobile phone subscribers worldwide, and notes that pay phones are "still common and heavily used"[9] throughout the country, despite unprecedented cell phone use. Pagers have also been a widely sought consumer item — the Matthews report estimated more 60 million pagers in use in 1998,[10] and the figure continues to grow.

These statistics reconfirmed the observations we had while staying in Nanjing in 1997, and revisiting that city (along with Beijing and Shanghai) in 2001. In large cities, one cannot walk a block without either hearing the ringing of someone's phone or watching them make a call. And among our new friends in Nanjing, there were several young professionals who carried their cell phones wherever they went. When asked, one of them told us that the activation fee was usually about $125 USD, and he generally paid about $60 USD in monthly charges. We were stunned, given what we knew about a typical Chinese worker's income.[11] As it turned out, the young man had a job at a multi-national company, which paid all the fees. And while this may account for much of the cellular phone use in China, it's not the only explanation. Sometimes, several families actually contribute to share one phone, simply to create an image of wealth and position (which will be discussed later in this chapter).

*Television.* Since the mid–1980s, the sociology of mainland China has changed dramatically, replacing some of the more established forms of music, art and oral history with icons from the West. Some scholars refer to this phenomenon as China's "second" cultural revolution, and television is a big part of it. Television has been essential to unify a nation of highly diverse populations; it has also served to familiarize all Chinese with the culture of city life, although most of China's population still lives in rural areas. Most startling in the development of this phenomenon has been the short time in which it has been accomplished. In the mid-1980s, there were large differences between the numbers of TV sets found in the cities versus those in the countryside. In urban areas, one generally found one television set per 8.7 people; outside the cities, only 7 TV sets (and usually monochrome) per 100 households.[12] As China entered into the next millennium, its ratio has grown to one TV set per 4 people throughout the country, and almost all are color televisions.[13] In addition, the Matthews Report cites newer means of network transmission through China Central Television:

> There are thousands of registered ground receiving stations in China which, as well as providing access to broadcasts from Beijing, enable some users to watch foreign programmes and record them for sale.... There are [also] over 750 cable television stations in China with an estimated 100 million customers.[14]

This large growth rate in consumer media consumption has also ignited an interest in western products and programs. With satellite and cable television now available, some Chinese can receive signals from all around the world (Malaysia, US, Japan, India, Australia, Singapore, and Great Britain, just to name a few). True, these are the exceptions— most Chinese must satisfy their media appetites with programs from only three or four channels of CCTV network (Central China TV) and several local stations— but even China's domestic programming has a western "look."

For example, the CCTV nightly news report appears much like anything one might see on ABC, CBS, NBC or CNN. Typically, it consists of 20–25 minutes of national news, a bit of local news, a few mentions of international headlines and an Asian weather report. The news items vary from political events (like a recent visit from Jiang Zemin) to some more human interest stories (like a botanical display, an auction, or perhaps the troubles surrounding the opening of Hong Kong's newest airport). And, as with western television, it's often unnecessary to know the language because the visuals tell the story well.

In addition to news and information, entertainment programming is very big in China, especially music videos from Hong Kong. Most are found on MTV Asia, but are often used at the end of movies or as series openers. Then there's drama and comedy. One of the most popular type of drama is the "serial"— shown in multiple episodes. The Chinese call these shows "inside dramas," because the first programs of this type were taped inside studios. Westerners, on the other hand, know them as "soap operas." Unlike American soaps, these are "closed serials," meaning that they have a definite number of episodes. American soap operas, as we all know, can and do last for decades.

Soap operas, whether domestic or foreign, are one of most popular program genres on Chinese television. They can usually be found on some channel almost every hour each day. American soaps like *Texas* and *Bold and the Beautiful* are very popular and translated or dubbed in Mandarin. However, other imports, especially those from Japan, India and Latin America, are equally well received. In addition, there are large numbers of the indigenous soaps, which are embraced by both producers and audiences for several reasons. Viewers watch them because they demand little formal education; they are easy to follow; and they feature people, locations and products to which many Chinese have never been exposed.

But producers and state-owned networks use them for their potentially persuasive message content — a feature which, incidentally, has been utilized by many political leaders in Latin America, Eastern and Central Europe, Africa and other Asian nations.

Of course, all programming (news as well as entertainment) is interspersed with commercials for such "necessities" as snacks, appliances, video disc players, phone cards, express mail services, muscle ointments and complexion cream for teens. The Chinese government has placed several restrictions on its format, and content, including extra fees for foreigners and the proviso that the message should be written in Mandarin and say nothing offensive about the state.[15] Despite these apparent limitations, though, the campaigns are highly successful. According to a February 2002 *New York Times* article written by Elisabeth Rosenthal, there are now more than eighty McDonalds in Beijing alone, about 600 Kentucky Fried Chicken restaurants throughout the country and numerous other popular stores and restaurants such as PriceSmart, Starbucks, T.G.I.Fridays and Esprit.[16] Many Chinese (in the cities) also ride around in luxury Buicks, Audis, and Mercedes-Benzes, and drink imported wines or Coca-Cola while watching movies on their DVD players. Clearly, unlike

Russia in the 1990s, where Western advertisers created a need for a product but none were available, one can buy anything shown on Chinese television ... as long as one can afford it.

*Cyberspace.* More and more Chinese are acquiring personal computers each year, and have become very active in Internet communication. The 2001 market reports showed that more than 26 million Chinese are enthusiastic e-mail users and enjoy surfing more than 260,000 Internet web sites available to them — an almost unimaginable technological evolution, considering that just ten years before, the country claimed fewer than 10 million telephones.[17] Indeed, China is moving quickly toward conspicuous cyberspace consumption. According to financial analyst Scott Savitt, China's web usage should surpass that of the United States and be the world's largest by 2005.[18] ChinaOnline confirms Savitt's prediction with its own forecast — 300 million Internet users by 2005 (as compared to 200 million in the United States), with a Chinese Web base larger than the English Web by 2010.[19]

Given the figures, it is not surprising that companies such as Microsoft, the giant computer software corporation, have become heavily involved in China.[20] It's also not surprising that e-commerce has surged to the top of many entreprises. For example, in December 1999, China launched Dangdang.com, its own version of Amazon.com, creating online sales for over 200,000 books in Mandarin and Cantonese.[21] According to James Kynge in London's Financial Times, the rewards are many:

> It can save money on physical infrastructure, and customers may find that the convenience of shopping online outweighs the cost of delivery. In this aspect, the labyrinthine lay-out and surly service in state-run stores is the web site's greatest competitive advantage. The company is also aiming at a market of 70 m[illion] Chinese who live beyond China's shores, as well as universities and libraries abroad which keep up with Chinese scholarly works.[22]

The idea is certainly commendable, although, unfortunately, perhaps ahead of its time. As Kynge notes:

> Attractive sales prospects may be frustrated, at least in the short term, by embryonic credit card systems, the lack of personal cheques for payment and the fact that postage costs would typically amount to about 10–20 per cent of the cost of a book, industry analysts said.[23]

In addition, as Scott Savitt observes, the government is anxious to have greater control over the growing number of "netrepreneurs":

> [In January 2000] Beijing ... announced seemingly harsh new controls

on encrypted software, news on Chinese websites and overseas public
listings by Chinese firms.... The new rules require that information not
already printed by official news organizations be cleared by the government.... The rules also proscribe Internet providers from distributing
information the government deems "state secrets." This includes information posted on electronic bulletin boards, news services and in on-line
chat rooms. Another alarming pronouncement requires Chinese Internet
companies to apply for and receive approval from three separate government entities— The China Securities Regulatory Commission, the Ministry of Information Industry and the Information Office of the State
Council — before they are allowed to carry out initial public offerings on
foreign capital markets.[24]

Some argue that this is simply an attempt to get more revenue from
the burgeoning Internet industry; others maintain the decades-old cold
war mentality of communist brainwashing. Reporter Martin Regg Cohn
subscribes to the latter theory. In his July 2001 *Toronto Star* article, he discussed the "new face" of China's *People's Daily*:

Now it's a mouthpiece looking for fresh eyes. Click a link for the latest
news, or join an online chat forum with 20,000 people in real time. Have
your say and let off steam. But be careful. Behind the hot hyperlinks and
snappy Web pages, Big Brother is watching more closely than ever.
A smiling President Jiang Zemin looks down from a colour poster in
the third floor offices of the Web site, where 10 full-time censors scan the
screens with their fingers poised on the delete button. Known colloqui-
ally as "cleaning ladies" because of their sanitizing duties, they patrol the
online chat room looking for offending comments on taboo subjects.
Taiwan independence, the banned Falun Dafa movement and criticism of
the Communist Party are all off limits. So are state secrets, sex and porn.
Offenders are tracked down and reported to the Public Security Bureau
for prosecution....
Sensing its enormous potential, Communist Party officials rely on the
Internet to keep tabs on the chat rooms as a way of taking the pulse of
public opinion. With street protest banned, the information highway
allows government analysts to take regular soundings so they won't be
caught off guard.
"The pressure of public opinion is expressed mainly on the Internet,
and the government pays close attention," says Wang Xiao Dong, an
author on Web issues. "The Internet is the only place where people can
comment on political affairs so freely," he adds. "Without the Internet,
the government wouldn't have any idea what people were thinking about
and they really want to know. It's a window for people, and the government, to look in on each other."[25]

In addition to online "supervision," thousands of Internet cafes have
been either shut down or ordered to suspend operations in 2001–2002.

Depending on one's point of view, however, the reasons for this action are varied. Some characterize the crackdown as yet another attempt to censor free speech, nontraditional perspectives, and personal freedoms. The Chinese government counters its critics by arguing that many of the Internet cafes have been ordered to close because these web outlets were not properly registered with the state's ministry, and as such, became havens for pornographic "surfing" or dissident rebellion by such groups as the Falun Gong sect.[26]

Whatever one feels about China's governmental policies on Web site politics, there also exists the very practical issue of consumer protection (i.e., controlling the amount of "junk e-mail" or "spam") assaulting cyberspace in every country today. As reporter Connie Ling observed in February 2000,

> Spam, the junk e-mail named after the luncheon meat-in-a-can, has been a headache for most Internet users since e-mail first began to grow in popularity about a decade ago. The unwelcome missives might be promotional offers from a health-food company or "invitations" soliciting visits to porn sites. But if you thought you had your share of spam and know how to deal with it, you obviously haven't tasted the new spam, made in China.
>
> I first began noticing Chinese spam in my e-mailbox about six months ago. Like most people I normally just hit "delete" when I see a junk mail message, and that's exactly what I did in the beginning with these short e-mail messages in simplified Chinese characters, asking if I wanted to make a million dollars or download pictures of hot girls. But a few weeks later, I started receiving these messages at my other e-mail addresses.... At first, I received two to three spam messages a month; as of last month, I was getting close to 60 spam messages a week from China.... Normally, the best way to get rid of annoying spam is to e-mail the sender and remove yourself from the mailing list (by law in many countries, junk e-mail or snail mail senders have to give the recipients an option of deleting their address from the mailing list). However, in the hundreds of junk e-mail messages I've received from various sources in China, none provides the option. Instead, most simply note at the end of the e-mail, "if this e-mail bothers you, please ignore and delete it." ...As in so many other aspects of China's business climate, the international rules of "netiquette"— or net etiquette — just don't apply here. It's so early in the development of the Internet in China that people don't even know or care about the niceties of e-mail communication. In a smaller country, such brashness wouldn't matter as much. But in China, spammers have found fertile territory.[27]

As Ling notes, the challenges, pitfalls, risks, and potential rewards for e-commerce entrepreneurs are actually quite representative of most fledgling "new" businesses in China, as infrastructures begin to change and the globalization of commerce continues to emerge.

## Business Ventures and Transactions

In his Foreword to *Business Decision Making in China*, Professor John Thanopoulos makes a strong comparison between Chinese and western business philosophies, noting:

> The Chinese have been traders for thousands of years. They have perfected the art of business dealings and negotiations. Since they have a drastically different perception of the deity than we have in the West, they adopt a very realistic attitude toward the earthly world. However, they do believe and accept powerful leaders. They do follow command. A case in point is Mao Zedong, who twenty years after his death is adored by many as almost a deity. Moreover, basic tenets of life's understanding are embedded in their laws, history and tales.
>
> For example, the blind acceptance of Mao's strong leadership is attributed to the fact that for hundreds of years the Chinese have been conditioned to readily accept the government's policies and viewpoints. It is interesting that this manifested behavior is affected by two seemingly opposing tendencies: to accept change and to be inflexible. In the West, we would have preferred to state our predispositions as being flexible and tolerant. In the Chinese thinking, however, the inflexibility construct[s] aims to accept flexibility within a process that "does not rock the boat," that allows for gradual change, and that even ignores modern-era information collection in inclusion in the decision-making models.
>
> The yin and yang concepts are anchoring these polarities: to be simple and complex, predictable and unpredictable, straightforward and double-faced, positive and negative.[28]

Given this context, it should come as no surprise that China has been extremely cautious to take a simple, market-based approach to its economy. History continues to leave its mark on the current Chinese political system, where Soviet influences, especially on organizational structure, have predominated for over thirty years. Chief among these Cold War vestiges are the state-owned enterprises, responsible for over 40 percent of the nation's gross industrial output.[29] Other entrepreneurial initiatives such as foreign-owned businesses and joint ventures have flourished, but they still must work within the infrastructural constraints of the system.[30]

In April 1999, the Monetary Policy Committee of the People's Bank of China (PBOC) — the central bank of the country — outlined its guidelines for commercial lending, including:

　　1. backing areas "helpful for economic growth or crucial in the structural adjustment of the economy," including agriculture, infrastructure, technology, exports and small-town construction;[31]

　　2. expanded renminbi loans given to foreign-funded businesses;

3. an established credit rating system to enable lenders to assess credit merit more easily; and

4. the growth of a market-based credit system to allow financial institutions to borrow money and exchange bonds with each other.

These guidelines were just part of Premier Zhu Rongji's objective to execute strong economic policies in China in the next several years, "without fear of offending any people."[32]

Should foreign banks do business with the Chinese, they were required to adhere to several proscriptions, including

> enlarging domestic demand, with this the priority economic task....
> [P]lanning and price departments must make use of comprehensive measures to improve macroeconomic control, using price policies, enlarging domestic demand, stimulating consumption and deepening reforms of grain and cotton circulation.[33]

More recently, in April 2002, the State Development Planning Commission (SDPC) issued new rules for general foreign investment, corresponding with China's recent induction into the World Trade Organization.[34] These rules have replaced the nation's 1995 provisional rules on foreign investors, and include the following directives (according to *Asiainfo Daily China News)*:

> The country hopes foreign investors start businesses in the western regions, where they will enjoy more favourable taxation policies for the next 10 years.... From 2001 to 2010, income tax will stay at 15 per cent if enterprises invest in industries encouraged by the government.... The government encourages foreigners to take part in key State-owned enterprises (SOEs) reform.... Overseas investors are expected to become shareholders in key SOEs ... [and] will even be allowed to hold the controlling stake in large SOEs, except for those of key importance to national or economic security.[35]

In short, this is the new China — looking forward to a millennium of change as it continues to grow as a significant force in global economics.

Besides foreign investment, other concerns in China's infrastructure evolution are energy consumption, water conservation and environmental protection. Breathtaking industrial growth, population changes, rising consumerism and an urban migration trend have all contributed to an ecological and economic imbalance in both metropolitan and rural areas. According to a January 2002 Global News Wire report, more than 100,000 square kilometers of fertile land have turned to desert since the

1950s.[36] While some of the erosion has been due to natural, climatic factors, much has been attributed to "the irrational, profit-driven human exploitation of land."[37] In addition to mineral resource erosion, a colossal economic divide between life in the lavish coastal cities and that of the countryside has evolved. As *Guardian* reporter John Cassy notes,

> It is the ultimate symbol of China's new economic virility. An area on the edge of Shanghai that, just a decade ago, was little more than farmland and paddyfields is now home to a forest of skyscrapers. Running through the heart of the city's Pudong district are ten-lane freeways with hundreds of thousands of cars using them each day — routes that a generation ago were dirt tracks.... [But] beyond the wealthy, urbanised eastern seaboard lies a broadly agrarian society where wages are minimal and what little heavy industry there is remains state run and financially unreconstructed.[38]

Economic strategists believe the best way of addressing these problems is through an intelligent management of outside resources as well as conservation of internal consumption. These "outside resources" can also be defined as "foreign venture opportunities," creating a win-win environment both inside and outside of China. The city of Hebei (which increased its GDP by 14 percent from 1990 to 1997) provides a good illustration of this trend. According to Provincial Party Secretary Ye Liansong, Hebei was able to survive the '90s Asian financial crisis because of billions of dollars of foreign fixed asset investments earmarked for "basic industry, infrastructure, facilities for State grain reserves and reform of the residential housing system, transportation and communications, and technology."[39]

Using Hebei as a case study for foreign investment management, China is optimistic about large gains in natural resource production and management as well as increased per capita growth in GDP, higher literacy rates, and an overall improvement in quality of life for its population of more than 1.29+ billion.[40] Nevertheless, forecasters from economic sources such as *The Financial Times* also suggest caution along with this rising optimism:

> China's economic scenario ... will be influenced by the tough global economic environment, especially the economic slowdown in the European Union, the United States and Japan. The downturn will send a heavy blow to China's exports. Moreover, membership in the WTO will increase the country's imports, reduce the trade surplus and weaken incentives that foreign demands will provide to China's economy.[41]

## *Transportation*

Perhaps one of the most dramatic improvements in China over the last twenty years has been the growing ability and ease of travel and transportation throughout the country. Railways have both expanded and improved, as have highways, shipping operations and aviation. Today, many Chinese enjoy travel luxury heretofore known only to the rich and influential.

Trains. In 1999, railway tracks covered 64,900 km of the country. Still, analysts estimated that China needed to expand this network by at least a third. In response, government officials increased their investment as well as sought monies for foreign investors.[42] In 2001, almost 2,500 miles of new railway lines—including 1,235 of double-track lines and 660 miles of electrified railway lines—were completed.[43] After five years of deficit railway spending, analysts saw a profit for the first time in 1999.[44] According to the minister of railways, Fu Zhihuan:

> [In that year] 976 million seats or beds were sold, 4.9 per cent more than in 1998. Railway cargo hit 1.57 billion tons, a 2.4 per cent increase.... The speeding-up of passenger trains across China — up to 90 kilometers per hour in eastern China — has won over road and air travelers.[45]

As Fu has suggested, China's economic success with its railways is due in large part to its growing technology. The first "bullet" train system came in 1996.[46] This was followed by several similar projects, the most ambitious of which will be a high-speed rail link between Beijing and Shanghai, most likely to cost over $12 billion USD, but already heavily supported by the Japanese government.[47] (Incidentally, the Japanese had to lobby strongly for this pact. They found themselves in close competition with both France and Germany, who are also interested in future high-speed train routes as well as other infrastructure projects such as electricity, telecommunications, bridges and elevated tracks.[48])

Another significant railway project in China's plans is the construction of a second Euro-Asia continental bridge. In a BBC broadcast, journalists reported that the 577-km railway would run between China, Kyrgyzstan and Uzbekistan, passing through China's eleven provinces and autonomous region as well as Turkey, Greece and Italy. Journalists noted that "opening the south passage is in line with the Chinese government's strategy to develop the west[ern part of the country]; it will also speed the opening-up of the inland and deepen the political and economic relationship between China and its neighbours."[49]

Shipping. In 1994, China claimed eighteen major ports, including

Dalian, Qinhuangdao, Xingang, Qingdao, Shanghai, Huangpu, Canton and Ningbo. Its merchant fleet numbered nearly 900 freighters, 272 bulk carriers and almost 200 tankers.[50] By 1995, building and repair sites were added to handle ships over 10,000 tons, as well as adequate dry docks, floating docks and ports to support other vessels for trade.[51] However, the resource supply was still not able to meet the incremental growth in need for shipbuilding and embarkation sites. As a result, there was severe strain on the current facilities as well as the eroding navigable waterways. To address these needs, the Chinese government has invested millions of dollars in restoration and redevelopment.[52] While this effort is still inadequate, 2001 customs records showed that China's major port of Shanghai reported a 17.2 percent growth in business from the United States and a 28 percent rise from Europe.[53] Moreover, shipping revenues throughout China increased more than 10 percent from Japan — its largest foreign market.[54] Despite the instability of world markets, the shipping industry continues to thrive in China.

*Highways.* In 1995, China had constructed more than 640,000 miles of paved roadways.[55] Four years later, paved roads linked 97 percent of China's cities and towns, and 78 percent of the rural areas.[56] By 2002, China claimed the 4th longest road system in the world,[57] with more than 15,800 miles of new highways (including almost 5,000 miles of expressway travel) opening to traffic the year before.[58] According to a 2002 report from *The Financial Times*:

> The fast development of China's roads is attributed to its huge spending on road construction. The Chinese government's annual expenditure on road construction had been over 200 billion yuan (US $ 24.16 billion) for three successive years from 1998 to 2000, while the expenditure in 2001 reached 260 billion yuan (US $ 31.14 billion).
>
> This huge expenditure enables the Chinese government to speed up the road construction, to improve the technology used in the road construction, to spread the roads throughout the counties and towns, and to finish building the Beijing-Shenyang expressway, Beijing-Shanghai expressway, and the southwest highway to the sea.[59]

As both foreign investors and local entrepreneurs continue to develop industries outside the coastal cities, the need and support for these roadways will continue to develop.

*Aviation.* In 1994, China confirmed 204 useable airfields, with only 86 paved runways of 8,000 feet or more.[60] But just five years later, 206 airports were operational, 192 with paved runways; in 2001, 37 airports were either newly constructed or expanded.[61] By 2002, the China Aviation Industry Corporation claimed a $6.04 million USD profit,[62] with continued expanse in all major cities, especially Shanghai.[63]

Thus, in air travel, as well as other areas of infrastructure reform, most scholars and analysts would credit China with remarkable growth in its market economy over a relatively short period of time. In addition, this growth curve continues to rise, making China a formidable partner in future world trade.

But China is not only evolving in global commerce and international identity. Its domestic persona is also quite different from earlier decades. Much like the clearly defined demographic groups found in post–World War II America, today's China is characterized by three definite "generations"— each with unique perspectives, goals and personalities.

# GENERATION DIFFERENCES

Never before in China's history has there been such immense generational distinction within its population. Prior to Premier Deng Xiaoping's government, China's people were defined by their location (urban versus countryside) or work unit more than by age. This was because, unlike many western societies, each group (within these strictures) generally belonged to the same economic class, had been educated in the same traditional way, and was exposed to the same information on propaganda. Today, because of changing government policies, social mobility, new technologies and global politics, the old classification systems don't really apply. While there is still great distinction between peasants and city dwellers, the more compelling distinctions are found between generations, namely: (1) children and young adults (the "baby boomers" of China); (2) their middle-aged parents; and (3) the elderly grandparents.

## Children Born Under China's One-Child Policy

This population segment is often referred to as "China's spoilt child (or 's') generation" of "little emperors," famous for enjoying the "most privileged upbringing of any generation in China's history."[64] To better understand the mindset of this age group versus that in older generations, one need only to read their background (or lack of), as described by *Los Angeles Times* reporter Maggie Farley:

> Most of China's 1.3 billion people were not alive to experience the Communist movement that produced the country's historic leadership. Many barely remember the bitterness of the 1966–76 Cultural Revolution. China's new generation was shaped by Deng, who was behind both the 1989 crackdown on protesters in Beijing's Tiananmen Square and the

seductive fruits of the country's economic reforms. China's development has brought today's youth a sense of confidence and entitlement — along with hints of alienation — that is by envied and resented by their elders.[65]

To the outsider, many "s" generation children tend to be overfed, overindulged, and overidealized. As one Canadian reporter has observed,

> In cities, where incomes have risen in that period [over twenty years], a 2–4–1 syndrome is frequent; two loving parents, four grandparents who can't say no and one very spoiled, and often fat, child.... Pot-bellied children are a common sight. So are parents taking their children out for brisk runs and calisthenics in parks. In summer, the well-off even send their offspring to fat camps, where children spend the summer exercising and limiting their intake of hamburgers, a western food young Chinese have learned to relish.[66]

When the child matures, food often gives way to money. According to information gathered by British journalist Damien McElroy,

> A newspaper survey of first-year college students found that a quarter received more than pounds 80 — double the average urban wage — as spending money each month. Another survey found that 90 per cent of secondary students have never cooked a meal, and half have never made a bed. Some parents take devotion to their children to ridiculous extremes. Dormitories at music academies have even been adapted specially to accommodate anxious mothers and fathers who have forsaken careers in order to watch over their precocious progeny.[67]

Indeed, much is sacrificed for them; but today's children in China are also expected to study hard, get a good education, and make something of themselves to enhance a family's status. As Craig S. Smith reports in *The Wall Street Journal*, there is a rising trend toward an accelerated education through either boarding school, after-school tutoring or private weekend courses. One example of this movement is little Zhao Wei-jie, whose father

> forks over $120 a month to send his daughter to Shanghai's intensive Soong Ching Ling Kindergarten, which keeps young students on its premises weeknights even if the family lives a short bus ride away. All children should undergo the same regimen, school officials figure; letting some go home at night would disrupt this.[68]

Even for successful businessmen in China, this investment is a hardship; it affects not only the child's immediate family, but the grandparents, aunts and uncles as well. The long-range goal is clear: to beat the heavy competition for coveted seats at prestigious universities, and go on to prominent, respected professions. No sacrifice is too great. As Smith explains:

> Mr. Zhao [Zhao Weijie's father] hopes the Soong Ching Ling Kindergarten, named after the wife of the revolutionary hero Sun Yat-Sen, will help his daughter get into one of Shanghai's private primary schools, and later into a private high school. While Shanghai has some highly rated public schools, enrollment is restricted to neighborhood residents, a system that leads to shuffling of households within some families as grandparents, aunts and uncles swap homes to get children registered in a good school district. For those without that option, money will buy entrance to a private school of equal caliber — though high test scores and strong references are also required.[69]

As with other changes in perspective, the new, individualistic attitude towards education often spills over into other dimensions of young Chinese life. For one thing, children learn to want — and get — things for themselves; they're not very interested in saving for others. This behavior is very unlike previous generations, where people saw themselves as others saw them, and lived for others rather than themselves. Among the "others" to consider in those years were neighbors and professional colleagues, in addition to family.

Another change in the "s" generation's way of thinking is the tendency to look for outside signs of success, rather than wisdom from within. A manifestation of this attitude is the desire to follow the latest trends (like cell phones), showing the world how good they can look, with an emphasis on material worth. As a result, the "little emperors" also tend to buy more imported clothes and other foreign consumer goods than their parents or grandparents.

Finally, it's important to recognize that China's youngest generation, in general, enjoys a greater disposable income than other population groups because they are apt to live at home longer than people in previous generations. Consequently, they spend comparatively great sums of money on such things as video disc players, notebook computers, clothes, cosmetics, cars, exercise bikes, cosmetic surgery and vacations in foreign countries.[70] In addition, they are more likely to search for relationships through personal ads rather than through the time-honored traditions of family associations or matchmaking. Reporter Erik Eckholm gives a few examples of such ads:

> "Female, divorced, has two-room house, good figure and appearance, looking for healthy, open-minded man." And "Male, 29, manager in for-

eign enterprise, humorous, open-minded, good at computers, looking for pretty girl who loves life."[71]

The anticipated reward of "getting ahead" is not without other drawbacks, however, as Craig Smith notes:

> Shanghai's city government recently announced that it will add psychology to its primary-school curriculum in an effort to help students cope with the increasing pressure. And several Chinese cities have banned electronic pets, because anxiety-ridden kids become dangerously obsessed with the keychain-size computer games. While no figures have been released, China's state media report that the number of school-age suicides has risen steadily since the 1980s.[72]

In addition, there is no longer a guarantee of the "iron rice bowl"— lifetime employment — which forces these Chinese "baby boomers" to reassess their lives based on new rules and expectations.

## Middle-Aged "Children" of the Cultural Revolution

Much like the generation of American World War II veterans, this age group finds itself "sandwiched" between two very different generations— their children, who are living at home longer, as well as their parents, who are living longer and expecting to reside with them. Like many Americans who gave birth to the baby boomers of the late 1940s and the decade of the '50s, these people must worry about earning a living while trying to take care of both parents and children. As a consumer group, they think little about fashion and technology trends; instead, they are known to buy the largest number of health supplies, medicines, etc. They could not, as reporter Erik Eckholm notes, imagine "spending $50 or $60 dollars on an item such as a shirt."[73]

This anti-materialism trend does not apply to institutions of learning, however. Most middle-aged adults tend to value education highly, since they were denied the opportunity to go to school during the Mao's Cultural Revolution. In fact, illiteracy is still a problem with many within this age group, although the percentage of illiterate middle-aged adults dropped from 10.4 percent to less than 5½ percent in 1997.[74]

Finally, another significant difference between the attitude of this era's 40–55 year olds and those from previous decades is their perspective on tending to their extended family. With a growing economy and two incomes, more and more middle-aged adults are sending their parents to nursing homes or assisted living facilities rather than caring for them at home. This can be a traumatic decision for a generation that has known no other life but that of family living — China's "over sixty" population.

## Senior "Survivors" of the Cultural Revolution

Surprisingly, elderly people (most identifiable by their somber, dark clothing and revolutionary Mao jackets) are rapidly becoming a much larger demographic than ever before in China. Author Conghua Li predicts that by 2025, at least twenty percent of the nation's population will be over sixty.[75] Just as important as its statistical presence, however, is the seniors' attitude toward younger generations. Money is not to be spent on one's own creature comforts. Rather it is to be saved for children and grandchildren, either to improve their health, their education or their social status. In addition, it is important to "leave" them something after one has died, which explains why the per capita rate of savings of China's senior population is one of the highest in the world.[76]

Older Chinese, more than any other age group, perceive themselves through the eyes of their peer group (or work unit). They formulate their sense of "self" by what neighbors say about them much more than both younger generations, who seem to identify with those they'd like to emulate rather than by those who are closest to them. This sometimes creates a sort of "generation gap" with kids being told to behave a certain way to avoid being the center of gossip from fellow citizens.

Surprisingly, elders in China also tend to be more politically active than many of their grandchildren. This can sometimes be troublesome, as noted in an August 1999 *South China Morning Post* article about members of the recent Falun Gong movement:

> The Chinese leadership, itself a self-perpetuating gerontocracy, has long worked on the assumption that it was the under-20s, the majority, who would be trouble. Yet 10 years after Tiananmen, it is a band of old-age pensioners, not students or democracy activists, who are the first to organize a national organization which has unnerved the party.... At any rate, the Communist party has now decided to deal with these old folk who can no longer be left to their devices. In old China they might have been kept busy looking after their descendants but not now with the one-child policy. Now the party is proposing that they be given something to do. They are "lonely and desolate" people isolated from the rest of society by the generation gap, warns one expert, proposing higher spending on better health-care and entertainment facilities. "Society must do more for them," says *Beijing Youth Daily*. Perhaps they should all be sent for a spell in the countryside, the solution resorted to when the cities were full of millions of idle "educated youth."[77]

Perhaps this is due to the politically charged atmosphere of the Mao's Cultural Revolution in their younger years. Still, it seems ironic that the suggestion to "educate" senior citizens by exiling them to the countryside would come from a younger, presumably more liberal generation.

# PUTTING IT TOGETHER

Clearly, the changing cultural climate and market-based economy as well as rising technology and evolving infrastructure has made China a very different place than ever before. One cannot make simple assumptions about social customs, ethnic traditions or political perspectives. Anyone interested in forming a joint venture or investing in a collective enterprise should study at least two cultural constants which have remained throughout China's evolutionary transformation: a strong sense of national identity and the ability to adapt to most situations.

## National Identity

For most of its multi-millennium history, China has had little contact with much of the rest of the world. As a result, it has developed its own unique identity along with a strong sense of ethnocentrism. In fact, according to author Conghua Li, the "isolation has reinforced the strength of its underlying social and cultural values and created a nation uniquely confident of its own identity — so confident that outside cultural influences do not compromise China, they become part of China."[78] This aspect of national identity is most evident when looking at Chinese reactions to the recent influx of western consumer goods (especially food). A 1999 survey taken in Beijing, Shanghai, Guangzhou, Wuhan and Shenyang showed that despite the obvious popularity of hamburgers, potato chips and pizza, over sixty percent of those questioned still preferred Chinese fast-food to western fare. People were very grateful for the introduction of restaurants such as Kentucky Fried Chicken and McDonalds in the 1980s, however — without their help, the Chinese might never have come up with the concept of "fast food, much less the western management techniques used to help them with their own businesses."[79]

## Adaptation

Indeed, the ability to innovate and adapt to change has been one of the major factors in China's identity and endurance during the many crises of its 5,000-year-old history. Hence, businesses looking to succeed in this country must acknowledge its age-old reputation as a great imitator. As those companies that have not been successful in China have acknowledged, the Chinese are known to fashion outside products and businesses to fit their lifestyle; if they can't, the business or product will ultimately fail. And after the "outsider" has come and gone, if the concept is still useful to consumers, some local entrepreneurs will most likely make their own which, in turn, will take over the market. Author Conghua Li makes this point dramatically with his example of the soft drink industry:

> Presently, Coca Cola and Pepsi sell their products at higher prices than in the West. A great deal of their success and popularity however, comes from the novelty value of the products. Novelty value eventually wears off, sometimes sooner rather than later.... Chinese consumers are shrewd and they will assimilate. Foreign goods may whet the appetite and tickle the fancy, but it takes more than novelty value to have long-term success.[80]

As Coca-Cola and Pepsi and other foreign investors have learned, China is still a dragon — worthy of respect, caution and care.

# 4

# Case Study: Educational Programs and Exchanges in China

*In this case study we primarily utilize the expertise of one of the authors. Nancy Street worked in the Chinese university system in 1985-1986, 1988 and 1989 as an exchange professor in Linfen, Shanxi Province at Shanxi Teacher's University. Sent by her college and accompanied by three undergraduate exchange students, Street taught in that educational work unit and traveled through China, primarily by train. Later, as a Fulbright group study grant recipient, she also participated in an educational and cultural study tour in China in 1990. In 1997, she was a visiting professor at Southeastern University in Nanjing. During these sojourns into the Chinese workaday world, she continued to do the basic fieldwork of interviewing and participant observation over time. At home, Street continues working with undergraduate and graduate Chinese students from both Taiwan and the PRC.*

*Street has been following the development of modern China for the past 17 years, living, working and visiting educational milieus in Linfen, Beijing, Xi'an, Shanghai and Nanjing, while charting the development of some of the most important ingredients in modern nation building—the educational, legal, attitudinal and physical infrastructure of a people and their country. Here she writes about her experiences as one of the first professors in Bridgewater State's exchange program with Shanxi.*

## OVERVIEW

The discussion that follows is influenced by my longitudinal reflections on various infrastructure issues in modern China. As one will also observe through the case studies, e.g., Foxboro and Crowne Plaza, presented in this book, much of the work of American business in China relates to cultural and physical infrastructure. In both areas, each side comes from a different perspective. Further, an American company can only benefit in productivity, profit, and acceptance if it considers the fusion of these perspectives. This is possible through thorough groundwork and the opportunity to be culturally immersed, if only briefly. Thus, cultural immersion is important for all persons hoping to work, in whatever way, in China — and has a learning curve which depends a great deal upon the available resources. The available resources for American business persons and American students and academics are often quite different. In this chapter, we will illustrate typical arrangements for educational seminars and faculty-student exchanges.

# THE COUNCIL ON INTERNATIONAL EDUCATIONAL EXCHANGE

The Council on International Educational Exchange (CIEE), located in New York City, offers study abroad and faculty seminars around the world "to help people gain understanding, acquire knowledge, and develop skills for living in a globally interdependent and culturally diverse world."[1] In 2001, Dr. Marilyn Matelski and I elected to participate in International Faculty Development Seminar (IFDS) for China for several reasons.[2] First, CIEE has its headquarters in the United States, making it easy for us to enroll and plan our trip. Second, it offered us the opportunity to update ourselves on China's culture, business and economy since our last trip to China in 1997. Third, traveling with IFDS was compatible with our methodology-in-use, i.e., participant observation and interviewing. Finally, as participants in IFDS, we would be spared the arrangements of our daily living and travel in China — something that in our past experience required time, energy and dedicated intercultural skills and focus. The China Seminar enabled us to peacefully continue our interviewing in Beijing, Xi'an, and Shanghai, and also observe and participate in a variety of Chinese-American relationships in the classroom and on the road. We also wanted to explore the available infrastructure — banking, the educational system and facilities, the communication system (phones, faxes, computers)—the physical and attitudinal infrastructure necessary to the new, seemingly market-oriented and "globalized" China.

Overall, the IFDS seminar proved to be an enriching, invigorating experience with well-qualified lecturers (see Appendix D) offering glimpses of important issues for further reflection. Additionally, our faculty leader, Dr. Mingzheng Shi, was very familiar with foreigners like us, having obtained his advanced degrees in America. Born in China, Ming received his Bachelor of Arts degree from Peking University in intercultural studies. Mingzheng Shi embodies the ideal leader for foreign folks in China, as he understands both cultures. Some of the aspects of the trip that I enjoyed most were the program flexibility, Mingzheng's unfailing good humor, as well as the breadth and depth of his knowledge, not to mention his helpfulness in aiding each of us in our various professional pursuits. After this experience, I would recommend that prior to creating an exchange program or enhancing international education, one would benefit from a professional development tour such as this, or a teaching assignment in one of China's many educational institutions.[3]

# BACKGROUND—EDUCATIONAL TRAVEL IN CHINA DURING THE PAST TWENTY YEARS

While the economic and banking infrastructure in general has improved dramatically in China over the past 20 years, it is still, with a limited time frame and limited resources, quite difficult to get around in China without the aid of expediters such as IFDS. In the eighties, foreign teachers or "English missionaries" could utilize several different ways to research and travel in China. About twice a year, the regional Office of Foreign Affairs would arrange a trip for its "foreign experts." For a very small fee (around $25 to $50 American dollars), one could join the planned group travel which usually lasted from three to five days. The regional office planned the trip, arranged for interpreters, ordered the buses or cars, ordered the train tickets and provided breakfast, lunch, dinner and a farewell banquet, as well as free pick-up and delivery to and from our various work units. In Shanxi Province in 1989, we had a delightful trip by train from Linfen to the home of Confucius and his temple (*kong miao*) at Qufu in Shandong Province. We also climbed Taishan, a sacred Taoist mountain.

On the train, we were in a "hard sleeper"—initially, a bit of a shock, since one never knows which of the three bunk beds one gets. If you are on the top, it's a long climb. If you are on the bottom, everyone for three aisles over tends to join you until long past bedtime. It's best to be in the middle bunk.

About twice a year, the local Office of Foreign Affairs would also provide a similar travel plan for its unit's foreign experts, such as a trip to the Yangtze River or nearby Buddhist temples (like the Temple of the Hell). These outings were orchestrated and essentially paid for by the local Chinese Office of Foreign Affairs. However, they were often cancelled due to impassable road conditions during winter or the lack of adequate transportation within the work unit. Too many elites, not enough cars — and party officials (not foreigners) were high on the list for the available transportation. One could also hire one's own taxi for an outing and also take a colleague as interpreter, paying all expenses. This second venue available for foreign experts was not implemented by many, as most foreign experts in educational systems received little pay. As an exchange professor, I received my pay at home, but my salary in China was deducted from my gross, so I had no extra money while I maintained my obligations in the States. Thus, though I often wanted to access my checking account or my credit cards or even my traveler's checks, this was not possible — another roadblock to possible travel.[4] At every turn, the rules, regulations and policies had to be investigated prior to making hotel reservations, train reservations and exploring where and when one might exchange traveler's checks, if at all. Not easily daunted, I was determined to visit as many of the Taoist and Buddhist holy places as I could afford. As a result, I worked hard to establish relationships within the Office of Foreign Affairs (as well as with several of my colleagues) to obtain the various seals, permissions, tickets and bribes needed to travel to these sites.

Persons working for international companies located in Beijing, Shanghai, Nanjing, and Guangzhou (and other coastal cities in China) did not, and do not, experience the same issues as TEFL teachers or educational touring groups might in the country. International corporations with a strong presence in China and other Third World countries iron out such difficulties for their employees. However, I offer the example to bolster my argument that lesser-funded corporations without international expertise and with an inadequate understanding of the everyday living issues in China might not prosper. It was, and is, expensive to maintain the lifestyle of foreigners in China.

In those early days, just obtaining money from (perceived) valid sources was a hardship in time, energy and frustration for the worker on his or her own in China. International corporations have a different climate. First, the people sent there usually have an international background and may be from the region, as in one of our case studies, the Crowne Plaza. Two of the general managers of Crowne Plaza hotels in Shanghai and Nanjing whom we interviewed, Mahmoud Masood and Grace Lau, are from other countries. Masood is from Afghanistan and Lau is from Singapore. While interviewing, they presented a distinctly different attitude than that of an American CEO. Each demonstrated an understanding of the Third World community and placed themselves in relation to that community and China. American experts, on the other hand, tend to place themselves in relation to the United States. This can lead (or not) to perceptions which are not necessarily "politically correct" in America.

Skewed perceptions were also more likely for traveling academics than for Foxboro Company personnel and others who have a global organization behind them, as well as worldwide experience. Having been away from America for many years, they tend to be equally relaxed amongst their Chinese counterparts. Hence, being huge and international, rather than your ordinary American student or scholar, seems to provide not only greater insights into a certain Chinese lifestyle and the global economy, but also greater productivity. One need not be concerned about the details of daily life (clean water, washing clothes, trying to copy materials, making hotel and train reservations) — these things are taken care of by others.

# IFDS — INTERNATIONAL FACULTY DEVELOPMENT SEMINARS

IFDS is a good example of harnessing and utilizing international skills to develop and produce a good product. In their materials, they say,

> Hosted by prestigious academic institutions abroad, the seminars provide short-term, intensive overseas experiences, offering focused updates on global issues and regions that are shaping the course of world events, while introducing participants to scholarly communities overseas....
> Over the last decade, Council's International Faculty Development Seminars have spanned the globe with over 100 programs in 28 countries....
> CIEE is a nonprofit, non-governmental organization whose mission is dedicated to helping people gain understanding, acquire knowledge, and develop skills for living in a globally interdependent and culturally diverse world [Introduction, 3].[5]

Ever vigilant and ready with our tape recorder, Marilyn and I recorded some of our observations as we, trouble-free, followed our IFDS guides throughout our pleasant and informative ten-day odyssey[6] from Beijing to Xi'an to Shanghai.

# TEAM OBSERVATIONS

NS:   OK, this is day 1. It is Wednesday, June 6th, and we are in the Shaoyuan Hotel, Building 7, located on the beautiful Peking University campus where I stayed in August of 1985. Only then, there was no elevator to the 4th floor. This hotel has been redone — fresh paint, new furniture. This, our first stop in an educational institution in China, offers top-of-the line accommodations. In fact, I have never before seen such accommodations at a university hotel in China. We finally found the building for breakfast, but left the breakfast there.

MJM:   This has to be the worst food since we arrived [we had already been on our own in Shanghai for 10 days]. We had such a great dinner in the hotel dining room last night. I had none of this breakfast, which appeared to be toast, noodles, soup and seaweed. We then made our way from our hotel, practically leaving a trail of breadcrumbs [we had no map of the university] to find our way back home.

NS:   We followed Mingzheng, our leader. The first hour was highlighted by questions and answers concerning what one should have brought to China to give away. I was much more interested in when the coffee break would happen, having had none.

MJM:   Of all the many written materials we had received, we didn't get anything like this and it seemed a little late to be giving things unless you have the shirt off your back to give to people.

NLS:   This morning's lecture was to have been on verbal and non-verbal communication.[7] Instead, we spent 98 percent of the time talking about what kind of money we should have brought and how we were to obtain Chinese money. So we solved that one.

MJM:   I want to say that there should be a campus map included in our package. Since all the signs are in Chinese and almost no one speaks English, I could easily get lost on this campus. So, I made this suggestion to the person who has coordinated this program on this campus for two years. Within minutes, we had campus maps— in Chinese characters! No pinyin, no English. So, we still don't know which lecture hall to go to or how to reach it along the way. The other thing is, the people who were delayed in Tokyo were not told they would not be able to cash any funds.
   They were also told that their relatives and friends could make long distance calls directly to their rooms, although the numbers that they gave us wouldn't link directly to our rooms. And obviously, there is no

way that people can contact them with the staff on board, none of whom speak English. So far I have not met one staff member here who speaks English, whether it is in the laundry room or at the reception desk or at the greeting tables. Not that they should speak English, but if anyone is going to try to get in touch with us, chances would be slim to none that we would be able to receive anything, call, e-mail or fax.

This is a perfectly nice hotel but without having the tools to understand, it's one thing to ask people to accept the Chinese ways, but it is another thing to understand that the audience here is American — and probably two or three have never been to China before. So, these people are clueless and they are trying to get clued in. It isn't that they don't understand and refuse to understand, they just don't understand the Chinese language. So, I just don't know what will be done about that.

NS:    The pre-trip letters should have explained what kind of cards could be used in the telephone machines which would have allowed people to call out by themselves. So Marilyn had a difficult time at the desk, as she wanted to be shown how to dial out of her room.

However, I do want to comment on the post office service, which is truly great in this hotel. We had been to the Beijing Hard Rock Café and wanted to mail some t-shirts home, so I went to the post office and using very basic Chinese I was able to get a box and mail some stuff very quickly and efficiently, unlike some previous experiences in the 1980s when they actually had to measure what was being sent and build a wooden box to hold it. Today, it's a simple and efficient experience, although I noticed that people were still using the old paste jar and a stick to put stamps on their envelopes.

That about covers it for our first forays into university hotel life in Beijing. Soon we felt at home. Our first lectures were quite interesting. Despite having been to the Temple of Heaven, Tiananmen Square and the Forbidden City many times, I had never heard such a clear explanation of the structure and the relevance of their positioning. Mingzheng Shi explained that the emperor's location was the center of the world. The world was represented by a square, and heaven by a circle. The Forbidden City was in the center of Beijing in the form of a square and running through that is a line which divides the city, the bell tower and the drum tower, usually on that line (all cities have bell towers and drum towers). In the *feng shui* belief system, the gate of the door to the Forbidden City or to one's home should face south. It should not face north. The reason (he said) for this has to do with the Chinese concept of *yin-yang*, which is sometimes described inaccurately as polar opposites, like good and evil. That however is incorrect, they are not polar opposites; each partakes of the other.

In any event, Ming went on to say that the imperial city is a square and within that square there is a gate at the south and a gate at the north. The gate at the north is not used to enter because it is the *yin*. The gate at the south is used for entrance because it is the *yang*. The *yang* is the good wind. The *yin* at the north entrance is the bad wind or evil forces blowing in. So in fact, at the Forbidden City, they built a hill in front of the north gate so that the winds could not cross the wood and would instead go into the hill in front of the north gate. As one walks out of the Forbidden City through the North gate, there is indeed a hill gradually building as you go. So the concept of *yin-yang* and the code of feng shui are clearly built into both the Temple of Heaven and the Forbidden City. In the center of the Forbidden City is the sacred Hall of Harmony, which is the most important of the buildings which are found inside the For-bidden City. So one sees how fundamental *yin-yang*, the tenets of *feng shui* and the concept of harmony are to Chinese culture. If one takes only a glimpse of this architecture, one literally does not know what one is see-ing, unless one has guides well versed in Chinese thought and architec-ture, as we did. This was the first of many lectures that I thought were exceedingly well done by our IFDS lecturers.

> NLS:   Later, we were taken on a walking tour of Peking University. One of the sights I found fascinating was the market, which was located directly beneath the student buildings. These buildings looked bleak and inhospitable, just as do most of the student buildings at any of the uni-versities I have visited. Students crowd 6 to 8 to a room, cook in the hall-ways, freeze in the winter (and Beijing winters can be extremely cold), and roast in the summer. It's not an easy or happy life for Chinese stu-dents. However, in this market place, the melons were wrapped in rags and fruit and eggs came in baskets! Quite an advance over the markets I shopped in during the 1980s when there were no bags or cartons for any-thing. At that time, I sent home for plastic bags and egg cartons, any-thing to put my purchases in to carry home. Sometimes, forgetting they were there, I squished the eggs in my jacket. Since I only wore jackets in winter this meant that the jacket would take at least a week to dry after washing it on the rocks in the River Fen.

> MJM:   That afternoon, we visited Tiananmen Square; but unfortu-nately, could not go to the rostrum. If you can see Tiananmen Square from the rostrum, you get a feel for the huge crowds and leaders such as Chairman Mao addressing the Chinese people at the founding of the People's Republic of China. However, our guide, Ming, didn't disappoint us, and explained the meaning and positioning of the various halls in the Forbidden City.
> Unfortunately, due to the heavy traffic in the center of Beijing that day, we could not go to the Temple of Heaven. Also, Mao's mausoleum was closed. With others in our group, we made plans to visit the mausoleum

early the next morning. The next morning at 6:00 a.m., four of us went by taxi to Tiananmen and stood in line with many Chinese citizens to view Mao's body.

NLS:    Major complaints of the group at that point had to do with the blazing heat and the fact that there was no time to take pictures or just stop for a bit. Obviously, there was little to do about the heat; but we did take a more relaxed pace. The next day, the rest of the group went to the Badaling Great Wall (*badaling changchen*) and the Ming Tombs (*shisan ling*). Having seen both sites more than several times by now, I enjoyed going to my carefree post office and to revisit the *Gong He Miao,* the famous Beijing Lama temple, which I never tire of visiting. We also went to my old home away from home, the Friendship Store (*youyi shangdian*) to purchase souvenirs. While more elaborate, and now allowing Chinese nationals to enter, the department store hasn't changed all that much since I first saw it in 1985. It's still the best bet for one's money in Beijing. There, we found some Chinese t-shirts which read "Beijing Olympics 2008." We bought some to help the cause and to be among the first to wear them.

Leaving Beijing, we flew seamlessly to Xi'an to visit, amongst other sites, the Xi'an warriors. This is a sight not to be missed. I think I have been there about 8 times. (Anytime anyone came to visit me in either Linfen or Nanjing — my sister, my father and mother, my friends — I whisked them away by train to Xi'an.) With IFDS, we stayed at the China Northwestern University Guesthouse. Lunch (bring your own chopsticks) was followed by a lecture from Professor Li of China Northwestern University.

MJM:    On the first day, we had a lecture on geography and then we went to the Stele Forest and the City Walls. Returning, we discussed the amenities of this guesthouse, which is really more typical of the accoutrements of a university guesthouse than our quarters at Peking University in the Shaoyuan Hotel. The accommodations and meals were good, but with 20 people and luggage, all trying to crowd into one tiny elevator to reach the 4th floor, things were a bit testy at first. The campus of China Northwestern University was attractive and pleasant. The people at the post office were really helpful when we tried, once again, the ultimate test of change in China, to mail a parcel. It was a pleasure.

On our second day in Xi'an, June 10, we visited the Xi'an Warriors and the neolithic site at Banpo Village. On the road to Banpo Village, we had to turn around and go to the Warriors first to avoid crowds of protestors. They were apparently protesting the fact that they were not receiving their unemployment money from the government. They receive 200 to 300 yuan a month to live on. Normal wage for the month would be 500 yuan or approximately $62 U.S.D a month. At half that for unemployment (if they had received it), they would be living on 31 American dollars a month. According to the most recent statistics I have found (see Appendix A), the average wage in China is $850 U.S.D a year. This protest highlighted the social unrest, occurring all over the country as the state-owned enterprises are either dismantled or sold off. Many years before, the Emperor Qin Shihuang may also have made his workers angry while he was tomb-building and creating the horses and warriors he would take with him to the next life. For within a short time of the creation of the Qin dynasty (221-206 BCE), it was overthrown and followed by the Han dynasty.

> MJM:   The Emperor Qin Shihuang[8] left us these priceless life-size clay warriors. The sight of them and their horses, unearthed in the vast covered archaeological site from which they were recovered, is breathtaking. Although Xi'an is in the interior, a visit to the warriors and that part of China is a must. Between going to the warriors and the neolithic Banpo site, we did something I have never done before — we visited some cave dwellings. Millions (exact numbers not readily available) of Chinese live in caves. They actually "build" these caves. That is, they take a cave, hollow it out and create a home, complete with windows and floors and heating. Caves are cool in summer and warm in winter. IFDS arranged for us to go visit some of these cave dwellings. Animals are kept in separate caves. I was mobbed there by the children all pleading to take a picture and asking for money. Women with babies at the breast were begging for money. Nowadays in the streets of Xi'an, Beijing, and Shanghai, one often sees people begging. This is the new society in China, there are no more "iron rice bowls," free housing and free health care. It's every man and woman for him or herself. Welcome to the world of globalization.

On our last day in Xi'an, June 11, we went to the Big Goose Pagoda (*da yan ta*), where I found the prayer beads and the saffron monk's robe I had been searching for throughout our trip. Of course, we also went to the Great Mosque (*da qingzhensi*) which is near the Drum Tower (*gulou*) and the Shaanxi Provincial Museum (*shanxi sheng bowuguan*), which is the home of the Forest of Steles.

Xi'an does not look like either Shanghai or Beijing, despite its great tourist appeal. It is a lovely "middle city" and not to be missed. While in Xi'an, we also had a lecture on Chinese calligraphy and painting. This lecture, conducted through an interpreter, was quite excellent. I had never before thought so carefully about the four constituent parts that every scroll must have: a poem, a picture, calligraphy and a chop. We also had a lecture on the legal system in China which was informative and focused on China's rapidly changing legal system, given their entry into the World Trade Organization (WTO).

Regretfully, we left Xi'an, which is a treasure trove of Chinese history and culture, and flew from Xi'an to Shanghai (also a treasure, albeit somewhat different in demeanor). During the flight, I sat next to Ming, who told me a little about IFDS. When we arrived in Shanghai, we would be staying in the same building on the same floor as the IFDS headquarters in Shanghai, located on the grounds of East China Normal University.

> MJM: We were looking forward to Shanghai primarily for another look at the incomparable Shanghai Museum. Quite by accident, we discovered that right next door to the Crowne Plaza, they were holding an international film festival. So, a few days after arriving for the second time in Shanghai, we viewed films in Shanghai (where we were often asked for our autographs — why else would *weiguoren* be there?). Meanwhile, our IFDS itinerary called for a visit to the Shanghai General Motors (GM) facility, where they make Buicks for internal consumers. The company is known as the Shanghai General Motors Corporation Ltd. which is a joint venture with Shanghai Automotive Industrial Corporation or (SAIC). Partners since 1995, Shanghai GM aims to "introduce technologically advanced cars to the China market as an alternative to imported sedans and to ensure that the new company would deliver high quality vehicles and services for many years to come." Their facility is awesome and ultra-contemporary, utilizing robots for some of the assembly.[9]

Thus, we had another chance to visit the Pudong area and to take the riverboat cruise on the Huangpu River. When the IFDS trip ended and we still had a few days in Shanghai to wrap up our interviewing. Shanghai literally means "on the sea," and it is one of the world's largest seaports, as well as the major industrial and commercial center of the People's Republic of China. The City of Shanghai lies on the western coast of the Pacific Ocean and at the central coastline of China. Also, Shanghai is home to 16.74 million people (March 2001), who live, not in a province, but an administrative entity equivalent to a province, reporting directly to the central government. Shanghai has long been the hub of many industries and educational institutions, including Jiao Tong and Fudan.[10]

We had become very certain that we wanted to include AmCham or the American Chamber of Commerce in this book, so we located their facility in the Portman Towers and stopped in to see what they had to offer. This opened up a whole other world. To keep receiving their materials, we joined the Shanghai Chamber of Commerce. We were also able to interview their managing director, Mr. Shane Frecklington, and learn more about the work of the American Chamber of Commerce in Shanghai, which we will discuss in the concluding chapter. In the next few pages, based upon my observations as an exchange professor in China, as well as the Fulbright study tour and my more recent IFDS professional development tour, I explore the parameters of researching and setting up both educational tours and educational exchanges. I begin with the historical context, without which we cannot begin to understand contemporary China.

## THE (RELATIVELY) LONG VIEW—
## 20TH CENTURY CHINA

China, as any Chinese happily will tell you, has a very long history—nearly 5,000 years—while that of the United States is less than 250 years. While only slightly larger than the United States, China now has 1.26 billion people while the United States has 280 million people. In China, 70 to 80 percent of the population live in the provinces, far from China's coastal cities, in vision, kilometers and living standards. The "China" one tends to see on TV is the China of the young university student and the successful Chinese businessman or woman. These groups sport European and American clothing, buy DVDs, videos, computers and electronic equipment and often enjoy discos, pizza and Kentucky Fried Chicken. With each passing year, the gap widens between the rich (many of whom live in China's cities) and the poor (nearly one billion Chinese live in the provinces). Reasons for this split are numerous and potentially dangerous to social and political stability.[11] This is why the Chinese Communist Party has not always responded positively to criticism of its policies by the United States' government.

As I see it, one of the major problems still hindering U.S.–China relations is our skewed perception of China, which is derived from a combination of the myth of the "mysterious Orient," latent racism, virulent anti–communism and a leftover Cold War mentality.[12] These factors tend to affect our good judgment when dealing with Chinese companies and the Chinese government. We tend to pretend in our media that all Chinese live as we do in America. Thus, they should be as "responsible and advanced" as we are. We assert that they are but a step away from world dominance. Apparently the government and media would like to turn China into another "evil empire." I would like to share here an up-close view of China's development over the past 17 years to counterbalance that attitude and at the same time demonstrate the difference in the attitude of successful American businesses in China. In further case studies, the need to overcome this parochial perspective will be highlighted.

# CHINA IN THE '80S

My views result from experiences and issues arising in teaching intercultural communication over the past 17 years to students both in the People's Republic of China and in the United States. I have also worked with Chinese colleagues and students from Taiwan. In 1988, I participated in a Fulbright group project studying economic development in both South Korea and Taiwan. Over time, one's teaching style, content, and lines of argument evolve based upon such intervening events and contexts. This is especially true in the case of understanding, interpreting and acting upon intercultural transactions and relationships in China, which has, since the 1980s, undergone significant changes in its social, political, legal and economic spheres (and in its transportation and communications infrastructure). That this is a road fraught with difficulties, Social unrest was best illustrated by the 1989 Tiananmen Square (Beijing) conflagration, in which many Chinese were killed (apparently no one knows how many) in confrontations between the army and the protestors. In short, some may perceive that China has undergone, at least in the coastal cities, and in its dealings with Westerners, a veritable sea change. Others make the assumption that the coastal cities of China today represent the new China. These assumptions are skewed as one will see by taking a train to Linfen in Shanxi Province or travel the rutted dirt roads to Gaoyou City in Jiangsu Province, as we "foreign experts" teaching in Jiangsu Province did in 1997.

Living standards have changed little in these rural cities since the 1980s, although basic infrastructure has improved (communications, transportation) somewhat. Per capita income is considerably less in the hinterlands, beyond the major coastal cities that receive the bulk of international trade via the vastly improved port and other transportation facilities. Chief amongst these cities is Shanghai and its partner city, Pudong, across the river. Multitudinous joint ventures flourish in these cities with international partners such as the Foxboro Company, Holiday Inn (part of the newly created Six Continents Group) and the ultra-sophisticated, robotized General Motors plant.[13]

Judging from the angry Cold War attitude of the American media in general in the eighties and nineties and its scathing indictment of every situation involving China,[14] others may think that so long as China continues as a communist nation, important changes (such as adopting American style democracy) can never occur. Here we have a conundrum. If we pose the question "has China changed," we must also ask ourselves "why do we care and into what should they change?" Change abounds in China from basic ideology to manufacturing processes, with the concomitant greater freedom of expression in everyday life and in the media. While this progress does not approximate that of the United States, does it have to? Particularly when we have had a much longer period — and more favorable circumstances— to achieve our lifestyle, and within that, our freedoms.

At the beginning of the 20th century, China's people — with the exception of the very rich and the foreigners who came to occupy various parts of China, including Shanghai — had a very low standard of living, did not own their land, rarely ate meat and often were beaten about by landlords and warlords. Contrary to the prevailing mythology of the exotic Chinese lifestyle, peasant dress, food, transportation, housing and workload was often inadequate or nonexistent. In times of drought, Chinese peasants often starved by the millions (as they did World War II and in the 1960s). At best, clothing covered the body — and if lucky, one might have 2 or 3 outfits. Houses were constructed of the available indigenous materials, which differed from North to South. Whole families slept on the *kang* (a brick bed covered with pallets and quilts). The *kang* abutted the cookstove and was heated in that way. Then and now, the *kang* is a household fixture, as is the coal stove, improperly vented so that in winter the house or cave house may be smoke-filled, causing cyclical bronchial and lung problems.

The peasant and his family could be uprooted at the whim of the landowner and evicted. That same peasant (or his wife) pulled the plow, in lieu of a draft animal. The peasant and his wife and children worked the rice paddies where giant leeches would attach themselves to the workers legs' and the workers would labor all day, bent in the rice paddy. Market prices were not stable. Most people had no electricity, but used lanterns and candles to get about. The water was not drinkable. There were no indoor toilets— there was no indoor running water (hot or cold) except perhaps in some of the larger cities in the homes of the very rich, or foreigners. If not, there was plenty of servant or slave labor available to endlessly haul the foreigner's water needs on one's shoulders in buckets suspended by a long pole. Even then, all water had to be boiled. Not to boil the water in China, then and now, means, if not death, then surely hepatitis. When automobiles came in, few but the foreigners and very rich could afford them. Rickshaws, drawn by patient men, or one's feet provided transportation.

More to the point, the ordinary Chinese person could neither read nor write. Men could rarely (except through the Confucian examination system) move out of the class into which they were born. Women could advance (as women have around the world, since the beginning of history) through marriage, by becoming the third or fourth wife or concubine of a rich (and older) man.

This inequality and the sheer drudgery of everyday life, as well as gross mistreatment of the peasants by the warlords and landlords, often gave rise to peasant uprisings. This is how new dynasties in China were formed. The old dynasty was deposed and another took its place (as in the Qin and the Han dynasties). When the Ching Emperor Puyi was deposed in 1911 and the government was taken over by the Nationalists, there was an attempt to begin a new dynasty which failed under the warlord Yuan Shi Kai. Both the Nationalists (Kuomintang or KMT) and the Communists (CCP) were revolutionary forces in China. Both subscribed to one-party government and both needed to address the severe question of land reform. The question was—who would control China? The two parties were more alike than different in their Confucian base, their commitment to land reform and their desire for a one party state, as well as their almost totally Chinese worldview. Yet the Nationalists were preferred by the United States. In part, the illusion of Western culture came from the perception in the United States of Dr. Sun Yatsen and his family. They were perceived to be (through connections and dress) westernized. While Sun Yatsen had been educated in Hawaii, Chiang Kaishek knew no foreign languages and was not educated abroad, though he did marry well and his and his wife and family did much to advance his cause with the Americans. As we have seen earlier, however, as Westerners, we would do well to shed our biases when contemplating other cultures. It is easy to be led astray, particularly when one assumes that the language being spoken—almost always English—represents the desired expression.

To explicate this breach in perception, a brief recap of China's evolution into modernity follows. Juxtapose the historical context of mainland China in the 20th century to that of the United States in the same time span in conjunction with the differences between the Western mind and the Eastern mind (discussed in Chapter 1), and China's growth pattern in the past 20 years demonstrates a compelling inner logic.

## Exchange Programs—"Being There"

The best way to study and experience a culture is by "being there."

In 1996, I arranged to teach at Southeast University in Nanjing while on sabbatical in the spring of 1997. I had several objectives in going to Nanjing, one of which was to gather data on the city to compare it to other cities I had visited in the past in regard to transportation and communication facilities, as well as sizing up what I call the "isolation" factor — proximity to other foreigners — as well as proximity to medical, communication and transportation facilities. In a previous exchange, I felt that while the experience of rural China was authentic and enriching, it was also isolating. If one is going to experience culture shock (and one will), that culture shock will be intensified if one is isolated, unable to communicate well in any language. Also, in a rural city, there may be few other foreigners. In Shanxi Province, some people had never seen foreigners before. Or, if they were old enough to remember, the last foreigners they might have seen would have been the Japanese, during World War II.

In our case, in 1985, we were "it."[15] When we went to market, crowds encircled us, people were laughing, pointing and touching us. After a while, this became a great irritation. So, in going to Nanjing, I also wanted to see how this "middle" city handled foreigners. The people of Nanjing tended to ignore us foreigners, they had already seen many of us over the years and we were no longer such a novelty.

My next objective was to observe the Nanjing students, their courses, their English abilities and their lifestyle. Nanjing has many KFCs, McDonald's and pizza places and my Chinese students went to these places once in a great while, but tended to prefer their mother's cooking or Chinese food in general, rather than great hunks of food. On campus, students lived many (6 persons) to a room, just as they had in 1988 in Linfen. In the classroom, I discovered much the same thing as one discovers in any classroom, anywhere. The students who want to sit in front do so. The students who want to sit in the back also do so. The trick for the instructor is to get all involved, which means reconfiguring the classroom, so that all are enabled to participate. Fortunately, there was one room in the department office building in which the furniture was not nailed down and one could develop an interactive classroom there. The students liked this better, just as students anywhere do. In small groups, all would speak.

This time around, I even taught public speaking[16] and prepped some students for the first ever public speaking contest in Nanjing in 1997. The topic was "The Return of Hong Kong to the Motherland," and the contest was held in downtown Nanjing with all the universities participating and a star-studded cast of judges which included some Red Army and Air Force officers, as well as two foreigners, Dr. Matelski and I.

My other major objectives for my sabbatical included: (1) gathering data on educational work units—the students, my colleagues, the work, the culture; (2) developing relationships with my colleagues at universities in Nanjing to discuss joint research projects and options for exchange programs; and (3) exploring possibilities and developing relationships conducive to distance education.

To do this work, I addressed the concerns listed below at four universities (public) and one college (private) in Nanjing. These opportunities were enabled through my longstanding relationship with my colleague Wang Keqiang (Chair of the English Department, SanJiang College), whom I have known and worked with since 1985.

My basic questions included the following:

1. What level of fluency is required of American students to come to study for a year (or a semester, or six weeks) in China?

2. What is the quality and diversity of the available living quarters? If students are housed off-campus, what affordable transportation is available to them? What is the traveling time?

3. What are the course loads (per semester, per year), possible equivalencies and academic expectations? How is testing done?

4. What is the computer and e-mail availability for students? How much integration with Chinese students is there, versus living on "an American island"?

5. What is the availability of field trips or outside activities with professors (or Chinese students)?

6. What "safety nets" are in place for foreign students, e.g., counselors, or quick access to medical and communication facilities in case of emergencies?

7. What specific courses are available to communication majors? To Asian studies students, to aviation and management science students?

8. What fluency in Chinese, if any, is required in these courses?

9. What is the ease of semester-equivalency and transferring credits between the two institutions, given the different semester dates and breaks? The first semester of the academic year in China does not end until Spring Festival (late January and February) while semesters in the U.S. tend to end just prior to Christmas. Thus, both the first and second semester endings are problematic. However, if courses begin in China in March and end in July, this proves to be the semester of choice for both students and professors, but cuts into summer vacation.

10. What are the possibilities of internships (for credit) at international businesses or institutions in China?[17]

As I visited the institutions selected, I also had questions regarding either summer study or teaching (4–6 weeks at an institution with perhaps 10 days for travel). These questions approximated those above.

Finally, as a former exchange professor and current visiting professor, I was, of course, interested in possible arrangements for faculty. Again, these approximated those questions asked above. Except, of course, that the course load expectancy, transportation and communication access, housing concerns and semester breaks would be in regard to the exchange or visiting professor. Language fluency for either group never seemed to be a significant factor. Visiting professors were "talking books" and were expected to speak English all the time for the benefit of the students, to enable them to "hear" English other than over the earphones in the language lab. Accommodations are often made for the low language fluency in Chinese for exchange students who speak English.

Most English-speaking professors teaching in a Chinese college or university have much heavier loads than their Chinese colleagues (this is, it is said, because it is our native tongue and therefore easy for us). Since professors are under the rubric of "foreign experts," we technically work for the state and our work and lives are overseen by the Office of Foreign Affairs, who also determine the pay scale, based upon rank and years of service. Unless one has a private income, or is on sabbatical or an exchange program, one will have to be frugal in China, as the pay scale is approximately $250 to $300 a month, depending on rank. Housing is mostly free and many universities have more than adequate facilities for their foreign professors. The quarters are usually not too large, so don't bring much with you. If you are single, the Chinese will try to make you make do with one single room in one of their campus hotels. This is almost impossible (for me) to adjust to. Therefore, when this happens, I protest until another arrangement is found. A good argument here is that it is impossible to receive either students or colleagues in one's bedroom. Since a "foreign expert" is rarely given an office, either another room or another venue should be easy to argue for — but this is time consuming.

While in Nanjing, I visited or lectured at five universities, including Nanjing University, Nanjing University of Aeronautics and Astronautics (NUAA), Southeast University, Nanjing Normal University and SanJiang College.

SanJiang College is a rare breed in China, one of the first private colleges. The college began as a three-year college in 1995. While there in 1997, I lectured there in its first incarnation. By the time Dr. Matelski and I went back in 2001 to lecture there, the college had moved into amazing new quarters outside of Nanjing. The new college campus has more than

750 acres. Projected investment in facilities was more than 60 million yuan. The classrooms are state-of-the-art by standards of both China and the United States. The students have access to computer facilities and to e-mail.

SanJiang College has six departments: Foreign Languages; Business Administration and Foreign Trade; Architecture; Computer Science; Mechanical and Electrical Engineering; and Chinese Language. The departments offer specialties in (amongst others) Foreign Trade English, Foreign Trade Japanese, Accounting, Modern Marketing Management and Computer Applications.

SanJiang was founded by a consortium of retired professors from Nanjing University and Southeast University. In 1997, it was one of eight private colleges in China and the only private college in Jiangsu Province. Following the educational policies of the Party and the State and under the leadership of the government educational department, the aim of the college "is to train morally, intellectually and physically develop, useful and professionally oriented students to meet the needs of China's economic construction and social development." Most of my educational research in Nanjing took place at four public universities. Again, my friend and colleague, Wang Keqiang, arranged the meetings and visits and also interpreted when necessary. Together, we surveyed the colleges in Nanjing, exploring for possible educational exchanges.

# SELECTED NANJING PUBLIC UNIVERSITIES

## *Nanjing University*

Situated on a lovely campus, Nanjing University is the third-ranked university in China and is known for its Chinese Language Department, Foreign Languages Department and School of Foreign Studies. Nanjing University operates directly under the State Education Commission. The School of Foreign Studies has 122 faculty members, most of whom have traveled abroad. In addition, further ongoing research is conducted by specialized institutes for "research on linguistics and literature ... centers for Jewish studies, Canadian studies, Australian studies and Cervantes studies." The School of Foreign Studies has many international students from all over the world and a large library, and subscribes to 110 journals (Chinese and other).

The School of Foreign Studies offers bachelor of arts, master of arts, and doctorate degrees. In the Department of International Business Communication, the bachelor of arts degree is offered in International Business (in English). In a lunch with Dr. Wang Shouren, Chairman, Dept. of English, School of Foreign Studies, Nanjing University, he explained details of the International Business major. It is a four year major with the study of English geared to business. Most classes are taught in English. From their junior year, students learn statistics, finance, accounting, marketing, math and international trade. In the fourth year, students have internships, e.g., China Daily (English language paper) or TV stations.

Nanjing University has ties with Harvard University and an exchange program with Boston College and other colleges in the United States and throughout the world. In regard to exchange programs, Nanjing University looks for materials exchange, information exchange, and textbook exchange.

Students at Nanjing University (in 1997) were not advised to go abroad — especially not to the U.S. If they wanted to study somewhere in the West, however, they were encouraged to study in England. In addition, desirable exchange programs might have included the possibility of sending one young faculty member for one semester to the U.S to attend lectures, audit classes and give courses, perhaps with payment. The sending side would pay airfare; the receiving side paid for health care, accommodations and a salary for teaching.

To conclude, Nanjing University has a wonderful reputation amongst Chinese universities, and has lovely grounds and buildings and a great faculty dining room. The university campus hotel is excellent for brief studies abroad. The Amity Foundation is located on this campus. One caveat (typical of most universities): Westerners may not come to teach for one semester only, but must come for one academic year.

## Southeast University

Like Nanjing University, Southeast University has changed its name several times during the 20th century. Its primary focus is on engineering and architecture. In thse areas, it has excellent facilities. Its Department of Foreign Languages is relatively new and developing rapidly. Many members of its faculty have gone abroad in recent years, returning after one year or after they have received master's degrees in England. This arrangement has been facilitated through joint research and writing projects (preparing teaching materials) with the British Council.

Southeast University like some other universities, agrees to Fall and Spring semesters of four months to fit Western academic calendars, e.g., late August to January 1 and late February to the end of June. While there, in 1997 I was given the following teaching assignments: American Literature and Film to majors; Thesis/Abstract Writing to doctorate students; American Culture to doctorate students; Conversation to master's students.

The basic issues under discussion at that time are listed below.[18] One thing about ongoing negotiations— they are ongoing. That's why the contract is such a nebulous concept in China. The terms of the issues continue to be negotiated and policies are in part promulgated by the Office of Foreign Affairs and in part by the specific needs at the time of the university with whom one is negotiating. Therefore, the terms which follow may have undergone a change but the basic issues tend to remain the same.

## Expectations of the Western Side:

1. Courses should be fixed and published (both sides);
2. Professors may be sent for one semester or one year;
3. For a one semester stay, Southeast should pay airfare one way;
4. For a one year stay, Southeast should pay round trip airfare;
5. Foreign experts will receive 2600 yuan (approx. $275), teachers will receive less (depending upon qualifications, degrees held);
6. Foreign experts will have accommodations with a bedroom, living room, bath and kitchen;
7. Foreign experts will have no more than 3 preps in a semester;
8. The University will provide health care;
9. The University will provide office space, computer and e-mail access.

In return, the American side offered:

1. Provisions for young teachers or professors to be sent for ten months to America;
2. Suitable living accommodations, with kitchen facilities;
3. No more than 3 courses a semester for young teachers or professors;
4. Pay for young teachers or professors for courses they teach;
5. The opportunity for young teachers or professors will be allowed to audit 2 courses per semester;
6. Some travel (to be negotiated);
7. Office space, computer and e-mail access;
8. Health care insurance.

Like Nanjing University, Nanjing Normal University and Nanjing University of Aeronautics and Astronautics, the Department of Foreign Languages at Southeast University was reformulating its objectives. In China in the late '90s, all objectives for learning English centered on science, trade, business and intercultural-international communication. In the Department of Foreign Languages at Southeast University, there were plans to offer courses in English, by foreign experts, in International Trade, Marketing, Western Economics, Trade Law, Export-Import (with lecturers from business organizations), English for Foreign Trade, Business Communication, and Current courses, e.g., literature, listening, reading, and grammar.

At Southeast University, computer facilities and e-mail were readily available. The campus is well maintained and the teaching buildings are in good repair. Foreign experts share offices and have adequate quarters. For foreign students there is an International Students' residence hall and foreign students from many continents live there. University conference amenities include a well-maintained conference center, good university hotel, a business center and an office for short term courses, e.g., 4-6 week summer courses for foreign students and faculty. With such good facilities, clear direction and the recently developed graduate programs throughout China, Southeast University and universities throughout China may reach their goal of 21st century excellence within the first 20 years of the century.

## Nanjing University of Aeronautics and Astronautics (NUAA)

NUAA is one of the leading universities of its kind in China. It operates under the leadership of the Aviation Industries of China (AVIC) and the Civil Aviation Administration of China (CAAC). It is also known as one of the top "100" universities in China, with 44 bachelor's degree majors, 32 master's degree programs and 11 doctorate degree programs. Of its 58 laboratories, one is a key laboratory for national defense and five operate under government ministries. As of Spring 1997, some 400 of its specialists and professors had been sent abroad to "give lectures, engage in advanced studies, [and] investigate or carry out cooperative researches." At that time, the university had cooperative relationships with over 30 foreign universities, institutions and enterprises.[19]

The Foreign Languages Department at NUAA was set up in 1988 and consists of 5 teaching and research sections: English in Civil Aviation; English in International Trade; College English; Postgraduate English (for non-English majors); and Minor Foreign Languages (Japanese, French and Russian).

Among other responsibilities, the department develops:

1. The examination in Business English for the Jiangsu Province;
2. The Self-study exam;
3. The papers in Mechanical English for the "English Project" of the Civil Aviation Project Administration of China; and
4. The training of personnel for Foreign Affairs and Economy and Trade.

Like other universities in Nanjing, NUAA is interested in materials and textbook exchange, summer study programs, personnel exchanges and scholars in residence. Despite China's rise as a trading partner and its potential as an economic power, there's still a long way to go towards financing educational institutions; and good, recent textbooks are in short supply.

Through the Foreign Languages Department and the Office of International Cooperation at NUAA, food, lodging and courses in Chinese culture and language can be delivered, in addition to some travel to, e.g., Beijing, Xi'an, Hong Kong or Jiangsu Province which have facilities for summer programs of 10-15 students, faculty or administrators for up to 6 weeks (July-August). The campus is pleasant, with good facilities. The Department of Foreign Languages is well-equipped and staffed. Negotiations with NUAA cover the same issues as those with other universities, particularly in the cases of exchange students or professors. However, it is my impression that NUAA is slightly more flexible than other educational institutions. At NUAA, the Foreign Languages Department is in charge of teaching "sky talk" to China's aviation professionals. Working with NUAA may offer some foreign institution a unique opportunity.

## Nanjing Normal University

I visited Nanjing Normal University (NNU) fairly often to meet friends, to discuss goals with the Acting Chair of the Department of Foreign Languages and once to give a lecture on intercultural communication. I had the opportunity to visit the student and faculty quarters, eat in the dining room and research the campus facilities. Nanjing Normal University has a beautiful campus with diverse departments. In addition, NNU has many departments which may prove compatible and may provide exchange options with U.S. normal colleges and universities. Among them are:

1. The Department of Adult Education — this program encompasses both the two-year program and the 4-year college;
2. The Department of Foreign Languages and Literature and its affiliated Linguistic and Cultural Studies Institute;
3. The Department of Education — the Research Institute of Education and Science;
4. The Department of Computer Science; and
5. The College of Mass Communications.

Collaboration on, and exchanges of, video programming is an area that needs implementation. One way of beginning distance education (if too expensive or difficult to achieve initially) is to develop a joint project that can be videotaped and simply sent to China or the U.S. by the research-project team. For the Chinese, this poses no problem; if we cannot videotape and translate to their system, they easily can do it with their state of the art equipment.

Nanjing Normal University was founded in 1902 and is one of the most respected of the many universities in Nanjing and in China. Like the others discussed here, it is part of the central government's project "211," has many professors educated abroad, employs many foreign experts and has excellent graduate programs. I have had dinners and discussions with a friend and colleague, Dr. Gu Jiazu (Charles),[20] who received his master of arts from Michigan State University and who has written intercultural communication textbooks (in Chinese). Gu Jiazu introduced me to other leaders in his department for preliminary discussions regarding possible joint research projects, exchanges and other options beneficial to both sides. Issues and terms were compatible with those discussed earlier.

Like the other universities discussed here, Nanjing Normal University has international students (over 300 a year from over 60 countries on either one-year or four-year programs and 3-week to 3-month programs). This university has good international student housing, and a reliable campus hotel to accommodate foreign teachers. Foreign experts have a bedroom, bath, and small living room, and share kitchen and recreation room facilities. At the time, NNU had 7,000 to 8,000 students, 43 master's programs and 6 Ph.D. programs.[21] In addition it had exchanges with, amongst others, Union College, Kennesaw State University, George Mason University and California State University. Nanjing Normal University is a pleasant place to live and study.

After conducting the above research of the above universities in Nanjing over a six-month period in 1997, I concluded that all the public institutions included here share the following characteristics:

1. All would welcome some form of faculty exchange;

2. All would welcome joint research and projects;

3. All would welcome materials and textbook exchange (a pressing need);

4. All would welcome limited opportunities for teaching and study abroad;

5. All have facilities, teachers and courses for summer or intercession courses (for students, faculty or administrators), available through the Departments or through their Offices of International Cooperation;

6. All have good campus hotels and restaurants at reasonable rates;

7. All have conference centers with a business center;

8. All have fax, telephone, e-mail and computer resources;

9. International flights are available at Nanjing International Airport — book through CITS or the Office of International Cooperation;

10. All have international dorms for international students;

11. All Departments of Foreign Languages have many English speaking faculty as do all Offices of International Cooperation;

12. All offer the BA, the MA and the Ph.D. and each Department of Foreign languages has (unlike in the '80s) qualified faculty with advanced degrees. Many faculty members have been abroad or are preparing to go abroad — to England, Singapore, Canada, Austria, Holland, Germany, France, Japan, Australia and the United States;

13. All belong to the chosen "100" selected by the State Education Commission for "Project 211"; and

14. All have dynamic faculty, able to teach in English.

The four public institutions and the one private institution described above are located in Nanjing, the capital city of Jiangsu Province. Nanjing is located about 2½ hours from Shanghai by superhighway or fast train. With more than 70.2 million inhabitants, it is one of China's "more attractive major cities."[22] Nanjing has a population of 5,298,200 inhabitants—one-third that of Shanghai. Nanjing is highly industrialized, as is Jiangsu Province in general, spurred on by its proximity to Shanghai. The city has twice been China's capital, the last time in the early years of the 20th century, when it was home to the Republic of China.[23] Nanjing's location, its history, museum, and temples, all contribute to its charm.

## CONCLUSION

In this case study, through our travels with IFDS, through my sabbatical in 1997 and our lecturing in Nanjing in 2001, we have explored not only getting around China and considerations and issues with conducting educational tours and exchanges, but also what a student or academic can anticipate at various universities across China — in Beijing, Xi'an, Shanghai and Nanjing. This is not a concept we often think about in the U.S., that is, universities and exchange programs. However, in developing countries exchange programs are necessary, just as they are in the United States. If the world is getting smaller, then intercultural communication — learning about other cultures and learning other languages — is more important than ever. In an interrelated, multinational and globalized world, it is imperative that we work together and through experience, lessen the mystification of the "other," for fruitful lives around the globe.

# 5

# Case Study: Two Art Exhibitions Cross the Pacific

*This chapter is, in part, the result of Dr. Nancy Street's second sojourn in the PRC in 1988, as a "teacher of English" and exchange professor from Bridgewater State College (BSC) to Chinese juniors and seniors at Shanxi Teacher's University (STU) in Linfen, Shanxi Province. This second teaching assignment was considerably different from her first such assignment in 1985 in several ways: (1) she now had supervisory responsibility for American students abroad;(2) she taught American History, British History, American Literature and British Literature to classes of 75 juniors and 80 Chinese seniors (as compared to basic public speaking and English grammar in her prior experience); and (3) BSC added a new level to the academic exchange with STU, asking her to oversee the cultural exchange (American art and artifacts) initiated between the two educational institutions.*

*The art exhibition was sent from Bridgewater to Linfen in the fall of 1988. Fortunately, she had participated in a similar cultural exhibit sent by the Chinese to Bridgewater in 1987; thus, she was acquainted with some of the transportation and communication problems that might arise on either side of the Pacific. Further, Dr. Street knew most of the persons involved in this interaction — on both sides of the agreement. Her story follows.*

# OVERVIEW OF SHANXI PROVINCE

STU is located some eighteen hours by train from Beijing (at that time, virtually the only way into Linfen, which until 1986 was a closed city.)[1] Shanxi Province, according to my colleagues in Linfen, was a kind of Chinese Siberia for political exiles. It seems that Shanxi has always been (because of its geographical location in central China, and mountainous terrain) a place of exile. For instance (so the story goes), when Xu Ting Ze, an Air Force officer from Taiwan, decided to defect, he escaped from Taiwan in a U.S.–made fighter plane and was sent to the Linfen Air Force base. Yet another Taiwanese, Wang Zi Cheng, hearing the Fujien Broadcast in Taiwan, also defected and was sent to "our" Air Force base in Linfen. These incidents took place in the late fifties. From time to time, during the various revisionist phases of China's post-liberation era, intellectuals were sent to the countryside in Shanxi.[2] During the Cultural Revolution, thousands more intellectuals and cadres followed, unable to return to their homes in the coastal cities of China until the early 1990s.

*People's Daily Online* describes Shanxi's physical location as "along the middle reaches of the Yellow River in the western part of north China."[3] Inner Mongolia is nearby. The province has a population of 32.97 million (March 2001) inhabited by Han, Hui, Mongol and others; in total more than 34 ethnic groups engage in farming some 3,656,500 arable hectares, or 23 percent of the available land. In truth, I felt quite at home in the dry and dusty Shanxi landscape — it reminded me of the San Joaquin Valley in California where I grew up. In Shanxi, they grow everything from tobacco to rice to beans, and raise, among other animals, pigs, sheep, chicken, rabbits, cows and mules. Additionally, they tend to silkworms and bees. As of March 2001, Shanxi had more than 12,000 industrial enterprises.[4]

Like most provinces in the interior, Shanxi's facilities and infrastructure cannot compare to those of the coastal cities, such as Shanghai. Shanghai has a wealth of shipping facilities and high technology industries, made possible through the creation of infrastructure considered as a given to participate in a globalized world economy. Further "airbrushing" of the city may be next, as lamented by Jim Scotton of the *Shanghai Star* in "Sad Farewell to Ten Thousand Flags." Scotton begins by saying,

> Spring has come to Shanghai and we can again see flowers blooming and trees budding. We can also see, perhaps for the last time in some parts of Shanghai, laundry drying on balconies, on trees and on utility poles. What Shanghainese call "the ten thousand flags" are flapping in the breeze as city residents dry their shirts, pants, socks and underwear in their outdoor clothes drier.[5]

The sight of clothes drying in the wind is a hallmark of old Shanghai. Tongue in cheek, Scotton makes the point that if things keep going in this direction, people may not flock to Shanghai if it is no longer a Chinese international city, but an international city which looks and acts like London or New York. He says, "We need to save its Chinese character."[6]

In the pages that follow, I will use the case study of an American art exhibit to further explain both the Chinese and American "characters."

## THE AMERICAN ART EXHIBITION IN SHANGHAI

By 1988, China was in the process of evolving from a near-technology-free environment (few phones, almost no major highways and existing roads subject to the vagaries of weather), towards developing significant communication and transportation infrastructure. However, then — as now — there were wide discrepancies between Shanghai and Linfen as cities. Shanghai was sophisticated back in the 1920s when it housed the "foreign concessions" on the Bund. After more than six decades of virtual capitalistic dormancy under Chairman Mao and his Long March companions,[7] Deng Xiaoping revived the city in the 1990s, enabling it to reclaim its earlier panache. Linfen, however, had no such resurgence during this same time.

For example, how did I do my laundry in remote Linfen with no washer and dryer? I found a Chinese woman, Yongmei, who rubbed my clothes on the rocks at the Fen riverbed behind her house.[8] They often really needed scrubbing every day. Everything was covered with coal dust in minutes—furniture, clothes, floors— it was even in the water supply. In winter, she dried my clothes on a line in her home near the coal stove that polluted the entire house. Yongmei's family coughed all winter and often, like most Chinese, had terrible colds and bronchitis from the insidious coal dust, the damp, and the fierce dusty winds howling in from Inner Mongolia. But that was everyday life.

## WEST MEETS EAST—NEGOTIATIONS FOR THE EXHIBITION

The revolutionary policies promulgated by the Chinese Communist Party (CCP) hierarchy in Beijing in 1988–1989 were avidly studied and articulated by the cadres and comrades in our work unit at Shanxi Teachers University (STU).[9] To learn about the West was good. Still, the lack of understanding of then-modern communications technology and transportation systems, as well as intercultural communication skills, led to unhappy situations on both sides.

On the one hand, the Chinese in Linfen, unlike their Shanghai brethren, had been isolated from the outside world — if not exactly forever, then perhaps for twenty or thirty years. Due to many restrictions (not the least of which was the lack of money), they had rarely left Shanxi; nor did they have access to foreign television or magazines. They could not easily visualize the world outside of Linfen.

On the other hand, Shanghainese tend to be canny and worldly, by comparison. In 2002, for example, to eradicate such visual pollution as the "10,000 flags," the government accelerated its earlier efforts to persuade the Shanghainese to move across the river to the industrial and residential areas in Pudong (a sterile environment, compared to bustling Shanghai) as well as other, less noticeable, places. But the people of Shanghai do not want to move. There is much status in coming from the leading commercial city in China — better, even than Hong Kong. Shanghai is also exciting and has popular culture from around the world. One can smell money on the Shanghai breeze.

By comparison, many of my colleagues in Linfen told me that, until we foreigners arrived and with us more opportunities to apply for graduate school in the United States— a horrendous process requiring nearly a year — they had never been to Beijing or Shanghai. During this time, students would make many visits to Taiyuan and Beijing for the necessary stamps, letters, seals and interviews.[10] There was little need to know about commerce and its conduct in Shanghai or the United States. No one could buy anything from America — they could not know what there was to buy, and there was no money to buy. Or, there was no American money to buy American products with, even if they could have ordered from a catalog, which they had never seen.

On the other side of the globe, my colleagues at Bridgewater State College had no understanding of this "cultural" partition. They simply *assumed* that all parts of the country were equal. Thus, there was no concern, for example, of what might happen to an art exhibit once it had arrived in Shanghai. Perhaps, they surmised, there would be a FedEx (or similar organization) to send the exhibit on to Linfen. In point of fact, the entire shipment could have been lost and there would have been no recourse.

This situation required important information, constant communication and serious negotiation; but neither side was adequately prepared to understand the real world circumstances of the other back in those early days of the BSC-STU relationship. Interestingly, in retrospect, the Chinese side learned how to negotiate with the American side far more quickly and efficiently than the American side ever understood.

As I explain later, these conflicts and failures in understanding, particularly on the part of the American university, proved detrimental to the work of the two institutions and especially to the Chinese work unit and its aspirations for its professors and students. Perhaps a more cautious step-by-step approach might have proven to develop into a more lasting relationship between the two institutions. Instead, to the credit of each side, they undertook the cultural exchange very early in the relationship. The Chinese, when discussing their trajectory during the 20th century, will often say, "Mistakes have been made." Certainly, through our mistakes, we learned.

In this case study, I approach the telling and analysis of the story utilizing concepts of self, hierarchy, thinking style and face. I also include "culture shock"—a very important consideration in all international negotiations. During both exhibitions, I was the only American academic present familiar with the procedures and persons involved on both sides. Some of my graduate students, especially Yu Shihao, whose thesis deals with the first Chinese art exhibition, and Shi Jingshun, had some knowledge of the expectations on both sides, as well as life experience with the deployment of both American and Chinese norms and forms. In short, we could share perceptions and analyses of the processes we were involved in as we sought to facilitate and understand the nuances of these exchanges.

## CULTURAL PATTERNS IN NOT-FOR-PROFIT ENTERPRISES AND FOR-PROFIT ENTERPRISES: THE U.S. AND CHINA

Information about Chinese-American cultural patterns, e.g., concepts of self, hierarchy, thinking style and face, are often gathered through participant observation. One area of particular value for this method is the study of international art exchanges by public institutions as described above. The worldview of not-for-profit public enterprises is considerably different than that of for-profit enterprises developed in other case studies in this book. The American government and for-profit organizations may have had more difficulty acclimatizing to the slower, relationship based, collectivist and hierarchical, high context negotiating style of

Chinese government and business than similar negotiations between educational institutions in both countries.

Public education in China, contrary to popular perception, is as undervalued (and woefully under-funded), as in the United States.[11] Like American professors, Chinese professors are poorly paid. Academics in both the U.S. and China, as a rule, tend to value collegiality and group consensus. At the university, we also live in a collectivist world, where the individual (professor) and the collective (members of the department) ideally work somewhat in concert to enhance the discipline and ensure the well-being of the students. In both settings, "rogue" professors, like "rogue" states, are little tolerated in the group. I do not mean that we always succeed in tempering these individuals or cabals and that there are not "rogues" or entrepreneurs amongst us, I simply explicate one vision of the ideal educational state.

Our product or desired outcome is the well-educated student, one who is prepared to meet the challenges of day to day life, sometimes as employee, sometimes as employer. At that point, the former student enters into the world of "for profit." In business, as we will see later in the Foxboro case study, teamwork is often not only encouraged, but mandated for the entire product development and manufacturing processes. Here again, however, the ultimate goal, in addition to worker satisfaction, is profit. I think from this explanation, one can see that both stages—the student as product in the not-for-profit realm and the employee creating a product for profit—are simply evolutionary, non-contradictory and complementary stages of an individual's life which he or she must reconcile at the appropriate time. In short, for the professor, the well-educated, secure and successful student (all it takes is one or two a year) is the reward, or "profit."

In the exchanges, the West wanted a glimpse of the "exotic" culture that was—and is—the cultural heritage of 5,000 years. The Chinese, on the other hand, wanted a glimpse of what the *waiguoren* (foreigners) could provide aesthetically (pop culture aside).[12] In 1987 and 1988, I witnessed the process of delivering two such exhibits: the first art exhibit, sent to the United States from China; and, reciprocally, the second art exhibit sent to China from the United States.

As an exchange professor to Shanxi Teacher's University, I was a participant observer in both art exhibit exchanges. Taking a systems perspective, I view the cultural exchange described here as interacting structures, and therefore, symbiotic. Accordingly, I first describe the intercultural communication behaviors of participants in the Peking Opera exhibit, followed by a description of the intercultural communication between participants of the U.S. art exhibit when it finally reached China. In each discussion, I use concepts of self, hierarchy, thinking style and face to structure the description. Finally, I analyze the interaction between the two interacting, interdependent systems. The analysis, on the Chinese side, assumes a dominant Confucian and traditional Chinese authoritarian model (the antithesis of American-style individualism) coupled with communist ideology; on the American side, the analysis presumes individualism and capitalism as the worldview.[13]

# THE PEKING OPERA EXHIBIT (1987)

## The Importance of Relationships in Chinese Society

The definitive Chinese perspective on the Peking Opera exhibit sent from Linfen, Shanxi Province, in 1987 can be found in Yu Shihao's "Managing Intercultural Rhetorical Communication."[14] In this master's thesis, Yu illustrates some of the problems of the Chinese delegation accompanying the Peking Opera exhibit from Linfen to Bridgewater, Massachusetts. Yu deals with those problems which illuminate clashing value systems, e.g. (perceived) selfishness and individualism, contrasted with the Confucian value system. Though changing somewhat, this system, in which the collective is more important than the individual, has not yet undergone radical transformation (despite the articulated "to get rich is glorious" motto of the 1990s). On the whole, the culture still sees the individual primarily in relation to the collective. Recall that the five relationships described as basic to a stable society are: (1) father-son (the relation of love); (2) emperor-subject (the relation of righteousness); (3) husband-wife (the relation of chaste conduct); (4) elder-younger (the relation of order); and (5) friend-friend (the relation of faithfulness).[15]

Given the demise of the Qing Dynasty with the last Emperor Puyi in 1911, we know that the literal emperor-subject relationship is not "on" in China, though it is implicit in the rule of the CCP (Chinese Communist Party). The Chinese citizenry remain steadfast in respecting authoritarian leadership, even in these changing times of globalization and the move from a state socialist economy to a market socialist economy "with Chinese characteristics." The concept of obligation remains in Chinese party ideology and the relationship of the Chinese citizen to the ideological leader. This was perhaps most clearly seen in the relationship of the people to Chairman Mao Zedong (d. 1976) and to a lesser extent, his successor Deng Xiaoping (d. 1997). Thus, the emperor-subject relationship clearly articulates the relationship between the state leader and the individual.

In CCP ideology, the above Confucian concepts define the relationship of the work unit (collective) to the individual. One example of the strength of this value became immediately apparent early in the Chinese delegation's visit to the United States (most of the university's delegation members were middle-aged men and some were Communist Party members). The delegates needed a Chinese videotape of Peking Opera converted to American video line standards. Given the magnificent and authentic Peking Opera costumes on display, the videotape would enhance the audiences' understanding of the art form in music, dance and rhetorical expression. Requesting this video conversion service of the American university's hierarchy, they were told that a university employee would gladly undertake the mission — if they would give him three Chinese neckties in return. The Chinese delegates were aghast at such an undisguised display of individual interests. They, of course, did not voice this to their American hosts; but privately, the delegates expressed their opinion to their interpreter, Yu Shihao, who says,

> Personal interests are important; however they should be subordinated to collective interests ... then the delegates regarded [his] request of Chinese ties as a self-centered demonstration, which they dislike. In other words, the Chinese believed that [his] behavior revealed his selfishness, which the Chinese considered to be contemptible.[16]

Yu's analysis can be somewhat puzzling to the Westerner familiar with the predilection of the Chinese to use gifts to initiate desired help or activities on the part of others, through the cultivation of relationships. The situation may be clarified by remembering that the Chinese have complicated rituals for processing requests and, perhaps most important, one never makes a request directly. In part, it was the directness of the employee's request that made it so unpalatable to the Chinese delegation. Further, Yu points out, even the "new Chinese self" (an evolving product of Deng Xiaoping's "open door" policy) realizes that

> personal interests should be given a great consideration when there is no conflict between the collective (or public) interests and personal interests. They believe that they should place collective (public) interests above personal interests because they think that collective (public) interests represent the fundamental interests of people in a broad sense.[17]

To illustrate, the Chinese have a saying, "*shui zhang chuan gao*," which means "when the river rises, the boat goes up," or, "particular things improve with the improvement of the general situation."[18]

Thus, despite the magnitude of changes that were occurring in China in the 1990s, significant changes in underlying assumptions were not occuring so quickly. In "The Cultural Context of Negotiations," Shenkar and Ronen discuss "the [Confucian] tenets of harmony, hierarchy, developing one's moral potential, and kinship affiliation having relevance for interpersonal behavior." They extend the analysis to include "recommendations for preparing, conducting, and concluding negotiations with one's counterparts."[19] Recommendations for preparing and conducting negotiations include a deep understanding of the concepts of face, harmony and hierarchy. This analysis points to the necessity of understanding these factors as grounding the Chinese worldview in all endeavors.

## Concepts of Face and Hierarchy: Expectations

During the Peking Opera exhibit in America, there were (sadly) many cultural clashes regarding "face." One such episode occurred when the Chinese delegation decided to forego an evening at the circus in Boston to attend a reception for Bridgewater State College alumni, held at the site of the Peking Opera exhibit in the Art Building at Bridgewater State College. As the Chinese delegation read the situation, the alumni had come to see the Peking Opera exhibit — and also to greet the delegation. As the alumni perceived the situation, they were attending a reunion and only incidentally viewing a somewhat esoteric exhibit. These clashes in expectations caused the Chinese to "quit the exhibition" that evening, feeling offended and having lost face as the alumni ignored both the exhibit and the delegation in favor of heartily greeting one another.

Further, the Chinese delegation was comprised of three high-level STU people: a full professor (who was on the board of directors of the Chinese National Association for Traditional Chinese Opera Research); a Shanxi Teacher's University (STU) administrator (both a vice-president and a high-ranking CCP member); and an STU associate professor.[20] In the Chinese educational work unit, these delegates were highly placed in the hierarchy. Their status was comparable to those American persons with whom they developed the exhibit and outranking many of the American academics and alumni present. Yet, I observed that they were not even introduced. As Yu puts it, "The Chinese delegates, who were placed in the American milieu and unaware of the American cultural norm, considered that the alumni treated them with contempt."[21] This and other similar episodes led to great stress on the part of the Chinese, who were still in some culture shock in part resulting from a series of similar episodes since their arrival in the United States. In part, the culture shock ensued simply from being in the United States and not at home — where they would have been accepted as the experts and in control of events.

Following the end of the exhibition, I discussed the visit of the Chinese Opera delegation with an American colleague who had been involved; he reacted with surprise when I explained some of the stress and anger expressed (privately and to me only) by the Chinese delegation. Thus, we see some of the communication problems in this situation. First, the Chinese were enculturated not to show or express distress in public, as this would incur loss of face. Second, the Americans involved were enculturated to express distress, for if one does not, one has lost the right to protest.

Put another way, in American culture, if one does not stand up for one's rights in an assertive or aggressive manner, then one deserves to lose face. Under the circumstances, each group went its own way feeling uneasy and unable even to discuss what had occurred, never mind manage the situation, as they do not approach management of such issues from the same perspective. One begins to see that negotiations can go astray from assumptions held unaware by each party, thus not examined. Placed within a context of culture shock (as when Americans are negotiating in China, or Chinese are negotiating in the United States) I think it a given that Westerners and Easterners do not always share the same thinking styles or worldview, therefore visits require preparation beforehand to minimize culture shock, distress, conflict and loss of face —for all concerned.

## Culture Shock

I have now studied, conducted research and taught in China five times (for extended periods of time) in the past 17 years. During these visits, I have experienced varying degrees of culture shock. What is culture shock? According to Dodd, it is part of the early adaptation experience and "refers to the transition period and the accompanying feelings of stress and anxiety a person experiences during the early period upon entering a new culture. Several terms apply to this concept including culture stress, adaptation, transition shock, adjustment, socialization and so on."[22] For me, the first time was the worst. I think I finally settled down and felt like myself again after five months. I went through all of Dodd's stages of adaptation: Predeparture stage — Simultaneously wary and excited; Stage 1— Everything is beautiful; Stage 2 — Everything is awful; Stage 3 — Everything is OK.[23]

As Dodd notes, following this is the long-term adaptation phase in which one adopts suitable behavior and lifestyle and makes further decisions about reliance on the host culture and decisions about involvement in the culture.[24] Dodd further articulates why a person who is staying awhile might become involved in the culture and thus adapt more fully. The analysis includes: acculturation motivation; linguistic competence; education; dual membership; occupational status; uncertainty reduction; mass media usage; and communication skills.[25]

I can attest to the authenticity of Dodd's framework. When one moves into a radically different culture (as did the visiting Chinese delegation, the Chinese graduate students in America, the BSC students in China and me), it's a given that there will be culture shock. From talking with American colleagues, I realized that they sometimes had no clue that the Chinese would suffer from culture shock in America, because we are such an "advanced culture." When I attempted to explain that, actually, given the students' circumstances in the United States (no phone, no bike, no familiar foods, no family, no real home, unfamiliar smells, lack of familiar clothing, bedding and cooking utensils, etc., etc.), they were in fact much more comfortable and happy at home. Here, in the United States, everything had to be learned all over again — in English, not Mandarin. In spite of it all, it was my impression that our Chinese exchange students who came to the United States tended to adapt better than did our American exchange students in China.

In the 1980s, life was difficult for our Chinese graduate students; they lived below "our" poverty line. That there is a line in the United States is obvious, while at the time, in China, life tended to be more egalitarian. To realize that China might be more egalitarian, more caring of daily needs than their counterparts in the Western world, no matter how much one disliked the CCP or Chairman Mao — was off-putting for those who had suffered during the Cultural Revolution. My Chinese colleagues, for the most part, had never reflected in quite the same way upon the Cultural Revolution or other episodes and concepts in Chinese life before experiencing life in the United States among the poor.

For our visiting Chinese delegation, in America for just three weeks, the cultural differences may have been overwhelming, and thus exacerbated their anger at being treated "contemptuously" by the local people. When one is in the throes of culture shock, everything goes wrong.

For example, the American students in Linfen in 1985 (and again in 1988) were always ill, as I was during the first semester in 1985. The stress of the new culture makes one vulnerable to illness, depression and anger. One initially thinks that everything in America is wonderful; everything in China is deplorable. But one gets over it … or not. Upon returning home, after some time (six or more months), there is yet another surprise — reverse culture shock or reentry.

## Reverse Culture Shock

Reverse culture shock is similar to entry culture shock. Having experienced it, I believe that it may be worse than entry culture shock. Surviving the worst in the "other" culture, one comes to appreciate it and may accept the values of that culture. For me, I learned to look and listen and reflect in China. Talking was what we did in the evenings, particularly in 1985–86 when there were few televisions on campus and all the films were in Chinese with no subtitles. I also lived with very few things (though my Chinese friends thought I had quite a lot of stuff in my house). The Chinese, in contrast, lived simply — nothing was wasted. Food was carefully chosen in the free market, lovingly washed, chopped and cooked; dinner was painstakingly prepared, not taken from a package in the freezer and thrown into the oven (my style in the United States). Time slowed down, one could no longer visualize the other life, nor long for it. Civility was the norm. One kept "face" and helped others to keep "face."

Arriving home in the United States after one year in Linfen and finding few of the Chinese values practiced, I felt especially the lack of civility, the stunning excess and a relentless emphasis on time and money. My world crumbled. I would sit and cry in my office, resenting my return home, and wishing to return to China. Why? In part, because I felt that in China, with all my mistakes, I had been useful in a way I had never before experienced.[26] I finally understood — less is more. I also had the advantages Dodd describes: acculturation motivation; education and occupational status.[27] Sometimes I think that I truly "grew up" in China, I know that "being there" was invaluable to me, both personally and professionally.[28]

## Thinking Styles — Analytical and Relational

American and Chinese thinking styles are perceived to be different. Ben-Ami Scharfstein, in *The Mind of China*, says that "the Chinese are merely interested in the inter-relations between the different signs...."[29] Unlike Westerners, the Chinese do not analyze things by viewing them as parts to be "added" together, as "one plus one equals two," but that the whole is more than the sum of the parts (as in the *Yin-Yang* symbol or in contemporary Western systems theory). As Yu Shihao explains,

> the principle of *yi fen wei er* (literally, "one divides into two") is commonly used in China. The Chinese people believe that this principle can guide people in understanding that (1) everything divides into two — the opposites (e. g., good and bad); (2) there is only one leading opposite; and (3) there is the unity of opposites.[30]

This analysis is also reinforced by this fact: the Chinese people are more likely than Western people to think by using analogies or metaphors or similes in their discussions, as Ames and Hall have pointed out in their book *Anticipating China*.[31] One further thought on this. Thinking by analogy, metaphor, example or storytelling is common, though not always acknowledged in the Western world. In our post-literate world, it is not yet commonly noted that we no longer (if we ever did) think "logically" and persuade through rational argument. The twentieth century understanding of Aristotle's *Rhetoric* for some reason does not seem to include both the "artistic and inartistic proofs" of argument, which are clearly laid out in Aristotle's work.[32]

On the other hand, Plato's proofs are often devastatingly dialogic, yet thoughtful and evocative, at the same time offering balanced proofs through argument, storytelling and myth. In the West, we moved away from this model. For better or worse, we chose a different, less evocative and more "scientific" path than our counterparts in the East.[33] Interestingly, as science evolves, we, in the West, no longer seriously maintain that a thing is the sum of its parts, as we sometimes did until the latter quarter of the 20th century. In addition, alas, as in chaos theory, nothing is "predictable," and as a result, we agree, knowingly or unknowingly, that "the path that is marked is not the way" (from the *Tao*).

## Hanging Scrolls: Spatial Awareness and "The Whole"

During the Peking Opera Exhibit (while videotaping with Dr. Matelski),[34] I had ample time to notice variations in thinking styles within my own cultural milieu. One example of differences in thinking styles, or perceptions of "how things should be," as well as the importance of relations, occurred when I was hanging scrolls in my apartment with Yu Shihao. I had no real plan except to hang them amongst other prints. Yu firmly put an end to this by removing my Western prints from the wall and hanging the scrolls in pairs, from exactly the same height around the room and not permitting me to hang one scroll (leftover) by itself. Further, he was distressed with the shape of the room and the available wall space that was cut in places by windows and doors; this design prohibited hanging scrolls in the prescribed fashion. I became very aware that there must be a procedure or rationale for hanging Chinese scrolls, a rationale which involved the relationship of one scroll to another; and those to the whole; and the whole to the shape of the room. Further, the placement of windows and doors (to the west, east, south and north) was interrelated to the whole. These are not "parts" but relationships within the whole, which is more than the sum of its parts.

At the Peking Opera exhibit at BSC, I further realized the importance of scroll hanging according to a particular way of seeing. A conflict erupted between the Chinese delegation and the American art professors assigned to help hang the exhibit. Following "the logic of correlative duality,"[35] the Chinese delegates proposed hanging the scrolls from left to right, in part because in China, "a large horizontal heading, under which the relative exhibits are also arranged along a horizontal line, is always put up to emphasize a unity between the events depicted by the exhibits or the objects on display."[36] Since Chinese characters in the heading of the scrolls go from left to right, this makes good sense and has become the accepted practice. Further, all scrolls are hung from exactly the same point, they relate to one another, following the Chinese belief in unity of content and form, as they do not see them as isolated or separate from one another, unlike the typical Western perspective.[37]

Not wanting to prolong the discussion and not accustomed to public confrontation and conflict, the Chinese delegates reluctantly agreed to allow the Western professors to hang the scrolls according to Western tastes and rationales—of which the Chinese had not a clue. The scrolls lost their meaning by being hung in the Western tradition. Again, the size and shape of the room precluded hanging the exhibit in the Chinese fashion. Reflecting upon the exhibits I had seen in China, I realized that the space in Chinese halls and homes tends not to be cut up as it sometimes is in Western fashion. Traditional Chinese architecture rarely has windows on all sides of the structure and often has only one door (sometimes there is a second door directly opposite the front door), as in traditional Chinese temple or palace architecture. Thus, Chinese architecture contributes to the whole, grounding aesthetic style, enhancing and extending the relational concept central to Chinese thinking patterns. The art of placement, or *feng shui*, is a highly developed Chinese art (or science).[38]

*Feng shui* evolved "from the simple observation that people are affected, for good or ill, by surroundings: the layout and orientation of workplaces and homes ... the aim of *feng shui*, then, is to change and harmonize the environment—cosmic currents knows as *ch'i*—to improved fortunes."[39] The concept of *feng shui* permeates Chinese culture in its material and psychic dimensions, playing into the mores and norms of the culture and aiding in the development of rituals for maintaining social order, civility and aesthetics.

Within the above framework, people must also be placed according to unspoken but well-known rules that contribute to maintaining social order and civility. For instance, Chinese meeting halls or rooms are often rectangles designed so that the leader sits at the head of the room, facing the door. Honored guests sit to the right and left of the leader. Other participants line the sides of the room, in descending order of importance. No one may stand, sip tea or leave without the signal or encouragement of the leader. Banquet rules are similar, with the exception that banquet tables tend to be round, and the same logistics apply. In China, one will always be told when and where to sit — and seating is a mark of rank, as well as an acknowledgement. In the more informal American dining rooms and meeting rooms, one might feel threatened by the lack of acknowledgement, enhancing one's culture shock.

# THE AMERICAN ART EXHIBIT IN CHINA (1988)

In *Dynamics of Intercultural Communication*, Carley Dodd makes the point that if one is to adapt in a culture, one must try to understand the elements of that culture, including the material culture (which consists of, among other things, travel, technology and communication).[40] By 1988 — and unlike the 1987 Chinese delegation in America described above — I had the advantage of experience of travel, technology and communication in the PRC and understood and tried to accommodate the differences between the two countries in those aspects of culture. However, I found it difficult to convey to the American side the intricacy of the steps necessary to mount a successful American art exhibit in Shanxi Province. One clear aspect of American thinking is that we often do think in parts; we also focus on the short-term and neglect to reflect upon consequences or the whole. The American side failed to focus on the pragmatic issues of transportation and communication. Ironically, these aspects of cultural exchange were anticipated by the Chinese delegation, which took responsibility for what would happen to *their* exhibit when it reached America. In turn, they made no provision for the American exhibit once it arrived in Shanghai. Or, if they did, the message was lost in translation. Neglecting to provide for what appeared at first to be a small problem was to have consequences for both sides relating to face and hierarchy, as well as illustrating differences in thinking styles. Whatever was negotiated was lost in the mist of time.

To provide a completed set of paperwork (with seals and appropriate signatures), one needed to travel (by train) to Taiyuan, the provincial capital. After these preliminary steps, it was essential to go to Shanghai by train to scout out the exhibit, paying the necessary fees, finding transport from Shanghai to Linfen, and accompanying and paying for the exhibit to its final destination. Neglecting these dimensions during any cross-cultural contract negotiations were to have consequences, some of which cannot be explained. Others were simply hilarious.

Prior to my departure for China I inquired about my participation in the preparations for the art exhibit, which was to be shipped to Shanxi and was to arrive shortly after I arrived in Beijing in September 1988. I was advised that I was to help "in any way possible." Fortunately, lacking prior experience in this area, I could only speculate as to what this might mean. Chinese educational work units work their foreign professors hard. My teaching load in 1985 often exceeded fifteen hours a week, and after 6 weeks, I was frequently assigned to a new set of courses—I assumed this would still be the case. In addition, after the first trial run of the exchange program in 1985, the BSC administration was convinced that the exchange professor should also advise the American exchange students. Therefore, besides teaching and advising Chinese students, I was to advise and counsel the four American exchange students, particularly in the initial stages of adaptation. These assignments were communicated to the Chinese administration, who, in turn, promptly added to my list of responsibilities, asking that I write promotional copy (to be translated into Mandarin) to advertise through the mail and the media the Western art exhibit—the first of its kind in Shanxi Province, ever. The task of creating promotional literature was soon overshadowed by the practical nightmare of bringing the exhibit to Linfen.

## Communication and Transportation Infrastructure

Confusion, bewilderment, and blunders loomed from the beginning. The American side shipped the art exhibit as far as Shanghai, expecting the Chinese side to arrange for shipping from Shanghai. In Linfen, we were duly notified that the shipment had reached Shanghai, where the Foreign Affairs Office notified me of its arrival and asked me how best to bring it from Shanghai. They also wanted to know why the Americans had not made financial provision for shipment from Shanghai. While the Chinese delegates to America had not physically accompanied the Peking Opera shipment all the way, they had arranged to send it to its ultimate destination. Apparently those in charge of the shipment from America decided, without consulting a map of China, that Linfen was "down the road a piece" from Shanghai. In fact, it was a twenty-four hour journey from Shanghai to Linfen by train. The transport of an important art exhibit from America would also cost a great deal and the Americans had not sent money, nor an escort, nor, as we would discover later, had they provided for the return shipment of the art exhibit to the United States.

Clearly, we (my Chinese friends and I) had significant problems to solve: (1) we had no clue as to where in Shanghai the shipment was; (2) we had no money to release the shipment from customs (or to pay bribes if necessary); (3) once the shipment was released, we had no person to accompany the shipment; and (4) we had no money to ship the exhibit from Shanghai to Linfen.[41] We discussed the options for several weeks, unable to decide what to do to actually ship the art to Linfen. It's important to remember, this occurred in the days before e-mail or quick access to overseas telephone lines, not to mention the itinerant international telegraph person whom I never was able to meet. To make matters worse, Shanxi Teacher's University was experiencing (at that time) a great financial crisis— so severe that, while there was a shortage of petrol, even if there had been plenty, we could not afford to buy it at black market prices.[42] There was certainly no money for transporting the art exhibit and yet, if both sides were to save face, we would have to find a way.

On the one hand, the Chinese could not plead poverty to the American side (or lose face), nor could they express indignation (no direct confrontation) that my institution had not thought to complete the entire undertaking (as the Chinese had with the Peking Opera exhibit). To add to our difficulties, we then received a letter from the United States telling us the date of arrival of my colleague in the art department, Dr. Roger Dunn, which was only two weeks away.

Immediately, Dean Cheng (head of the Foreign Affairs Office and a former graduate student at Bridgewater State College and therefore knowledgeable about us foreigners) dispatched Comrade Zhong to Shanghai to locate the shipment, discuss the arrangements with customs and find out the cost of transporting the art exhibit from Shanghai to Linfen. We clearly had no time to waste. Meanwhile, I continued to revise advertising copy and advise people on details of what our expected visitor (my colleague) might want to see in the way of art and temples in our province.

I was then prevailed upon by my good friend, the Dean of the Office of Foreign Affairs, to call the United States and explain, as diplomatically as possible, i.e., create a cover story, that the shipment was late in arriving in Linfen and therefore my colleague should postpone his trip for a month while we investigated the problem. I would then advise him when the shipment arrived and we would arrange to have him met in Beijing (eighteen hours by train north of Linfen), have a bit of travel, and arrive to open the exhibit in leisurely fashion. My colleague agreed and we relaxed. As it happened, we relaxed for quite some time, for Comrade Zhong remained in Shanghai for one month. Leaving Shanghai, he left the art exhibit there. He also neglected to secure the name, address and phone number of the firm employed to put the exhibit on the train. Our telegram inquiring the status of the shipment was returned to our work unit unanswered and undeliverable.

Understandably, Comrade Ma (one of the most powerful CCP leaders in our work unit) gave vent to his rage at this situation (Chinese do, from time to time). The Foreign Affairs Office (FAO) staff ran around in a panic, querying the foreign experts on what to do next. As a foreigner myself, I felt unequal to the task of explaining Chinese procedures in these matters to the Chinese and suggested that someone — preferably not Comrade Zhong — be dispatched to Shanghai to stay with the shipment while it was loaded onto the train and perhaps travel with the exhibit to Linfen on the same train.

Now I was worrying about face for all of us. I did not want to tell the American side what was happening, yet I also felt that we shared responsibility since it appeared that they, unlike the Chinese, had not taken responsibility for shipping the exhibit to its destination. Since only two or three persons from the American side had ever been to China, they could not really anticipate the difficulties inherent in this situation.

In many ways, American culture and citizens, despite our wealth and power, suffered from the effects of isolation during the Cold War, just as the Chinese had. Much of the time during the Cold War, Americans could not easily go to either Russia, China or Cuba. Since we learn to appreciate others by interacting with them, Americans had not had the benefit of casting a wide net, experiencing life in other cultures, and altering our perceptions of what constitutes the "world."

Learning to examine our closely held assumptions can only come with practice. Couple this with the exploration of the world of the "other," and it becomes possible to see options and explore consequences. If all we know is our own world, options are limited, consequences are perceived to be within established parameters and imagination — and potential relationships—fail. Those who sent the art exhibit might as well have sent it into space. Or, perhaps the administration had looked into the matter, decided it was too complicated to deal with from the States and left it at that. Whatever, we were all caught in the middle of a potentially difficult situation, especially those of us who wanted this educational and cultural exchange program to succeed.[43]

Finally, Comrade Zhong (!) was once again dispatched to Shanghai, where, with the aid of endless packs of American cigarettes and countless phone calls, he finally succeeded in getting the exhibit to the train. There were, however, further complications. As it turned out, one of the major factors in this drama was the request of customs officials in Shanghai for

100,000 yuan (at the time $20,000 U.S.D). This money would provide surety against the artwork being sold in China; it was pay up or they would not release the shipment. As the Foreign Affairs Office (FAO) in Shanxi had no "back door" (big or little) in Shanghai, they could not bypass this requirement, nor (apparently) come up with a large enough bribe to get the shipment released. Instead, Shanxi Teacher's University turned to the customs officials in Taiyuan, capital of Shanxi Province, where they did have *hou men* — back door relationships or *guanxi*.[44]

The FAO persuaded the customs officials to come to Linfen when the shipment arrived, to actually open the exhibit and view the contents, thus bypassing having to pay the 100,000 yuan to the customs officials in Shanghai. Face had been saved on all sides.

We could now contact my colleague in Bridgewater. Dr. Dunn had been waiting patiently to hear when he should arrive to open the exhibition. Acting on the information regarding when the shipment would arrive in Shanghai (not Linfen), he had booked to arrive in China in October. Since we were still awaiting word from Comrade Zhong, this would not work. Therefore, periodically, I had been in contact with him to postpone his flight. Looking to further disasters, I also asked him to plan to stay longer in China, just in case. Who knew when the shipment would actually arrive in Linfen? If Dunn were to come before the exhibit arrived, the Chinese would lose face and all would be (an even greater) disaster. Roger Dunn was agreeable, again postponed his flight and arranged to stay for three weeks. Alas, the shipment still did not arrive.

During these weeks which were turning into months, my colleagues in the Foreign Affairs Office could think of nothing but the exhibit, living in my living room, seeking advice, and in general, creating widespread panic. Responding to my instructions from my college to help "in whatever way," I continued to revise promotional copy and tried to make countless phone calls to the United States smoothing the waters (each call consumed hours, if not days).

During this period, we foreigners were told that all resources (money, petrol, banquets, etc.) would have to be saved for Dr. Dunn's visit; therefore, we could not take weekend trips, we could not even leave the work unit. Looking back, it was fortunate that they thought ahead to this. Dr. Dunn arrived in Beijing around the first of November. With the art exhibit shipment still not in Linfen, the Chinese FAO could hardly keep him in dreary Linfen for weeks and so spent a large portion of their budget for that year setting up an extensive travel program for him. All in all, he eventually spent about five days in Linfen before returning to America.

Roger Dunn and the members of the FAO were not in Linfen when the shipment finally arrived, along with the customs officials from Taiyuan — they were travelling through China. Instead, I was called to come to the library and watch while the shipment was unloaded, checking each piece against the packing list, checking for any damage. At length, the entire exhibit was unloaded. Now we would wait for Dr. Dunn. The FAO team travelling with Dunn was located and urged to come back to Linfen immediately to set up the exhibit. They came, the exhibit opened with appropriate fanfare and Dr. Dunn left. Later, I helped pack up the exhibit, which was then stored in the Foreign Affairs Office. Worn out and having no money to ship the exhibit back to the States, our Chinese friends simply ignored the requests from the States regarding the return of the shipment. It was a year before it was returned. Meanwhile, we used the shipping cartons to sit on during our impromptu gossip sessions in the FAO office — many lessons learned.

## CONCLUSION

In the above descriptions and analyses one becomes aware that intellectual awareness of differing concepts of self, hierarchy, thinking style, face and culture shock barely scratches the surface of intercultural quagmires. First, the participants must examine the ground of their assumptions. In short, one must do phenomenology (or an archaeology) of the many dimensions and layers of both the self, one's culture and the cultural milieu one is entering.

From the example above, one sees that in America, the Chinese delegates had no significant problems with the technology of communications and transportation, yet had an incredibly difficult time with seemingly simple issues such as hanging the scrolls. More often than not, if one accepts Yu Shihao's analysis, what caused the most distress was the lack of understanding (on both sides) of the cultural context of decision-making.

More effort on the part of each side was needed to even allow discussion (an exchange of ideas); instead, the Chinese felt hurt, and given their (culturally induced) inability to confront directly, the episode did not enhance their experience of the exhibition or of their time in America. Clearly, according to the Chinese view of the world, harmony was lacking in the exhibit as hung; just as the seeming disdain of the alumni at the reception was offensive to the Chinese, further disturbing the harmony of the exhibition — and their hierarchical positions within that world.

In the second description, I show that concepts of face, hierarchy and thinking style affected the way the Chinese and I handled the American art exhibit. In fact, we were all trying to maintain face. This instance is particularly interesting in that the issues were not black and white as in "us" and "them." This may reflect positive movement in the development of the cultural exchange negotiations, as my Chinese colleagues and I were united in preserving face for at least four different and potentially hostile entities: STU, my college, the educational-cultural exchange program, as well as the customs officials. Instead, we were united in our efforts, realizing that if one group lost face, we all lost face.

By 1988, my Chinese colleagues and I had interacted enough that we better understood one another. Dean Cheng of the FAO had been a friend in Bridgewater during his master's program in the English Department in 1986-1987. Further, many of the individuals involved in the cultural exchange had studied in and about the culture of the other. We shared common experiences, both in the United States and China; we had developed a knowledge of the iconography of everyday life in each culture and thus, in the end, we were able to meet the crisis.

The pragmatic study of cross-cultural negotiation requires more historical critical emphasis, more descriptive fieldwork and open-ended interviewing and a holistic, contextual approach to cross-cultural negotiations. One significant example of the very real need for this approach can be understood by looking at the word "harmony." The significance of the word, from the Chinese point of view, is pointed up by the scroll-hanging episodes. In developing this idea I was struck by the architecture I have seen in China, the relationship of the exhibition to the front door, of the scrolls to one another and to the calligraphy which unites the exhibit; as well as the absence in many houses and other buildings of a "back door" and the significance of the Chinese expression "I have no back door," when referring to lack of relationships. It is not "stuff, nonsense." As Carl Jung has pointed out, "sets" like this may seem (to the Western mind) "stuff, nonsense." The Chinese mind (or the relational mind) faced with an old shoe, a hat and a dead fish on the sand at the shore, asks, "What can it mean?" Those of us interested in nurturing cross-cultural relationships must seek that which lies beneath the surface and accept that the process is both long and rewarding. One never arrives.

# Case Study: General Electric and *Sesame Street*— A True Joint Venture

Since its 1969 premiere,[1] *Sesame Street* (produced by the Children's Television Workshop, or CTW) has grown to be one of the most highly acclaimed children's TV programs in the world. Long recognized as an educational icon in the U.S., the series is currently exported in its American form to more than 143 countries. In addition, indigenous, culturally specific co-productions have been developed in at least 20 other countries, including China.[2]

In February 1998, after three years of careful deliberation, determination and diplomacy, Shanghai TV became CTW's latest partner in one of *Sesame Street* most ambitious joint ventures, *Zhima Jie*. But building an intercultural bridge to *Zhima Jie* was, at times, quite difficult; and it might have never happened but for some much-needed assistance from a surprising resource — the General Electric Company — as well as careful negotiations between the Children's Television Workshop, Shanghai TV (STV) and the Chinese government.

## GENERAL ELECTRIC AT HOME

While underwriting a children's television series in China was clearly a new venture for General Electric, it was typical of the corporation's innovative approach to business. Begun as the Edison Electric Light Company in 1878 (to fund research on incandescent bulbs), its founder, Thomas Alva Edison, quickly realized the enormous potential of his creation. Within four years, he merged with Thomson-Houston Electric to form the new General Electric Company. By 1896, it was included in the Dow Jones Industrial Index,[3] and for many years afterward, maintained its reputation for quality, performance and durability in everything from turbojet engines to toasters.

In the 1970s, however, the influx of foreign-made goods began to erode GE's stronghold in many of its U.S. manufacturing markets. By the end of the decade, it faced its worst recession since the Depression era.[4] In 1981, a new chairman and chief executive officer came on board, John F. (Jack) Welch. Equipped with visionary talent as well as a charismatic presence, Welch redefined corporate culture, and recaptured General Electric as an American icon.

One of Welch's first challenges was to downsize the company, divesting it of some "traditional businesses" like mining equipment and small appliances. In fact, from 1981 to 1986, 73 plants were closed; ultimately 232 different product and service lines were sold. Next, Welch reorganized GE's existing corporate structure (a process he labeled "delayering"), and looked ahead to new markets and technologies, including financial services and fiber-optic products as well as company acquisitions.[5] He also created a new paradigm for his company — an amalgamation of technology, service and manufacturing. Finally, and perhaps most importantly, Welch gave his employees a personal stake in GE, by letting them brainstorm with managers in regular sessions called "work outs," which, in turn, made them more accountable for its successes or failures. *Los Angeles Times* reporter Linda Grant describes this strategy in 1993 through the eyes of Bob Gedeon, a mechanic at GE's Lighting Division in Cleveland:

> "Welch is our Jimmy Johnson," says Gedeon proudly, comparing the coach of the champion Dallas Cowboys with the executive many businessmen regard as the nation's most successful CEO.
>
> A compact 5 feet, 8 inches tall, athletic, the fiery Welch could in fact be the motivational Dallas coach as he jawbones, inspires, pressures and intimidates his minions into giving GE every last ounce of effort. Repeating a wrenching message over and over, Welch has convinced ... Gedeon

and other GE workers to accept searing truths: In today's business climate, only satisfied customers can guarantee their jobs, and only the best
will survive. He has persuaded them to seize the initiative, to be innovative, to turn out top quality at rock-bottom cost. While other CEOs bite
the dust daily, Welch's company prospers and most of his employees
believe in him, despite his heavy hand.[6]

According to Grant, Gedeon and his co-workers were somewhat confused when Welch began his "campaign" to cut red tape and allow people in the factories to make daily decisions on how things should be run.
But it didn't take long to convince the GE employees in Cleveland (as well
as throughout the U.S.) that Welch was both serious and right:

> "I'm in control of my job," he [Gedeon] says. "We're given parameters,
> goals and objectives, and we figure out how to achieve them. This leeway
> allows me to think. I take ownership. I'm always questioning."
>     The about-face was apparent when union workers in Lynn joined with
> local managers to reorganize a plant scheduled to be closed. Today
> [1993], they run the plant with self-directed work teams that have estab-
> lished a lofty goal: six-sigma quality, a mathematical measure of faulty
> parts per million pieces manufactured. Six sigma is perfection, or 3.4
> defects per million, a number that theoretically cannot be bettered. The
> Lynn plant is now at 3.5 sigma and still climbing.[7]

With this "new look" firmly in place, General Electric quickly
regained its reputation, and within ten years was once again listed among
America's most successful corporations, receiving kudos from *Forbes* as
"the world's most powerful corporation based on revenue, profit, market
value and assets" in 1990.[8] It has remained on the industry's "A list" ever
since, even dubbed "the most admired company in the U.S." by a *Fortune*
magazine survey for three years in a row (1997-2000).[9]

Today, GE operates in over one hundred countries, employing more
than 340,000 people around the globe. It is a highly diversified company,
comprised of ten divisions:[10]

(1) Aircraft Engines (both large and small engines for commercial
and military use; various aviation services as well);

(2) Appliances (all major appliances such as refrigerators, freezers,
ranges, conventional and microwave ovens, washers and dryers, dish-
washers, garbage disposals, waste compactors, air conditioners and water
purification systems);

(3) Capital Services (a wholly-owned diversified financial services
company, including long-term care among other things);

(4) Industrial Systems (equipment to operate and manage electrical power);

(5) Lighting (the complete spectrum of lighting products and equipment for both consumers and industry);

(6) Medical Systems (all areas of diagnostic imaging technology, including CT scanners, x-ray machines, MRI systems, ultrasound devices, mammography and ultrasound equipment);

(7) NBC (a multifaceted global media producer and distributor);

(8) Plastics (components for computers, office equipment, data storage, automobiles and construction, among other things);

(9) Power Systems (equipment, service and design assistance in most areas of energy consumption, including gas, steam, hydroelectricity and nuclear fuels); and

(10) Transportation Systems (diesel engines, freight locomotives, railway signaling systems and electrical propulsion equipment).

## THE CHARISMA OF JOHN (JACK) WELCH

While few companies have been "personality-driven" after the late 1960s, Welch was clearly the "man" behind the logo at GE. One need only skim the voluminous articles written about him to appreciate his drive, ambition and persona. For example, *Christian Monitor* Staff Writer Mark Clayton drew this portrait in 1987:

> The intense Mr. Welch is frequently described as a "dynamo," sometimes throwing off business ideas faster than he can write them down or describe them to others. But Welch is more than just a good idea man; he's a hands-on manager with a vision.[11]

Michael Maccoby once labeled Jack Welch a "narcissist" in his 2000 analysis of current business leaders in the *Harvard Business Review*. But Maccoby was quick to qualify his category, describing the differences between a simple narcissist and a productive one:

> Productive narcissists—people who often have a dash of the obsessive personality—are good at converting people to their point of view. One of the most successful at this is GE's Jack Welch. Welch uses toughness to build a corporate culture and to implement a daring business strategy, including the buying and selling of scores of companies. Unlike other narcissistic leaders such as Gates, Grove, and Ellison, who have transformed industries with new products, Welch was able to transform his industry by focusing on execution and pushing companies to the limits

of quality and efficiency, bumping up revenues and wringing out costs. In order to do so, Welch hammers out a huge corporate culture in his own image — a culture that provides impressive rewards for senior managers and shareholders.

Welch's approach to culture building is widely misunderstood. Many observers, notably Noel Tichy in *The Leadership Engine*, argue that Welch forms his company's leadership culture through teaching. But Welch's "teaching" involves a personal ideology that he indoctrinates into GE managers through speeches, memos, and confrontations. Rather than create a dialogue, Welch makes pronouncements (either be the number one or two company in your market or get out), and he institutes programs (such as Six Sigma quality) that become the GE party line. Welch's strategy has been extremely effective. GE managers must either internalize his vision, or they must leave. Clearly, this is incentive learning with a vengeance. I would even go so far as to call Welch's teaching brainwashing. But Welch does have the rare insight and know-how to achieve what all narcissistic business leaders are trying to do — namely, get the organization to identify with them, to think the way they do, and to become the living embodiment of their companies.[12]

When asked which negotiator he admired most, conflict-resolution expert Michael Gibbs answered emphatically:

If I had to tell you who, over the past ten years, has demonstrated the best ability in getting results by working with people and negotiating, I would say Mr. Jack Welch, chairman and CEO of the GE company. I worked in GE for a few years, and saw that he was an extraordinary negotiator. He was able to pay attention to detail, and yet at the same time keep the big picture in mind; he could zoom in and zoom out. He was ruthless. He was what I call "thick-faced, black heart." That can be used for good or for bad. He always used it for good. His black heart was always resistant to pressure and always in the best interest of other people.

He has been able to turn the GE company into a company worth U.S. $80 [billion] to U.S. $90 billion. Many people believe he is one of the best — if not the best — mainly because of his ability to negotiate. He brings people together, builds a relationship, keeps his focus on the goal and then relentlessly and persistently follows through until he gets it.[13]

But perhaps the greatest compliment paid to GE's most revered — and sometimes reviled — CEO occurred when Jack Welch announced his April 2001 retirement — twenty years after accepting the job. After his statement, *Financial Times* reporter Andrew Hill voiced the opinion of many:

Jack Welch, chairman and chief executive of General Electric, makes some unbelievable claims. He says divisions of the U.S. conglomerate often give up part of their budget to help out needier GE operations. He

says the bigger the company gets, the easier it is to run. And he says there
is absolutely no internal politicking over who will succeed him.

Of the three, the third may be the most credible, for who would want
to step into the shoes of Mr. Welch, one of the most successful and most
admired businessmen of the late 20th century?[14]

## GENERAL ELECTRIC OVERSEAS

While GE's multinational feats are legendary, they have not always
succeeded in understanding the subtleties of working in another culture.
*Financial Times* writer Jean Louis Barsoux gave this account of a rather
disastrous *faux pas* in 1988:

> Consider the example of a French medical equipment maker, taken over
> by General Electric in 1988. GE decided to boost the morale of its new
> French employees by organising a training seminar for French and other
> European managers. In their hotel rooms, the company left colourful T-
> shirts emblazoned with the GE slogan "Go for One." A note urged the
> managers to wear the T-shirts "to show that you are members of the
> team." The French managers wore them, grudgingly, to the seminar, but
> as one of them recalled: "It was like Hitler was back, forcing us to wear
> uniforms. It was humiliating."[15]

But despite the occasional misunderstandings, GE is known worldwide as a company committed to addressing the long-term goals of the
countries where they do business as part of being a respected "corporate
citizen" within a boundary-less culture. One of the best examples of this
pledge occurred in Hungary in 1989, when the conglomerate began its
aggressive campaign of investing in Eastern Europe. In that year, GE Lighting purchased a 50 percent share of Tungsram, a century-old Hungarian
lighting manufacturer, renowned for its scientific accomplishments
(including the first tungsten filament light bulb). The move was a
significant one, marking General Electric's first European site for its lighting business as well as a platform for expanded marketing in other divisions, especially GE Capital.[16]

GE's rationale was quite simple. The company saw the enormous
potential of the Eastern European market — much more "mature" than
some of the emerging Asian markets, but malleable nonetheless. However, management was not quite prepared for the massive effort needed
to make the Hungarian investment work. In 1989, Tungsram was over-
staffed, with an indelible stamp of Soviet-style supervision — politically-
motivated executives with little or no expertise in the field. Further, the

condition of the facilities and equipment was appalling, in need of major upgrades and repair.[17]

GE's first move was to hire a longtime employee and native Hungarian, George Varga. Varga had fled from his home in 1956, when the Soviet tanks moved in to crush a rebellious populace. Besides being devoted to his mother country, Varga also understood the possible problems GE might encounter by interfacing its corporate culture with the Hungarian mind. And moving too quickly with Western-style management might do more harm than good, as he observed in a March 1998 interview with John McClenahen:

> A sweeping layoff would have virtually shut down Tungsram — because under communism, decision-making was concentrated among very few people, and everyone else had a specific, small task in a daisy chain arrangement. Pull out any of those and the whole chain collapses.[18]

Instead, Varga proposed a combination of American-style management with the European work ethic, creating "the right alloy — part American, part Hungarian, and part European."[19]

In the first few years, GE's investment return was minimal, to say the least. Friction between Hungarian workers and American managers was everywhere along the production-distribution line. Americans saw Hungarians as shiftless, lazy and uninterested in their work; conversely, Hungarians felt their American bosses to be egotistical, heavy-handed and overbearing. Further, the GE concept of "work outs" — ongoing communication between labor and management — was a foreign concept to those raised under the communist system. Thus, according to *New York Times* reporter Jane Perlez, the "grand expectations [of 1989] collided with the grim realities of an embedded culture of waste, inefficiency, and indifference about customers and quality."[20] Vargas was ultimately replaced by a more aggressive Welch-style CEO, Charles Pieper, who required Tungsram workers to attend management and productivity workshops; learn English (to better communicate with American personnel); and continue to support "work outs." This last requisite was perhaps the most important to Pieper, who once told *Financial Times* reporter Vanessa Houlder, "I have never seen a group of people [that] is not interested. Never, never, never. Whether you are Chinese, Hungarian, Japanese or Swedish, people love to go and make their workplace better."[21] Shiela Vinczeller, a native Hungarian human resources manager at GE-Tungsram, agreed, citing the example of pooled electricity buying as the result of an idea discussed at a "work out."[22]

But interpersonal issues were not enough to make a difference. Pieper also employed the GE "formula" for efficiency by authorizing major cut-backs in the workforce. However, many of the positions removed were those on extended leave or retired. In addition, Pieper offered generous severance packages to those near retirement as well as training and coun-seling to those being laid off—two extremely popular initiatives to the Hungarians.

As a result, Tungsram gradually was able to turn itself around, and serves today as an example of eventual success in long-term investments. Jack Welch now sees the Hungarian "experiment" as a prototype for all of his foreign ventures as well as a validation of his formula for success-ful, "boundary-less" management:

> You have to take the initiatives and you have to understand they've all become broader and deeper. Every one of them. So if you take globaliza-tion, we started out doing aftermarkets and expanding our horizons. And that was quite successful. International sales have grown two or three times the rate of domestic sales. And that was quite positive. Then we took globalization to the next step, which was globalizing compo-nents, products, sourcing in Mexico, sourcing in Eastern Europe, sourc-ing around the world. That was the next step of globalization. And you take the third step, which we're in now in the last year or so, it's globaliz-ing the intellect. Building research labs in India; dealing with Russian scientists and materials; having medical centers of excellence in China, India, and Korea. Lots of engineers.... So we've gone from markets, products, and components—we have forty-four plants in Mexico, we have thirteen plants in eastern Europe. We have better metallurgists in Czechoslovakia than we can find in some businesses here. So this intel-lectual expansion has opened up big new horizons.[23]

As part of cultivating intellect — and ultimately, the quality of life — General Electric has invested in several areas of social service. Among its ongoing programs are: (1) the GE Fund, money set aside to improve the "quality of life" either through such initiatives as educational scholar-ships, daycare facilities and health maintenance; and (2) GE Elfun, a vol-unteer organization of more than 40,000 company employees who perform community service in building and grounds renovation, mentor programs and food distribution.[24]

Finally, to better understand other cultures, Welch was one of the first CEOs to internationalize his Board of Directors, choosing highly respected people from outside America for their national perspectives as well as for their business acumen. Included in the list of appointments over the last ten years have been Claudio X. Gonzalez (Mexico) and Paolo Fresco (Italy).[25] Today, many multinational conglomerates employ more non–Americans on their advisory boards, which has generated some criticism against Welch for not making more foreign appointments. According to the GE icon, the lack of international presence is more practical than philosophical — the difficulties in synchronizing travel schedules from far-flung global locations can sometimes be overwhelming.[26] And, considering Welch's other innovations, it seems only a question of time before this challenge is met.

## GENERAL ELECTRIC IN CHINA

General Electric was one of the first American companies to do business with China, investing in its lucrative local market as early as 1910. Unfortunately, the resulting political climate from two world wars impeded the growth of further capital ventures in this area for several decades. In the mid–1990s, GE's Lighting Division began to penetrate the Asian market, broadening its previous presence in Japan, India, Korea, Taiwan, Hong Kong and Indonesia, as well as creating the GE Lighting Technical Center in Shanghai.[27] Creating and managing a new operation in China was no small task, and Jack Welch needed someone with both management expertise and an understanding of the Confucian mind. His ultimate choice for the position was James McNerney Jr., president and CEO of the GE Lighting Division in Cleveland, Ohio.

McNerney was well-grounded in the "Welch" college of field management, having successfully mastered the concepts of "delayering," "boundary-lessness," "work outs," "six sigma" and "quality initiatives." He also had an understanding of Asian culture from his earlier assignment at GEAsiaPacific, making him a perfect match for the formidable task. When interviewed by Shari Sweeney in 1997, McNerney reflected on his prior experience as well as the challenges of his new responsibilities:

> When I first went to Asia, I brought a harder, New York edge to a lot of my interactions.... I had to learn that that doesn't always get you where you want to go in many Oriental settings. I think that having been forced to adapt and build my management style, it built my portfolio of skills.[28]

These skills, according to Sweeney, were more complicated than producing dependable light bulbs:

> McNerney says his challenges in Asia are broader than simply ensuring that every line worker understands his or her contribution to quality standards. While most North Americans and Europeans take for granted the presence of outlets, switches and light bulbs, the average number of bulbs per household in some areas of China is two (in the United States,

it's more than 100). Energy is very expensive in most parts of Asia, so to win the Asian-market lighting game, McNerney says, a company must produce "the same number of lumens using a lot less energy."[29]

Assisting McNerney in his perspective was Cheng Mei-wei, a Chinese-American born in Taiwan, educated in the United States, and highly experienced in joint ventures, having worked with AT&T for twenty-two years before joining General Electric. Cheng's ethnic background as well as his familiarity with U.S. corporate culture proved invaluable to GE China's success in the PRC.[30] And successful it was. As it entered into the new millennium, General Electric claimed twenty-four wholly owned or joint ventures (totalling $1.1 billion U.S.D and employing over 7,000 nationals in 1998), making its corporate presence in China beyond question.

However, "business" has not ever been GE's only concern. The long-term value of being a responsible citizen within the community is equally important. Thus, in China (as in other countries) the company makes a point of integrating itself within the local society, analyzing its needs, and trying to improve current conditions, most especially in education — a policy, incidentally, not unknown in the United States. GE's corporate advertising manager Jim Harman points out: "Historically the company has a rich tradition of support for education and non-commercial sponsorships. GE has been a supporter of public television and public radio in the United States for more than 20 years."[31] The uniqueness of this particular "marketing mix" was working with both Chinese and American production companies — the Children's Television Workshop and Shanghai TV — to achieve the needed results.

## SESAME STREET — THE BEGINNING

*Zhima Jie* was not the Children's Television Workshop's first foray into China — only its most sophisticated. Chinese children first took a walk on Sesame Street in 1981, when the American version was dubbed in Mandarin. Since that time, politics, the economy, culture and society have changed greatly in both countries. So too have Big Bird, Bert and Ernie. During the 1950s and early 1960s, the world of educational broadcasting was often seen as colorless and uneventful, consisting largely of bespectacled professors, monochromatic photos and slides, and a sterile academic setting. Children's television wasn't much better, although kids seemed more impressed with the likes of Howdy Doody, Miss Frances (of

*Ding Dong School* fame) and Kukla, Fran and Ollie. In short, any TV program associated with "children" or "education" was akin to a root canal without Novocaine. As puppeteer Caroll Spinney once told *Chicago Tribune* reporter Ron Grossman, "In 1968 conventional wisdom said children's television was a lost cause. The teaching profession assumed preschoolers weren't ready to read."[32]

Realizing that both children and education were an important part of our nation's future, members of the U.S. Congress set about to change the image of instructional TV as well as children's programming. At the same time, a new network, the Corporation for Public Broadcasting, was being formed to address audiences who may not fit into the advertisers' portfolio of "preferred" viewers. The syncronicity of these two waves of public concern set the stage for what soon developed as the Children's Television Workshop (CTW), commissioned by the federal government and funded by both public and private agencies.[33]

CTW's first assignment was to design educational TV shows for preschoolers from disadvantaged urban households. As a self-described "applied research laboratory that creates experimental television programs which have specific educational or informational goals presented in interesting ways,"[34] the challenge to excite youngsters in their early years was enticing. As a result, CTW, under the directorship of Joan Ganz Cooney, began its mission to produce a daily, hourlong educational-entertainment show for 3- to 5-year-old ghetto kids.

The educational objectives of the project seemed quite clear, if complicated, and included the following:

(1) to recognize basic visual symbols (i.e., letters, numbers and geometric forms);
(2) to identify different parts of the body;
(3) to discriminate similarities and differences between objects, including finding matches and opposites;
(4) to rhyme similar sounds;
(5) to associate certain sounds with objects, animals, etc.;
(6) to understand size and spatial relationships;
(7) to sort or group objects, animals, people together;
(8) to problem-solve;
(9) to understand both natural and man-made environments;
(10) to interact in a social environment, understanding customs, common practices, etc.;
(11) to understand and appreciate similarities and differences between social environments; and

(12) to adopt a cooperative attitude in friendships, social relationships and work projects.[35]

The format of the show, on the other hand, seemed less obvious. After holding a series of seminars for teachers at Harvard University, producers agreed to adapt the successful strategies of commercial advertisers to the educational mission of the project, incorporating a creative mix of puppetry, animation and music. Still, the program title remained elusive. Among the original suggestions were *104th Street* and *Columbus Avenue* (both allegedly inspired by the production staff's lunch hangouts) as well as *Open Sesame! Sesame Street* became the compromise choice.[36]

Once the team settled on a name and format, the subsequent structure developed quickly, and remained largely the same for more than three decades:

> The programs are nonsequential, with short segments of a few minutes each followed in rapid-fire order by totally unrelated segments. Slow-motion action and cartoons are mixed to enhance the "reality" and the impression of speed. Stop-action, zoom closeups, repetitions, instant replay, and frequent songs further minimize the need for viewer concentration.[37]

The format remained fairly constant up until 2002, when significant changes were introduced. The audience, however, changed and expanded soon after the show began in 1969. Originally targeted for urban ghetto youths, the show rapidly gained popularity with a mainstream national audience. The series was not without its critics, but most viewers found themselves happily involved (and sometimes highly motivated) by the characters and their message. In fact, *San Diego Union-Tribune* reporter Greg Joseph gave several such examples in a 1989 article:

> A medical student at Boston University, saying that *Sesame Street* always made him feel comfortable with school and learning, credited the series with propelling him toward his intended career in pediatrics.
> A Charleston, S.C., woman told how her parents at first forbade her to watch the show because it had "colored people" on it, but because she begged to keep watching, they finally learned — like her — that the race of the teachers didn't matter.
> A woman who was the 15-year-old sister of a 5-year-old brother in a poor, dysfunctional family related that the series kindled a thirst for knowledge in both of them — and that she went on to earn a master's degree (doing a thesis on *Sesame Street* along the way) and that he became a registered nurse.[38]

Within a few short years, *Sesame Street* had not only become a staple for American audiences, it had also been widely adopted by a diverse global market. In the mid–1970s, producers from the Children's Television Workshop forged joint partnerships with Mexico, Canada, Germany and the Netherlands; a decade later, they negotiated similar arrangements with Portugal, Turkey and Norway.[39] When the international cast of indigenous Muppet characters gathered for a New Year's Special in 1993,[40] Oofnik the Grouch and Kippy the Porcupine (from Israel's *Rechov Sumsum*) shared treats with Alpha Bjarne and Max Mekke (*Sesam Stasjon*, Norway), Tita (*Rua Sesamo*, Portugal) and Tiffy (*Sesamstrasse*, Germany).[41] Today, *Sesame Street* is seen — either in its dubbed American form, or as a joint-produced local series — in over 140 countries. Included among them is one of the Children Television Workshop's most ambitious efforts to date — China's *Zhima Jie*.

# THE LONG ROAD TO CHINA

When *Zhima Jie* premiered in Shanghai in February 1998, Chinese children were already well-acquainted with Grover, Kermit the Frog, Cookie Monster and the rest of their friends on the American version of *Sesame Street* — the show was first dubbed into Mandarin in 1981.[42] Within two years, the "joint venture" was successful enough to forge another co-production effort — this time for American viewers. The title was *Big Bird in China*, a ninety-minute special created by the Children's Television Workshop and China Central Television.[43] *New York Times* columnist John J. O'Connor described this landmark show in great detail:

> The action begins in New York's Chinatown, where Big Bird, on skates and accompanied by Barkley the dog, discovers a scroll about the legend of the phoenix, China's most beautiful bird. Determined to find this creature, Big Bird and Barkley sail for China, with Big Bird inevitably asking, "Say, Barkley, doesn't this strike you as an awfully slow boat?" Meanwhile, Telly and Oscar the Grouch begin digging their way to the other side of the world.
>
> In China, Big Bird finds exotic boats floating on tranquil rivers. Children and grown-ups exercise in public squares. Big Bird and friend traipse through the street, visiting such sights as the Forbidden City, always to the obvious delight of onlookers. When it becomes evident that they have a language problem, they manage to find help in the form of an adorable 6-year-old girl named Xiao Foo. Does she speak American? She speaks English. That's close enough, decides Big Bird.
>
> The new friends set out in search of the legendary bird, a journey that will take them to the Great Wall and other landmarks. At each stop a new

clue about the location of the phoenix is offered by a monkey, which just happens to be the Monkey King, a popular character among Chinese children.[44]

*Big Bird in China* received both critical and popular raves as one of the most innovative programs in television history. The series had now broken new ground in cross-cultural programming — one of the first steps in creating a template for more indigenous Asian versions of the "most widely viewed children's series in the world."[45]

However, as in world diplomacy, the path from CTW's "vision" of a Chinese *Sesame Street* to its TV reality became much more complicated than anyone could have imagined. Politics, economic considerations, educational goals and cultural changes each played a significant role in the local series concept. Finally, in 1994, after years of discussion and negotiation, the Children's Television Workshop announced a joint venture with Shanghai Television (STV) to produce 130 half-hour episodes of *Zhima Jie.*

Shanghai Television was the obvious choice as the Chinese representative, given its recent history. According to author Junhao Hong, Shanghai was not only a major economic, technological and cultural center, it had China's second largest TV station, broadcasting to more than 100 million potential viewers.[46] It was also known as the most liberal, import-friendly television facility in the country, as Hong notes:

> In the middle of the 1980s, the climax of the reform period, China's central government even blueprinted a plan to let Shanghai be an experimental special cultural zone, implying that the city could have more freedom and autonomy in importing/exporting cultural products. Although the plan was killed in the cradle later on because of the "anti-spiritual pollution" campaign initiated by the Party hard-liners, Shanghai did take the opportunity to expand its import scale considerably. STV was eventually able to set up several overseas offices in the United States, Japan, and Hong Kong.[47]

With the organizational structure set in place, both Shanghai Television and the Children's Television Workshop were extremely excited about the heretofore unexplored possibilities. "This is an adventurous way of teaching children. China needs this," enthusiastic STV children's television producer Ye Chao told *The Ottawa Citizen*.[48] CTW Shanghai producer Kathy McClure concurred, adding that the move had culminated years of negotiations with the Chinese government which had been particularly sensitive to politically or culturally objectionable images.[49]

# BIG BIRD FINALLY MEETS DA NIAO

As discussed earlier, Chinese children were already familiar with the *Sesame Street* format through previous efforts of the Chinese Central Television (CCTV). In the early 1990s, CCTV authorized a number of satellites to be aimed toward households in rural areas to provide equal TV opportunities for everyone. This was part of the government's overall plan to better assimilate two very dissimilar populations— urban residents and peasants from the countryside. One means to this end was to teach English through American programming,[50] and *Sesame Street* was one of the shows with a proven track record in this area.

But *Zhima Jie* would not be a Mandarin replication of the popular American program previously seen on CCTV. Rather, the new series was to reflect China's unique cultural qualities. In 1996, a highly impressive 18-member team (comprised of educators, philosophers and health specialists throughout China) was asked to create such a curriculum. In the Preface to their final report, they underscored their commitment to the special nature of this project:

> China is a country with thousands of years of splendid culture, where children are born and grow. Their "development" is realized in this uniquely oriental cultural environment. In order for Chinese children to appreciate the program fully, it is essential, therefore, for the creators of *Zhima Jie* to consider how to incorporate the best of Chinese culture into the program, so that children will find it familiar, intimate, and naturally acceptable.[51]

Within this framework, the academic "task force" created a list of curriculum objectives to be met in the 130-episode series. Like the American version, children would receive instruction in five specific curriculum areas. The specific lessons would embody Chinese philosophy and lifestyle. The areas included: (1) symbolic representation (e.g., learning to create Chinese characters and knowing what they represent, using numbers); (2) cognitive organization (e.g., recognizing patterns, classifications and quantities); (3) the child and his or her world (e.g., knowing both the powers and limitations of their bodies, learning safety and coping mechanisms); (4) family and society (e.g., understanding different family structures, relationships to peers versus authorities, cultural diversity, conflict management, environmental respect); and (5) aesthetics and arts (e.g., cultural awareness, creativity, nature appreciation).[52]

The last programming area, aesthetics and arts, needed to be most specifically Chinese, the experts agreed. They also wanted to reserve the right to choose which segments to produce and which to simply dub:

> Except for "aesthetics and arts," different portions of the original curriculum of *Sesame Street* are preserved for the other four units, since those goals are suitable to Chinese children as well. With regard to the specific content of scripts, we will have to decide whether to keep the original segments or to produce the "Chinese" segments. There is a degree of commonality across the five units due to their shared elements such as children's development of their self-concepts, mutual care, understanding, respect, and their sense of responsibility and love.[53]

The curricular goals were also to be incorporated with larger reform measures set forth by the Party's Central Committee in 1988, namely:

(1) to play a positive function for society by publicizing and explaining the policies of the Party and the government, and by motivating people to work hard towards certain social and economic goals;

(2) to offer a set of socio-moral standards based on Marxism-Leninism and Maoism and to encourage and educate the people of the entire nation to strive to create a socialist civilization that is both materially and culturally rich;

(3) to help the Party and the government in [the] smooth running of the country and maintaining established social order and stability; and

(4) to follow the Party's and the government's guidelines, and to prevent anti–Party and anti–government coverage.[54]

The combined sociopolitical and educational objectives were then to be interpreted into scripts "completely created, written and produced by Chinese educators and television professionals."[55] Equally essential were the sets, characters and dramatic storylines, which would mirror China's culture and society. As STV Producer Ye Chao emphasized, *Zhima Jie*, while cloned from America's *Sesame Street*, would not be its identical twin: "We take the format and adapt it to our children's needs in accordance to the culture of China. All its setting, environment, language and characters are entirely Chinese."[56] Big Bird, for example, was hardly around as often as his Chinese cousin, Da Niao, who spoke Mandarin and played with the kids in the busy Chinese neighborhood.[57] Muppet characters Bu Hu Hu Zhu (a blue pig) and Xiao Mei Zi (a furry red monster) were Da Niao's friends, as well as Chinese actors portraying storekeepers, doctors, police, etc.[58] The sets on *Zhima Jie* featured typical icons found in all Chinese towns and cities—a noodle shop, a public phone booth, a bicycle repair stand and a recycling center.[59]

According to *Time* reporter Jaime A. Florcruz, the show's title was the easiest cultural barrier to overcome:

> *Zhima Jie* translates literally as "Sesame Street." The average Chinese
> child consumes more sesame seeds, cakes and oil than even the most avid
> American Big Mac aficionado.[60]

On the other hand, teaching Chinese writers to incorporate comedy
in their scripts was a bit more challenging ... but ultimately successful.[61]
The Chinese do not employ such devices as puns or jokes in traditional
prose, and hence, were unused to it. However, their ability to learn quickly
was to their advantage — they soon picked up on the advantage of humor
as an educational tool, and managed it well.

Another important factor to be addressed was China's one-child policy and its implications. Many children (at least those living in the city)
are spoiled "only" sons and daughters— affectionately known as "little
emperors." They must learn to respect others as well as the environment
in which they live. *Vancouver Sun* journalist Malcolm Parry reports this
"interesting challenge":

> With Beijing mandating one-child families, *Sesame Street* there is devised
> to take the place of siblings in developing social skills. And, given the
> lingering harshness of China's Cultural Revolutions, officials there
> reportedly want the television show to help children understand and
> appreciate beauty.[62]

Once again, after some reflection and discussion, writers at Shanghai Television were able to address these issues openly and artfully.

The original air date for the series was targeted in early 1996 (for
Shanghai only; later, the series would be expanded to include the entire
country).[63] Unfortunately, financing the series soon became a more critical problem than previously anticipated, and the project was temporar-
ily shelved ... but not for long. In 1995, CTW renewed its pledge to Chinese
children's television, declaring that *Zhima Jie* would premiere in 1997, the
three-year, multi-million dollar investment underwritten almost in its
entirety by General Electric.[64] GE's Vice Chairman and Executive Officer
Paolo Fresco made these comments at the press conference:

> We are committed to long-term involvement in the Chinese marketplace,
> and as a corporate citizen of China, we believe this sponsorship is an
> important investment in the future of Chinese society. *Zhima Jie* will
> provide Chinese children with high-quality, locally developed educa-
> tional programming that will help accelerate the learning of the next gen-
> eration. CTW is a preeminent programming source that has set the
> standard for quality children's programming around the world, and we
> are pleased to become a part of their tremendous *Sesame Street* family.[65]

STV President Sheng Chong Qing was equally optimistic about the final product:

> Cooperation between STV and our friends at CTW began more than two years ago. We quickly learned that both of us shared the same philosophies and goals of creating a quality educational TV program, such as a Chinese language *Sesame Street* series. This program will meet the needs of young viewers in China by drawing from the rich and enduring cultural heritage of China as well as CTW's 25 years of successful experience in research-based production. We are also grateful for GE's long term support for the children of China by committing to sponsorship of this great project.[66]

Children's Television Workshop President and Chief Executive Officer David Britt added these words:

> China has the largest number of pre-school children in the world, and we're delighted to provide tools to help them learn. We're especially pleased to be partnering with Shanghai TV, and to have the sponsorship of GE, a worldwide industrial leader. *Zhima Jie* will help to educate Chinese children, and its impact will be multiplied by the transfer of the technology of quality educational television to STV.[67]

For its part, General Electric was not only progressive in its commitment to sponsor a Chinese-produced series; it was unprecedented in its desire to underplay its advertising prerogative in this situation, and instead, concentrate on its aim to be a "good corporate citizen." Thus, rather than producing commercial messages during breaks in the show, GE used a simple logo at the start and finish of the program and paid CTW to produce thirty-nine 30-second "mini-lessons" under the moniker *It's Time to Discover*, which would accompany the corporation's logo at these times. These brief information capsules featured topics such as floatation and magnetism. In keeping with the "Muppet" vision, GE even created several characters to give the lesson — "Omni," a frenetic character known by his hair shaped as a question mark, and "Beacon" and "Watt," two friendly incandescent light bulbs to talk to the children. According to a June 16, 1998, report in *Business Wire*, the format was designed as follows:

> Five young children on location in China hook into Omni's science lab via video screens and explore the world around them, asking such questions as: "What floats?" "What sinks?" "What can you do with a magnet?" and "Bubbles! What are they?"[68]

Jim Harman, GE's manager of corporate advertising, explained the rationale for this strategy:

> Instead of the traditional adult-oriented commercials, we wanted to create memorable and fun sponsored educational spots that appealed to children's inquisitive nature and their sense of humor; after all, GE is sponsoring *Zhima Jie*, an entertaining and educational program.[69]

David Jacobs, regional vice president for CTW Asia and Latin America, seemed a bit surprised at the extent and character of GE's commitment to *Zhima Jie*, since it was the company's first sponsorship of this kind — using on-air corporate billboards only (rather than commercial interruptions) in a Chinese series. However, Jacobs predicted that the long-term gains would far outweigh any short-term disadvantages of the decision: "Support of this educational program projects GE as a 'good corporate citizen' — important in China — and could serve as a model for other markets in Asia."[70] He added (at a later date):

> Despite the hiccup of the Asia crisis, a fundamental change has occurred in the Chinese broadcasting market. TV has become a business, but China is very much a developing market when it comes to promotions. The types of venues that we [are] using in the U.S. to do promotions either don't exist in China, or they are just starting to evolve. For example, there are virtually no on-air promotions, so you come to rely much more heavily on special events.... When we tour the characters in the U.S., people don't get as excited because they are used to seeing them on TV. But in China, it's so new and unique that it draws crowds. The ability to do special events, although sometimes technically difficult, is something we were able to capitalize on in a big way to promote *Zhima Jie*.[71]

*Zhima Jie* did not actually air in 1997 due to more production difficulties and bureaucratic red tape. However, in March of that year, pre-production planning began in earnest. After a two-week orientation workshop in New York, STV and CTW started the tedious process of casting for the new Muppet characters, including Big Bird's Chinese counterpart, Da Niao. After the actors had been chosen, a team of CTW technical advisors accompanied STV staff to Shanghai to "consult, train and transfer skills relevant to all aspects of the project from early research through production."[72] CTW Vice President Gregory Gettas was excited about the process as well as its promise:

> We are honored to work together with STV on this great project in China — one of the most magnificent countries in the world. We are also

grateful to GE for their belief in the project and their generous support. Sesame Street begins at Hooper's Store and now extends to China's Great Wall; truly making this the longest street in the world. Yet, regardless of country our objective remains the same — to provide the world's children with a program that delights and entertains.[73]

Thus, armed with a total commitment to Chinese curriculum, philosophy and culture, supported by CTW's expertise and production values, and sponsored by one of the foremost multinational conglomerates in the world, Shanghai TV began shooting the series. In February 1998, after over a decade of plans to create an indigenous Chinese version of *Sesame Street*, *Zhima Jie* finally premiered on Shanghai Television. When interviewed by the *New Straits Times*, CTW's Associate Director for International Licensing, Asia International TV & Products Group, Rita Nelson, alluded to the merger as symbolic of *Sesame Street's* ongoing philosophy, which "began as an experiment in 1968 in New York and [is] still an experiment [today]."[74] Shanghai TV felt the "risk level" to be quite low in the "experiment," however, estimating an initial audience of 300,000 in China, and expanding greatly as the program reached other areas of the country in the future.[75]

And Shanghai TV was right — the initiative met with overwhelming immediate success. In fact, in 1999, after a year's programming, General Electric and Children's Television Workshop announced their intentions to continue the series as well as to produce sixty-one new *It's Time to Discover* spots. Corporate Advertising Manager Jim Harman gave his reasons for the decision, citing the value of the first thirty-nine *Discover* mini-capsules:

> Children responded so positively to the spots last year that we wanted to build on that momentum. We are pleased to be in a position to help children in China learn concepts that are not easily understood and to make it fun for them at the same time. With their proven expertise in developing educational and entertaining programs, we welcomed the opportunity to strengthen and expand our relationship with CTW.[76]

Indeed, the first cooperative commitment between the Children's Television Workshop, Shanghai TV, and General Electric — 130 completed episodes over three years[77] — exceeded everyone's highest expectations. According to GE publicists, *Zhima Jie*

> has been put on in 39 TV stations all over China and been [a] favorite [of] preschool children. Just like its 17 other versions in different countries, it is full of miracles and wonders. One episode in 30 minutes, not

only is attractive to preschool children to increase their knowledge and inspire their intelligence, but also caters to parents, [the] elder generation, relatives and teachers of the children as well as [those] who love and care about children.[78]

In addition, the *It's Time to Discover* segments on *Zhima Jie* were so rewarding to both GE and CTW, they are now seen as a prototype for future co-production projects in other countries. CTW Group Vice President for International Television and Licensing Steve Miller comments:

> GE's efforts in responsible sponsorship has resulted in a unique opportunity to create a whole new brand of programs and products that can be enjoyed by children and families around the world. There is tremendous growth potential for lessons that appeal to children's inquisitive nature and for lively characters that appeal to their sense of humor. *It's Time to Discover* does both and does it well.[79]

It is an example of "true" joint ventureship in every way.

# 7

# Case Study: The Holiday Inn®
# Network in China — More Is Better™

In May 2001, the Crowne Plaza Nanjing Hotel debuted amid great anticipation in China. The hotel had been previously known as the "Golden Eagle," jointly owned by a Chinese American company and the Industrial and Commercial Bank of China. However, times had changed since the Golden Eagle's inception in 1991: Nanjing sought a new emphasis on "internationalizing" the hotel image, which also meant brand renaming. Within the domain of hotel companies, the safest bet in name recognition would be "Holiday Inn" or one of its sister brands (including Crowne Plaza® Hotels and Resorts, Inter-Continental® Hotels and Resorts, Holiday Inn Express® and Staybridge Suites®), all part of the "world's most global hotel company."[1] In 2001, the owner of the Holiday Inn brand, Six Continent Hotels, Inc.,[2] either owned, operated or franchised over 3,200 hotels in almost 100 countries.[3] Surprisingly, just fifty years before, it would have been difficult to find even one.

The Holiday Inn brand started out simply enough. In the summer of 1951, the company's future founder, Kemmons Wilson, was irate to discover that moderately priced motels, geared toward vacationing families, were virtually nonexistent. In addition to an extra fee for children, the typical roadside inn was often unclean, with few amenities. Wilson then told his wife,

I didn't think this was fair. It wouldn't encourage people to travel with their children. I told her I was going to build a chain of motels, and I was never going to make a charge for children as long as they stayed in the same room as their parents.... I also told her I was going to build a brand name that you could trust. And I told her I'd build 400 of these things across the country before I was through.[4]

Within a few months, Wilson had researched all the items he wanted to include, and hired a designer to create the prototype of his dreams. As it happened, the draftsman watched an old Bing Crosby movie while he was working, and sketched "Holiday Inn" at the top of his drawing. Wilson liked it, and decided to keep it as his brand name. By August 1952, the first of many Holiday Inn hotels was opened in Memphis, Tennessee. Ten years later, 400 more could be found along major highways throughout the United States.[5] But the growth of Holiday Inn was far from over — it had barely begun.

## HOLIDAY INN—THEN AND NOW

Kemmons Wilson's original vision of the "Holiday Inn concept" was to parallel the development of the U.S. interstate highway system, creating a standardized group of franchised hotels along most major routes in the country. In the 1970s and 1980s, this image of "roadside travel stops" had been internationalized and re-shaped to include urban and suburban properties.

Despite Wilson's remarkable expansion, the hotel industry had begun to decline during the mid– to late 1970s. The 1973–1974 recession and subsequent energy crisis stymied the previous years' massive building. Wilson, himself, became a casualty at this time, and in 1976, stepped down as CEO after twenty-four years and 1,710 properties at home and abroad.[6] As a result, Wilson's successor, L.M. Clymer, re-focused the market strategy of Holiday Inn, opting instead to manage — rather than own — most of its units. Management contracts involved an outside investor building the facility and turning it over to Holiday Inn for brand name recognition and professional management. Holiday Inn, in turn, received a percentage of the property's gross operating profits and "a negotiated percentage of revenues."[7]

In addition to its management contract approach, Holiday Inn moved away from the "roadside" concept, and re-directed its development efforts toward cities and towns. In a 1976 *Business Week* article, Michael D. Rose, then president of Holiday Inns, Inc., explained, "We will probably be going to properties that have a broader mix of business so that we're not dependent on just one kind of traveler. The 'buzzword' is multi-market location."[8]

Operating under its new mandate, Holiday Inn expanded its horizons— both literally and figuratively — to practically every country in the world. Along with the establishment of a different hotel brand for different clientele, the old company name, "Holiday Inns, Inc.," had evolved to become part of "Holiday Corporation" to reflect its revised persona. Business continued to grow.

In 1990, Bass PLC (U.K.) — now known as Six Continents PLC[9] — acquired Holiday Inns, Inc., and moved its U.S. corporate headquarters from Memphis to Atlanta, adopting the trade name "Holiday Inn Worldwide." The strategy here was both practical and symbolic: Bass wanted a more recognized cosmopolitan environment, with easier access to both sides of the Atlantic. This change in location was accompanied with plans to establish a new brand category — Holiday Inn Express — a no-frills, mid-market value, providing a continental breakfast with lodging (but no other food service). Consumer segmentation was beginning to take hold.

In 1994, Holiday Inns, Inc., refined its brand-category recognition by redesigning its Crowne Plaza hotels to become more upscale hotels, attractive to foreign independent travelers as well as for individual business travelers and meetings, as distinguished from convention clientele. In addition to serving the targeted group, the name "Crowne Plaza" now signified a specific "image," limiting the risk of "brand creep."[10] More elegant than before, this category featured more sophisticated facilities— meeting rooms, a business center, fax connections, and other amenities for corporate clients.

But the road to brand recognition was far from completed. In 1997, Holiday Inns, Inc., was succeeded by Holiday Hospitality Corporation, which identified yet another traveler category — persons requiring extended (five nights or more) stays. This new brand group, called Staybridge Suites, featured studio, one- or two-bedroom designs, with kitchen amenities, a study, and other "residential" facilities. Within a year, the first model opened in Alpharetta, Georgia.

The announcement of the new Staybridge Suites grouping was followed shortly by a press release revealing Bass PLC's acquisition of the luxury Inter-Continental Hotel chain from a Japanese company. After adding this "preferred hotel brand of the world's business community for more than 50 years"[11] to its list of diversified brand categories in 1998, Holiday Hospitality changed its name to Bass Hotels & Resorts, Inc. Then, following its parent's disposition of Bass Brewers and the Bass trademark, it changed its name to Six Continents™ Hotels, Inc., in 2001.

In July 2001, the Six Continents Hotels system encompassed over 3,200 hotels in almost 100 countries, including 134 Inter-Continental, 152 Crowne Plaza, 1,541 Holiday Inn, 1,173 Holiday Inn Express, and 26 Staybridge Suites hotels.[12] Future plans include "new designs for living," reflecting the Six Continents' identity (as voiced by its Chief Executive Tim Clarke): "a name which emphasizes the global spread of the company and a name which will soon become synonymous with our strong hospitality service brands."[13]

## HOLIDAY INN WORLDWIDE ... AND IN CHINA

Much of the development of Six Continents Hotels abroad — and especially in China — has reflected its corporate evolution in the United States as well as the growth in infrastructure of the host country. As a writer for a May 1993 *South China Morning Post* article observed, "It is one thing to open hotels in China, but another to market them successfully, and Holiday Inn has been particularly innovative in campaigns designed to both raise awareness and fill rooms."[14] Holiday Inns, Inc., became a strong presence in China almost immediately after the nation's doors were open to the West, establishing its centerpiece hotel, Beijing's Lido, in 1984 and growing steadily, even in remote areas like Lhasa and Urumqi.[15] It was also the first hotel chain to work together with local authorities (called Joint Marketing Committees, or JMCs) to target domestic audiences as well as regional and global markets.[16] By 1994, Holiday Inn Worldwide was managing at least ten hotels in China, including two "floating hotels" on the Yangtze River in Sichuan province.[17] But clearly leisure-time vacationers were not hotel management's primary concern in the 1990s — the investment potential in Asia (and especially China) had begun to re-emerge when political stability seemed likely after Tiananmen Square. As then general manager for Bangkok's Holiday Inn Crowne Plaza, Mahmoud Masood,[18] observed, the needs and desires for this audience segment were far different than those of vacationers:

> The business traveller is looking for trouble-free service that is timely and accurate. There is also a desire for recognition of the needs of the business traveller versus the leisure traveller, who does not have the same sort of deadlines to meet.[19]

However, money was still "thin" in China as well as in other parts of the world. Consequently, Marc Tay, then director of sales and marketing at Holiday Inn Guangzhou, described the shift in the hotel chain's emphasis in 1993–94 Asia:

Business travellers are looking for cheaper hotels, largely due to tighter travel budgets in most companies due to recession; they are looking for a cheaper booking source, as most find it cheaper to book through travel agents than directly with a hotel, and particularly for Guangzhou, business travellers are travelling less and staying for shorter periods as the [Chinese] economy slows and completion of the Guangzhou-Shenzhen superhighways cuts down travelling time to Hong Kong.[20]

Not deterred by the temporary setback, Holiday Inn Worldwide (now officially named Six Continents Hotels) continued to invest in China. In the next five years, the hotel chain claimed twenty-five properties in China — a mosaic comprised of Inter-Continental, Crowne Plaza, and, of course, Holiday Inn hotels.[21]

In addition to its recent acquisitions, top management at the Atlanta corporate headquarters decided to re-evaluate and upgrade some of their existing facilities in the mid– to late 1990s. The Shanghai Holiday Inn, for example, was one of the properties selected for renovation and upgrade to a Holiday Inn Crowne Plaza hotel ("Holiday Inn" was later dropped from the name). Conversely, the Holiday Inn Lido in Beijing was renovated but kept its brand name identity as the flagship Holiday Inn in China.

Ravi K. Saligram, Six Continents Hotels' current Brand President for the Americas, was president of the company's Asia Pacific region during this exciting growth period. He described some of the challenges— and rewards— of being a hotel pioneer in China as well as creating the Holiday Inn University in Beijing, where managers are taught to integrate corporate culture with local custom. Excerpts of this October 2001 interview follow:[22]

> RS:   For us, I think, the Lido was actually a "flagship" for the Holiday Inn brand in China — and in Asia — because it really demonstrated great value, while at the same time, showing tremendous scope. Holiday Inns in America, as you probably know, were really founded upon "innovation"— the first "family" kind of atmosphere ... the first to put TVs in all the rooms. In China, the Holiday Inn Lido illustrated how far the Holiday Inn brand could stretch. And even though it is a very extensive property — with a large number of restaurants, a supermarket, bowling alley and apartments— as well as the rooms— the values of that hotel are more centered on friendliness than on facilities. It's important to have a friendly staff and good values and good locations and everything that the Holiday Inn name stands for.
>
> NLS:   I agree. I was teaching in China in '85, '86, '88, and '89. I was there again on a Fulbright in 1990, and it was my "home away from home" because it was the only place for a long time that you could actually get

groceries easily. There was a grocery store, and it had food, and it was friendly, and it was a Holiday Inn. I stayed there a lot in those years. To me, it was the best place in China.

RS:   Yes, we've heard a lot about that. The Lido has a really nice atmosphere — very warm and yet, not pretentious. It is not an Inter-Continental or a Crowne. It is very much a Holiday Inn, and I think we are very proud of that fact because we believe that "mid-market" does not mean "mediocre." This is true throughout China. We have many excellent Holiday Inn hotels in terms of extensive facilities and great product. Nevertheless, all of our hotels truly reflect the essence of the brand in terms of friendliness, value for money, and importantly, a home away from home where you can be yourself.

NLS:   So, how did you begin to expand after the Lido?

RS:   At first we decided to expand our holdings in the major gateways. We were obviously in Shanghai and in Beijing. We found that while we had a very high quality reputation, we were still not big. Importantly, we had breadth of distribution but not depth or critical mass in any one country. Consequently, we wanted to refocus. As you know, Asia is a huge, huge region, with so many countries and so many diverse cultures. In order for us to leverage scale, it was really important for us to be focused. Based on our strategic insights, we decided that China and Australia would be our top priorities.

MJM:   What year was this?

RS:   This was around 1996.

NLS:   Why China?

RS:   Part of the reason was not only the improving economy of China but its huge potential for domestic business. Saturdays were declared holidays to establish a full weekend, more highways were available in many areas of the country, and restrictions to travel from province to province were relaxed. We started seeing slowly that there was an increase in the number of domestic consumers in our hotels. We then decided to adopt a strategy like that in the United States— to get a dominant share of the market, really get critical mass, and build the name of "Holiday Inn" as an American brand, an international brand, and, on a third level, a local brand. If you ask people in China what nationality the Holiday Inn is, I don't think they would say American or Chinese. I think they would just say international.

MJM:   So, it's not seen as an American place?

RS:   It's really international. Some of the attributes are Americana, which are very positive. In fact, when we did a consumer research study in China four years ago, we found that amongst hotel brands, Holiday Inn's image ranked highest amongst domestic consumers. Further, when Chinese traveled outside their country, the brand they would look for most was Holiday Inn. I think that had a lot to do with us having a "focused" strategy on China, which evolved over time. We started in the gateway cities with a wonderful product. We were already very fastidious about the product quality and good facilities and great value. The most important thing for us— the key factor for our success— was that we recognized, very early on, that the business model in China should be in management contracts. Our ability to manage the hotels allowed us to build the brand according to its values, maintain a high level of customer service and quality, and drive brand recognition. We have been steadfast in adhering to a management strategy, and it's been a very important feature for us. In China, our operational expertise has been a major success factor for our success....

NLS:    Can you go into further detail about management properties versus franchises?

RS:    There are really four major business models in this business. One is a franchise — the real estate or the ownership is with whomever owns the property, but whoever owns the property also manages the property himself or herself, so that the running of the hotel is entirely under that person's control. The owner, of course, may choose to appoint an independent management company. When a hotel property is "franchised," the franchiser doesn't carry the burden of real estate, the physical assets, nor do we actually run the hotel ourselves. What we stipulate is that the owner runs the hotel according to our standards. We have a set of physical and service standards. We then use a "quality" group that checks the franchisee's performance against our standards. If the hotel is not adhering to our standards, we go through a standardized process of improving the quality of the hotel.

In franchising, our value proposition is a result of driving heads into beds through our reservation system, our technology platform Holidex, our sales force who call on global customers, and our marketing programs and the brand's critical mass. Holiday Inn has enormous brand power with universal awareness and ubiquity. More people stay at Holiday Inn on any night than any other lodging brand in the world.

In the case of a management contract, we actually run the hotel on behalf of the owner. We do not own the real estate. We appoint the general manager, the financial controller and other key management members for the hotel. We build an operating team, who are experts at leveraging the power of the brand to maximize EBITDA potential of the hotel. It is all about creating an operating culture that focuses on guest satisfaction and retention while maximizing the bottom line to drive ROI for owners. The rest of the staff is not necessarily "ours" from a legal standpoint — the owner is legally responsible for them. Thus, like a franchise, the hotel would be run according to our quality standards but, in addition, we would control the "operating culture."

The third business model is a joint venture, in which we would own a portion of the hotel along with someone else. But we would manage. The fourth model would be to own the hotel outright.

In China, we have a very unique system of managing hotels, because many of these hotels are owned by government enterprises. The owners create a "parallel" operating system, using a "foreign" general manager (typically, the person from us) teamed with the deputy general manager (a mainland Chinese).

The role of the GM [general manager] is to be a business manager *cum* hotelier. His or her responsibility is creating the right service culture, retaining customers, positioning the hotel with the right marketing programs and pricing ... in essence, driving profit growth and keeping guests happy. The Deputy GM gets involved with the welfare of the local staff and dealing with local regulations, laws, government policies and political issues. Although it can act as a check and balance system, it also provides a complementarity of skill sets. This structure can be a challenge, but our successful GMs have worked hard to make the relationship with the Deputy GM fruitful and productive.

China is a tough and complex operating environment. The ex-pats who are flexible, business-oriented ... those who are very good with relationships but are still bottom-line focused ... can operate well in this sort of environment. If you are a very "black-or-white" person, you might not be successful. You have to be able to operate in shades of gray without compromising one's integrity. I am proud to say our GMs in China have been a key contributing factor to our success.

NLS:   Why did you choose management contracts over ownership?

RS:   We wanted to get rapid distribution and at the same time control quality and service. By offering a management model, we were able to work with a number of owners simultaneously who had land and wanted to make real estate investments. Also, real estate ownership is quite complex. Management contracts allowed us to focus on our core competency, building the brand through operations, customer service and marketing to generate a high ROI for our owners. We have also not franchised in China because of lack of critical mass, infrastructure and lack of operational expertise.

MJM:   And, how does this model fit into the Chinese business community?

RS:   You bring up a very good point, Marilyn. The general manager of a hotel, especially of a big hotel like a Holiday Inn or a Crowne Plaza, is really a community leader. They play a key role in ensuring that the hotel is run according to brand standards and values. Furthermore, they work hard at building the right image for the hotel to ensure that it runs at an optimal level.

In addition to community leadership, we decided to make a commitment to management education for the locals. As a result, we launched the "Holiday Inn University" in China. The University was aimed at developing the managerial skill sets, especially at the supervisory level of our local associates. This was particularly important as we started gaining distribution in both primary and secondary markets such as Dalian, Hefei — the sorts of places that really attract the domestic market. It's important to distinguish between "managerial skill sets" versus "functional skill sets" for front line staff. The latter were developed through training programs "in hotel," e.g., cleaning rooms, setting tables, taking reservations, etc. Remember, a lot of the front line staff in these cities had never been to a hotel and it was important to train them well to ensure that our guests received world class service.

MJM: Grace [Lau — GM of Crowne Plaza, Nanjing] said that the hotels must often furnish shower facilities for the staff to use, as well as a place to have their uniforms cleaned and pressed because they don't have that "luxury" in many cities.

RS: In order to treat our guests right, we needed to treat our employees right and give them the appropriate facilities and amenities. We were able to standardize a lot of our practices because of our operational scale.

NLS: And, like you said, the infrastructure — the ability to travel on highways, and the trains going to different places — also added to the possibilities of doing things.

RS: Indeed. There's one other thing that I should mention in terms of key success factors. While we used ex-pats for most of our management teams at the hotels, we gradually started to change the hiring profile of the ex-pats in order to improve communication with the owners. In the past, a lot of our GMs were Europeans; over time, we also started to hire more and more Singaporean Chinese, Hong Kong Chinese, Indians since they were able to speak the language of the owners. We also wanted to develop mainland Chinese nationals to become the GMs of the future (which I am pleased to say that has now started to happen). Ultimately, we were able to develop a team of strong and diverse GMs, including Americans, European, Hong Kong Chinese, Singaporeans, etc., who were not only excellent operators, but also had a high degree of cultural sensitivity. Our development team was also unique — they were all local nationals. This was something none of our competitors had. They were — and are — the best. They were able to really sell our product, our operational expertise and were great at building relationships and having contacts. These guys were the best in terms of bridging and understanding — to use a very hackneyed phrase — the East and the West.

The development team knew how to build the relationships with the mainland Chinese owners. To reward their diligence, they received performance bonuses based against clearly set goals.

But we didn't just reward our people monetarily ... we also recognized them through awards and training programs in Hong Kong and the U.S. Also, our developers realized that my door was always open — that they could talk to me without worrying about hierarchical boundaries. There were no barriers. Many of them were courted by our competitors, offering more money, titles, etc., but they were very loyal to us because we were loyal to them.

NLS: I'm curious, what were the requirements for your mainland developers and how did you find these people? Were they educated in the United States or in Europe?

RS: None of them were educated outside of China. It's not how well someone speaks English, but what's in their heads and what's in their hearts, and really being able to understand what they bring. They were smart, focused and results-oriented. They had strong operational backgrounds, but were great negotiators and salespeople. They had built their skills over time because we had sent them for owners' conferences and training programs for us. We would also bring them to Hong Kong and the U.S.

Localization is a very important thing. You have to have global strategies and values, but you have to have local people who believe in those values ... because values are values. This is how we started to build the talent pool in each of the major countries that we operated in.

In conclusion, we are profitable in China because we have been patient, taken a long-term view and invested for the future. We have built a profitable business through reputable brands, developing and training people with an emphasis on localization, bringing operational expertise and giving it back to the community. We are proud that Holiday Inn is a true brand icon in China.

# Holiday Inn Hospitality and Shanghai

Because of its reputation in Asian trade ventures, Shanghai serves as both prototype and forerunner for future hotel development in China's main cities. Accordingly, Six Continents Hotels has concentrated some of its most ambitious efforts here. One indication of its most recent advances toward market domination in the city occurred in March 1998, when the company opened a Holiday Inn in Pudong's Lujiazui Finance and Trade Zone. Located in the 33-story $68 million China Coal Mansion (and owned by the Ministry of Coal Industry),[23] it was the first hotel to be managed by an international group in this rapidly developing area. And because of its site — home to most multinational corporations — its primary goal was to accommodate corporate personnel with generous travel allowances.[24] Not to ignore other business travelers, however, the city's

Crowne Plaza opened its new club and business center during the same year.[25] Both moves were intended to maintain the Holiday Inn stronghold in Shanghai, with almost seven percent of the market share — the highest among its competitors.[26]

But Six Continents Hotels was far from finished in Shanghai. Within a year after the Pudong site and Crowne Plaza upgrade, it announced its third managed Holiday Inn property in downtown Shanghai (in the Zha Bei district, north of Shanghai International Airport), as well as the addition of the city's Inter-Continental Hotel to its list of brand name categories. As Steven Young, Regional Vice President for China, told *Asia Pulse* in 1999:

> Shanghai is the main economic focus for Northern China and is among the top ten Asian cities of strategic importance....With visitor arrivals in Shanghai at 1.4 million per annum and the city's GDP growth running at 8 percent, we are delighted that we now have a strong presence in this vital city.[27]

Mahmoud Masood, general manager of Shanghai's Crowne Plaza in 2001, was present for these benchmark changes in the evolution of Six Continents Hotels' worldwide reputation. In a May 2001 interview, he shared some invaluable insights on the development of Asia's hotel industry; China's unique position within the region; Shanghai's importance to multinational investment with China's rapidly emerging infrastructure; and Six Continents Hotels' strategies to meet the changing needs of clients along the way. Here are some excerpts from this interview:[28]

> MASOOD:   I think in almost every case I know of, bar one or two in our company, the party A (which is typically the owner of the property) has bought a state owned company. This may be a bureau, which means it is a direct government organization or it may be a state owned enterprise — an SOE — which is like this hotel. This hotel is owned by the Film and TV Bureau, Shanghai Film Studios — which are the subsidiary of the [State] Film and TV Bureau — which, in turn, eventually comes under the Ministry of Information. Shanghai Film Studios owns this hotel. However, they in turn have a joint venture with a Hong Kong group of investors. Typically — and this is not unusual — Shanghai Film Studios provided the land and the Hong Kong investors built the hotel, provided the money, and created that joint venture. And then they looked for a management company, which was us. That happened in the case of this hotel in 1991.

> NLS:   Do you come in after the hotel is built; because, if that is the case, maybe they wouldn't build it according to what you need?

MASOOD:   Exactly. It's unusual for us to come in after the hotel is built, although on occasion, that does happen because there is a fallout between the developer, and perhaps the original intended management company. But typically, we come in either prior to, or during the building of the hotel, in time to assist in some of the planning of the layout, design and other specifications.

MJM:   Who determines what hotel brand is going to go on that building?

MASOOD:   I think it's a combination of events. Primarily, if we have enough representation of a particular brand in our city portfolio and we feel that the city is able to support one of our other brands, then we will look for a suitable opportunity. The Intercontinental is typically a "main city" or a "gateway city" product. A Holiday Inn is much more flexible. A Holiday Inn can be in a main gateway city, in a secondary city, in a resort, or out by the airport etc., etc.—there is a lot more flexibility of location in the Holiday Inn hotel than there is in Inter-Continentals. Crowne Plaza is somewhere in between. Crowne Plaza can typically be accommodated in main cities and in secondary cities, but perhaps not in the sort of emerging cities. That's how we look at it. Typically, we'll have a three-to-one ratio when we look at Holiday Inn hotels, Crowne Plazas, and Inter-Continentals. For every three or four Holiday Inn hotels, there might be one Crowne Plaza and for every ten Holiday Inns there might be one Inter-Continental. That's just simplifying it but it makes it easier to understand.

MJM:   Following up on that ... in 1991, the current Shanghai Crowne Plaza started as a Holiday Inn. Then, you made a decision a few years ago—for lack of a better phrase—to upgrade to a Crowne Plaza. When did that happen and what elements went into that decision?

MASOOD:   This hotel actually only existed as a "pure" Holiday Inn for a very short time and was almost immediately converted to a Holiday Inn Crowne Plaza—in line with our then global strategy to position these as the best and most upscale Holiday Inn hotels. As we gained scale, we made a global decision to reposition Crowne Plaza as a true upscale brand, competing with the likes of Hilton, Sheraton and Marriott. Hence the decision to take the Holiday Inn name off the brand.

NLS:   I was also wondering about the profile. You gave us a profile of where each hotel would go—that is, a Holiday Inn would go into a more emerging town, whereas a Crowne Plaza would go into an established town ... and Inter-Continentals would go into gateway cities. What are the profiles of each of these that make them significantly different from one another?

MASOOD:   I think some of the differences are subtle and some are more pronounced. Obviously, like any product, when you are trying to offer an upscale experience, everything in the hotel should reflect that experience from your arrival throughout your stay, including dining and entertainment experiences. The kind of level of attention and services you are provided with determine the kind of positioning of the hotel. Typically, Inter-Continental hotels would have a more comprehensive concierge function than a typical Holiday Inn would. Inter-Continentals are geared more for the needs of a senior executive, typically, business leaders who are international travelers, whereas Crowne Plazas would come into mid- to upper-management, and Holiday Inns would be for middle managers seeking value. Also, Holiday Inn hotels would typically cater on the leisure front to group movements, families with young kids. The needs and the level of attention and the number of options available, whether we are talking about a breakfast buffet or whether we are talking about an in-room vanity, would reflect the needs of the different profiles that I have suggested.

NLS (to MJM):    Didn't we stay at the Inter-Continental in Istanbul?

MJM:    Yes, and we also stayed in the Inter-Continental in Athens.

NLS:    I was just trying to remember whether or not I found them very different from this hotel.

MASOOD:    A lot of this has to do with individual market needs and competitive position. Also, major differences are present with service levels, the number of suites, etc. Having said that, one of the major challenges we constantly work on is "brand creep" in order to truly keep our brands distinct.

MJM:    I was just going to ask about the Holiday Inn Lido. It was just gorgeous. I could have lived there for years!

MASOOD:    Holiday Inn is a great brand. And ultimately, the Holiday Inn Lido, despite its extensive facilities, does a great job of representing value for money and friendliness. The brand and hotel have been great for each other, making this a great flagship for us.

NLS:    How do you train your personnel for these diverse experiences?

MASOOD:    Cross "exposure," or cross training on a more regional basis. In Asia, we move people around all the time, to give them more experience, to give them more exposure. But it is far less easy to move someone from Asia to Europe for a cross-exposure or cross-training experience. It has nothing to do with cost. It has more to do with our understanding that in Asia, our figures show that 70 percent or higher — sometimes 80 percent — of the business comes from within Asia. So, if you want to cross-expose someone, do you want to send him somewhere

where perhaps only 10 percent of the business is coming from, or do you want to send him somewhere where 20 percent or 30 percent of the business is coming from? If we look at Australia, at least 80 percent of the business in any Australian hotel is domestic. It makes more sense to cross-expose within Australia — from Sydney to Perth. You are still covering major distances, and there are some differences in people's habits, etc. If you look at China today, 20 to 25 percent of the business in any one of our hotels in China is domestic. In another five years, maybe 40 percent will be domestic. But in addition to domestic, if we include Taiwan, Hong Kong and Singapore, that probably covers 60 percent or maybe even 70 percent of our business. When we send people around for experience and exposure we send them within the region rather than across continents. On the Inter-Continental brand, we do cross-training and exposure on a global basis since this is truly a global brand.

Masood's experiences in Shanghai, however, are both a model and an anomaly for the rest of China — a sort of *yin-yang*, if you will. As one of the primary driving forces in China's economic development, it is decades ahead of most other major cities in the nation, and (literally) centuries ahead of many interior towns and villages. Perhaps a better picture of hotel expansion in greater China can be found in Nanjing — specifically, the 2001 opening of Six Continents Hotels' (then) newest management property, the Crowne Plaza Nanjing.

# NANJING AND SIX CONTINENTS HOTELS' EXPANSION

Nanjing — current capital of Jiangsu Province and former capital of the Ming Dynasty — is deeply based in Chinese culture and tradition, as well as in economic identity. Birthplace of Dr. Sun Yatsen (the Father of present-day China) and a major city on the Yangtze Basin, Nanjing was an obvious focal point for silk production, industrial manufacturing and trade. In addition, as one of the nation's "three furnaces,"[29] the city also attracts many domestic and international tourists.

Given this distinction in both business and leisure travel, it is not surprising that a fledgling domestic (as well as international) hotel industry was attracted to it in the early 1990s. Among the most impressive "outside" entrepreneurs during this time was California's Transpacific Management Company, Inc., which joined forces with the Industrial and Commercial Bank of China to fund a 60-story multi-purpose building. Designed by France's Frederic Rolland Architects and Nanjing's Building Design Institute, the structure (completed in 1996) included a "boutique" hotel, a department store, banks, apartments and entertainment venues.[30] The complex was named "Golden Eagle Plaza."

Golden Eagle enjoyed great popularity and name status in Nanjing, but within a few years, the hotel segment reached its domestic limits, and required a more experienced, international management company to take charge. Accordingly, in May 2001, Six Continents Hotels re-opened the renovated, renamed Crowne Plaza Nanjing, to an enthusiastic public. Shortly afterward, General Manager Grace Lau agreed to be interviewed to provide a historical context to the changeover. She also discussed the challenges of redesigning an existing hotel to meet the corporate objectives of the Crowne Plaza brand, introducing the newly packaged entity to both domestic and international travelers, hiring and training local personnel to meet international criteria, and being a good "corporate citizen" within the Nanjing community. Portions of our discussion follow:[31]

> NS:   What is the relationship that you have to Golden Eagle, in terms of the structural hierarchy of the company?

> MJM:   And the building?

> LAU:   At the beginning of May — not more than one month ago — we converted the name to Crowne Plaza, no longer GE plaza. The previous hotel had been privately run, privately owned, and privately operated by local owners. Several months ago, they decided that they wanted to internationalize the hotel and began to look for an international management company to do that for them professionally. I came into this hotel in January to help them set up all the systems, and we launched the hotel — under the new name, Crowne Plaza — in early May. By now, there should not be any signage showing that this is a GE plaza hotel, but because the public had difficulty with the Crowne Plaza hotel name, we had to put a caption stating that it was formerly the GE plaza hotel. It's actually the same owner, but with a different management company now.

> MJM:   Are you ultimately going to remove the GE, and what is the time frame for this period?

> LAU:   As soon as we find that the market is mature enough, we will remove it.

> MJM:   So, you're representing the management of the company?

> LAU:   Right. In Asia, the number of franchise hotels is marginal because the market is not as mature here. The reason behind this is that either the city or the management culture is not up to the pace we feel necessary for a good franchise, and there is the issue of critical mass. That's why in Asia, we do not usually have a franchise.

NS:   Is the Golden Eagle International a state-run company?

LAU:   No, it's a totally private company. The owners are American-Chinese.

NLS:   So, it's a different type of structure than a state-owned company?

LAU:   It's different, because a state-owned company belongs totally to the government. Most enterprises in China — maybe 95 percent — are state-owned. In the past, most businesses were owned by the state. Only relatively recently — maybe less than twenty years ago — we have seen the emergence of private ownership.

MJM:   How do you maintain brand standards — particularly quality? And what actions do you take when hotels do not meet these standards?

LAU:   Every year, the corporate offices send people to inspect your hotel. You must also send figures, guest comments, your hardware and software standards and employee opinions on a monthly basis ... sometimes even on a daily basis. Quality control personnel then evaluate your management record. If you are constantly below the standard they've set, they usually give you a time frame for you to turn things around. They would then monitor improvement continuously, and if they do not see marked development after that, they would take the appropriate actions, including termination.

MJM:   And that's built into the agreement? In other words, if there are certain quality standards problems that are not improved after some time, Holiday Inns are free to terminate?

LAU:   Our license agreements and management contracts clearly spell out the terms of how the hotel needs to meet brand and operational standards, including penalties if they don't.

NLS:   What things do you think you do to contribute to running a successful operation, in terms of understanding the needs of your clients?

MJM:   And understanding where you are in terms of the local culture, the client culture, and the corporate culture? What kinds of things do you think put you above other companies?

LAU:   Let me see how to tackle these questions. I will say that I do think this is a personal comment, and it is true from my heart. I think the Crowne Plaza is one of the most successful global hotel chains, in terms of understanding the culture and needs of the local community. Six Continents manages the highest number of hotels in China. This is a reflection of success — not a reason for success — but a reflection of success. We have more than thirty hotels in China, which are open already.

Most other companies have no more than five or ten. A lot of management companies, I find, fail not only because they can't understand the local customer needs, but because owners' needs differ. For some owners, profitability is everything; for some, hotels epitomize service excellence; and for a few, they are showcases of success.

MJM: Owning a hotel is more of a status symbol than a money-maker?

LAU: For some. But our focus is always on driving bottom-line profitability as well as customer service. We want our brands to have the highest respect in their markets.
　　We excel in customer comfort. Take the Holiday Inn Lido— one of the biggest hotels in China and even in Asia — despite its size, you feel cozy inside, because we take you as friends. This is where I think we really have the winning edge. This is where we distinguish ourselves from the market. Even for a hotel that big, we are still able to make people feel that they enter into a community. They don't have to go outside to buy anything, and the staff can answer all the questions that you have. You have a supermarket, schools....

MJM and NLS:　And a post office! The post office is so wonderful at the Lido. I wish you had one in Shanghai. Do you have one here?

LAU:　We have a postal corner ... a postal station ... but not really a post office. They basically do what customers need.

MJM:　You are absolutely right, though. For people who are traveling, you make them feel that their world is not overwhelming.

LAU:　At the Holiday Inn, we do not try to sell luxury. We just try to sell good service to make the customers feel comfortable. These are things we try to plan into the local needs.[32]

　　Coincidentally, Lau was interviewed during a week when China honors its children. The preparations for this event at Nanjing's Crowne Plaza Hotel were clearly a priority, including the allocation of dining room space to accommodate parents and children, special buffet treats containing both Eastern and Western foods, and hotel staff to supervise and entertain the children. In addition, Crowne Plaza staff presented small gifts and treats (through a tie-in with Nestlé) to everyone, creating an atmosphere of joy and amusement.
　　While the Children's Day Brunch Buffet was open to the public (i.e., anyone who wanted to pay for it), the Crowne Plaza–Nanjing had also devoted many of the same resources to host children from local orphanages several days earlier.

NLS:   We were fascinated with the way you treated the national children's day in China. Was that a special promotion? The kids were delighted with everything that you had done. I was watching very carefully — everything went very smoothly, despite the confusion of serving two different types of customer. That strikes me as one of the examples you mention also.

LAU:   We try to be good citizens within the community every chance we get. Actually, two days ago, we also invited two hundred children from a local orphanage to spend Children's Day together with us. The hotel staff union took complete charge of the operation. Our employees joined together to contribute half the monies needed for the orphans' celebration. In the end, we were able to invite these children for lunch, do a small show, and give away tricycles, bicycles and other toys. This was only one in a series of promotions for the holiday. For the children with families, we've also had a big blue bear giving out flyers in the last two days, advertising today's buffet. The buffet is not the only treat, though — they can enjoy the pool until 4 p.m. We opened it up free of charge for the children for their special day.

MJM:   I noticed that the children also received little blue bags with the Nestlé logo on them. Was that a cooperative arrangement you initiated?

LAU:   Yes. We started talking with Nestlé about a month ago, especially for the event with the orphan children. They donated all the ice cream.

This commitment to children reflects a larger sense of social responsibility expressed in Six Continents Hotels' mission statement. As articulated by Chairman and CEO Tom Oliver,

> Six Continents Hotels strongly believes in supporting communities in which our hotel brands have a presence and, through our charitable giving programs, we are able to positively impact the well-being of our consumers all over the world.[33]

Equally significant, Six Continents Hotels seems committed to bettering the quality of life for its employees, as evidenced by Ms. Lau's comments to our questions:

NLS:   We'd also like to talk about your staff. How do you select them? Are most of them from Nanjing? Do you train them here?

LAU:   Yes, most of them are found and trained in the local area. Local people love to work for international companies because they receive a great deal of training ... possibly more training than they might receive in U.S. hotels. That's because, here, we must train them from scratch — how to set the table, for example, because spoons and forks are foreign to them. Also, you must teach them about shaving, proper grooming and overall hygiene. In our hotels, we provide all these facilities—hot water, a shower twenty-four hours each day—and we encourage them to use these.

MJM:    So, not only do you want them to do this but you give them the opportunity as well?

LAU:    They all have the opportunity to use these facilities. That's why they love to work for international companies or international hotels. We provide them with food ... we give them uniforms ... we also give them allowances to take home.

Based on (1) building scale synergies; (2) localization; (3) a dedication to quality; (4) attention to community needs; and (5) understanding global market trends, it's clear that the success of Six Continents Hotels has been neither serendipitous nor incidental. In China, the company's measure of accomplishment has been even more dramatic, considering the nation's special circumstances of infrastructure development and growth, amid cultural change and political and economic upheaval. It appears that a considerable energy and empathy, coupled with good business skills, have bridged the chasms exhibited in the more typical scenarios of frustrated negotiation often endured by American entrepreneurs seeking instant gratification.

# 8

# Case Study: DaimlerChrysler — Silence in China After the "Deal Heard 'Round the World"

In their May 2000 *Detroit News and Free Press* article, reporters Bill Vlasic and Bradley A. Stertz summarized the anticipation, expectation and ultimate frustration experienced by the 1998 Daimler-Chrysler merger:

> It was the deal heard 'round the world. In May 1998, a stunning $36 billion merger was announced by Chrysler Corp., the all-American maker of Jeeps and minivans, and Daimler-Benz AG, the German maker of Mercedes-Benz luxury cars. The deal rocked the global auto industry and ushered in an epic era of consolidation.... The merger was hailed as a "merger of equals," but the hype backfired amid a clash of cultures and personalities. When the dust settled, Daimler had bought Chrysler, and the shock waves reverberated on both sides of the Atlantic.... Daimler-Chrysler, applauded as the grandest of cross-cultural experiments, instead became a cautionary tale of the risks and rewards of going global.[1]

As the authors point out, some of the disappointments faced by the new entity were uncontrollable elements of fate. Clearly, no one could have foreseen the economic and political turmoil occurring in the half-decade after the deal was made. However, DaimlerChrysler's Achilles' heel — social differences between Americans and Germans — was noted by many observers at the outset. This, in turn, affected the newly merged conglomerate's development in other countries, especially China.

To better understand the current position of DaimlerChrysler in today's China, it is crucial to ascertain the motivation and mindset of those who envisioned the corporate merger in 1995.

## ORIGINS

In an age of market economies, mergers and multinational conglomerates, the notion of combining the forces of two auto giants from different countries was clearly not an exotic concept. In the case of Daimler-Benz and Chrysler, one company's weaknesses seemed to be the other's strengths. As a 1998 *Financial Times* article observed:

> Chrysler and Daimler were a perfect fit. Geographically, their core activities were in different areas: Chrysler was dominant in the U.S., while Daimler's strongholds were Europe and South America.
> The two were equally suited in products. Most of Chrysler's output comprised sports utilities and multi-purpose "minivans." Although it was still the smallest of Detroit's "Big Three" carmakers, Chrysler's focus on such high-margin vehicles had allowed it to report profits which, at best, had been more than those of GM and Ford, its bigger rivals, combined.
> Daimler, by contrast, was a byword for luxury limousines. It also made vans and trucks — which Chrysler had long dropped — and had made forays into smaller cars and other industries, notably aerospace.[2]

But how should these companies come together? The three most likely options were: (1) participating in regional joint ventures; (2) merging the two corporate entities; or (3) orchestrating a company buyout.[3] After brief discussions, the idea of a corporate merger surfaced as the clear choice.

Because of the delicate nature of negotiations, however, secrecy and limited access were essential to the overall success of the alliance. As a result, the potential merger was dubbed "Project Gamma," with legal and financial representatives from "Cleveland" (the code name for Chrysler) and "Denver" (the code name for Daimler-Benz) meeting frequently at undisclosed locations to resolve the specifics.[4]

Included among the "talking points" of the finalized deal were creating a single "identity" for two companies with different corporate personalities, operating in different countries. Robert Eaton (Chrysler's chairman) expressed concern that his company's distinction as an American landmark in Detroit's automotive history would be diminished by its connection to a foreign company. Daimler-Benz had similar concerns with the success of its major luminary — Mercedes—crossing the Atlantic and receiving American "citizenship." In 1998, *New York Times* reporters Edmund L. Andrews and Laura M. Holson aptly characterized the Daimler image as

> elite and European. Most Mercedes passenger cars range from $30,000 to more than $100,000, and most of its sales are in Europe. Though sales by Mercedes in the United States soared 65 percent last year, it commands less than 1 percent of the American market.[5]

Mercedes would not easily be re-instituted as an American car — nor did its manufacturers want it to be. This problem was later resolved by creating a separate and autonomous board of directors for the vehicle group.

Equally challenging to the solving potential identity crises was the practical issue of merging two corporations with different authorization and tax systems. Daimler-Benz had its greatest difficulty addressing *Aktiengesellschaft*— its registration as a joint stock company in Stuttgart. Chrysler, on the other hand, belonged to the Securities and Exchange Commission (SEC) and was registered in Delaware. Ultimately, both parties decided to incorporate to base the new company in the Netherlands, with a two-tiered board of German and American executives.[6]

The legal intricacies of Project Gamma were soon overshadowed, however, by the dilemma of naming the new company (or "Newco" as it was called in preliminary negotiation). *Financial Times'* reporters characterized the proceedings in this way:

> "Everything was going fine, and then the name came up," says one participant. The Germans were adamant the title should reflect Daimler-Benz's history, and the fact that their company was the bigger part of the merger. They pushed for Daimler-Benz-Chrysler. Apart from being a mouthful, Mr. Eaton was equally determined to have his company at the front. Chrysler-Daimler-Benz, was his suggestion.
>
> While the latter was "unacceptable" to Daimler, recalls Mr. Eaton, the former was "totally unacceptable to us. There was a stand-off. Neither side would budge."
>
> In the end, common sense prevailed. DaimlerChrysler was the solution. Mr. Lutz and Mr. Stallkamp decided the name was "really classy."
>
> Mr. Schrempp was sad to drop Benz, [saying] "some local papers accused me of betrayal." However, the Benz name would live on, as the products would continue to be called Mercedes-Benz.[7]

The "naming" issue not withstanding, deeper, even more volatile culture clashes were on the horizon. And these were less likely to be resolved as easily.

## CULTURAL CONTRASTS

In 1998, the *St. Louis Post-Dispatch* published a *Wall Street Journal* compilation of significant differences between Daimler-Benz and Chrysler employees before the merger. Included among them were average hourly wage (Daimler-Benz — $18 U.S.D; Chrysler — $20.31 U.S.D), average vacation time (Daimler-Benz — six weeks; Chrysler — four weeks); average hours of work each week (Daimler-Benz — 35; Chrysler — 50.5); and number of plant workers (Daimler-Benz — 38,500; Chrysler — 4,370).[8] And labor standards revealed only the tip of the cultural variance iceberg. As Vlasic and Stertz contend,

> the great divide between the Germans and Americans seemed as deep as it was wide. They didn't just make cars differently. They lived in separate worlds. Bringing them together required a measure of education, changes in behavior, and a willingness to accept the other side's cultural biases. The Americans attended classes on German meeting protocol and personal interaction. The Germans took a course on the meaning of sexual harassment in the U.S. work environment. ("A German male should always keep the door open when meeting with an American female.") The cultural divide extended beyond attitudes and mores. The yawning gap in pay scales fueled an undercurrent of tension. The Americans earned two, three, and, in some cases, four times as much as their German counterparts. But the expenses of the U.S. workers were tightly controlled compared with the German system. Daimler-side employees thought nothing of flying to Paris or New York for a half-day meeting, then capping the visit with a fancy dinner and a night in an expensive hotel. The Americans blanched at the extravagance and resisted quickie trips overseas simply to meet face-to-face.[9]

Further, cultural views of hierarchy, assertiveness, individualism versus collectivism and risk-taking were more diverse than similar.

Elements of culture within the workplace have been studied for several decades by scholars like Geert Hofstede and Fons Trompenaars, Dutch researchers interested in social psychology. Hofstede is particularly interesting to this discussion, having begun his study of intercultural differences in attitudes in the mid–1970s. While his findings have shifted from year to year, he has clearly established contrasts between cultures in four areas: power distance; individualism; gender roles; and uncertainty avoidance.[10]

"Power distance" is defined as the way in which hierarchical status and mobility are addressed in organizations (and society in general). Cultures with a "low" degree of power distance tend to expect consensus in decision-making, scorn status symbols and try to minimize class differences at the workplace. Conversely, those with a "high" degree of power distance see executives as autocratic (if benevolent), expect inequities in the organization (as it is outside the organization), require obedience from subordinates; and see "perks" and privileges as necessary rewards for corporate officers.

"Individualism" (as compared to "collectivism") emphasizes the singular contributions of persons, rather than the aggregate result. Highly individualistic organizations are very task-related, having specific rules to follow. Employees are encouraged to be direct, even confrontational, to "get the job done." Collectivism (on the opposite end of the spectrum) stresses the importance of relationships over tasks, avoiding overt conflict, and contributing to overall harmony within the organization.

"Gender roles" (or masculinity vs. femininity) identifies values closely associated with society's definition of males or females. In highly masculine organizations (or societies) for example, characteristics such as assertiveness, competitiveness and decisiveness are encouraged; in highly feminine organizations (or societies), emphasis is placed on nurturing, compromise, humility and quality of life.

Finally, "uncertainty avoidance" reflects the emphasis on rule-making to reduce anxiety levels in businesses (or nations) that are either newly established or somewhat volatile. "Low uncertainty avoidance" environments usually have few rules, pay little attention to time, and seem relaxed (even shiftless). "High uncertainty avoidance" settings, on the other hand, are time-conscious, usually stressful and busy, and sometimes aggressive.

As cultural diversity continues to grow, all corporations must learn to understand and adapt to a mosaic of different cultural perceptions and values. In 1998, London's *Financial Times* observed that "the problem is that much greater for multinationals such as Chrysler and Daimler-Benz where the merging businesses must fuse the characteristics of their countries of origin."[11] For example, many management scholars would classify both German and American organizations as highly individualistic (although the United States is seen as "the most individualistic society in the world"[12]). Both Germany and the U.S. are also highly masculine, although Germany reflects a somewhat higher degree of masculinity than the United States.[13] In the other two areas, however, the similarities become less clear. Americans seem more comfortable in a "low power distance" milieu, with "weak uncertainty avoidance." Germans are also at ease within a "lower power distance," but desire a strong "uncertainty avoidance" environment.[14] While seemingly minor, these small differences would catapult into much larger issues as the DaimlerChrysler merger became reality.

Within a year of their historic alliance, *New York Times* journalist Keith Bradsher reported trouble on the horizon:

> The merger in November of Daimler-Benz A.G. and the Chrysler Corporation, presented at the time as a merger of equals, is producing considerable unhappiness among some American managers at DaimlerChrysler A.G. who contend privately that the combined company has come to be dominated by Germans....
>
> American managers still at DaimlerChrysler also complain privately that more and more decisions are being made at Daimler's former headquarters in Stuttgart, Germany, even though DaimlerChrysler officially has dual headquarters, there and in the Detroit area. Gerald C. Meyers, the former chairman and chief executive of American Motors, which Chrysler bought in 1987, said that Germans were dominating Daimler-Chrysler now and that this was hurting company morale in the United States. "To have to go and kneel at the altar of Stuttgart has to be demoralizing," Mr. Meyers said. DaimlerChrysler executives acknowledge that some employees here are worried about the effects of the merger. But they say that these concerns— particularly the persistent and anxiety-causing rumors that more plum jobs will be going to Germans— are unjustified....
>
> Some German managers have been fretting that American executives have too much influence, and DaimlerChrysler executives use this to suggest that the merger must therefore be striking an appropriate balance between the two nationalities. "Among the guys who are sitting in departments where the boss is American, there is also frustration, particularly among those who are not able to speak English clearly," said Roland Klein, a former spokesman for Daimler-Benz who is now the chief spokesman for DaimlerChrysler.[15]

Warren Brown, *Washington Post* staff writer, discussed similar laments:

> The public relations operation is controlled by the Germans. Sources said Detroit usually defers to Stuttgart in the release of any important information about the company, such as the expected favorable earnings report due out today. Before the merger, "We were having this magical time at Chrysler where we [on the staff] could make quick decisions on our own and make things happen," said Steve Harris, a former public relations official. After the merger, "every day there was a battle between the Germans and the Americans" over how press releases and news events would be handled.[16]

By March 2001, 19 of the 31 senior executives at Chrysler before the merger had either quit, chosen an early retirement package, or been driven out.[17] In addition, six plants had closed and 26,000 American jobs were eradicated. Clearly, a general economic decline accounted for some of the losses, and corporate restructuring objectives explained other changes. However, attitudes that "Germans ha[d] taken over Chrysler lock, stock and barrel"[18] continued to abound as well, despite vehement denials.

And the feeling of being overrun by outsiders was only more complicated by other cultural challenges such as language, social mores and seemingly insignificant "rules." In a May 2000 article in *Automotive News International*, writers Jeff Mortimer and Chris Wright chronicle DaimlerChrysler engineer Bob Emick's first visit to Austria (to prepare for an upcoming assignment there):

> He thought it appropriate that he pay a social call on his predecessor. Emick and his wife walked up to front door, knocked and got an unfriendly reception. "Hello. You just did it all wrong," his predecessor said. "In Austria, you're supposed to wait at the front gate." "When we looked," says Emick, "we saw that both the mailbox and the doorbell were by the gate next to the street. For us to push through the gate was tantamount to breaking into his home."[19]

Mortimer and Wright go on to describe other *faux pas* committed by automotive expatriates (either from the United States or elsewhere), who learn more by "doing" than by a cultural awareness course. Who, for example, could have advised the newly arrived Brazilian executive at Nissan that getting onto a packed elevator at the first floor could be a maze of misunderstanding? As he watched it stop at every floor — and saw no one getting off— he only realized later that not pushing a button for a specific floor (even if he thought it was unnecessary since the button had already been pressed) would not tell those with lower status where he was going. "So at each floor they were being — in typical Japanese fashion — respectful to me by allowing me to get off first."[20]

Language also plays an integral role in understanding a culture; but beyond words, one must learn to "think" in the language. As a GM senior manager told Mortimer and Wright,

> Our relationship with our Brazilian dealers required it. Being in sales and marketing, I couldn't rely on translators to establish that kind of relationship. It had to be something where I could understand what they're saying — not just the words but the emotions behind it. I had to be able to get my thoughts across spontaneously.[21]

As everyone knows, the task of integrating diverse cultures — in business, politics or personal relationships—can be difficult and tedious at best. At DaimlerChrysler, there were three cultures to address initially — German, American and corporate. The notion of incorporating a fourth — China — through a joint venture agreement at this delicate time may have been more than anyone should have been expected to tackle.

# THE CHINESE THROUGH HOFSTEDE'S EYES

As discussed earlier in this chapter, Dutch scholar Geert Hofstede is one of the most recognized researchers in the field of multinational corporate negotiation. His cultural comparison studies in perception have bred numerous replications and expansions in different geographic areas, including conflicting "world views" of Westerners in China.[22] Authors Terence Jackson and Mette Bak, for example, apply Hofstede's design (collectivism-individualism, power distance, uncertainty avoidance, masculinity-femininity) when discussing attitudes foreign companies should have when employing Chinese locals:

> Power distance ... is high in China.... The respect for hierarchy and authority may well be rooted in Confucianism, together with a regard for age as a source of authority which is largely unknown in business in the West.
>
> A view of uncertainty avoidance in China is not so clear cut.... But Hofstede in his later work argues that uncertainty avoidance may be an irrelevant concept ... linked to the question of "truth." Truth is not a relevant issue in Eastern thinking. The Chinese manager may well be motivated to save "face" and to tell the other person what they want to hear, rather than what may be regarded as the absolute truth in Western eyes.
>
> Masculinity-femininity is also a value dimension for which there is little direct information in China.... The concept of masculinity represents an emphasis on competition and the centrality of work in one's life.... It is the degree of working which influences employee motivation, and this is an area of information which is lacking in the context of China.
>
> As one would expect, collectivism is high in Chinese cultures, with the main group of reference being the family. This is rooted in both Confucianism and the ancient land system which ensured the farmer and his family were immovable for economic reasons....
>
> Rather than the short-term achievement orientation of many Western societies, China is characterized by long-term values such as thrift and perseverance.... A connected factor is that of locus of control, where Eastern cultures have a fatalistic view of destiny, where cause and effect is more likely to be attributed to external factors than internal factors which can be controlled by the individual. With a view that the individual has little control over short-term objectives, goal-based individual reward systems may not be appropriate.[23]

Business consultant Elizabeth Scholz offers some thoughtful advice on joint ventures in China in a 2001 article in *Human Resources*:

> In China, the negotiating team is usually larger than the American team. The Chinese team may be insulted by a small American negotiating team and may question the seriousness of the American alliance....
>
> In Asian societies, what is said or even implied may hold more weight than what is written. It is important to understand what body language means in different cultures, and be prepared to hold up your end of a verbal agreement....
>
> There may also be differences in methods of logic and perceptions of time. Asians tend to analyze situations in a spiral, interactive, holistic fashion. Americans are typically more linear thinkers who move from one analysis to the next in a structured sequence. Americans view time as sequential and absolute. Asians generally perceive time as nonlinear, infinite, and repetitive. Given these differences, it may be very difficult to follow each others' logic and thought patterns....
>
> It is vital to the success of any organizational intervention — or business alliance — that you have a clear understanding of a foreign company's basic values, as well as the foreign country's culture.[24]

The lack of clarity in American-German relations at DaimlerChrysler should have persuaded business leaders to cancel — or at least table — talks in China at this time. It would have seemed that negotiating with yet another culture (and one far different than the other two) would have further complicated an already complex situation. But the allure of nearly two billion potential Chinese consumers was tantalizing, if not precarious.

# DAIMLERCHRYSLER IN CHINA

China has always held a special "exotic" quality for Westerners — it is both mystical and menacing, compelling and frightening. Ironically, the Chinese have often been equally perplexed by many Western cultures, especially in business relations. Jim Mann, author of *Beijing Jeep: A Case Study of Western Business in China*, uses an old adage to describe the uneasiness: "*Tong chuang yi meng*" — "Same bed, different dreams."[25] Mann goes on to explain the conundrum after Deng Xiaoping opened up China's doors for trade:

> For the most part, the Western corporations starting up in China were dreaming about a market of one billion people. This was the same dream that has beguiled Western companies since the Industrial Revolution, since one British writer declared more than 150 years ago: "If we could

only persuade every person in China to lengthen his shirttail by a foot, we could keep the mills of Lancashire working round the clock." The products had changed — the West now wanted to sell the Chinese personal computers, Jeeps, baby food, shampoo, razor blades, Tampons, and Ritz crackers — but the dreams were essentially the same.

China had its own dreams, which also date back to the nineteenth century. China wanted to try once again to obtain the technology it needs to modernize and to catch up with the West and Japan. In 1860, the Chinese scholar Feng Guifen wrote, "There ought to be some people of extraordinary intelligence who can have new ideas and improve on Western methods. At first they may learn and pattern after the foreigners; then they may compare and try to be their equal; and finally they may go ahead and surpass them — the way to make ourselves strong actually lies in this." After 120 years of turbulent history, China was still trying to fulfill these dreams.[26]

When American Motors agreed to build a joint venture to manufacture Jeeps in Beijing in 1983, they knew things would be different from projects in other parts of the world, but they had little idea *how* different. At the end of a very frustrating experience, coupled with the political turmoil of Tiananmen Square, they looked back to see that basic negotiations and operational constraints had not changed much in a decade. As Mann noted in 1996,

> In the never-ending dance between China and foreign investors, the Chinese of the 1990s still seek to obtain as much foreign technology as possible, while the visitors from abroad try to obtain permission to sell as much as possible in the Chinese market. In negotiations, Chinese leaders still play off one company against another and one country against another.... Once a contract is finally signed, the company still discovers ... that the process of negotiating has only started.[27]

Such was the case of DaimlerChrysler as it prepared to introduce one of its new designs — the Z-car.

Daimler-Benz had experienced a long history of successful business dealings with the Chinese — starting in 1936, with a small truck assembly line, and growing continually until it had become China's major European trading partner in the mid–1990s.[28] As Daimler's president, Jurgen Shrempp, proclaimed to President Jiang Zemin during one of his visits to Germany in 1995, "We see China as an extraordinarily important and meaningful market. We don't want short-term, rather long-term, partnerships with China."[29] Shortly after Zemin's visit, Daimler announced it had beaten then-competitor Chrysler and the Ford Motor Company for a $1 billion contract to build 60,000 mini-vans and 100,000 engines in Nanfeng. At the same time, Daimler was also given permission to forge an additional $50 million joint-venture deal with a Chinese company to manufacture buses.[30] While some political pundits argued that the move was a clear reaction against America's favorable treatment of Taiwan and its public disdain for China's apparent neglect for human rights, trade experts assessed the move as "business as usual." Probably a more accurate assessment came from *New York Times* reporter Nathaniel Nash, who noted:

> The contract awards to the Germans also underline a European approach to business, in contrast with that of some Americans. European governments are less inclined to risk commercial interests in Asia over political areas like human rights, and present themselves as less bellicose, more tempered trading partners to governments that find themselves in political fights with Washington.[31]

Political differences aside, however, no one could be prepared for the Asian market collapse that followed almost immediately after Daimler had begun its Nanfeng project. In addition, Chinese consumers were simply not ready to invest great sums of money in Western-designed cars. In short, Shrempp's declarations of long-term relationships with China would be tested soundly. In a 1997 *Financial Times* article, James Harding described the challenges in foreign auto ventures throughout China:

> Nearly half a million Chinese thronged to the Shanghai International Auto Show earlier this month, caressing the leather upholstery on executive saloons and having their pictures taken behind the wheel of the latest sports car. Few, if any, were looking to buy. With an average wage in Shanghai of around $100 (£60) a month, most visitors could only dream of owning one of the shining models displayed by the world's leading car companies. The event encapsulates the Chinese challenge for the car industry. China is the world's most promising automotive market but, until it fulfills its potential, manufacturers must invest billions of dollars and endure untold frustration to cultivate future consumers.[32]

By 1997, Daimler's $1 billion joint venture was at a virtual standstill, due to difficult relations with the company's Chinese partner. Peugeot was forced to abandon its plant in Guangzhou, and both American and other European automakers suffered unanticipated slowdowns. Unhappy venture partners, the difficulties in financing cars through Chinese banks, and the lack of desire by typical Chinese consumers for simple, subcompact passenger cars all contributed to the Western carmakers' distress. The last factor — disinterest in economy cars — was perhaps most devastating, since most automotive analysts predicted a high demand for such vehicles. Instead, the Chinese preferred either mini-vans (to carry multiple families or baggage) or high-priced executive cars to show status. From this desire for prominence as well as substantial growth in Western expatriate executives, GM Shanghai ultimately emerged as the number one American producer of luxury cars (Buicks), Ford took a distant second place, and the "Chrysler" portion of DaimlerChrysler was hardly even recognized as a contender. This is due to the fact that Daimler concentrated on bus and mini-van production, Benz marketed luxury Mercedes,[33] and Chrysler's major contribution was the 2-seater, subcompact cars ... which stayed on the lots, virtually ignored by the local consumers. Not an impressive start for the newly formed alliance of Daimler and Chrysler.

As a result, many of the subcompact car manufacturing plans for China were scrapped by foreign carmakers in the late 1990s—DaimlerChrysler's Z-car being among the first to go. (Incidentally, the "Z-car" has since found a profitable marketplace in Europe, where the design is now know as the "Smart" car.[34]) For its part, DaimlerChrysler has concentrated on what's worked best for them over the past several decades—building buses and trucks for commercial transportation. Not to be discouraged, DaimlerChrysler is also teaming with Mitsubishi to market an "urban car" in 2004, along with its own collection of mini-vans and luxury cars. The "urban car" would be a derivation of the old "Smart" car, but with four seats (instead of two), and sold under the Mitsubishi name.[35]

But the question still remains—will China be a successful venture for the "new" DaimlerChrysler? And will DaimlerChrysler be able to resolve its internal problems well enough to venture further into a market that requires long-term commitment, minimum short-term gain, and trust through *guanxi* (relationships)? Only time will tell. Many critics see the prospects as dim, due to the clash of multiple cultures. But, as *Daily Telegraph* reporter Peter Dron writes, the potential of success—however small—is still there, due to the enormous market possibilities of the Chinese consumer:

> A while ago I had a discussion with Jurgen Hubbert. He's the man who will, in all probability, neatly sidestep personal blame for the fiasco of the Chrysler acquisition and assume control when the DaimlerChrysler board finally tires of the other Jurgen, chairman Schrempp. For some reason, the subject of China came up in the conversation. Not crockery, but the big Asian country where they execute their political prisoners. "What the typical Chinese car buyer wants," said Hubbert (currently responsible for Mercedes-Benz passenger cars and Smart non-passenger cars), "is a conventional saloon with five seats. And then he wants to put eight people in it."
> 
> I later relayed this comment to a senior Audi executive, who said

scornfully: "That's the kind of remark made by people who know nothing whatever about the Chinese market." Warming to the topic, he went on to detail various other areas of which he felt that DaimlerChrysler board members were comprehensively ignorant.

But let us not mock the afflicted. They have suffered enough; and it has not yet finished.... The Chinese car market is potentially huge, but it is also notoriously difficult to break into (there'll be no puns about cracking China here).[36]

Same bed, different dreams.

# Case Study: The Foxboro Company — Infrastructure's Hidden Jewel

Founded as an "American" business in 1908, The Foxboro Company[1] (like many of its contemporaries) later merged with other companies outside the United States to adapt to changing environments and challenges. As a result, it has become

> the world's leading supplier of 'sensor-to-boardroom' solutions for industrial automation systems, and advanced software applications, plus comprehensive engineering, maintenance, training, and ongoing performance services.[2]

Foxboro is especially known for its development of instrumentation and software systems for industrial automation. These are desperately needed by evolving countries such as China. Ironically, because these nations possess so little modern infrastructure at the outset (transportation, communication, water systems, etc.), companies like Foxboro can both create and customize new concepts, ultimately providing more efficient infrastructures for "Third World" countries than found in many "First World" cities and towns.

One example of this phenomenon in a different area is the obvious comparison of newly built or refurbished "high tech" international hotels in China to many American hotels, which offer only basic amenities such as lights, cable TV and hot, running water. In cities like Beijing, Shanghai and Nanjing, it is not uncommon to have access to satellite television (with more that 200 channels), towel rack warmers, and light dimmers— all controlled from the bedside night table. In fact, when staying at the JinLing Hotel in Nanjing in 1997, we actually needed help from the staff to discover how to use all the amenities of our room.

As one of the first joint venture companies in China, a study of the Foxboro Company provides a useful map for other companies with a substantial backup system, appropriate and much needed product, as well as the ability to understand and communicate the hardware, software and training needs of its clients and its employees. Finally, Foxboro places a premium on the welfare and needs of its employees, both at home and abroad, illustrating its understanding of intercultural norms and nuances and a grounding in communication and culture. What follows is the story of Foxboro in both Massachusetts and in China. Foxboro in the 20th century adds to the long tradition of New England trade in China. As one senior executive whom we interviewed put it, "The founders of Foxboro came over on the Mayflower."

# WE DISCOVER FOXBORO IN OUR OWN BACKYARD

In 1997, while teaching at Southeast University in Nanjing and observing the hustle and bustle of a rapidly growing city, author Nancy Street became acutely aware that things were quickly changing— that the transportation and communication infrastructure could now accommodate much of the industrial growth in this small city. The construction of the Three Gorges Dam was highly publicized, and one could hardly miss the "cranes" on the Shanghai skyline as more and more companies established manufacturing facilities in Shanghai and Pudong.

Further, many universities in Shanghai and Nanjing now offered advanced degrees in engineering and other technical disciplines. Fifteen years prior, there were almost no universities in China offering the M.A. and the Ph.D. In 1997, however, Street taught thesis and abstract writing to a class of master's candidates— all in technical or scientific disciplines. At commencement, Ph.D.s were awarded in many disciplines. At the

same ceremony, representatives of major companies from the Netherlands, France, England and the United States also awarded scholarships
to students taking degrees in engineering, chemistry and biology, directly
benefiting the increasing cooperation in China with joint ventures from
abroad. This exposure made Street think that perhaps it might be time
for a book on communication and business in China. She shared this
observation with Marilyn Matelski when she arrived in Nanjing as a visiting scholar at Southeast University in June 1997. The idea, at first,
seemed easy — but both authors soon discovered a series of stumbling
blocks.

One of the problems in developing our prospectus was how to select
the best companies for our case studies. We finally arrived at a simple formula — each corporation was to have a relatively long (10-15 years) track
record in China as well as a home office we could tour and visit, either
before or after our interviewing in China. Further, each company should
benefit Chinese economic and social development in some way, aid in the
acquisition of the Four Modernizations and be a "good citizen" to the Chinese people.

Initially, we didn't really consider the financial aspects of the company's record (though later, this, at times, would seem to significantly
impact upon a company's viability in the China market — see Daimler-
Chrysler, Chapter 8). We were much more interested in location — American companies in China with home offices in eastern United States— as
the research and interviewing for each company would have to take place
both in China and in the United States. As luck would have it, the headquarters of The Foxboro Company — one of the first American corporations to do business with China — was just fifteen miles from both of our
colleges. More importantly, Foxboro was in the business of working with
other manufacturers, builders and engineers (as in power plant projects)
to deliver and maintain product flow (whether electricity, water, cookie
dough, beer or oil), most efficiently. Clearly this company was perfect for
our purposes; its story is a blueprint for those interested in joint venture
development.

Unlike most of the other case studies in this book, the history of
Shanghai-Foxboro was researched primarily from interviews at home and
abroad. As such, it is best told through an array of voices from The
Foxboro Company, describing their first experiences with Chinese negotiators in 1978, their successes (and failures) in the next decades, and how
the company perceives itself now — some 25 years later.

# MANY VOICES—AN ORAL HISTORY OF FOXBORO IN CHINA

After describing our book idea to The Foxboro Company in February 2001, we were invited by Public Relations Manager Paul Miller to tour the corporate headquarters during our March semester break. This would give us a baseline understanding of the company before interviewing in Shanghai in May and June. The senior administrators in Foxboro first gave us a vigorous review of the scope of the company, the importance of the Six Sigma Program (or Lean Transformation) to their ongoing facility and product makeover, as well as the background on their joint venture in China.

After our initial briefing, we were taken on a tour of the Foxboro facilities (both the plant and the open space offices), had lunch in the dining room, and were able to talk to a half dozen upper level executives from various divisions as well as other skilled and long-time employees. This was a mind-boggling day for us, but it demonstrated the quite excellent communication skills and training afforded many employees of Foxboro. These qualities are in part a function of and the result of the impact of globalization; assimilation into the Invensys organization;[3] and the implementation of Lean Transformation or Six Sigma principles (based on cybernetic system theory) into the physical, visual and conceptual workplace. Portions of our conversations follow:

> NLS:   Our question to you is: How did you do it? Big question. How have you hung in there (in China) for so long?

> MG:   My name is Mike Godek and I am the General Manager of M&I [Measurement & Instrument] manufacturing across the street. I've been with Foxboro for 21 years, and have worked with China from the get-go. Basically, we started with stuff that utilized high labor content and very low complexity. Gradually, we moved up on the complexity scale.

> DC:   My name is Dan Carrie and I am the General Manager of Systems Manufacturing. I've been with Foxboro for over 20 years. I've been working with China for over 20 years. We also have a staff of full time Chinese employees.

> MJM:   May I ask a question about the Chinese who are here? Do they come for a certain period of time and then return? Or, are they permanent residents?

> MG:   When a new product is introduced, they come over and spend

three to six months working with our engineering people to ensure that there is a proper start up. They need to understand the technology and what is necessary for all of the testing and everything else, and be able to replicate that in China. This is easier and a far more efficient way to do business rather than by phone or e-mail.

RP: My name is Ron Pariseau, and right now I am Vice President of Purchasing for Invensys Process Automation, in which Foxboro Company is the main player. My relationship with Shanghai dates back to 1983. I am going to tell you how the relationship developed, what we are currently doing, and some of the steps along the way that made a difference in terms of the success of continuing this relationship. Basically, parts come out of this facility and are used to run power plants, refineries — to make Anheuser-Busch beer, to make Nabisco cookies, to make pharmaceutical products and so on. Our product is very important to building the infrastructure of many different commodities.

PM: Paul Miller, Public Relations Manager. If you want to control any industrial process in which you have a fluid flowing through a pipe you have to first be able to control that fluid — you have to be able to measure the flow. And Mike's plant makes the transmitters that measure the rate of flow, or the instruments to measure other variables. Then that signal is transmitted to another system and the system opens and closes valves and controls that flow. That is just one process variable in a plant and it is usually very complex — you have pressure levels, temperatures, pH measurements. There are many different variables.

RP: We get involved in a lot of different things. The Foxboro Company was founded in 1908 by the Bristol family, specifically to go into this "process control" industry that was evolving at the time. They found[ed] a facility in Foxboro, MA, and that's why the name of the company is Foxboro Company. From 1908 to 1981 we were pioneers and invented many of the products that you see today. We invented them and patented them for the industries that we serve.

In 1981, the president of our company (then Colin Baxter), attended an Instrument Society of America show (a big deal in our business) and the talk of the convention was the exploding growth between America and other countries around the world and that we should plan to double our business in five years. At that time we were a 500 million dollar company, our expectation then was to be a billion-dollar corporation. In some of the presentations, they discussed the emerging markets.

In the 1950s, we developed a relationship with Japan. We formed an alliance with a competitor who was manufacturing our products for distribution in the Asian Pacific, and we were doing some joint development work on the instrument type products that Mike's factory makes. That didn't work well. The company actually copied some of our patents and also competed against us in the marketplace. Our experience in Asia Pacific in the 1950s and 1960s was not a good one. With the emerging market in 1981, though, we decided to revisit the Asian Pacific —

Malaysia, India and China — for the purpose of developing a local capability or a joint venture. We started planning, and went to China in 1983.

Basically there were two purposes in our visit. First, we wanted to be the market share leaders as the infrastructure was being developed. As I explained earlier, our products are a core to developing power plants and refineries — all the things you need to build an infrastructure. Second, we wanted to develop a manufacturing capability so when our power product patents ran out (and in the early '80s we were starting to get more and more competition), we could manufacture our products more economically than we could in the United States or in the Western hemisphere.

I happened to be one of the first ones to go to China. I probably spent three weeks traveling around China. During that time, I visited 45 factories. One of my purposes was to increase foreign currency resources. Even today, China does not have a world-recognized currency. What they needed to do was to generate some world recognized foreign exchange to be able to buy the raw materials needed to produce inventory. My job was to adopt a purchasing fulfillment role in visiting factories to see what we could buy from China to generate U.S. dollars for them. They, in turn, could then buy the electronic components they needed to build the products we wanted them to build for the Chinese products. The generation of foreign exchange was really the key issue in this project.

# AT THE FOXBORO COMPANY
# IN SHANGHAI (PUDONG)

According to a senior spokesperson for Foxboro Company in Shanghai, however, the American-based corporation's decision to go to China was made before 1983. Preliminary discussions actually were begun several years earlier by a visiting Chinese delegation to the Foxboro facility in Massachusetts. This senior administrator (SA) continues the story:

> SA:  It started in 1978, when a high level group of Chinese people from the ministry level came to visit corporate headquarters to discuss the possibility of building a joint venture company in the field of industrial instrumentation. Why did the Chinese choose industrial instrumentation? Well, for one thing, it was a key to the development of all infrastructure projects including power generation, water purification systems, sewage treatment, transportation and oil refineries. Obviously it was a key project in terms of the Chinese situation at that time.[4]

The Chinese followed this visit with trips to several other Foxboro facilities. In turn, Foxboro sent delegations to search for sites and joint venture partners in China. The company's representatives put enormous energy and time into their search. After three or four years, they found a partner.[5]

SA:    The partner we selected was here in Shanghai because we felt that was the easiest place to do business at the time, and if we wanted to have a reasonable chance at success, we would have to do it in the Shanghai area. We wanted to do business, and they wanted our technology to improve their country. Everybody won. It was a win-win situation. Our business has grown every year since 1982. When we first started in 1979-1980, there was no such thing as joint venture rules and regulations. We wrote the book here and the book has been modified, but we were pioneers for sure.[6]

MJM:    The company that you decided upon for a joint venture — was it run by the state or a private enterprise?

SA:    It was a state enterprise. Back then, in 1978, there were no private enterprises. It was a state-owned conglomerate, called Shanghai Instrumentation Industry Company. This was a group of state enterprises in the instrumentation industry and there were probably 130 or 140 companies within that group.

MJM:    You said earlier that it took three to four years to find a joint venture partner. Did it actually take three to four years to find this partner, or did it take three or four years to actually work out the details?

SA:    We found the partner within the first year, but the rest of the time was taken to see how we were going to do it, what we were going to do … kind of laying down some groundwork for the joint venture agreement which we finally signed. The difficult time was in negotiation. It was not finding the partner — that was easy; it was trying to determine who was what. Up to that point, China had been closed for thirty years so there was a tremendous lack of knowledge about the United States and China … and China and the United States, especially at the business level. No one trusted anyone back in those days.

NLS:    We were (each side) uninformed and mystified. Often, when my college was negotiating our exchange program in 1984–85, we were not negotiating with the right person. Often that person was in the room, but we had no hierarchy chart.[7]

SA:    That is still a problem we have in 2001— you don't know who the decision-makers are over here. Every single person you end up negotiating with turns out to be a decision-maker and everything has to go right up the line.

MJM:    Did the negotiating team have its own translators or did you have one person interpreting for both?

SA:    We relied solely on Chinese translators. Sometimes we would invite an independent interpreter from a research organization to come in. We had the ability in the United States to check accreditation services but we felt that we could trust the interpretations provided us.

MJM:   That probably went a long way to establishing a relationship with the Chinese side.

SA:   Of course. The "relationship" is just as important today as it was twenty years ago. This trust and mutual understanding has not gone away and will never go away.

NLS:   Who advised you on cultural norms at that time? Your interpreters? How did you feel your way through the differences between the way Americans communicate and the way the Chinese communicate?

SA:   We didn't. We learned our way as we went along. We learned by our mistakes. I think that the people we were dealing with in those days knew little, if anything, about the corporate situation. So, mistakes on both sides were easily forgiven. Protocol had not yet been determined so quite a bit of knowledge of the proper things to do was not a problem for either side.

MJM:   You mentioned that you were one of the pioneers in this venture. How many people from Foxboro where actually involved in these negotiations?

SA:   There were six people from Foxboro and one from Singapore. That comprised the core negotiating team. Back at corporate headquarters, we had all kinds of people as supporters in a specific discipline. However, there were six coordinators working on the Shanghai negotiations at that time.

MJM:   Did each of the coordinators come to this team having some specific specialty?

SA:   Yes. Each member had a specific technical expertise or financial expertise or business expertise.

MJM:   How many Chinese were on the negotiating team?

SA:   Their negotiating team had many more members and included many people whom we did not know. We didn't know what they were doing or what their titles were; nonetheless, they were there.

MJM:   That would have been scary for me and thrown me off. Did you experience dismay at not knowing with whom you were negotiating?

SA:   We were in their country; on their turf. And they could do whatever they wanted. Just as in the U.S., if a team of six people came to us, we might have more or less people. This requires understand[ing] something of the culture before one begins.

MJM:   Your group was constant, but theirs might change?

SA:   Our group was always there. The Chinese side might have visitors from foreign affairs, foreign ministries, municipal people. But the core was always there. And, we were negotiating for a place in their territory, so it seemed only fair that others would show an interest.

MJM:   One of the things that we always emphasize in intercultural affairs is the concept and perception of time. One of the things that first impressed us about Foxboro is that unlike many of the other corporations we have looked at, you have been in it for the long haul.

SA:   Yes, definitely a different ballgame and in for the long haul. Our primary reason for being here is to gain market share and, of course, to make a profit. We were very careful in the beginning in selecting a partner and negotiating the contracts and in the way we did business. We were extremely careful in other areas as well. In the last twenty years, our results have proven that it worked.

NLS:   What is it about Foxboro that it succeeded in China, as compared to other companies who have tried and failed in China?

SA:   I think the biggest thing is that Foxboro is flexible. We have a joint venture contract now with unlimited time, and the transfer of technology is continuous. We are not going to do something that is worldwide obsolete here in China. The Chinese have a lot of money to spend. They are going to only spend it on the latest and greatest technology. Many companies that have failed are companies that have tried to introduce into the China market products that the Chinese won't use, can't use, or will never use.

NLS:   Can you give us examples of such products?

SA:   Many consumer goods like ladies cosmetics ... things of that nature. People are simply not used to using them over here, and many cannot afford the prices.

NLS:   I noticed that very thing in Nanjing when I was teaching at Southwestern University in 1997. Developers kept putting up new department stores, and each one had cosmetic centers to rival department stores in Western countries. However, there were no American products there ... just French and Japanese cosmetics. Finally, one day I walked into my favorite department store and there, amongst many, was the Maybelline counter. Maybelline is a relatively inexpensive product in the American market (and may be as international as Foxboro). But only tourists and the Chinese elite can afford any of these products.

SA: Usually, Chinese women use Chinese cosmetics, such as pearl cream, if they use much at all.

NLS: Yes, I also noticed that at that time there were no designer clothing lines found in American department stores, like "Liz" or DKNY. The labels indicated merchandise from Western Europe or Japan.

SA: No clothes from America, but you go to America and you find no clothes from America. They're made in China.

MJM: I was also curious about the fast food industry in China. Unlike the American population, I think it is dubious that any but the rich could afford to eat lunch at McDonald's or KFC once a month, never mind every day, especially when the average wage may be the equivalent of 100 to 200 American dollars a month.

SA: I think certain franchises such as McDonald's or KFC, TCBY yogurt do really well over here and will continue to do well. Starbucks coffee shops are all over the city and a lot of the young Chinese people frequent these places; not so much because they like the food, but because it is a status symbol. It is a social thing to do to go to Pizza Hut and have pizza.

MJM: Getting back to your company. You know, I came across Foxboro quite by accident. I was reading *Beijing Jeep*;[8] and on page 116, there was one line mentioning that President Reagan visited the first joint venture company in 1984 — and this [Foxboro] was it.

SA: When President Reagan was here I had the distinct honor of taking him around the factory. He also gave a major speech here and Mike [Michael Godek] had a private audience with him and Nancy. We have some photographs of that event downstairs on the third floor.

MJM: Your program here has been tremendously successful, yet little has been written about your capabilities, products and expertise, particularly in the China market.

SA: The core business community and both the governments — both the Chinese government and the U.S. government — know the success that this company has created, not just through increased sales and profit but success in helping to develop China's infrastructure. This isn't the biggest company in China by any means. But it is probably one of the most important, because we provide metals and mining, and other basic infrastructure projects (e.g., water, power, oil) that go a long way to helping the country develop, and to help the peaceful transformation from a planned socialist economy to a cultural democracy in a very peaceful way.

## Mediating Culture and Communication

The issue of peaceful transformation from planned socialist economy to a cultural democracy is significant politically as well as economically in China.[9] Companies such as Foxboro develop a credible presence in China by hiring and training Chinese employees in the work of developing infrastructure in China. The Chinese people also realize tangible results during this very difficult transition period. Companies such as Foxboro provide the necessary infrastructure to make the lives of the Chinese easier and safer, without the need to change the culture or imitate the West in some onerous fashion or fad.

For example, Chinese culture may change greatly as a result of utilizing products that make clean drinking water available to most (if not all) the people. Certainly, the lives of Chinese women would be different — no more carrying (often on poles with hanging buckets) and boiling drinking water or washing clothes on the river bank. The culture may also change due to the availability of electricity and gas in many (if not all) homes in China, just as the lives of American women changed with clean water, washing machines, and dryers, and the use of gas and electric stoves. However, getting to this point will be more difficult for the one billion, two hundred eighty million Chinese than it was for the then less than 200 million citizens of the United States.

It isn't just that China is such a "vast" land (slightly larger than the United States), but that the nation has many truly serious issues to deal with as it moves toward the evolving social and political culture of privatization. Environmental needs are often acute, resulting from hundreds, if not thousands of years of overuse, plus the removal of topsoil (*loess*) as the winds from inner Mongolia sweep across Shanxi and other interior provinces. Vast areas of China are unsuitable for farming without proper equipment and irrigation. Farmers must utilize more efficient farming techniques, more trees must be planted to halt serious erosion of the land, power plants and dams must be built. Further, China's one billion, three hundred million citizens (one billion more than live in the comparable borders of the United States) continue to complicate the equation.

Factoring in the last century's wars, the Cultural Revolution, the Four Modernizations, Tiananmen Square and the burst of development in the coastal cities, one sees that China has come far in the past 20 years — but this growth does not extend significantly to the interior nor to the peasants. Instead, the villages have been given voting rights in an attempt to alleviate distress in the rural regions. The plan is (and has been) to develop the cities first (let them get rich first), which makes sense at certain levels.

Once cities develop fundamental industries through joint ventures with other countries, these lower technology industries can be moved to the interior while more sophisticated technological industries replace them in the cities. In this way and over time, the "big brothers" of the coastal cities will help the "little brothers" of the cities in the interior to also become rich. It's a nice gentle plan but the process of implementation can be — and is— very difficult. Obviously, cities with ports have greater access to world trade and the facilities available for foreign business ventures are consistent with what is needed to develop the manufacturing potential of such cities as Shanghai, Pudong and others.

Contrary to popular American belief, should there be yet another "peasant revolt," or intellectual-worker-military revolt, there is little reason to believe that China's government would be replaced with a more liberal government.[10] More friendly to the U.S., perhaps, but more liberal to its people? Doubtful. Thus, it may be incumbent upon us not to incite further unrest in China. Pragmatically, this is a matter of economics— ours as well as the Chinese. Too much "foreign investment" would be at risk in any major political or revolutionary struggle. Too many Chinese have already died (30 million, 40 million?) in the past century in their desire for good government. Yet another struggle will not yield better results politically for the masses of people. Another revolution will simply mean a transfer of power, with no short or long term gain for the people, socially, economically, or politically. In short, it is in everyone's best interest that all cultural spheres continue to evolve over time. Ultimately, given cultural differences, there is not a 1:1 ratio of understanding of "democracy" and how it works.[11]

The current unrest is, of course, a combination of social, economic and political factors exacerbated by the privatization of many of the state industries. Often in the American media, these factors are ascribed primarily to the communist government, i.e., the fact that the government is communist is responsible for the social unrest. This is not necessarily a correct reading of the situation. In any country, when millions of workers lose their jobs and simultaneously have their benefits cut, there is social unrest and despair. In addition, China, having no democratic tradition, has virtually no institutional infrastructure in place to ease the ills of the evolutionary economic and social changes, as well as develop the political infrastructure. The nature and scope of these problems is multiplied many times over that of similar issues in tiny Taiwan and Korea with their, relatively speaking, minute populations. However, in March of 2002, the BBC News announced China's "details of what is to become the world's largest social security system."[12] That the new program will not cover all

Chinese is obvious. According to a Chinese spokesman, the new program will cover some 200 million people, "but not the majority of the population — more than 800 million rural-based peasants."[13] China's Minister of Labor and Social Security Zhang Zuoji said: "In rural areas ... the main form of insurance is still provided by families which completely conforms to the national condition and ethics of China." China watchers say that the government is intent on "social stability in cities, where potential labor unrest is seen as a threat to the Communist Party's rule."[14] As the above discussion indicates, one might also worry about, should a conservative anti–Western government come to power, the "domino effect," if foreign investment or joint ventures were put at risk through social unrest.

Both Russia and China, as the chief developers of communism and state-owned enterprises, serve as models of this malaise at the end of the Cold War that was won by capitalism. During our talks in Shanghai, we also discussed this perspective and the impact upon the Russian and Chinese societies in the 21st century.

# BACKGROUND OF THE COLD WAR

Following World War II, the Chinese and the Russians both adopted variations of communism as social, political and economic ideology.[15] This was, of course, in direct contrast with the development of democracy (however dubious) and capitalism in the so-called Western World. A line was drawn, cutting the world in half, setting up the battle line between evil (communism) and good (capitalism). Both doctrines are economics-based, but turn on whether that economic base is state ownership or private ownership. This line in the sand was backed by an ever-increasing defense build-up, including nuclear weapons on both sides of the line. On the communist side, enterprises were said to be state-owned. On the capitalist side, enterprises were said to be privately owned. Several times during the almost 50 years of the Cold War, there were "police actions" around the world, small "skirmishes" between client states of the Soviet Union, China and the United States where newly developed weaponry could be deployed, tested, and kill — but there were no formally declared wars.

At another level, supplementing the military buildup, was the economic challenge of competing ideologies. After a while, it became increasingly apparent (even to the governments of the Soviet Union and China) that their state-owned enterprises were not going well and the people were dissatisfied. Unwilling to risk bloody revolution yet another time in the

20th century, both the Soviet Union and China had capitulated to Western economic and military might by 1990. The question was— what to do next? In the case of the Soviet Union, she shed the union and Russia emerged once again, no longer communist in commitment after roughly 75 years. In the case of China, she remains communist at certain levels (as do the republics of the former Soviet Union), but is moving from a state-owned enterprise economy to privatization, following 50 years of state-owned enterprises.

The implications of this seemingly innocent change in ownership are complex and hugely political. First, the change signals the end of the Cold War and wars traditionally have a victor. Using this model and with the triumph in the Western world of capitalism as economic ideology and the failure of communism as economic ideology, then the West "won" the Cold War. Traditionally, when someone wins and someone loses, the victor dictates the terms of the surrender. In this case, the United States (promising aid to the Russians) and its entrepreneurs moved into Russia to impose the "true believer" syndrome on the vanquished and impoverished Russians. The "true believer" syndrome, articulated in the book of that name by Eric Hoffer,[16] asserts that there is inherent instability in the ability of "true believers" to flip flop from one extreme to another.

Alas, this proved to be the case with Russia in the 1990s as capitalist entrepreneurs, Western scholars, businessmen and bankers sought to overhaul the Soviet system without the benefit of appropriate internal legal, social, political and economic infrastructure in place. Many "former" communists managed to skim the available money, as well as manage and divert to foreign banks much of the aid money coming in. The predictable result was that the Russians lost everything. In 2002, the average Russian is worse off under the new regime than under communism and no new plans are forthcoming, despite the intentions of President Valdimir Putin.

Unlike the Russians, the Chinese have fended off the West's accusations that they are moving too slowly. Even so, many, if not most, of the Chinese (especially the 800 million outside of the major coastal cities), are worse off than during the full-blown communist era of Chairman Mao Zedong. Nonetheless, the Chinese are slowly putting the requisite infrastructure in place. But they resist having it imposed upon them —for if the legal-political-economic system is not their creation, they will suffer the dismal fate of Russia. Russia's story is a cautionary tale for the 21st century.[17]

# Interview at Foxboro in Pudong— Business, Governments and Culture

While at the Foxboro facility in Pudong, we also approached this topic with both Chinese and Western employees. What follows are some excerpts from this dialogue:

NLS:　I think the key is "planned" and small stages of development as opposed to attempting to flip-flop from communism to democracy overnight as did the Russians. This had truly disastrous results for the people, the culture, the economic and legal systems, as well as the development of infrastructure compatible with modernity.

SA:　That's a different system. I have made some trips to the Soviet Union. We tried to do a similar thing there that we have done here, but we decided not to do it for many reasons. Going back to the history of China and the Soviet Union, if you follow the history closely you can see why there was a break between them in the 1950s. The Chinese people told the Russian people to go home.

MJM:　I have a question for you and you may want me to turn the tape recorder off. So, I'll ask the question and then, if you would like me to do so, I will turn the recorder off. Your company deals not just with the Chinese, but also with the American government. Given all the diplomatic ups and downs between China and America over the past twenty years, has this ongoing uncertainty affected your work in China?

SA:　No, you can leave it on the record. Obviously in a company like ours with high technology, the industries that we work with often have dual roles, oriented toward both the commercial and the military worlds. Still, we have never had any real problems with the United States government. We work very closely on sensitive technology ... technology that is licensable. We go through the regular channels getting menus and applications. We have never really had any problems.

In the early years, licensing review that we had with our people at DLC required inter-agency review. We never had any major difficulties. But we do have to explain our reasons for doing it and show them the technology. Right now, this company in Shanghai makes the nuclear reactor safety control system for most of the world's nuclear power stations. We have approval from Washington to do that. We recently supplied the reactor and safety control system for the nuclear power station here in China. We supply systems for the United States, the Soviet Union and South Korea. In the case of the controllers in United States, we export the products to our company in the U.S. and then they redistribute it for control purposes to other areas of the world.

MJM:　So there's never been a major problem?

SA:   Never been a major problem in what we deal with. We've always been very honest with what we are doing, who we are doing it with over here, and why we are doing it. Again, back in the early years, even certain integrated circuits required licenses. These days, the Chinese are at a very, very high level technically. There is nothing that we have other than software that they don't currently have in this country.

MJM:   This is a business venture, but I have to believe that you get a great amount of personal satisfaction taking a look at the growth of this country. It seems a business relationship and also much more than that. It seems to me that there must be a great deal of satisfaction over having had a part in the development of China, particularly its infrastructure.

SA:   I think one of the reasons we are still here is not just business satisfaction, though we perceive that in the steps we take each day, or even hour by hour. A big part of it has been the personal satisfaction. It is not a 9-to-5 job, where you work until you are 65 and then you retire. The personal satisfaction of helping someone — seeing changes in the industry, in the society, in the culture — and assisting in the change is a very special feeling that few people would understand.

NLS:   From the mid-eighties on, one recognized that the core issue in China was infrastructure — promoting transportation, communication systems, sewage systems, power plants, oil and water projects, catapulting (or leapfrogging) the Chinese into modernity and later into cyberspace. In 1985-1986, there was little in the way of modern communication and transportation systems. When I would try to describe this world to my [American] students, they would wonder, "Why didn't you buy frozen foods?" They, and all the people I talked with, were so used to the products of infrastructure, they were unable to assess the infrastructure needed to produce frozen foods—clean water, equipment made for the production of frozen foods, refrigerated trucks, good roads to put those trucks on. Not to mention a communication system which allowed people to learn about a shipment on the way in a timely fashion. Trying to help my students visualize this wonderful, yet different world, I would sometimes say, "Oh, this is much too complicated to explain to people who had everything in place when they were born, including highways, trucks, trains, airplanes, frozen and canned food and all the t-shirts one could want in this life."

SA:   You have to understand that Chinese people don't particularly care for frozen food. For thousands of years they have gone to the market twice a day to buy their fresh meat and their fresh vegetables. It's the young people that find it more convenient to go buy something that is frozen and put it in the microwave when they get home.

NLS:   I think that I am trying to make a different point. Students in America don't understand why everybody in the world not only doesn't live as we do, but also doesn't necessarily want to live as we do. So, you have a real gap in understanding that most of the world's peoples have lived for thousands of years without the sophisticated infrastructure which we take for granted (but which was not taken for granted when my father, who is 86, was young).[18]

SA:   That's correct. I think people in general in most Western countries take everything for granted. They have all these things and have never really experienced anything else. So, they think the situation now in America is normal for the rest of the world and that's the benchmark that the rest of the world needs to be measured by.

MJM:   And they often make the decision, at least the students that I deal with, that if a person doesn't take a shower everyday, it's because they choose not to. It's not because they may not have the resources to be able to do that — or to wash their clothes in a certain manner, in other words, for them it is a choice made, as opposed to a way of life or a necessity they may not have the opportunity to have. They may say, "Well, why don't they like frozen food? Don't they understand that the microwave is the way to go?" And you have to say, "Well, not really." They really have no clue in terms of time or history and that stands in the way of understanding the impact of culture on perceptions of choice.

SA:   That's correct. Not too many years ago, in many Western countries—America included—your grandmother and your grandfather probably came over from Europe somewhere. What did they do? They didn't have frozen foods, they didn't have showers, they didn't have this or that and this is a very recent change in the last fifty or sixty years.

NLS:   My grandmother just died at 101. She didn't have shoes when she was a girl, she didn't have a car, and she didn't own a freezer until 1955 or so. Her life spanned the 20th century and the changes were incredible from her birth to her death.

SA:   Well, I have a microwave over here, but haven't used it in 7 years. I have no desire to energy zap the food before I eat it!

NLS:   I wanted to ask you about the context of your business here in the larger context. For instance, have you gone into other developing countries and done essentially the same thing as in China through Foxboro?

SA:   We have over 500 locations throughout the world, many of which are just sales offices. We have 18 different operations. This one in China is the biggest [outside the United States].... Here in China, we have over 200,000,000 U.S. dollars invested in operations.

# KEYS TO SUCCESS IN CHINA—AND AT HOME

Given the considerable investment in U.S. dollars by Foxboro in China, as well as its clear ability to succeed in delivering products suited to the Chinese client needs, the authors felt compelled to "dig" a bit further, and discover the parameters and infrastructure of Foxboro Company. We were also interested in learning, in addition to its corporate structure, more about its integrated tools and strategies for success— market share and profit — in a global market.[19] First, we asked for general advice on how to approach international development from a marketing perspective. Second, we felt it important to discuss training strategies and specific training available to Chinese employees, as well as those American employees sent abroad. Finally, we had been exposed to the concepts of "lean transformation" and its "no inventory" counterpart back home in the Massachusetts Foxboro facility. Would the Chinese facility approximate the U.S. facility in these latter dimensions? We began our questions with our American interviewee. What follows are his answers to some of our questions.

# IMPORTANCE OF MARKET SURVEY, PLANNING AND TRAINING

SA:    Probably one of the most important things to understand is that it is necessary to do a good market survey guided by what you are trying to do here in China. Also, involve your very best people, your specialists, your financial specialists, your technical specialists. Any good plan is short-term, medium-term, and long-term. I think you obviously need to have a short term plan of what you need to accomplish, a sense of equality in the joint venture in the first couple of years, but also you need a medium range plan, as a five year plan or longer. You have to have vision and you need a strategic objective. Ask yourself, "Why am I doing business in this particular country?" "What am I trying to accomplish?" "What are my goals?" Good people must be involved.

You also need to spend a tremendous amount of time training in all the specific disciplines. If you don't spend time on training, most companies will have trouble. One of the reasons that we have been so successful is we have trained hundreds and hundreds of people around the world. Training doesn't stop. Right now I have three engineers in the United States. In August, six more will be going. This isn't a one-week vacation. This is for two, or three, or four months. And in particular, our philosophy here is to train the trainer. Send a few people over and they come back here to Shanghai and they train the rest of the company.

NLS:    I'm impressed that you have put in place the open, well-lighted, clean and clear areas as part of the plant and office's "lean transformation." How do you feel about this program?

SA:    In reality, in any company today, there is one program or another and it really doesn't matter what you call it. But the fact is that savvy companies have programs all the time — forever — whether you realize it or not. That is the only way that you are going to be competitive. Don't forget that we are a global company. We are competing globally, so we are expected to be the best.

# The Lean Transformation and Six Sigma— Mental and Strategic Infrastructure

While visiting the Foxboro, Massachusetts, facility, we were first introduced to the idea of "Lean Transformation" described in Henderson's and Larco's book as "the ultimate strategic weapon."[20] In describing the merits of this transformation, the authors assert:

> You can be the first to deliver precisely what your customers want when they want it with products that are virtually defect free. Unless you are starting a business from scratch, this will not be easy. Nevertheless, we are certain that the benefits to you, your employees, customers, and shareholders, will be worth the effort…. Perhaps the most notable ingredient of a lean organization is a winning attitude…. The first step toward mastery is to master the basics. Here they are:
>   *The lean producer will be exceptionally neat, safe, and clean….*
>   *In the lean producer, products are built just in time (JIT),* and only to customer demand…. *Six sigma quality is designed into the products of the lean producer and built into its manufacturing process….*
>   *Empowered teams make decisions….*
>   *Visual management is used to track performance and to give workers feedback.* Information flows freely… .
>   *The final fundamental of the lean enterprise is the relentless pursuit of perfection.* The primary goal is to provide value. This pursuit is ensured by procedures that institutionalize the search.[21]

The authors warn, however, that "A lean factory alone does not make a lean enterprise."[22] The concept must illuminate every area of the company to insure corporate and customer satisfaction.

Both Foxboro facilities have implemented the "lean transformation" throughout the company from design engineering to human resources to purchasing.[23] During our visits to facilities in both Massachusetts and

Shanghai we saw evidence of this lean transformation. In both facilities there was no clutter, no mess, no dirt or grease, no equipment lying around. Reference charts for production were visible at all work stations. The plant facilities were clean, bright and well-lighted. True to the "lean transformation," there was no visible inventory. There were however, cards indicating specific orders from customers. In Shanghai, we watched customers being trained in the usage of the equipment — hardware and software — which they had ordered. In both facilities, the atmosphere was focused, yet tranquil and without unnecessary noise or dangers. In an interview during our visit in Massachusetts, one senior executive (SE) explained:

> SE:    As we walk through the factory, we will see the various techniques in visual management. A visual management tool is a concept that we use to be able to status the works out. Whether it be a material issue, a quality issue, or even a people resource planning issue, the lead people and the supervisors in the factory manage their work cells to the extent that they will do resource planning and all of these things are displayed on the visual board. So, it's a tool for those folks that work in the cell, for those folks that work in other cells that may complement that cell to understand the status of it. Visual management is important.
>
> In addition to visual management, there's employee empowerment, which is again what we practice and demonstrate that by allowing these folks to make their own decisions, they make their own plans for project completion. This includes the decision to work overtime or to judge if a part does not fit correctly. In the latter case, they may partner with a process engineer and come together (in the group meeting place) to assess what is right and then go forward with that decision.
>
> Part of the process that we use to improve processes is to map out information flow and material, or product flow. We want to make sure that they're *in sync* with each other and that's one of the Six Sigma tools, it's one of the Lean values stream mapping tools. It's a real closed loop philosophy and it involves everyone.
>
> NLS:    And communication is the underlying concept pulling it altogether.
>
> SE:    The paramount requirement is to communicate this stuff, and we launched this effort probably 15 months ago. We all had to study and read books to get on board.... This factory has always been on the leading edge of these initiatives. As testimony to that, you can see all the awards we've won over the last 10 to 12 years.
>
> MJM:    May I ask a dumb question? I may actually ask many but this will be the first of many. I first came across the Six Sigma concept through reading a book about Jack Welch.[24] Did he originate the Six Sigma concept?

SE:   The principles of Six Sigma have been around for about 20 years. What Six Sigma does is to package them in such a way that you have these principles in a toolbox. Our program is very similar to the ones that GE and Motorola have and they have been very successful. We started this program in late 1996. At this facility we have both green belts and black belts.

NLS:   That sounds like karate. Is this an East-West concept you have put in place?

SE:   Certification is very important when you do business globally. You cannot sell products into Europe if the company is not certified. Therefore we employ techniques and strategies to attain and surpass global standards. To attain this, we pay attention to the workplace, down to the smallest detail. In our next interview, we learn how this is accomplished with the aid of skilled Chinese engineers, translators and other workers, closed-loop training and the leadership of the green belts and black belts.

NLS:   How much do you emphasize globalization here?

SE:   Quite extensively. From a purchasing perspective, we gather material from companies all over the world. We also have customers all over the world. In this day and age, if you are not global, then you're not competitive. Our products cater to the chemical, oil, gas industry, food, pharmaceutical, pulp, paper and utility companies. You find those all over the world.

NLS:   Does that mean that when you grow, you grow by countries? Or do you stay here? I know there is the economic factor and the worker factor — how do you deal with globalization regarding economics, workers and outsourcing to other countries?

SE:   Let me give you an example. We've just recently decided to outsource all of our [surface-mount] production to another Invensys company in Mexico. This is happening as we speak [March 2001]. We partnered with them and resource sharing was a part of it. First, we needed to communicate and learn about their capabilities. They needed to see what our capabilities are. There's been a continuous exchange of that transfer of knowledge over the last two or three months when this project first started. We also have a facility in Shanghai.

NLS:   When your people go abroad to either China or Mexico, how are they taken care of? That is, who makes their arrangements for visas, hotels, cars and other travel?

SE:   It's a mutual effort.

# FOXBORO COMPANY AS GLOBAL COMPETITOR

Following up on the above interview when we arrived in Shanghai, we talked with a Chinese engineer, Lu Yun, product manager and lean manufacturing coordinator for one product family at the Shanghai facility, called SCADA. The full name for Lu Yun's product family is "supervisory control and data acquisition." Lu Yun's background is in engineering (automatic control engineering). Lu Yun and his colleagues provided us with our tour of the Shanghai (Pudong) facility, a great lunch and fascinating talk.

> NLS:   Let's begin with you. Tell us a little about your background, if you will.

> LY:   I am actually one of the local people. I was born in this city, and I got my degree from JiaoTong University. I'm proud of graduating from that school because it is almost the MIT of China.

> NLS:   When did you graduate?

> LY:   I graduated in 1993. Since that time 7 or 8 years, I have worked here. When I came to this company I was a product engineer. I was responsible for some products and also for some of the manufacturing processes. Since then, I have been promoted to product manager of SCADA products. This is a product assembly, utilizing the technology from the Foxboro Company in Australia.

> MJM:   Do you spend much time in Australia?

> LY:   I have made several trips there, yes. Sometimes for training because there is a necessary technique transfer from there to here and also sometimes for other issues.

> NLS:   Because I know nothing about engineering, I am curious about how the process goes from your hearing about a project, going to that site and visiting the project, to what happens in your engineer's mind as you try to create a workable system for the project? Take, for instance, a power plant.

> LY:   Some of our products will go to power plants.

> NLS:   Then please describe to us what you do when you first receive such a project. What considerations come first?

> LY:   OK. First the decision is made by the Foxboro family, maybe because they think that it will be less expensive to make this product in

China, rather than Australia or some other country. My product comes from Australia. This is a project in which we transfer a product to Shanghai to manufacture. Because this Shanghai facility is a joint venture, we must evaluate whether or not it will be profitable for us to do this. So the first thing we do is obtain the drawings to see what this product is like and if we already have this capability. When we discuss capability, we mean many things. Do we have the right equipment? Do we have the right people? Do we have testing capability? The drawings help us decide this. In the case of the new product, we have most of the ingredients right here. It's just a new product family but not a brand new technique. Because the drawings indicate the component parts needed (or to be ordered), we will build the whole bill of materials for each market system. This way, we collect and connect with all the companies needed to complete this job. Then we calculate and see the cost involved. We then ask for Australia's cost calculations. If negotiations go well, we reach a financial agreement and decide that we can do the project. Then we start to slowly transfer the information.

NLS:    However, in the beginning, you must confer with the joint venture partner?

LY:    Yes.

NLS:    Physically, is your joint venture partner operating from here at this facility? Mr. John Sun, your managing director, explained to us that the Deputy Director is always from the Chinese side, while the managing director is from the Foxboro side. Unfortunately, we were unable to meet with the deputy director.

LY:    Actually, the China partner is now a holding company. A few years ago we didn't call it a holding company. As you know, the rules and regulations governing business arrangements are rapidly changing in China.[25]

NLS:    The director and the deputy director — they can question whether or not you have the right equipment and the right people and that you are part of the decision-making process?[26]

LY:    Yes.

NLS:    So, may we go back to the process? You've explained that technically and financially you agree to make this happen in Shanghai. What comes next?

LY:    First, the people from Foxboro Australia visit Shanghai to see our capabilities and to find out what we may need from them. Also, our people visit Australia, tour the plant and get an idea of the steps in the process. Then, some people like me (and other product engineers) go to

Australia for training. The training focuses on diagnosis, testing — the whole process. At that time, we will develop the drawings. Drawing is important — we have to know all the information contained on the drawing. We then make certain that we have lines of communication. That is the first phase. Then, we return with the drawings and calculate what components need to be purchased, which brings in purchasing at that point.

As product engineer, I may have to order test equipment or other equipment. Then I must train the operators. For this, we use the team approach: purchasing, training, courtesy people, operators and engineers. We demonstrate what must be done to produce the product. All the drawings are in English but the operators cannot read English. So we do translations and also write out a worksheet, which will tell them how to do their job.[27]

MJM:   So, who is in charge of making all these pieces come together?

LY:   As product manager, I am responsible for what happens.

MJM:   In addition to all of this, I understand that you have the "black belt" in lean transformation. How is that tied in to what you do as product manager?

LY:   You mentioned GE and Motorola earlier. In 1997, Foxboro introduced the Six Sigma program to improve the competitiveness of the company. They first started it at Foxboro in the United States. Then they extended the program to all their companies around the world. Each company has one or two champions. In this company, two senior administrators received their training in the U.S. Their job is to make a commitment to all that happens. They are the top level. At the second level is the lean manufacturing coordinator. That's my job, in addition to product manager. A coordinator is also a program manager. So, that person is responsible for all the projects that happen here and reports to headquarters (in the U.S.) what happens here. Now I am the coordinator. Level three is the black belt, the most powerful in karate. Mr. Wong, the deputy chief engineer is a black belt also, and then we have the green belt.

Lu Yun then described the arrangement within the Shanghai plant. Each department has at least one black belt, e.g., purchasing and quality control. Each is thoroughly trained over a period of 4 months. The candidate attends classes for one week each month taught by champions or black belts, either from the States, China or elsewhere. A project following the principles of lean transformation (described above) serves as an exam. At Foxboro Shanghai, there are six black belts. The black belts in turn train the green belts. LuYun, as a black belt, trains about 20 green belts. Again, each green belt must a project illustrating mastery of the concepts and applications of Lean Transformation. When asked how people were admitted into the program, LuYun said that they were generally identified as potential black or green belts. First, both black and green belts must be able to use the computer as a tool. Second, one needs analytical skills so a background in mathematics is desirable. Not all the staff at any company have such skills. Lacking them, they would not be identified for the program. The quality of the project accomplished helps the decision-makers determine whether the candidate is at a management or supervisory level. Theoretically, candidates may select their project; pragmatically, the project will be about some product the candidate is working on. We then asked Lu Yun to give us an example of such a project:

> LY:   OK, let's take my project. SCADA products is a product family. It is not just one or two products— it is several hundred products. My project was how to control the quality and save on cost. When we said OK to this project, we quoted a cost of … let's say $100 … and Foxboro Australia said $120. On this we have a 10 percent margin. So what we wanted to do here is to reduce the manufacturing costs so that we can get a better profit margin. My project was to improve the quality and improve delivery. To be competitive, you must meet the customer's requirements, and the customers always need their product as soon as possible. We wanted to reduce the cost — this was my target. First came the measurement of where we are right now. Then we analyzed the situation to determine how to improve the outcome in cost and product. Third, we developed improvements to make this happen. We go through all the phases and meet our target. For developing and implementing this process in cost reduction and quality improvement, I succeeded in attaining my black belt and certificate. Afterwards, I also initiated such projects to completion.

Not only did Lu Yun explain the process of product improvement and the impact of lean transformation and the hierarchy of command implicit in that process, i.e., champions, to black belts, to green belts, to teams, he also is an example of efficient and equitable utilization of available resources. Lu Yun is a product of one of China's best universities (the MIT of China), and has a place in the development of China, through the integration of international resources, trainers and training programs which contribute to China's growth through the development of infrastructure compatible with China's needs. While it is true that, like all developing countries, China offers a less expensive labor force, it is also true that he works in an industry which makes products which contribute to a better life for all Chinese. Further, the Chinese government, planners and educators had the forethought to include programs in their universities (which are still state-supported, though not totally, as in the past), which would enable Lu Yun and others like him to prepare for this millennium. This is especially important given the dearth of educational opportunities from 1966 to 1976 when almost no one was educated in China.[28] Anyone travelling through China in those days or until roughly 1990 would have seen a different world, especially in education in China. Those who chose to work in China back in the eighties often faced severe difficulties in adjusting to the culture and lifestyle. Thinking about this, we inquired into the policies of Foxboro Company regarding the training and living quarters available to those who went to China from the U.S. in the early days of Foxboro in China.

## CULTURE SHOCK AND BEYOND

In talking with senior administrators at Foxboro Company and given our own experiences as professors in China, we wanted to know what preparation Foxboro people had for living and working in China, short-term and long-term. As we have observed in other instances, culture shock may lead to depression and other illnesses. However, with personnel like one of the secretaries we met — Chris Du — it seems less likely in this environment than in other venues. This is no accident, as we discovered from further questioning:

> NLS: Another question. When you bring your people over here [to China], do you have to deal with culture shock, and if so, what do you do?
>
> SA: Yes, especially in the early years. We had many people who would come over here. Those of us who were here for some time simply molded ourselves into the environment. But people who came for a short time often had trouble adapting. I had one person who came over for about one month, and he brought three seaman trunks full of food. I said, "You don't need that." After a week, he couldn't manage himself on the job so we had to send him home. I think that the selection of people that do come here, even in these days [2002], is done quite carefully. We want people with the right skills yes, but also people with the right attitude, with an open frame of mind, people who aren't too far to the left or too far to the right. One always has to be aware of these factors.
>
> NLS: And how do you determine whether they have the right attitude or not or if they have an open frame of mind? Is there some process that you go through to identify these people?
>
> SA: It's all the same process. In my case, I've been around the company

for 35 years, so I know mostly everybody who's going to come over here, so we make a judgment call. A guy with the seaman trunks full of food is a warning that things will not work well. Best to bring someone else in.

Today, it's quite different, especially in Shanghai, which has name brand shops, is a big city and offers the amenities of any big city. Also, our people here [China] have been going over there [U.S.] for 20 years so there is a lot of understanding between the two facilities. You've got a commitment to a common cause.

NLS: When you bring your people in from abroad, do you take care of settling them in? In short, does your personnel office handle the day to day living arrangements prior to their arrival?

SA: Basically that is correct. All you have to do is land here. We take care of the necessary work permits, green cards, brown cards, that sort of thing. You don't really have to be too concerned about it. In my case, I just landed. I didn't tell anybody in America I was coming here. I just got here and everything was taken care of for me. I have to report different places, find different things, supply different information, but other than that, no trouble for me whatsoever. Zero. Not a concern at all.

NLS: And the living quarters — people are happy with their quarters?

SA: I've had no complaints. I've heard real horror stories from other companies but Foxboro people have not had difficulties. When I relocated to Shanghai, the second time I came over, two suitcases, that's it, nothing else. Zero. It's a very simple lifestyle.

MJM: It seems to me that the company takes a realistic look at the whole, not only the Chinese company itself, but also your employees. It's not just about working, but about how one lives.

SA: You have to. You have to take reasonable care of your people, whether they are from the U.S. or China. There are times when machines are absolutely required to do the job and it cannot be done by hand. Then there are other times, when you need human intervention to do the job. So, we have a mix here. People are our biggest asset, not machines.

NLS: Your people [Foxboro] helped to write the basic rules and laws in China for joint ventures in cooperation with the Chinese government and I realize that they are very complex. Could you give us some significant rules that are an absolute must for companies coming here to be able to work with?

SA: That's a difficult question now that China is about to enter into the World Trade Organization (WTO). Many rules and regulations are being relaxed in anticipation of this. Rules are changing daily. Many of the requirements for setting up different enterprises or joint ventures are being changed now because of the entry into the WTO. It will continue to get easier and easier to do business. However, that doesn't mean it is going to be easier to be successful.

MJM: Exactly. Because running it and setting it up are two different things.

NS: I think you are right about training being a major requirement for success.

SA: In the early days of the joint venture, we had a whole training department and we basically had teachers here with different skills and we taught everything. We taught everything from finance to communication skills to English language to translation from Mandarin to English and so forth. Right now we continue to have training at that level but we also have a training center here for our customers. We have a classroom. We have computers. We train our end users on the use of the product. Training is crucial.

# SUMMING UP

As part of the global community, Foxboro Company has demonstrated excellence here and abroad. Unlike many American companies, Foxboro is not peddling "meaningless growth;" rather, it produces the "invisible" infrastructure necessary to aid in both infrastructure maintenance and the implementation of infrastructure where there is none. Clearly, while making a profit, they also make a difference in many ways, particularly in China. Unlike McDonald's or KFC, the Foxboro product infrastructure will enable the Chinese to achieve their goals for this century. Through attention to people, product, communication, the ability to adapt and listen to the culture, as well as to create cross-cultural commitment to excellence, Foxboro is still in China after 20 years.

# Final Thoughts: Getting to Yes Between East and West

> Confucianism, the moral and religious system based on the teachings of Confucius, began with the family and an ideal model of relations between family members. It then generalized this family model to the state, and to an international system (the Chinese world order).[1]

Even after the smog and debris of the old Soviet Bloc had dissipated, the new "world order" was not clear-cut, due, in part, to the emergence of China and other Asian nations as major contenders in world trade. In short, the awakening of the "Confucian Dragons" in the 20th century mandated the Western world to pay close attention to them. Through our work with students and delegations in the People's Republic of China and in the United States, we have come to better understand not only Confucianism, but the vital relationship between perception, theory and practice, as practiced by Chinese societies, no matter what form of "ism" they may follow. In an essay entitled "On Practice," Mao Zedong says,

> The perceptual and the rational are qualitatively different, but are not divorced from each other; they are unified on the basis of practice. Our practice proves that what is perceived cannot at once be comprehended

and that only what is comprehended can be more deeply perceived. Perception only solves the problem of phenomena; theory alone can solve the problem of essence. The solving of both these problems is not separable in the slightest degree from practice. Whoever wants to know a thing has no way of doing so except by coming into contact with it, that is, by living (practicing) in its environment.[2]

Mao's observations are pertinent to those persons practicing naturalistic methodology, with its emphasis on phenomenology, fieldwork and ethnography — and those interested in successful (equitable) East-West negotiations in today's rapidly changing alliances.

## CHINA'S DEVELOPMENT, GLOBALIZATION AND AMERICAN BUSINESS

The outcome of globalization is not yet in view, particularly in developing countries where it is sometimes seen as the latest incarnation of colonialism. (See Chapter 2 for further discussion.) Specifically, few would venture to predict the outcome for China's economic, social and political future, especially after its entry into the World Trade Organization (WTO). On the one hand, China has wanted to enter the WTO for a very long time; on the other, the massive legal and political ramifications of this act may start "a prairie fire." Social unrest may spiral out of control, as more and more state industries coalesce with foreign investors and strive to meet the conditions of entrance into the WTO. In turn, annihilation of the "iron rice bowl"— the backbone of China's social, political and economic system for nearly 50 years— has already cut deeply into the fabric of China's social order. Enmity between city workers and rural population may increase as the disparity between the two— the rich and the poor — grows greater. This is also true for other developing areas of the world — Africa, Asia, the Middle East, and South America — where most of the world's people live, often in abysmal poverty. The need for the West to become conversant with cultures of other countries is urgent. In the past, we in the West, particularly in the United States, have not felt it necessary to understand the lives of others. We are the world's largest purveyors of military infrastructure, coupled with many battalions and bases around the world. Until recently, many Americans felt invulnerable and powerful; immune to attack. Since September 11, 2001, however, we have learned that this is no longer true (if it were ever so). Belatedly, we see the wisdom of understanding "the other," even if only to protect ourselves against devastation. There seems to be more to gain than mere protection — a truly "interconnected" world would be both economically linked and militarily enforced as well as mutually committed to the care and enrichment of the disenfranchised — wherever they are in the world's power structure.

The authors of this book argue that knowledge — not unfettered military prowess— is power. Far less emphasis on military action to achieve economic goals is imperative for future survival. In addition, stronger emphasis on other cultural elements, as well as equitable arrangements amongst the world's nations— rich and poor — is necessary. For the sake of the homeless and hopeless men, women and children around the globe, we must learn about others in more than a superficial way, and step in to help.

This may mean helping to build basic infrastructure which provides clean water, electricity, transportation, education, and communications, and which incorporates environmental protection. Further, we must accelerate access of all nations to affordable medicines, vaccines or loans— whatever it takes to even approach (in many cases) a livable life (more than simply proclaiming a "free election.")[3] Globalization has this potential. As demonstrated through the case studies in this book, there are multinational corporations which, while making a profit, also promote positive impact in China (and elsewhere), through thoughtful and persistent application of the best in American business practices:

1. ethical and responsible business behavior;
2. corporate codes of conduct;
3. new ideas and information technology;
4. Western business practices;
5. environmental, energy efficiency, health, and safety standards;
6. compensation, benefits, and training;
7. volunteerism, charitable giving, and community activism; and
8. rule of law.[4]

In "Corporate Social Responsibilities in China: Practices by U.S. Companies," the authors note that the "DaimlerChrysler Corporate University provides cross-cultural conflict training seminars for executive managers of its joint venture in China to improve communications between both partners." [5] DaimlerChrysler (Chapter 8) also has an Integrity Code according to this report, which "establishes strict rules on managing supplier relationships, protecting the environment, and abiding by anti-bribery and export control laws. These rules are universally implemented by DaimlerChrysler."[6]

Similar comments can be made about the other corporate case studies in this book, researched in both the United States and in China. In Shanghai, as indicated in the Foxboro case study (Chapter 9), we toured the facilities and observed the working conditions for ourselves. We listened to the voices of employees tell us their perspectives on China and on the work of Foxboro in China. We observed clients being trained to use the product hardware and software. In addition, the products Foxboro generates help to make possible the implementation of much of China's sorely needed infrastructure.

The Holiday Inn hotel network (Chapter 7) is yet another example of corporate responsibility and the creation of infrastructure needed to boost China's economy, enhancing tourism through judicious integration into the local culture, including celebrating the Chinese holidays (Appendix B) and encouraging community involvement and service. In addition to business travelers and foreign tourists, Holiday Inn hotels have a large following with Chinese tourists. Further, as we have seen, the policies in place for utilizing local employees, in addition to training them as necessary for the tourist industry, adds credibility to the enterprise.

Other case studies included in this book help one to understand the challenges facing both the Chinese and complexities of business ventures in the People's Republic of China. General Electric's (Chapter 6) underwriting of a children's television series in China is typical of their innovative style. The metamorphosis of *Sesame Street* into *Zhima Jie* required creating an intercultural bridge between several unlikely players— the American Children's Television Workshop (CTW); Shanghai TV (STV); the Chinese government; and General Electric. This is a tribute to careful negotiation and respectful concern for cultural values. Twenty years ago, this coalition would have been fraught with insurmountable difficulties.

Intercultural relationships brokered by common interests have brought the United States and China closer. But, there is much more to do, particularly in understanding the impact of culture upon negotiation styles. In the next few pages we discuss intercultural negotiating issues and approaches.

# NEGOTIATING CULTURES

In generating the case studies in this book (utilizing conventional library and critical methodology, as well as extensive descriptive field work, including participant observation, interviews, and negotiations), the authors generate a feel for contemporary China.[7] We think that Chinese scholars and negotiators may also find this book useful to help probe the (implicit and explicit) Western *weltanschauung* so evident in this book.

The hidden difficulties in intercultural communication, and particularly in business and trade negotiations, can be overcome with some effort on the part of Western negotiators and the institutions that they represent. We have seen this in each case study discussed in this book. Though filled with untoward events and adventures, the art exchange (Chapter 5) was an aesthetic and intercultural achievement, remarkable in its time and place. Success in this endeavor quite literally depended upon the quality of communication generated by negotiators of good will, relying on a win-win strategy, rather than "hard-liners," from the East or the West.

Quality of communication necessarily takes into account both the verbal aspects of communication interactions and the non-verbal aspects of the communication process. Communication seen as a process— ongoing, without beginning and end, verbal and non-verbal — is at best complicated. At worst, it is chaotic. Within this context, understanding the communication process suggests that one explore two important concepts— perception and applied perspective — as fundamental to the successful intercultural communication and negotiation process.

## GETTING TO YES

The perspective advocated here is from Fisher and Ury in *Getting to YES*.[8] Known as "principled negotiation," as opposed to "positional bargaining," the style is not only principled but is the most pragmatic approach to negotiating with the Confucian-based culture in the People's Republic of China.[9] The grounding attitude is that of "principled negotiation," rather than "positional bargaining." Positional bargaining precludes a "win-win" ending. Fisher and Ury's concepts are especially significant when considering the negotiating process in Confucian-based cultures.

In addition, the norms, forms and non-verbals of Confucian-based cultures in relation to the actual negotiation process and context are important to consider. Pragmatic, yet crucial, non-verbal "signposts" and other seemingly trivial issues often take precedence over individuals and contractual issues.

Americans often feel that, unlike persons from other cultures, they are free to do as they like. Yet, we are all bound by rules and governed by our assumptions of "what ought to be," consciously or unconsciously.

On-the-ground contact with another culture makes us acutely aware of this in ways that no other experience can generate. Finally, regardless of the end state of the "new world order," the emerging order mandates an understanding of the social values grounding the negotiation styles of other market forms (such as the Four Dragons, but most particularly those of the People's Republic of China).[10]

## CONFUCIAN CONCEPTS IN NEGOTIATION

The five Confucian relationships (Chapter 1) are the foundation of the state — the linchpin of the Confucian-Chinese worldview. Coupled with the concept of *guanxi* (relations), the two concepts have been taken for granted by Western scholars. Thus, the either-or dichotomy continues, perpetuating the myth that the Chinese have no sense of self. This, in turn, fosters beliefs about the nature of the Chinese person as individual and Chinese society as a viable entity. These Confucian ideals may not always exist in fact, or in the act. Further, the authors of this book suggest that relatively few (and none of the above) interpersonal relationship or negotiation studies have been done in mainland China.

On the other hand, much of our work has been done in the PRC and all of our interviews are with students and colleagues from the PRC, conducted and recorded either on the mainland or in the United States. Historical-critical research has enabled us to glimpse some fundamental differences in the 20th century development of Confucian-based cultures such as Hong Kong, Taiwan, Korea and the PRC.

In the aftermath of the Cultural Revolution and the immediate cultural incursions of Western culture, it is possible that Chinese students began to think in terms of "I," and to conduct an altered version of traditional Confucian "relationships" (or *guanxi*). Based on the experience of the authors, this is a possibility (Chapters 4 and 5). At a deeper and more subtle level, the term *guanxi* has the additional dimension of relationships as resources (see comments by Shi Hong, a student, in Chapter 1). It includes the elements of "insiders" and outsiders," which are not necessarily part of the Confucian philosophy. This complex concept is often misunderstood by westerners and complicates negotiation with Confucian-based cultures. This discussion may be better understood within the context of the "win-win" orientation or Fisher and Ury's "principled negotiation" strategies.

## PRINCIPLED NEGOTIATION

Principled negotiation, under a number of different labels, has been advocated by many conflict and argument scholars in the communication journals, texts and books for well over twenty years.[11] In "The Win-Win Conflict Resolution Strategy: A Dramatistic Analysis," Diane Metthe[12] demonstrates that the "win-win" and "win-lose" conflict positions discussed by Frost and Wilmot (among others) are analogous to Fisher and Ury's position of "principled negotiation" and "positional bargaining."[13] Metthe describes the primary concerns of "principled negotiation as: (1) to separate the people from the problem; (2) to focus on interests, not positions; (3) to generate a variety of possibilities before deciding what to do; and (4) to insist that the result be based on some objective standards."[14]

Since the publication of *Getting to YES*, Fisher and Ury's premises have been discussed in scholarly journals and popular publications and subjected to critical review, in part, because the communication process aspect of negotiation was not given sufficient attention. Whether one calls the approach "win-win/win-lose" or "principled negotiation/positional bargaining," it has heuristic value, particularly in intercultural negotiations. At its base, principled negotiation calls for close attention to transactional communication concepts such as mutual respect, empathy, equality, relationships, listening, consultation and the realization that meaning is in people, not in words. Thus, one must look to the total communication exchange and bridge the divide between verbal and non-verbal communication, or, put another way, look to the interdependence and interrelationships of negotiation as a communication system.

## ACTIONS SPEAK LOUDER THAN WORDS

Intercultural negotiation seen as a relationship-building process necessitates that the participants (particularly Westerners) acquaint themselves with the deep context of the culture. Beyond the obvious, i.e., reading Chinese history, eating Chinese take-out and recognizing the names Deng Xiaoping and Tiananmen Square, what is needed to conduct negotiations leading to successful relationships for both parties? What are the expected norms of behavior for Westerners negotiating in Confucian societies, particularly the mainland Chinese? What are the assumptions held by the negotiators? What is happening that is implicit — not verbalized? In short, what does one need to know about the culture one is visiting? Some norms, such as business cards, seating arrangements at banquets, notions of hierarchy, and designated leaders, are common to all (not just Confucian) cultures. Other concerns, such as what to wear when traveling on a train in China and other pertinent travel tips apply in the People's Republic of China in 2002 only.

As fast as China is developing (and assuming that the trajectory is fairly smooth), many comments made here will not be applicable by 2008 — the year of the Beijing Olympics. The Beijing Olympics will significantly alter the face of China. Given the resolution of the Chinese people and their government, as well as their proven ability to undertake and achieve monumental change, they will be ready for the world to descend on China for the 2008 Olympics. Examples of the variety and depth of coordinated projects throughout China include the ongoing, thoughtful "restructuring-from-the-ground-up" of the entrenched and enculturated economic system. This is also being coordinated with the higher education system, transportation, communication and clean water, amongst a plethora of other concerns. Ironically, things may go easier (and faster) when a nation starts with virtually nothing — save one's people and a determination — to once again be a player on the world stage.

# NORMS FOR NEGOTIATION

## *Team Negotiation*

One of the most important points to stress at the outset of this discussion is that persons from all Confucian-based nations usually negotiate in teams. They also often use an interpreter (even when they speak English well), and rarely discuss business with only one negotiator, especially a non-native (i.e., a lone American negotiator). The Chinese seem to enjoy delegations, perhaps due in part to past delegations sent centuries ago to pay tribute to the Chinese emperors. More to the point, sending delegations to negotiate incorporates the Confucian principle of "the collective" over "the individual" in decision-making, seemingly unlike the American individualistic approach. A negotiator on his or her own cannot negotiate (or appear to negotiate) and make decisions for the (invisible) group. Representing a negotiating "team" demonstrates that the individual is a respected member of the collective, not a renegade or a self-aggrandizing Western clone. It's also important to remember that each person in a delegation is perceived to have a specific function — the seemingly designated leader may not be the leader.[15] As a result, negotiating on one's own tends to diminish status and therefore treatment — and both sides lose face.

A Western delegation should have at least three or four members. Clearly, some thought must be given as to how many persons are needed to complete the negotiations; however, most negotiations require a "chief" negotiator or leader, a "coordinator," and a translator.

The "chief" negotiator is the person empowered to make all major social and communication process decisions for the group. Both insiders and outsiders look to him or her, especially in the formal communication of the negotiation process.

The "coordinator" assists the chief negotiator by handling the specific details of daily life. (This is particularly important if the group plans to travel away from the major population centers such as Beijing or Shanghai into the countryside of the PRC; communication and transportation arrangements can become complicated and time consuming). This person should also be able to transcribe notes and know where to go for necessary supplies and help. In short, the coordinator will take care of the details and the daily schedule.[16]

The interpreter-translator, preferably bilingual as opposed to speaking English as a second language, should be able to speak both the national language (*putonghua* or Mandarin) as well as the specific dialect for the area, e.g., Cantonese.

Finally, except in very special circumstances, such as a woman's delegation visiting women in a Confucian-based country, it is important to note that a man should be selected as the chief negotiator, or leader. This may sound chauvinistic, but it is merely expedient. Few women hold high positions in any relevant hierarchy within China (not unlike America). With the many other dimensions of growth the country is experiencing at this time, a sexual revolution is not imminent. Do include a woman in the group, if appropriate.

A negotiating team should also allow enough time for the Chinese to highlight their history and culture to foreigners through visits to museums, temples and elaborate receptions in the homes of high-ranking officials. These cultural forays provide all members of the negotiating team the opportunity to learn other aspects of the culture, enhancing the negotiation process. Otherwise, you may be whisked from hotel to meeting place to hotel again, never seeing anything but the airport, the inside of a taxi or your hotel. Learning the history and culture of the society will aid negotiations, providing opportunities to develop the relationships central to Confucian negotiations and successful partnerships in joint ventures. Further, such interactions, with norms of behavior in mind, can enhance "face" for all concerned.

## Time

The concept of time also affects negotiations. In *The Dance of Life: The Other Dimension of Time*, Edward T. Hall describes what he calls monochronic and polychronic time.[17] He maintains that Americans live in monochronic time (M-time — doing one thing at a time), while Japanese and similar cultures live in polychronic time (P-time — involving people and completing transactions, rather than sticking to strict schedules). Hall says that nations with high technological involvement tend to "mix" the two times. Thus, as China continues to develop its technological capabilities, differences in the perceptions of time may have less impact.

## Space and Privacy

Finally, the concept of space and its utilization differs between East and West. When the Chinese build the foreign expert's quarters or guesthouses, they exercise the belief that smaller quarters are more functional. In a country that allows its citizens central heating in the north, but not in the south,[18] resources are scarce. Those amenities, which Americans take for granted, are for foreigners and a tiny elite.

The utilization of space is important in other ways also, as in "my space" and "your space." Non-verbal communication studies indicate that distance between people is different in different cultures. For instance, Middle Easterners tend to stand closer than do Americans. Americans, on the other hand, carry an enhanced "space bubble" around them. This may be connected to their high degree of individualism. When someone moves into an American's space, there is dismay and an attempt to realign the encounter, to regain space, even to the point of backing up.

In China, living in an expansive space is nearly impossible. Currently, there are more than one billion three hundred million Chinese living in a space approximately the size of the United States. (By comparison, only two hundred eighty million people live in the United States.) China's cities, with the influx of peasants and workers seeking "to get rich" like the city dwellers, have grown rapidly. For instance, in the late eighties, Shanghai had approximately 11 million people; it now has more than 16 million inhabitants. People tend to live whole families to a room and often share cooking facilities with others. Chinese seem to like living close together and sharing more than do most Westerners. This affinity for closeness may also be expedient, particularly in winter. Living in close quarters, the concept of privacy also differs.[19]

## *Business Cards and Banquets*

In addition to issues of space and time, rank and position are extremely important to Chinese negotiators. Make certain that each member of the negotiating team has business cards made, and that they carry them at all times. Not having a card readily available denotes lack of status and respect for the person and the situation. Also, it's important to remember to imprint cards on both sides—one side in English, in Chinese characters on the other side. Younger or less important people should offer their cards first to older or more important people.

Business cards are offered at first meeting after the handshake. Try to remember to offer cards at all times, though not to the same person twice. Offer the card with both hands, one slightly behind the other. Receive the offered card with both hands. Do not casually put the card in your pocket, nor fold it. Examine it carefully and remember the name, at least the last name and the main title. Put the card away carefully in your card case. The recipient of your card will do the same. Sometimes (particularly in Taiwan), in deference to Western custom, the last name is not given first but last. Your interpreter should clarify this for you. In China, names are usually written last name first; thus in the name "Tao Benyi," Tao is the last name, Benyi is the first. Therefore, if you cannot remember the entire name, call the person Mr. Tao. Benyi is the first name and reserved for close friends and family unless otherwise indicated.

As to the banquet itself, set your mind at ease — your hosts will provide you with a knife, a fork, and a soup spoon, as well as chopsticks. Therefore, you will be able to eat. If you can, practice with chopsticks prior to your trip. The effort will be noticed and if you have any problems with chopsticks, your hosts will help you. This is not a matter for embarrassment; rather the Chinese will be delighted that you have taken the trouble to try. Again, this small effort can only contribute to the communication process. Other suggestions:

1. Arrive at the designated banquet room or hall a little before time.

2. Shake hands and offer your card to all those newly presented; a slight bow is nice if you've mastered it. Repeat the name to yourself. Give your name clearly. Do not shake hands heartily.

3. Stand aside and wait until you are told where to sit. Chinese seating tends to be somewhat formal. Sometimes there are place cards. In any case, your hosts will make certain you sit in the proper place.

4. If you are the leader, you may be placed directly across from the Chinese leader (tables are often round). Or, in some cases, you may sit

next to the Chinese leader. The test of how important you are perceived to be is two-fold. If there is more than one table, leaders will sit at the first table, others will sit at the second or third tables; if there is only one table, the leaders will usually sit directly across from one another, or next to one another.

5. Interpreters are carefully placed strategically around all tables so that you will have no problem talking to your banquet partner.

6. After the most important person has arrived, all will sit. Never sit before the leader has arrived. Never eat before the leader indicates (by offering food to his or her opposite) that the meal has begun.

7. Toasting is an integral part of banquet ritual. Do not drink unless the first toast has been given. The host will give the first toast, the visiting leader should give a toast in response. Others may give toasts as they like.

8. Before giving a toast, indicate to your hosts that you would like to do so. Since many present will not speak both languages, an interpreter will be provided to interpret your toast as you make it. Speak slowly and distinctly, pausing to give the interpreter time to translate.

9. Accept a serving of each dish. Hosts will worry that you do not like the food, if you reject many dishes. You are only expected to eat a bite or two of each dish offered, so take a spoonful. If not to your liking, you may leave it on the plate.

10. From time to time, compliment a dish. Do not take large spoonfuls or seconds unless urged to do so. Remember that banquets may have from ten to twenty courses. You will have more than enough to eat.

11. Banquets may last for several hours. Do not schedule meetings or other affairs to interfere with this ritual. Leaving before the chief host closes the banquet is not good form.

12. The banquet will end when the host leader inquires of the guest leader if he or she cares for more. When the guest leader indicates that he or she has had sufficient food and drink, the leader will (sometimes seemingly abruptly) end the banquet. With the last of the food and the closing toast, the banquet is over. Chinese do not linger over coffee or tea to talk as do Westerners.

13. Usually, toasts are given in very small glasses with very strong liquor. If you do not drink alcohol, you may request water, soda or other beverage.

14. When the host stands, stand; be certain to shake hands all around and down the reverse receiving line. The banquet is over.

15. Usually, during the goodbye or final banquet, the hosts give gifts to their guests. They may give a gift to the leader or to all the participants.

Guests should be prepared for this and bring something from the United States to give as a gift. If you are the leader, prepare a speech to go with the gift. Gifts should be simple but elegant. You will receive quite remarkable gifts from various sources. Your hosts may give you scroll paintings, tea sets, jade pendants and other remembrances of their culture. In turn, the gifts that you select should reflect the American culture.

Different occasions obviously require different gifts. The head of a company should receive something elegant; gifts for others you would like to thank can be inexpensive but representative, e.g., coin sets or stamps. Give thought to the gifts you will bring with you. They are a necessary part of the negotiation process that you undertake. They are not bribes, but symbols of respect for the other culture and its customs.

For Confucian-based cultures, the intricacies of the arrangements will allow them to indulge in relationships and the judicious distribution of inducements to cement those relationships. Negotiators should remember that they, too, must indulge in significant inducements to develop relationships. To Westerners, this may seem odd and seemingly not in accord with the group perspective of the East. However, the reward is seen as being for the group, i. e., each person in the network of relationships must receive something. This may not necessarily be in the form of a material gift or money. Rather, it may be using influence to aid the son of one of one's friends to enter the college of his or her choice in the United States. For example, one may achieve desired results through the ability to offer graduate assistantships to deserving Chinese youth to go abroad to study. The negotiator will find this offer warmly received by nearly all to whom it is offered.

Always the Chinese will protest (three times) that whatever you offer is unnecessary. Do not stop at three times. On the fourth, the proposal will be accepted. Chinese rarely accept so much as a cup of tea without several refusals. This is traditional form. Smile and carry on. Traditional politeness requires three refusals— and the final fourth offer before accepting.

The negotiation process is a difficult one, requiring patience and good will on both sides. The process will only be enhanced if each side — and, in particular, the Western negotiators— makes the effort to know not only the assumptions, motivations, rituals and forms of the Chinese, but also make an "archaeological dig" into Western assumptions regarding motivation (individual and corporate), rituals and forms in Western culture.

# THE AMERICAN CHAMBER OF COMMERCE IN SHANGHAI (AMCHAM)

One of the best "finds" of our fact-finding trip to China in 2001 was the American Chamber of Commerce in Shanghai, which puts out a monthly journal called *AmChat: Journal of the American Chamber of Commerce in Shanghai.*[20] According to AmChat's chairman, Sydney Chang:

> There are ten committees that serve our members on a regular basis.... Most committees organize one event each month. AmCham has at least 100 or more committee and general membership events each year. These topics are centered on topics from the WTO to manufacturing, taxation and human resources. We discuss our problems, exchange ideas, and learn from others' mistakes and successes.[21]

Amongst the articles in the April 2001 edition of *AmChat* was one entitled "Leveraging Young Talent to Produce More," devoted to internships available to MBA students in China and the United States. According to its author:

> The U.S. Commercial Service in Shanghai has brought student interns from local Shanghai universities and from U.S. institutions for periods of several weeks or months to help facilitate the sale of U. S. goods and services. Interns work on international market research, develop industry sector data, build up the contact database, and work with the staff on trade events.... FCS's talented young Americans come from such leading schools as Columbia, MIT, Harvard, Wellesley, Brown, Dartmouth and Cornell. These students tend to do summer internships. They act as assistants to the commercial officers and specialists, and have the option of earning academic credit.[22]

In the same issue of *AmChat*, another article, "China's Shipping Industry," describes the 2,000-plus and the 600-plus deep-water berths available. More than 120 ports are open to foreign trade, accommodating 36,000 vessels from over 100 countries and regions each year. Shipping markets are open to foreign players and foreign investment to develop ports is encouraged.[23]

Yet another article, "Government Speaker Forum," deals with Shanghai's new pension and medical benefits programs, which

> include state-owned company workers, municipal government workers or large private firms as well as workers in small private companies and the self-employed.... Payments for outpatient and emergency services will be handled by Individual Medical Accounts (IMA) and the Unified Medical

Fund (UMF). The payment system requires a bank deposit book to reflect the amount in each patient's account.... The Social Medical Security System is composed of three parts:

1. Basic Medical Insurance;
2. Additional Insurance (Private Insurance/Mutual Aid Organizations); and
3. Medicaid.

Currently, the retired population of Shanghai has reached 2.35 million and their major source of income is their pension. The average pension in 1992 was 250 RMB (*renminbi*) and by last year it had risen to 750 RMB.[24] Payments are intended to ensure a basic standard of living for retirees and promote social stability. The original pension pool was established in 1986 and was the first such program in China.[25]

This program sounds remarkably like a U.S. program, less the American dollars. The point here is that Shanghai, as an autonomous entity in China, in the interests of foreign investment and by virtue of its supremacy on the mainland, has begun a process difficult to conceive of just 15 years ago.

Yet another topic in the June 2001 *AmChat* focuses on "Dispute Avoidance and Dispute Resolution in China," offering "three primary ways to resolve a commercial dispute in China: negotiation, arbitration, and litigation," proposing that "In China, arbitration offers many advantages over litigation." In addition, the article gives insights into drafting contracts in China.[26]

We were fortunate enough to interview AmCham's operations manager, Mr. Shane Frecklington, while in Shanghai. After spending some time there, we joined AmCham and have been receiving its e-mail and mailings for the past year. This is a vital organization and an essential contact for anyone considering doing business in China, especially in Shanghai. Founded in 1915 (3 years after the founding of the U.S. Chamber of Commerce), AmCham Shanghai was "resurrected after a hiatus of 38 years." Now, the Chamber is arguably the fastest growing Chamber in Asia. Current members number around 1,600, of which 850 are corporations.[27]

AmCham's principles include: free trade, open market, private enterprise, transparency, unrestricted flow of information and improvement on the development of policies and practices. During the past year, for example, AmCham has promoted seminars to help both sides to understand and create the needed policies required for China to conform to the WTO. AmCham participation can help any company understand China and give a leg up on current policies and laws.[28]

In their materials, AmCham offers these three regulatory consider-ations promulgated by the Chinese organizers of APEC 2001, to the delib-erations of the 21 member economies:

1.  Seek the greater benefits of globalization;
2.  Aim for greater liberalization of trade and investment; and
3.  Bring their economies and financial systems into closer alignment with global standards.[29]

Specific programming for AmCham members includes:

1.  Breakfast Briefings: Personal settings for companies considering entry into the China market to meet with experienced members in that industry (by invitation).
2.  Executive Speakers: Executive speakers are invited from private industry to discuss topics affecting current business trends.
3.  U.S. Government Delegations: AmCham hosts events for many various delegations, allowing member companies to engage in dialogue with U.S. policy makers who are trying to understand the issues affecting U.S. businesses.
4.  Shanghai Municipal Government Speaker Forum: Shanghai gov-ernment officials provide up-to-date information in changes on business practice issues.
5.  U. S. Consulate Briefings: The Consul General and staff brief AmCham members on the latest developments in Chinese and U.S. poli-cies, and U.S.–China relations.
6.  Training Seminars: Periodic seminars of interest and practical value to members.
7.  Publications: Membership directory biannually, main directory in Spring, supplementary directory in Autumn, monthly magazine, *AmChat,* local and expatriate salary surveys and position papers.
8.  Visa Referral Program: While granting visas is strictly the pre-rogative of the U.S. consulate, local employees of AmCham's U.S. corpo-rate members can be eligible to bypass the interview process, provided that the corporation has been a member of AmCham for at least 12 months.
9.  Independence Day Celebration: The only party of its kind in Shanghai in terms of scale and scope.
10.  Promoting Member Interests: AmCham works with the U.S. Chamber of Commerce and the Asia Pacific Council of American Cham-bers of Commerce to promote common interests and to speak on behalf of its membership on key issues affecting business in China.

If you are planning to do business in China, you will want to contact AmCham. Through participation in this organization your understanding of China's past and present will be enhanced. Given AmCham's resources and membership, the networking potential is significant.

# CONCLUSION

This book has been a long journey. We began tracking information on American business in China in 1997. We interviewed in China in 1997 and again in 2001. From Confucius to globalization to AmCham, we have enjoyed the journey. Earlier in this book (Chapter 2), we cited the Philippine Agenda 21 and the Center for Alternative Development Initiatives (CADI). CADI suggests that there are five types of unsustainable development in the wake of globalization: jobless growth, ruthless growth; futureless growth; rootless growth; and voiceless growth.

In the political dance between China and the United States over the past 20 years, the United States has criticized and been primarily concerned with only one dimension of unsustainable development in China — voiceless growth. Analyzing the five types of unsustainable growth in light of China's past and present economic, social and political worldview, it appears that these issues are intertwined and interdependent and cannot be looked at as totally separate entities. In short, concern for China's profitability for multinationals, as well as concern for China's sustained development, must include the four other variables.

The Center for Alternative Development offers a sixth concern: "meaningless growth" or growth which results in "loss in creativity, perspective, meaning, hope, and morality." One of the main critiques of China has been that the country is changing too slowly. We argue that, in light of uncertainty regarding the efficacy of globalization (as it is now structured) in the long run, China could change more slowly. China has so many people, all wanting to join the "to get rich is glorious" bandwagon — and few will make it. This will cause further social unrest, which will impact politically — how, one cannot say or predict. For now, it is best that China goes slowly, integrating technological opportunities slowly and carefully and analyzing situations and opportunities via the lens of sustainable growth. Sustainable growth must include full employment; a safety net for the people — health benefits and pensions; concern for the environment over sheer economic growth; retention and integration of the cultural "backbone" of China in the new Chinese order (whatever form that takes); and freedom of political expression.

With China's 1,300,000,000 people and its current resources, China's government and people face a daunting task. Given their 5,000 year history and hence a certain attitude towards time, China has all the time in the world to accomplish its goals.

# Appendix A: China Profile[1]

China is the world's most populous country, with one-quarter of the world's population in a landscape not much larger than that of the United States. Admitted to the World Trade Organization in 2002, China's influence is growing in the economic sphere.

**Population:** 1.26 billion

**Capital:** Beijing

**Provinces (23):** Anhui, Fujian, Gansu, Guangdong, Guizhou, Hainan, Hebei, Heilongjiang, Henan, Hubei, Hunan, Jiangsu, Jiangxi, Jilin, Liaoning, Qinghai, Shaanxi, Shandong, Shanxi, Sichuan, Taiwan, Yunnan, Zhejiang

**Autonomous regions (5):** Guangxi Zhuang, Inner Mongolia, Ningxia Hui, Tibet, Xinjiang Uygur

**Centrally Administrative Municipalities** (4)**:** Beijing, Chongqing, Shanghai, Tianjin

**Special Administrative Regions** (2)**:** Hong Kong, Macao

**Major language:** Standard Chinese

**Major religions:** Buddhism, Christianity, Islam, Taoism

**Life expectancy:** 68 years (men); 72 years (women)

**Monetary unit:** 1 *Renminbi (yuan)* (Y) = 10 *jiao* = 100 *fen*

**Main exports:** Manufactured goods, including textiles, garments, electronics, arms

**Average annual income:** $840 USD

**Internet domain:** .cn

**International dialing code:** +86

# GOVERNMENT

**President and Head of State:** Hu Jintao, General Secretary of the Chinese Communist Party. Hu Jintao has replaced Jiang Zemin as President General Secretary

**Chairman of the Central Military Commission:** Jiang Zemin, former president and head of state

# CENTRAL COMMITTEE OF THE COMMUNIST PARTY OF CHINA

**General Secretary:** Hu Jintao

**Members of the Standing Committee of the Political Bureau:** Hu Jintao, Wu Bangguo, Wen Jiabao, Jia Qinglin, Zeng Qinghong, Huang Ju, Wu Guanzheng, Li Changchun, Luo Gan

**Other Members of the Political Bureau:** Wang Lequan, Wang Zhaoguo, Hui Liangyu, Liu Qi, Liu Yunshan, Wu Yi, Zhang Lichang, Zhang Dejiang, Chen Liangyu, Zhou Yongkang, Yu Zhengsheng, He Guoqiang, Guo Boxiong, Cao Gangchuan, Zeng Peiyan

**Alternate Members of the Political Bureau** (*List of Members of the 16th CPC Central Committee [listed in the order of the number of strokes in their surnames]*): Xi Jinping, Ma Kai, Ma Qizhi (Hui), Ma Xiaotian, Wang Gang, Wang Chen, Wang Yunlong, Wang Yunkun, Wang Taihua, Wang Lequan, Wang Zhaoguo, Wang Zhongfu, Wang Xudong, Wang Qishan, Wang Huning, Wang Jinshan, Wang Jianmin, Wang Shengjun, Wang Hongju, Uyunqimg (Female, Mongolian), Deng Changyou, Shi Yunsheng, Shi Xiushi, Shi Zongyuan (Hui), Lu Zhangong, Tian Fengshan, Tian Chengping, Tian Congming, Bai Lichen (Hui), Bai Zhijian, Bai Keming, Bai Enpei, Ismail Amat (Uygur), Legqog (Tibet), Lu Fuyuan, Hui Liangyu (Hui), Zhu Qi, Qiao Qingchen, Hua Jianmin, Doje Cering (Tibeten), Liu Jing, Liu Qi, Liu Yunshan, Liu Shutian, Liu Dongdong, Liu Yongzhi, Liu Yandong (f.), Liu Huaqiu, Liu Zhijun, Liu Zhenhua, Liu Zhenwu, Xu Yongyue, Xu Qiliang, Sun Zhiqiang, Sun Jiazheng, Mou Xinsheng, Su Rong, Du Qinglin, Li Changjiang, Li Changchun, Li Zhilun, Li Zhaozhuo (Zhuang), Li Andong, Li Keqiang, Li Jinhua, Li Jianguo, Li Rongrong, Li Dongheng, Li Guixian, Li Tielin, Li Jinai, Li Qianyuan, Li Shenglin, Li Zhaoxing, Li Dezhu (Korean), Li Yizhong, Yang Yuanyuan, Yang Zhengwu (Tujia), Yang Huaiqing, Yang Deqing, Xiao Yang Wu Yi (f.), Wu Shuangzhan, Wu Bangguo, Wu Guanzheng, He Yong, Wang Guangtao, Wang Shucheng, Wang Xiaofeng, Shen Binyi, Song Fatang, Song Zhaosu, Song Defu, Chi Wanchun, Zhang Yunchuan, Zhang Zhongwei, Zhang Wentai, Zhang Wenkang, Zhang Yutai, Zhang Zuoji, Zhang Lichang, Zhang Qingwei, Zhang Qingli, Zhang Xuezhong, Zhang Chunxian, Zhang Junjiu, Zhang Gaoli, Zhang Weiqing, Zhang Fusen, Zhang Dejiang, Zhang Delin, Lu

Hao, Abul'ahat Abdurixit (Uygur), Chen Yunlin, Chen Zhili (f.), Chen Chuankuo, Chen Liangyu, Chen Jianguo, Chen Kuiyuan, Chen Bingde, Chen Fujin, Luo Gan, Luo Qingquan, Ji Yunshi, Jin Renqing, Zhou Qiang, Zhou Xiaochuan, Zhou Yongkang, Zhou Shengtao, Zhou Yuqi, Zheng Wantong, Zheng Silin, Meng Xuenong, Meng Jianzhu, Xiang Huaicheng, Zhao Keming, Zhao Leji, Zhao Qizheng, Hu Jintao, Niu Maosheng (Manchu), Yu Zhengsheng, Wen Shizhen, Jiang Futang, Hong Hu, He Guoqiang, Yuan Weimin, Raidi (Tibetan), Jia Qinglin, Jia Zhibang, Jia Chunwang, Chai Songyue, Qian Yunlu, Qian Guoliang, Qian Shugen, Xu Caihou, Xu Kuangdi, Xu Youfang, Xu Guangchun, Xu Rongkai, Xu Guanhua, Gao Siren, Guo Boxiong, Guo Jinlong, Tang Tianbiao, Tang Jiaxuan, Huang Ju, Huang Huahua, Huang Qingyi (f.), Huang Zhiquan, Huang Zhendong, Cao Gangchuan, Cao Bochun, Chang Wanquan, Fu Tinggui, Yan Haiwang, Liang Guanglie, Sui Mingtai, Ge Zhenfeng, Han Zheng, Chu Bo, Zeng Qinghong, Zeng Peiyan, Wen Zongren, Wen Jiabao, Pu Haiqing, Meng Jinxi, Lei Mingqiu, Yu Yunyao, Lu Yongxiang, Xie Zhenhua, Jing Zhiyuan, Liao Hui, Liao Xilong, Teng Wensheng, Bo Xilai, Dai Bingguo (Tujia), Dai Xianglong, Wei Liqun.

# MEDIA

**Print:** *Renmin Ribao (People's Daily)* — official Communist Party newspaper; *Zhongguo Qingnian Bao (China Youth Daily)* — state run; *China Daily* — English language; *Jiefangjun Bao* — People's Liberation Army Daily; *China Economic Times; Fazhi Ribao* (Legal Daily); *Gongren Ribao* (Workers' Daily); *Nongmin Ribao* (Farmers' Daily); *Nanfang Ribao* (Southern Daily); *Guangzhou Ribao*

**Television:** Chinese Central TV (CCTV) — national broadcaster, eight channels

**Radio:** China National Radio; China Radio International — broadcasts in 38 languages, notably to Taiwan and Korea

**News Agencies:** *Xinhua (New China News Agency)* — state-run; *Zhongguo Xinwen She (China News Service),* aimed mainly at overseas Chinese

**Other sources (Hong Kong):** *South China Morning Post*; *Hong Kong Mail Ming Pao*; *Hong Kong Hsin Pao (Economic Times)*; *Hong Kong Economic Journal*; *The Asian Wall Street Journal*; *The Far Eastern Economic Review*; Radio-Television Hong Kong (RTHK)

# Appendix B: Traditional Chinese Holidays and Festivals[1]

January-February — Chinese New Year — another name for the "Spring Festival" (or *Chun Jié*). The festivities for this major holiday last a little more than a month — usually from 22 days prior to the New Year date until 15 days afterwards. As with most Chinese holidays, food is a central element for celebration — including special treats as well as food with symbolic value (fish for "good luck," mustard greens for "longevity," etc.). Families are also expected to clean their houses and make sacrifices in honor of the Earth God; children usually receive red envelopes with "lucky money" inside. Families enjoy special meals and gifts, and firecrackers and rockets are lit to ward off evil spirits and revere the gods. The long holiday season closes with the Lantern Festival (*Yuánxiao Jié*), where lanterns are lit to see the celestial spirits flying in the light of the first full moon of the lunar calendar.

Here are the Spring Festival dates in the coming years:

Spring Festival — January 22, 2004 (Year of the Monkey); Lantern Festival — February 6, 2004

Spring Festival — February 9, 2005 (Year of the Rooster); Lantern Festival — February 24, 2005

Spring Festival — January 29, 2006 (Year of the Dog); Lantern Festival — February 13, 2006

Spring Festival — February 18, 2007 (Year of the Pig); Lantern Festival — February 3, 2007

Spring Festival — February 7, 2008 (Year of the Rat); Lantern Festival — February 22, 2008

Spring Festival — January 26, 2009 (Year of the Ox); Lantern Festival — February 10, 2009

March 8 — International Women's Working Day

April 4–5 —*Ching Ming* (Tomb Sweeping Day)— a special day set aside to visit the graves of relatives who have passed away and clean the gravesite. Usually occurs on April 5 each year; April 4 on leap years.

May 1— International Labor Day

May 4 — Chinese Youth Day

June 1— International Children's Day

June 15 — Dragon Boat Festival

July 1— Anniversary of the Founding of the Chinese Communist Party (CCP)

August 1— Anniversary of the Founding of the People's Liberation Army (PLA)

September 21— Mid-Autumn Festival

October 1-3 — The National Day of the People's Republic of China — a celebration of the Communist Revolution, establishing the People's Republic of China. At this time, those who can will visit Tiananmen Square, where Mao Zedong proclaimed the PRC in 1949.

# Appendix C: Contrasting Cultures

*In 1985–1986, one of the authors, Nancy Street, taught in Linfen, Shanxi Province, PRC. Near Inner Mongolia, this province represented the worldview of China's one billion peasants, which was (and may still be) quite different from that of the people of the coastal cities such as Guangzhou and Shanghai. Street taught American History, American Literature and other seminars as needed to the senior class at Shanxi Teacher's University.*

*At that time, the isolationism of China was reflected in the lifestyle and attitudes of the Chinese students and the Chinese Communist Party. In daily life, the genders did not mix. Female students walked hand in hand with other female students. Male students walked hand in hand with other male students. When Street attempted to take pictures of the senior class, males and females could not be standing next to one another. A female student could not be pictured with a male student. Any mixing of the genders would bring down "criticism" on the offenders by the communist party secretary who, at that time, was the senior official of the university.*

*Prostitutes, homeless persons, "child mothers," drug addicts and AIDS victims were not acknowledged within the society, either in discussions or in the media. This was a Maoist legacy. (What one did hear of was abortions— within marriage and most certainly in situations outside of marriage.) In 1985–1986, people in Shanxi Province were innocent of these issues. This was a legacy of the communist revolution, which outlawed prostitution, private property and drug use. The system also provided for all persons, so that all belonged to a "work unit," or the "iron rice bowl." This meant that (almost) all had access to health care, housing, educa tion and a right to work.*

*In 1997 in Guangzhou, Shanghai and Nanjing, Street saw many positive manifestations of the western influence and privatization, in addition to the welcome changes of globalization. She saw that males and female students could walk together, have pictures taken together and go to McDonald's and the movies together (though parents still had a say in with whom and where they might go). She also saw manifestations of negative impact of changes in the decade from 1986 to 1997.*

*Today in China, there are many recognized cases of AIDS, many homeless people and a failing health care system, as well as many millions unemployed as the "work units" are privatized. In the process of political, social and economic change, many of the "old ways" have been obliterated. Americans who were in China in the interior provinces as well as in the cities (Beijing, Shanghai, Guangzhou, Nanjing) sometimes have "culture shock" anew upon seeing the changes wrought through foreign influence and privatization.*

*What follows is the perspective of a Chinese exchange student from the mainland of China in 1986. The student addresses the issue of (perceived) cultural differences between China and the United States. While the writer may seem naive, the point of view (as well as the use of English) is typical of most college students throughout China during the mid–1980s.*

Chinese culture is an ancient culture that values cooperation, unity, interdependence, modesty, endurance and obedience to leaders. American culture, on the other hand, is a modern culture which values independence, freedom, democracy, equal opportunity, self-confidence and competitiveness. As all people are culture-bound, there exist the differences of habits, rules, outlooks, and values that are shaped by culture. When one crosses the "culture line" these differences will become obvious and shocking, in other words, there comes the culture shock.

## INDEPENDENCE AND INTERDEPENDENCE

American people value independence strongly. The independent "I" and "you" clash in argument as each tries to persuade the other. They go so far as to enjoy the argument and heated discussion as a sort of intellectual game. What others think and say is of little significance. In contrast, Chinese people value interdependence, generally "we" dominates over "I." What others think and say is of greater importance than what the individual does.

# Self Confidence, Economic Independence and Wasting Intelligence

Americans value self-confidence For example, college students in the United States almost all work, even many high school students work. They seem to regard economic dependence on their families as a kind of shame.

In China, however, almost no college students work, not to mention high school students. They consider that work and study conflict with each other. They are afraid that to work might interfere with their study and therefore waste their precious four-year college study time. College students in China get financial support from the government and they also ask for money from their parents.

On the other hand, parents don't encourage their children to work, instead, they urge their children to concentrate their mind solely on study, not to "waste intelligence in other extra activities." They would rather live frugally to save more money for their children than let them work.

# Individualism

American people value individualism. Self-assertion and self-reliance and frank expression of opinions are encouraged. Americans are apt to argue back when challenged, regardless of who the challenger is. In contrast, in China, people value group emphasis, cooperation and the insignificance of the individual. Individualism or egoism is regarded as something bad like being selfish. The opinions of others are of great importance for individuals in considering, forming and expressing their own opinions. Chinese people like to maximize the similarities while minimizing differences to achieve harmonious relations with others.

# Competitiveness

Americans value competition. Darwin's evolution theory "the fittest survive" is highly appreciated in America. As a result, a fast paced life marks this characteristic of Americans. Everybody is busy working, nobody wants to be a failure in the competition. Chinese value cooperation very much. Competition is something fearful.

Teachers, workers of state-owned factories, are regarded as possessing "iron bowls," that is, they are in a safety box. They will never be deprived of their jobs or go starving. And they can get a pension regularly from the government after their retirement. So everybody just enjoys the safe cooperation, nobody wants to begin the intense, fearful competition.

# SENSE OF HOME AND FAMILY

In America, the sense of home is not too strong. In China, the sense of home and family is very strong. No one wants to leave his or her hometown, away from his or her family and friends, unless for some important and "have-to" reasons. Americans have a weak family tie.

Also, everybody has his or her own ideas and makes his or her own decisions. In contrast, in China, people are extremely obedient to the government. This has something to do with the long history of China. China remained in a feudal society for over two thousand years, people are greatly influenced by the feudal loyalty, which is an important ideology of Confucianism.

The Cultural Revolution was a shocking example of the Chinese people's obedience. In 1966, Chairman Mao thought that the intellectuals in China were mostly from the old society, they received feudalist and capitalist education rather than communist education and to him that was very dangerous. In order to keep the People's Republic of China "red," that is, being communist forever, it was necessary to help the intellectuals to re-build their minds. As a result, intellectuals were assigned to farms and factories to change their feudal and capitalist mindset.

Meanwhile, Chairman Mao chose many workers and peasants who suffered a lot in the old society [pre-communist]; they had a deep hatred for the old society and a strong love for the new. Therefore, they were communist enough to be the leaders all over China, even in technological endeavors and to lead and teach in colleges and schools. The Chinese people just listened to Chairman Mao's words and did as Chairman Mao said without thinking if they were right or wrong. People thought that Chairman Mao was the greatest leader who saved them from the suffering of the old society during the fight for China between the Chinese Communist Party and the Nationalist or Kuomintang Party.

The people believed that what Chairman Mao said was 100 percent pure communist and true. One could not have even a little doubt about his words. All people answered the call of the government and took part in the revolution actively. The "Gang of Four" took the chance of Chairman Mao's mistake and people's obedience and undertook their conspiracy. This made the revolution last for ten years [Mao tried to call a halt in 1967] and caused an historically disastrous turmoil. Chinese people still have the impact of the Cultural Revolution in many ways today [1986].

# ATTITUDES TOWARD LOVE AND SEX

With regard to the attitudes toward love and sex, there are some shocking differences between the two cultures. Americans value freedom and egalitarianism in love and sex. There is nothing mysterious about sex for

Americans. TV, books, newspapers, magazines, even telephones are all available for learning about sex! There are prostitutes in America and some women get pregnant before marriage. Americans are somewhat too open about sex.

In sharp contrast, in China, people value prudence and loyalty in love and sex. Chinese people tend to be very cautious about sex. It is a forbidden topic, especially for young people. You will never hear people talking about sex in public places in China. Many people are very ignorant about sex prior to marriage. There are no prostitutes or baby-mothers in China. The sense of women's chastity is very strong in traditional Chinese morality. Chinese women would rather die than lose their chastity. And almost no men are willing to marry women who have lost their chastity.

You mention the word "homosexual" to an American and he or she will immediately link it to AIDS, but you mention the same words to a Chinese and he or she will not know what those words mean. Sex of any kind is very mysterious and shameful to think about for Chinese unmarried people. People who are in love are loyal to each other and are willing to sacrifice everything he or she has, even his or her life for his or her sweetheart. If an American young man goes abroad for two years, his fiancée can seldom wait for his return. But a Chinese woman can.

## OTHER PHENOMENA

Americans tend to be extroverts and to express their inner feelings and emotions openly. Chinese people, on the other hand, tend to conceal their inner feelings and emotions in an effort to maintain the harmonious relations with the people around them. Chinese people value endurance and can strongly restrain themselves under almost any conditions. For example, from 1960 to 1962, a big drought swept over China and at the same time, China severed her relationship with the Soviet Union. As a result, the Soviets withdrew all their technological experts with many projects still under construction. The Soviets asked the Chinese government to repay all debts and loans, which the Chinese had incurred in the Korean War. The Chinese government did not surrender to the Soviet threat, but paid all the debts, despite the weak economy, thus retaining face with the Soviets. But the Chinese people had to suffer starvation during this time, but they did not complain to the government. They faced the hard situation bravely and worked even harder to improve the situation. The Chinese were capable of bearing such a nationwide hard time without a coup d'etat or even complaining.

Americans value self-confidence and self-assertion. They are always confident in themselves; some are even arrogant. They are apt to overestimate themselves. On the other hand, Chinese people value modesty and tend to underestimate themselves. Some even go to the extreme of being humble.

Culture shock is the result of two cultures meeting. Different cultural backgrounds cause different cultural values. There is no right or wrong about a culture. Values are also changing within a culture. If you cross a cultural line, just learn about the other culture and adapt to it, then you won't be shocked anymore.

# Appendix D: Council on International Educational Exchange

East China Normal University
Academic Exchange Center, 2203
366 North Zhongshan Road
Shanghai 2006, P. R. China
Tel: 86-21-6286-3492
Fax: 86-21-6286-3747
E-Mail: mzshi@hotmail.com

**Faculty Leader CV**

Dr. Shi Mingzheng

**Education**

**Ph.D.,** Chinese History, Columbia University, 1993
**M.Phil.,** Chinese History, Columbia University, 1990
**M.A.,** American Studies, University of Connecticut, 1988
**B.A.,** Cross-cultural Studies, Peking University, 1986

In addition to his position as Regional Director for East Asia, Dr. Shi was the Program Director and Faculty Leader for the Faculty Development Sem-

240

inar "The Historic Cities of China" in 2000 and 2001. This involved leading the group of 20 American educators through 4 historic cities. Responsible for conceptualizing, planning, budgeting and liaison with Chinese host institutions. Lectures, site visits and cultural activities were also arranged.

## Brief Lecturer Biographies

*Cao Lindi*, Professor of Chinese Literature at Suzhou University. A scholar of classical Chinese gardens, she was a college student at Peking University during the Cultural Revolution.

*Jia Qingguo*, Professor of Political Science and Associate Dean of the College of International Studies at Peking University. After receiving his Ph.D. in government from Cornell University, he taught at the University of California at San Diego and also at the University of Sydney, Australia. Dr. Jia is the author of *Unrealized Accommodation: Sino-U.S. Relations During the Early Years of the Cold War and Thorny Cooperation.*

*Li Jianchao*, Professor of Geography at China Northwestern University. The author of, amongst other publications, *Ethnic Minorities in China*, Professor Li has conducted field research on ethnic minorities and led research teams to study the Silk Road.

*Tao Jie*, Professor of American Literature and Associate Director of the Women Studies Center at Peking University. She has published widely on American literature and was a Fulbright visiting scholar to the United States. Prof. Tao is a leading expert on women's issues in China.

*Wang Xixin*, Professor of Peking University Law School and Director of www.LawInfoChina.com.

*Douglas Grob* received his LLD from Stanford University and is now Senior Consultant to www.LawInfoChina.com.

*Xiong Yuezhi*, Professor and Director of the Institute of History of the Shanghai Academy of Social Sciences. Professor Xiong is a leading authority on the history of modern Shanghai. His publications include, amongst others, the edited, 15 volume *A General History of Shanghai,* published in 2000.

*Yin Xiangshuo*, Professor of Economics at Fudan University. Professor Yin is a renowned expert on Chinese economic reforms in the last two decades.

*Zhao Rong*, Professor and Director of the Center for the Study of Historic Cities of China at the Northwestern University in Xi'an. He is also an authority on the history and development of Xi'an, one of China's foremost historic cities.

## *Host Institutions*

## Beijing

Shao Yuan Hotel
Building No. 7 Shao Yuan
Peking University

Beijing PRC 100871
Tel: 011-86-10-6275-1818
Fax: 01-86-10-6275-123

## Xi'an

Guesthouse of Overseas Scholars and Students
Northwestern University
229 Tai Bai Road
Xi'an PRC 710069
Tel: 011-86-29-841-0941
Fax: 011-86-29-830-3511

## Shanghai

Academic Exchange Center
East China Normal University
3663 North Zhongshan Road
Shanghai 200062 PRC
Tel: 011-86-21-6286-3492
Fax: 011-86-21-6286-3747

## Other Contact Information

China National Tourist Office
350 Fifth Ave., Suite 6413
Empire State Building
New York, NY 10118
Tel: 212-760-8218
www.cnta.com
China National Tourist Office
333 West Broadway
Suite 201
Glendale, CA 91204
Tel: 818-545-7507

# Glossary

**"back door"**(*hou men*)—To survive in China, one must have a big "back door," i.e., powerful "relationships" to obtain whatever is needed or wanted. Maintaining relationships (and keeping the door wide open) requires access to those currencies needed to persuade others to help one. In 1990 currencies included: cigarettes, television sets, food (particularly meat), tiger bones, jobs, Foreign Exchange Currency (FEC) and American dollars.

**Beijing**—Formerly Peking and home of the last Chinese Emperor Puyi. The People's Republic of China was established in the capital city of Peking on October 1, 1949, following the victory of the Chinese Communist Party (CCP) over the Kuomintang (KMT) in the War for Liberation.

**Buddhism**—Founded in the sixth century B.C. by Sakyamuni, who achieved "enlightenment." The religion spread throughout Asia. Buddhism, Taoism and Confucianism co-existed in China, each supplying a needed spiritual or pragmatic dimension to living everyday life. On Taiwan and on the mainland of China, Buddhism is still practiced, as is Taoism.

**Chiang Kaishek**—Inherited the leadership of the Kuomintang (Nationalist Party) following the death of the founder of the republic, Dr. Sun Yatsen. Following the War for Liberation, Chiang Kaishek became the president of the Republic of China on Taiwan.

**Chinese Communist Party** (CCP)—Founded in Shanghai in 1921 by Chinese revolutionaries, including Mao Zedong. Since 1949, the Chinese Communist Party (CCP) has governed the People's Republic of China (PRC).

**Confucianism**—In China, Confucius (551-479 B.C.) is still known as

Kung-fu-tzu. In a disordered society, Confucius developed the rules for an ordered society and worked out the five basic relationships which still (to an extent) dominate Chinese society, despite the influence of the CCP. Temples to Confucius dot the landscape of both Taiwan and the mainland of China.

**Cultural Revolution (CR)**—Begun by Chairman Mao Zedong in 1966, and continued by others, including Lin Biao and Mao's wife, Jiang Qing of "Gang of Four" notoriety. It was meant to rekindle revolutionary fervor and dedication in the masses, the intellectuals and in the CCP. The strategies of the Cultural Revolution included the closing of schools and universities. It formally ended in 1976.

**Deng Xiaoping (1904-1997)**—Former leader of the People's Republic of China. Educated abroad in France and the Soviet Union, he was a political commissar in the Red Army during WWII. During the Cultural Revolution, he was "sent down" in disgrace three times. In the late seventies, he began to assert leadership in the CCP. Deng Xiaoping was in part responsible for the new economic policies (the combination of socialism and capitalism) implemented in China in the eighties. Since the Beijing Spring of 1989, he was branded a "hard-liner" in the West.

**Four Modernizations**—One of the main themes of Chinese rhetoric in the eighties (originally articulated by Premier Zhou Enlai) designed to motivate the people towards technological progress in China. The Four Modernizations are the development of industry, of science and technology, of agriculture and of national defense. Deng Xiaoping says that "Education must face [serve] the four modernizations, the world and the future."

**The "Four Olds"**—The parts of society thought by Mao to be detrimental to his Cultural Revolution. He encouraged his Red Guard to eradicate them. The "four olds" included: (1) old thought; (2) old culture; (3) old customs; and (4) old habits.

**Four Principles of "Right" Conduct**—Taken from Confucianism, these include: (1) *jen* (humanism); (2) *i* (faithfulness); (3) *li* (propriety); and (4) *chih* (wisdom or a liberal education).

**Gang of Four**—Sometimes perceived as scapegoats for the Cultural Revolution. The four included Mao's last wife, Jiang Qing. Others in the Gang of Four were Wang Hongwen, Yao Wenyuan and Zhang Chunqiao. They were "overthrown" in 1977 and tried and convicted in 1981.

*guanxi*—The importance of relationships to accomplish one's goals.

*hou men*—See "back door."

*hukou*—A "registration" system in China, where citizens were classified as either "urban" or "rural;" "agricultural" or "non-agricultural." Once classified, workers could not change either their professions or locale.

**iron rice bowl**—Chinese expression for a guaranteed job for life.

**Kuomintang (KMT)**—Also the Nationalist Party; founded by Dr. Sun Yatsen. The KMT and the CCP battled for control of China for approximately twenty-five years. The KMT was backed by the United States. After their defeat in 1949, the KMT set up the Republic of China on Taiwan (ROC). The

ROC was recognized by the United Nations as the legitimate government of China until 1971. Having common origins, the government of the KMT is structured much like the CCP.

**Lean Transformation** — See Six Sigma.

**MFN** — Most Favored Nation status in the World Trade Organization.

**Mao Zedong (Mao Tsetung) (1893–1976)** — The son of a middle peasant, Mao Zedong was one of the founders of the CCP. He conceived of the strategy of winning the peasants to the Communist cause. Mao became a cult figure in China and is famous for his strategies, poetry, and martial theories. Mao also began the Cultural Revolution which was to end in disaster. Chairman Mao, Premier Zhou Enlai and Marshal Zhu De all died in 1976. Their deaths ushered in a new order.

**Marxism** — The foundation of Chinese Communism. Karl Marx believed that capitalism offered less than "the best of all possible worlds." He was concerned that economic systems not overwhelm the human dimension. His major contributions to economic theory are found in *Das Kapital.*

**Mien Tze** — The concept of "face."

**Min Gong** — The "floating" population (migrant workers).

**monochronic time** — (also known as M-time) doing one thing at a time.

**People's Republic of China (PRC)** — The government of the mainland of China since 1949. The PRC is a socialist state of the dictatorship of the proletariat. This state is led by the working class in alliance with the peasants. The PRC has had a constitution since 1954. The second constitution was adopted in 1978. The constitution grants rights to education, to freedom of speech, to demonstration and also grants "women's equal rights with men in all spheres of political, economic, cultural, social and family life."

**Pinyin** — Endorsed by the government in the PRC. *Pinyin* romanizes Chinese words, replacing the Wade-Giles system. Both are an attempt to convert the tones and other differences between the English and Chinese languages into words that the reader can understand. Unfortunately, this poses further problems. Books written prior to 1980 tend to utilize the Wade-Giles system. Those written after 1980 tend to use the *Pinyin* system, leading to such differences as Mao Zedong (*Pinyin*) and Mao Tse-tung (Wade-Giles).

**polychronic time** — (also known as P-time) includes involvement of people and completing transactions, rather than sticking to strict schedules.

**Red Guard** — The Red Guards were organized in 1966. They were assembled by Chairman Mao Zedong in Tiananmen Square at the beginning of the Cultural Revolution. Many of these city youth were sent to the countryside "to learn from the peasants." Later, the Red Guard came from all ages and areas throughout China. By 1967, they were out of control. They were encouraged to seek out and punish those who did not adhere to Mao Zedong Thought and to destroy all old culture, e.g., art and artifacts of China's past, to include temples. In the eighties, China began to rebuild its temples and other historical sites.

**Republic of China (ROC)** — Founded on the mainland, the ROC government was transferred to Taiwan after the War for Liberation. At first recognized by the United Nations, that recognition was later given to the PRC. Taiwan is governed by the Kuomintang and until 1987 was under martial law. Economically, Taiwan is ahead of mainland China and is a major world trading partner.

**Six Sigma** (also known as Lean Transformation)—A quality initiative for all areas of the workplace—physical, visual and conceptual—based on cybernetic system theory.

*Taoism*—Lao Tzu is perceived to be the founder of *Taoism*, centuries before the advent of Christianity. Confucius is thought to have been one of his disciples. The *Tao* is the Way and the *Tao* is within. *Taoism* and its patterns of thought were influential in developing the Chinese civilization. Today, Taoist monks are once again seen in the temples in China.

**The Three People's Principles**—Nationalism, democracy and the people's livelihood. These were first put forward by Dr. Sun Yatsen.

**WTO**—World Trade Organization.

*Waiguoren*—Anyone who is not by birth Chinese (Chinese living abroad are "overseas Chinese," regardless of their citizenry). At best, the non–Chinese is a *waiguoren*, or foreigner; at worst, the foreigner is a "foreign devil."

**"Walking on two legs"**—Alternative way of saying "One country, two systems." This means (for mainland China) the combination of free enterprise found in the special economic zones and the traditional state economic control under the CCP. The concept has wider application when Hong Kong and Taiwan are included. In this case, it means that mainland China will continue as a primarily socialist country. Hong Kong will continue to be capitalist, even though in 1997 Hong Kong returned to the PRC. The phrase is expanded to include Taiwan. According to Deng Xiaoping, if they should reunify, Taiwan will retain the capitalistic economic system. Thus, through reunification of the mainland of China, Hong Kong and Taiwan, there will be "one country, two systems," or "walking on two legs."

**Work Unit**—The designation given to a communal work and living environment.

**Xi'an**—Site of the capital of the first emperor of China, Qin Shi Huang. In modern times, Xi'an is the bustling and pleasant capital of Shaanxi Province. Since the discovery of the magnificent clay warriors at the tombsite of Qin Shi Huang, Xi'an has become a major tourist attraction in China.

**Zhou Enlai (1898–1976)**—Educated in part abroad. An early Communist Party member with Mao Zedong and Deng Xiaoping. Zhou Enlai is well-known throughout the Western world as a statesman. He is also beloved by the Chinese people. He attempted to bring the Red Guard under control during the Cultural Revolution.

**Zhu De (1886–1976)**—Famous military strategist in China's modern revolutionary history. A close comrade of Mao Zedong. Not known for political intrigues. Marshal Zhu De was Commander-in-Chief of the People's Liberation Army (PLA).

# Notes

## INTRODUCTION

1. According to "China Labour Protest Suspended," BBC World News (March 22, 2002), a protest took place in Liaoyang in "the country's economically depressed northeast." The article also alludes to unrest in Daqing, China's "leading oil producing city." Both cities are north of Beijing. To ease the tension, oil companies promised more benefits. (Database on-line; available from http://news. bbc.co.uk/hi/english/world/asia-pacific/newsid_1886000/1886977. stm.)

## CHRONOLOGY

1. Information for this chronology has been obtained from several sources, including: (1) Randall E. Stross' *Bulls in the China Shop and Other Sino-American Business Encounters*; (2) Nancy Lynch Street's *In Search of Red Buddha*; (3) Hong Junhao's *The Internationalization of Television in China: The Evolution of Ideology, Society, and Media Since the Reform*; (4) Li Conghua's *China: The Consumer Revolution*; (5) Brittanica.com (http://www.britannica.com); (6) Jim Mann's *Beijing Jeep: A Case Study of Western Business in China*; and (7) *The Lonely Planet: China* guide.

## 1. THE CHINESE WORLDVIEW

1. Deng Xiaoping, "Opening Speech at the Twelfth National Congress of the Communist Party of China," in Deng Xiaoping: *Fundamental Issues in Present-Day China*.

(translated by the Bureau for the Compilation and Translation of Works of Marx, Engels, Lenin and Stalin Under the Central Committee of the Communist Party of China), 3. Part of a series of *The Selected Works of Deng Xaoping* (1975–1982) (Beijing: Foreign Languages Press, 1987).

2. Nancy Lynch Street, *In Search of Red Buddha* (New York: Peter Lang, 1992), 78.

3. Judith N. Martin and Thomas K. Nakayama, *Intercultural Communication in Contexts* (Mountain View, Calif.: Mayfield, 1998), 22.

4. *Ibid.*

5. *Ibid.*

6. Edward T. Hall, *The Silent Language* (New York: Fawcett, 1959), 41. Cited in Martin and Nakayama, 21.

7. Edward T. Hall, *The Anthropology of Manners* (San Francisco: W.H. Freeman, 1955).

8. Margaret Mead, "Some cultural approaches to communication problems," in L. Bryson, ed. *The Communication of Ideas* (New York Institute for Religious and Social Studies, 1948), 2–26.

9. September 11, 2001, is the date of the Al Qaeda "suicide missions." Nineteen terrorists hijacked four planes that day and flew them into the World Trade Center, the Pentagon and a field in Pennsylvania. Several thousand Americans died that day. The attack was attributed to Osama bin Laden, a wealthy former Saudi who, stripped of his citizenship, had set up terrorist training camps in Afghanistan. The attack was followed by the United States declaring a "war on terrorism," and intensive bombing of Afghan caves in pursuit of bin Laden and his men.

10. "China's Shipping Industry," *AMChat, Journal of the American Chamber of Commerce in Shanghai*, April 2001, 14. Web address: www.amcham-shanghai.org . International container transportation also increased in 2000 by 37.1 percent over 1999. Shanghai, Qingdao, Shenzhen, Tianjin and Guangzhou are listed as part of the world's 50 largest container ports.

11. Bruce Cummings, *The Two Koreas* (New York: Headline Series, Foreign Policy Assoc., Inc., 1984), p. 8.

12. Victoria Chen, "Mien Tze at the Chinese Dinner Table: A Study of the Interactional Accomplishment of Face," *Research on Language and Social Interaction* 24 (1990/1991), 109–140.

13. June Ock Yum, "The Impact of Confucianism on Interpersonal Relationships," *Communication Monographs* 55 (December 1988): 377.

14. Myung-seok Park and Moon-soo Kim, "Communication Practices in Korea," *Communication Quarterly* 40 (Fall 1992): 399; Oded Shenkar and Simcha Ronen, "The Cultural Context of Negotiations: The Implications of Chinese Interpersonal Norms," *Journal of Applied Behavioral Sciences* 23 (1987): 263–275.

15. Ringo Ma, "The Role of Intermediary in Interpersonal Conflicts in Chinese Culture," *Communication Quarterly* 40 (Summer 1992): 269–278.

16. Hui-Ching Chang and G. Richard Holt, "More than Relationship: Chinese Interaction and the Principle of Kuan-Hsi," *Communication Quarterly* 39 (Summer 1991): 251–271.

17. *Ibid.*, 253.

18. Nancy L. Street, *In Search of Red Buddha*, 30.

19. Chang and Holt, 256.

20. Street, 210.

21. *Ibid.*, 213.

22. Edwin C. Nevis, "Using an American Perspective in Understanding Another Culture: Toward a Hierarchy of Needs for the People's Republic of China," in *Journal of Applied Behavioral Science* 19 (JAI Press, Inc., 1983): 249–264.

23. Gilbert M. Grosvenor (editor), *Great Religions of the World* (Washington, D.C.: National Geographic Society, 1978), 414.

24. *Ibid.*, 158.

25. *Ibid.*, 89.

26. *Ibid.*, 94.

27. *Ibid.*, 128.

28. Kuan-yin is the Wade-Giles spelling used in Taiwan. On the mainland, the spelling is in Pinyin as Guanyin.

29. *Great Religions*, 94.

30. See for instance, Jonathan D. Spence, *The Memory Palace of Matteo Ricci* (New York: Viking Penguin, Inc., 1984).

31. "Jiangsu," *Lonely Planet China* (Victoria, Australia: Lonely Planet Publications, 7th ed., 2000), 310-313.

32. Yoko Mizui, "Looking Back on the Historically Inevitable," *The Daily Yomiuri* (December 11, 1997) [database on-line]; available from Lexis-Nexis.

33. *Ibid.*

34. During the Tiananmen tragedy, Hong Kong supporters supplied the Chinese students with tents, food and access to the media, aiding them in staying there despite the government's warnings; in the end some students were killed.

35. Frank Welsh, *A History of Hong Kong* (London: Harper Collins, 1993).

36. Street, 27–28.

37. As in Venezuela and the conflict between Hugo Chavez, the military and the elite in April 2002. Chavez wants land reform, education reform and economic reform. The "haves" oppose this, the "have nots" approve.

38. Mao Zedong, "Report of the Investigation of the Peasant Movement in Hunan," in *Selected Works of Mao Tse-Tung*, Bruno Shaw (editor) (New York: Harper & Row, Publishers, 1970), 17.

39. *Ibid.*

40. *Ibid.*, 19–20.

41. Street, 36.

42. *Ibid.*, 29.

43. See Jonathan Alter, "On the Road in China," *Newsweek* (June 29, 1998), 29. He says: "For now, the country's one-party state most resembles the regimes of U.S. allies like Taiwan and South Korea in the years before they became democratic. These nations opened stock exchanges, mistreated political prisoners—and lobbied Washington with campaign gifts. Sound familiar?"

44. Street, 76.

45. *Ibid.*

46. Jean Chesneaux, *Peasant Revolts: 1840–1949*, trans. C. A. Curwen (London: Thames and Hudson Ltd., 1973), 107.

47. "A Programmatic Document on the Great Proletarian Cultural Revolution," *Peking Review* 34 (1966), 19.

48. This social safety net no longer includes guaranteed jobs, house, food, salary, health care, education from birth through college, child care and the safety of relationships, among other concerns for everyday living.

49. Street, research for *In Search of Red Buddha*.

# 2. ISSUES IN GLOBALIZATION

1. Barry Lynn, "Unmade in America: The True Cost of a Global Assembly Line," *Harper's Magazine* (June 2002), 34.

2. *Ibid.*, 39.

3. Walker, Gordon R. and Mark A. Fox. "Globalization: An Analytical Framework,"

4. *Indiana Journal of Global Legal Studies* (Spring 1996) [database on-line]; available from http://ijgls.indiana.edu/archive/03/02/walker.shtml, 2.

5. "In China, the Rich Seek to Become the 'Big Rich,'" *Washington Post* (March 16, 2002)

[database on-line]; available from http://www.washingtonpost.com/ac2/wp-dyn/A38967-2002Mar 16. In the article, a reporter from the state-run Central Television said he shelved a documentary project about the rich in China because few wanted to be interviewed and most of them made their first million by breaking the law.

6. John le Carré, "In Place of Nations," *Nation* (April 6, 2002), 11.

7. *Ibid.*, 12.

8. *Ibid.*, 11.

9. The unfolding (in 2002) Enron scandal in the energy field may be a good example of this, especially in light of its use of government to strong-arm India.

10. Walker, 2.

11. *Ibid.*, 4.

12. And, by the way, where, geographically, culturally or financially, is Russia in this face-off?

13. *Ibid.*, 2–3.

14. In place of "underdevelopment," we will use the word "infrastructure" throughout this book as having the richer connotation applicable to China. Infrastructure will be discussed in two senses— the cultural and the physical.

15. The Center for Alternative Development Initiatives (database on-line); available from http://www.cadi.ph (June 14, 2000), 1–3.

16. *Ibid.*, 2.

17. "Why Do They Hate Us?" *Boston Sunday Globe* (September 16, 2001) [database on-line]; available from Lexis-Nexis.

18. The Arab-Israeli conflict has a long history. In modern times, this conflict was re-ignited when the UN declared the State of Israel in 1947. While this action gave the Jews a homeland, it at the same time displaced the Palestinians who now have no homeland. This bitter conflict has no end in sight. Terrorist groups may have selected the U.S. for terrorist attacks in part because the United States sides with Israel in this conflict. Just a week before the events at the World Trade Center, the Pentagon and the airplane crash in Pennsylvania on Sept. 11, 2001, the United States had walked out of the Racial Conference held in Durban, South Africa, due to a resolution calling for Israel to be branded a racist state, in addition to the call for reparations to the descendants of former slaves.

19. The targets chosen by the terrorists attacked several of our cherished symbols: the World Trade Center, symbol of New York, the financial center of the world and thus the hub of globalization, and the Pentagon, home of the mightiest army on earth. Both institutions have their detractors but are considered untouchable. They may do wrong at times, but only in the service of the good. The terrorists scored on two of our most cherished institutions and symbols: money and the military.

20. "China Unveils Huge Welfare Plan," BBC News/Asia Pacific (March 18, 2002) [database on-line]; available from http://news.bbc.co.uk/hi/english/world/asia-pacific/newsid_1212000/1213973.stm.

21. "China's Unemployment Challenge," BBC News (March 19, 2002) [database on-line]; available from http://news.bbc.co.uk/hi/english/business/newsid_1881000/1881153.stm.

22. Database on-line; available from http://www.amcham-shanghai.org/ english/positionpapers/agriculture.htm.

23. See glossary.

24. This is a term used to describe the hot summers in this area. More recently, Beijing has been termed the "fourth oven," due to its climatic change from desertification.

25. As one example, while the authors were in Nanjing in May of 2001, they knew that the film *Pearl Harbor* had been released just two days prior in the United States. It was already available in that Nanjing video store.

26. "Thousands Protest in Chinese City," BBC News/Asia Pacific (March 18, 2002) [database on line], available from http://news.bbc.co.uk/hi/english/world/ asia-pacific/newsid_1879000/1879005.stm.

27. "Thousands of Workers Protest in Chinese City," *Washington Post* (March 19, 2002) [database on line]; available from http://www.washingtonpost.com/ac2/wp-dyn/A52370-2002Mar19.

28. *Ibid.*

29. *Ibid.*

30. Compared to the now destitute Russians, who heeded U.S. advice and criticism, China has—in hindsight—been credited for choosing the wiser, more prudent course of its political and economic reformation.

31. *Ibid.*

32. "China Cracks Down on Worker Protests," *Washington Post* (March 20, 2002) [database on line]; available from http://www.washingtonpost.com/ac2/ wp-dyn/A52370—2002Mar20.

33. *Ibid.*

34. Lynn, 41.

# 3. THE CHANGING CHINESE CONSUMER

1. Li, Conghua, *China: The Consumer Revolution* (Singapore: John Wiley & Sons [Asia], 1998), 2.

2. Jianying Zha, *China Pop: How Soap Operas, Tabloids and Bestsellers Are Transforming a Culture* (New York: The New Press, 1995), 3.

3. Li, 23.

4. *Ibid.*, 28. Li's urban resident ownership assets graph, as well as that of comparative residential living space from 1980–1995, on this page are particularly impressive.

5. Damien McElroy, "International: China's Little Emperors Blamed for Juvenile Crime Wave," *Sunday Telegraph* (London) (February 7, 1999), 29.

6. "China: Economy," Janet Matthews Information Services; World of Information Country Report (September 14, 1999) [database on-line]; available from Lexis-Nexis.

7. *Ibid.*

8. "China: Country Profile," Janet Matthews Information Services; World of Information Country Report (August 28, 2001) [database on-line]; available from Lexis-Nexis.

9. *Ibid.*

10. *Ibid.*

11. According to the February 12, 2002, edition of *Nikkei Weekly*, the average income of a Chinese employee for a foreign firm in Shanghai is about $725 USD per month; the average monthly income of a Chinese employee for a domestic firm in Shanghai is about $325 USD; and those outside the city generally earn far less. ("Shanghai 'Yuppies' Lap Up Luxury") [database on-line]; available from Lexis-Nexis.

12. Lynne Schafer Gross, *International World of Electronic Media* (New York: McGraw-Hill, Inc., 1995), 281–284.

13. "China: Country Profile."

14. *Ibid.*

15. "China: Economy," 18.

16. Elisabeth Rosenthal, "Beijing Journal; Buicks, Starbucks and Fried Chicken. Still China?" *New York Times* (February 25, 2002), 4A.

17. Martin Regg Cohn, "China Seeks to Build the Great Firewall; Controlled Modernization the Mantra; Censors Patrol Chat Room," *Toronto Star* (July 21, 2001), 1A.

18. Scott Savitt, "AWSJ: China and the Internet," Dow Jones Newswires (February 1, 200), *Wall Street Journal Interactive Edition*; available on-line.

19. "Amazing Facts on China," ChinaOnline (database on-line); available from http://www.chinaonline.com/china facts.

20. "China: Economy," 18. According to the report, in 1999, Bill Gates, the company's founder and CEO, announced that he had entered into an agreement to link more than 40

government ministries to the internet in conjunction with the State Economic and Trade Commission

21. 1 James Kynge, "Companies & Finance International: Chinese Book Web Site Set for Launch," *Financial Times* (December 9, 1999), 33.

22. *Ibid.*

23. *Ibid.*

24. Savitt, "AWSJ: China and the Internet."

25. Cohn, 1A.

26. "Internet Police Shut Down Cafes Over Internet Pornography in China," EFE News Service (February 6, 2002) [database on-line]; available from Lexis-Nexis.

27. Connie Ling, "Junk E-Mail Flourishes in China as Fast Growth Bypasses Manners," *Wall Street Journal Interactive Edition* (February 15, 2000); available on-line.

28. Quanyu, Huang, Joseph Leonard and Chen Tong, *Business Decision Making in China* (New York: International Business Press, 1997), xvi.

29. *Ibid.*, 3.

30. According to Quanyu et al., joint ventures can be configured in several different ways: (1) foreign investment in a state-owned enterprise; (2) foreign investment in a collective enterprise; and (3) a joint venture between a foreign financier and a Chinese entrepreneur to build an entirely new business, either for international trade or the domestic market. (pp. 12–13).

31. "China: Monetary Policy Committee Weathering Financial Developments," China Business Information Network (CBNET), April 20, 1999.

32. "Zhu Asks Officials to Implement Economic Policies Without Fear," AFX News (November 24, 1999); available on-line from Lexis-Nexis.

33. Ibid. Zhu's vice-premier, Wen Jiabao, gave these specifics at the November 1999 national planning meeting.

34. These rules went into effect April 1, 2002.

35. "New Guideline to Attract Overseas Capital," Asiainfo Daily China News (February 28, 2002) [database on-line]; available from Lexis-Nexis.

36. "Law on Prevention of Desertification," Global News Wire Business Daily Update (January 4, 2002) [database on-line]; available from Lexis-Nexis.

37. *Ibid.*

38. John Cassy, "Capitalism, But Not as We Know It: The WTO Will Admit China But Skyscrapers and Rampant Consumerism Cannot Disguise the Slow Pace of Change," *Guardian* (September 11, 2001), 24.

39. "China: Public Spending to Bring Hebei to Growth Goal," *China Daily* (October 28, 1998); available on-line from Lexis-Nexis.

40. "China's Population Exceeds 1.29 Billion," Asia Pulse (March 28, 2001) [database on-line]; available from Lexis-Nexis.

41. "Stimulating Domestic Demand Cheers Retailer." Global News Wire (January 4, 2002) [database on-line]; available from Lexis-Nexis.

42. "China: Economy," 18.

43. "Xinhua Carries 'Full Text' of Report on Social, Economic Development Plan," BBC Worldwide Monitoring (March 17, 2002) [database on-line]; available from Lexis-Nexis.

44. "China: China's Rails Gleam with Gold," *China Daily* (January 8, 2000); available on-line from Lexis-Nexis.

45. *Ibid.*

46. Li, 43.

47. "China: Economy," 18.

48. "China: China's Rails Gleam with Gold."

49. "Railway Connecting East China with Europe to Open Soon," BBC Summary of World Broadcasts (December 31, 1999); available on-line from Lexis-Nexis.

50. "China Facts & Figures," ABC-CLIO, Inc. (includes information from Europa World Year Book, FAO Production Yearbook and The World Factbook); available on-line from Lexis-Nexis.

51. "China Bans New Shipbuilding Projects During Remainder of 9th 5-year Plan," AFX News (November 5, 1999); available on-line from Lexis-Nexis.

52. "China: Economy," 18.

53. "Shanghai Port Sees Growth in Imports from US, Europe," Asia Pulse (December 17, 2001) [database on-line]; available from Lexis-Nexis.

54. *Ibid.*

55. "China Facts & Figures."

56. Li, 43.

57. "The End of 2001, China's Total Roads Measured 1.698 Million," Global News Wire (March 14, 2002) [database on-line]; available from Lexis-Nexis.

58. "Xinhua Carries 'Full Text' of Report on Social, Economic Development Plan."

59. *Ibid.*

60. "China Facts & Figures."

61. "Xinhua Carries 'Full Text' of Report on Social, Economic Development Plan."

62. "Briefing: Asia Aviation — February 20, 2002," Asia Pulse (February 20, 2002) [database on-line]; available from Lexis-Nexis.

63. At present, Shanghai has two airports—one in Pudong and one closer to the city. Pudong International Airport is still being developed, but according to a March 2002 Hong Kong Imail report, Pudong will start handling all international arrivals, totaling more than 80 million passengers each year. ("Shanghai Pledges to be Flights Hub," database on-line; available on Lexis-Nexis.)

64. Damien McElroy, "International: China's Little Emperors Blamed for Juvenile Crime Wave," 29.

65. Maggie Farley, "Deng's True Heirs: The Ambitious Young; The Late Leader's Legacy Includes a Sense of Confidence and Entitlement that Worries Many in the Older Generation," *Los Angeles Times* (February 24, 1997), 1A.

66. "Parents Often Feed 'Little Emperors,'" *Arizona Republic* (December 6, 1998), A22. It should be noted, however, that the article emphasizes that this trend takes place only in the cities. As the author states, "This is still a country of great poverty. In rural areas, it is estimated, as many as 24 million children are malnourished."

67. Damien McElroy, "International: China's Little Emperors Blamed for Juvenile Crime Wave," 29.

68. Craig S. Smith, "Private Lessons: In China, Parents Seek to Give their Children an Advantage by Choosing Private Schools," *Wall Street Journal Interactive Edition* (October 20, 1997); available on-line.

69. *Ibid.*

70. Erik Eckholm, "Beijing Journal: Delectable Materialism Catching On in China," *New York Times* (January 10, 1998), 1A.

71. *Ibid.*

72. Craig S. Smith, "Private Lessons: In China, Parents Seek to Give their Children an Advantage by Choosing Private Schools."

73. Erik Eckholm, "Beijing Journal: Delectable Materialism Catching On in China."

74. "China: Nation Takes on Illiteracy," *China Daily* (December 13, 1999); available on-line from Lexis-Nexis. Most of the illiterate population, however, resides in rural areas as well as in regions heavily inhabited by minorities.

75. Li, 33.

76. *Ibid.*, 9

77. Jasper Becker, "Elderly Accused of Inciting Trouble," *South China Morning Post* (August 7, 1999), 14.

78. Li, 8.

79. "China: Generation Gap Opens Up in National Fast-Food Fight," *China Daily* (May 16, 1999); available on-line from Lexis-Nexis.

80. Li, 19.

# 4. CASE STUDY: EDUCATIONAL EXCHANGE PROGRAMS

1. CIEE also offers IFDS programs in many other countries, as well as other programs and services, including Work Abroad, International Volunteer Projects, Teach in China, Council Travel and Group Travel. For further information on Council, see www.ciee.org,e-mail info@ciee.org, or call 1–888 COUNCIL (toll free).

2. Dr. Street's research through the IFDS program was in part supported in 2001 by the Office of Academic Affairs and professional development money at Bridgewater State College. Her sabbatical research in Nanjing in 1997 was supported in part by Bridgewater State College, by Dr. Arthur Dirks, Acting Dean of Arts and Sciences, and by a Small Grant from the Center for the Advancement of Teaching and Research (CART) at Bridgewater State College.

3. See www.ciee.org, e-mail info@ciee.org.

4. Initially, we could not even use FEC (our legitimate currency) in closed cities such as Linfen, though eight hours by train away in Taiyuan, the capital of Shanxi Province, we could use FEC and exchange *renminbi*. In fact, by 1988, the blackmarket in FEC/RMB was scandalous, there was almost no relief from Chinese wanting to "change money."

5. CIEE materials. These materials also included the CV for the faculty leader, Mingzheng Shi and the lecturer biographies for each of the Chinese lecturers throughout China. See Appendix D for this list and the address of CIEE at East China Normal University.

6. The seminar met for three days in Beijing, three days in Xi'an and 4 days in Shanghai. Each day we had lectures and also went to see the primary sights in each city. At either lunch or dinner, or both, we usually went to "traditional" restaurants, in order to "have a taste" of local delicacies.

7. Scheduled lectures for seminar participants included: Face to Face with the Chinese: Tips on Verbal, Non-verbal, and Cross-cultural Communication Skills; China in the World and Chinese-American Relations; Understanding Chinese Laws, Legal Reforms, and their impact on Chinese Political Processes; From Imperial City to Socialist Capital: Cultural Traditions and Modern Transformation of Beijing; The Rise of Shanghai in Modern China; and

8. Economic Reforms and Environmental Protection.

9. Qin Shihuang, first emperor of China, was known as the "yellow" emperor.

10. From the Shanghai GM materials provided us during our tour of the facility in June 2001. According to *People's Daily*, "Drastic Price Cuts Shake Auto Market," Thursday, January 17, 2002, at http://english.peopledaily.com.cn/200201/17/ eng2002017-88828.shtml, "The drastic price cut in the compact Xiali cars made from Toyota technology, in Tianjin north China, has kicked off a price war in the automobile market one month after China's official entry into WTO.... The latest model, Xiali 2000, now sells for 97,000 yuan (11,680 USD), down 20 percent from 119,980 yuan (14,555 USD). An earlier model is now 39,800 yuan (4,795 USD) which is the lowest price on the market.... Meanwhile, other cars including Buick Sail, Citroen also lowered their prices but still could not compete with Xiali."

11. China Web, "Welcome to Shanghai,"5/11/01 online at http://www.comnex.com/ shanghai/shanghai.htm and "Country Profile: Shanghai Municipality—*People's Daily* online at http://english.peopledaily.com.cn/data/province/Shanghai. html

12. The move by the CCP from a socialist, planned economy with primarily state owned enterprises has proceeded with caution. However, there appears to be no solution at the moment to the serious unemployment generated by this move. With the breakup of state enterprises, persons no longer have access to the "iron rice bowl." This entitlement meant employment, housing, education and health care for life. Many were disenfranchised in this process which in effect dismantled the social and economic infrastructure of the coun-

try without replacing it or allowing access to similar infrastructure, particularly in the countryside. In China in 1985 there were no homeless, no jobless, few drugs and little prostitution. In 2002, one can see it all on the streets of China's major cities.

13. Following the events of September 11, 2001, things cooled off between the United States and China. However, in redefining the war on terrorism as a war on nuclear weapons, President Bush has now included China in his "rogue states" list.

14. From the CIEE booklet, 2001.

15. These include the Hainan Island "American spy plane" incident of April 2001 when a (clearly) American spy plane was forced to do an emergency landing on Hainan Island. Controversy erupted over whether or not the Chinese would return the spy plane. My take was that given the somewhat rudimentary conditions on Hainan Island (opened in about 1988), no one, least of all the Americans, had any idea how to dismantle or remove the American plane from the island.

16. In 1985–86, there were 3 exchange students, 2 Canadian professors and me. Six of us in a town of 300,000 souls. Believe me, people noticed — yet another irritation.

17. In 1988–89, I had been reprimanded by the Department of Foreign Languages for teaching public speaking — although there had been no objection when I put it in the syllabus, nor when I taught it in 1985–86. In retrospect, I better understand the university's position in 1988–89, the year of Tiananmen.

18. Dr. Marilyn Matelski and I formulated these questions for an earlier project in Italy in 1996. She was researching possibilities for internships for Boston College (BC) in Italy, where BC already had several. I was researching possible exchanges for Bridgewater State College. We visited universities in Rome, Florence, Milan and Parma. This rubric worked quite well during that project. So in 1997, I adapted it for my exchange research in Nanjing.

19. These are negotiating issues, not necessarily the completed details of an exchange program. There may be, for example, other issues which come up, though these tend to form the core and are based upon the past experiences of both parties developing a preliminary plan for a negotiated exchange program.

20. Most of the information in this case study having to do with Chinese universities in Nanjing was gathered during my sabbatical in 1997.

21. Gu Jiazu has spent many years in American universities, as have his sons. One of his sons, Gu Hao, is married to the daughter of my best friend in China, Wang Keqiang. His daughter, Yongmei, was also my graduate assistant in the nineties at Bridgewater State College. That's how Chinese relationships work — just like relationships in the rest of the world.

22. These figures are from spring of 1997. NNU may have grown since that time and added to its graduate programs as the Chinese government is acutely aware of the need for more highly trained and/or educated people in the 21st century.

23. *The Lonely Planet: China*, 310.

24. *Ibid.*, 310.

# 5: CASE STUDY: TWO ART EXHIBITIONS CROSS THE PACIFIC

1. Not realizing the implications of a closed city in 1985, the exchange students and I were unprepared for its restrictions. Essentially what is meant by "closed city" in China is a city which either is too poor to be seen by foreigners, has a military base, or both conditions apply. In Linfen, in 1985, both conditions applied. Pragmatically, this meant that foreigners (and others) could not leave the city — nor enter it — except under escort and

with proper paperwork. The consequences of this for foreigners at STU in 1985 was that we were objects of considerable speculation. (In Linfen, a town of some 350,000 persons in a county of three million, there were seven foreigners and we were it — we saw other foreigners infrequently. Most of the peasant population had not seen a foreigner since the Japanese occupation ended in 1945 — if they were old enough.)

2. As an example one of my colleagues had been "sent down" almost 30 years prior to the arrival of the Bridgewater State College foreign exchange students from the United States. This colleague, whom I call Yang Li, was able to return to his province at the end of the 1980s. His daughter, whom I had known as a young girl in Linfen, finished college and applied to our Communication Studies graduate program at BSC, where she was my graduate assistant. This friendship formed in Linfen almost twenty years ago has only blossomed over the years. With the advent of e-mail, China friends are no longer "far away."

3. "Shanxi Province," *People's Daily Online* (database on-line) available at http://english.peopledaily.com.cn/data/province/shanxi.html.

4. *Ibid.*

5. Jim Scotton, "Sad Farewell to Ten Thousand Flags," quoted in *China Daily Online* (March 21, 2002) [database on-line]; available at http://www.chinadaily.com.cn/star/2002/0321/vo3-2.html.

6. *Ibid.*

7. After suffering heavy losses in Jiangxi Province, the Red army retreated from direct engagement with Chiang Kaishek and the Kuomintang through the mountains and north to Shaanxi Province (next to Shanxi Province). "The march took a year to complete and covered 8000 km over some of the world's most inhospitable terrain.... Of the 90,000 people who started out in Jiangxi, only 20,000 made it to Shaanxi. Fatigue, sickness, exposure, enemy attacks and desertion all took their toll." *China: The Lonely Planet Travel Survival Kit* (Singapore: Lonely Planet Publications, 1996), 26–27.

8. Everyone washed in the Fen River near our university. Directly behind my house was an old pagoda. In ancient times, Linfen had been a capital of China.

9. See the glossary for the definition of the Chinese work unit.

10. The students also made these trips (up to 18 hours one way) sitting upright in crowded railway cars in "hard seats." Hard seats tickets were sold until no one asked for one. Thus, they were oversold. Hard seat cars, especially during the Spring Festival, are one's worst nightmare. As a spoiled foreigner, I had a rule, "No more than 8 hours by hard seat."

11. This financial aspect apparently eludes Americans. In 1985, 1988, 1997 or 2002, Chinese students could not begin to afford American textbooks. This problem has plagued Western and Chinese teachers in China since China opened its door to the West. In my classes in Massachusetts, students must pay approximately $50-$100 USD for texts for each course. Logically, if Chinese workers make $100 to $200 USD a month, or under $2,000 USD a year, such textbook costs are out of the question. What I have done in the past is to ship books by U.S. mailbag. One hundred books can be sent for one's courses for very little money. It may take 3–4 months, but they always arrive. China simply cannot afford these texts; hence they reproduce them. I understand copyright for the Western world. In developing countries, we need to rethink the issue as we have finally done with vaccines and medicines for HIV-AIDS in Africa and other countries. While people die or wait to become as rich as Americans, they may as well go generic and live.

12. I honestly believe that the Americans and the Chinese must be the most ethnocentric peoples on the face of the earth.

13. Richard H. Solomon, *Chinese Negotiating Behavior: Pursuing Interests Through "Old Friends,"* 2d ed. (Washington, D.C.: United States Institute of Peace Press, 1999), 163.

14. I first met Yu Shihao at STU where he was in the English Department. (He was one of the few professors at the time in that department who actually spoke English.) He was also the administrative assistant to then–President Tao Benyi, now (2001) the academic vice-president of Shanghai Teacher's University. After receiving his masters' degree, he worked in the Chinese Foreign Service. He was at university in Beijing for this purpose when the

Cultural Revolution began in 1966. Sent to the countryside "to be educated by the peasants," he later was employed as a professor at STU until 1987, when he came to the States (technically he was still employed at STU). After 20 years in the countryside, his opportunity to leave the bleak and culturally barren city of Linfen came with the exchange program between BSC and STU. Like many persons in his position, he never returned to the college which sent him but rather, as Chinese policies began to allow, returned to Beijing where he was recruited for the Chinese Foreign Service. In the nineties, he served at the Chinese consulate in Chicago. At the time of the Peking Opera exhibition, he was a graduate student at Bridgewater State College in the Department of Speech Communication and served as the interpreter to the Chinese delegation. I met Yu Shihao at Shanxi Teacher's University in Linfen, where he and I taught in the English Department in 1985–1986. He was selected that year for graduate study in the United States. From 1986 to 1988 I was his advisor. For purposes of his graduate work, he reversed his name in Western fashion. Thus, his thesis citation reads, Shi Hao Yu, "Managing Intercultural Rhetorical Communication: A Case Study of the Delegates from the People's Republic of China in the United States," unpublished master's thesis, Bridgewater State College, May 1988.

15. Hui-Ching Chang and G. Richard Holt, "More than Relationship: Chinese Interaction and the Principle of Kuan-Hsi," *Communication Quarterly* 39 (Summer 1991): 253.

16. Shi Hao Yu, 96.

17. *Ibid.*, 104.

18. *Ibid.*

19. Oded Shenkar and Simcha Ronen, "The Cultural Context of Negotiations: The Implications of Chinese Interpersonal Norms," *Journal of Applied Behavioral Sciences* 23 (1987): 263–275.

20. The Peking Opera Exhibit was the first of its kind outside of mainland China. The Chinese delegates could be justifiably proud of its significance — and their part in creating the exhibit. They spent nearly a year selecting, preparing and shipping the exhibits. The delegates were: Xu Chimin, administrator; Huang Zhusan, full professor; and Yang Taikang, associate professor, Shanxi Teacher's University.

21. Shihao Yu, 118.

22. Carley H. Dodd, *Dynamics of Intercultural Communication,* 5th ed. (New York: McGraw-Hill, 1998), 157–158.

23. *Ibid.*, 159–162.

24. *Ibid.*, 165.

25. *Ibid.*, 165–166.

26. *Ibid.*, 167–168.

27. *Ibid.*, 164–166.

28. I have written about these experiences in my first book, *In Search of Red Buddha* (New York: Peter Lang Publishers, 1992).

29. Ben-Ami Scharfstein, *The Mind of China* (New York: Basic Books, Inc., 1974), 138. Scharfstein is quoting Chang Tung-sun.

30. Shihao Yu, 132.

31. Ames and Hall, *Anticipating China.*

32. Aristotle, *The Rhetoric.*

33. Ames and Hall.

34. Dr. Marilyn J. Matelski of Boston College, co-author of this book. We produced a videotape of the Chinese exhibition titled "Chinese Opera: Art and Artifact," which was later shown at the China Conference at Bridgewater State College. The China Conference was the result of a Fulbright consortium study grant in 1990 to Massachusetts state colleges.

35. Scharfstein, 138.

36. Shihao Yu, 135.

37. This dichotomy pursued in Western cultures has been discussed often. Robert Pirsig, in *Zen and the Art of Motorcycle Maintenance,* argues for a synthesis. Pirsig's *Zen and*

*the Art* is useful for acquiring the "thinking out of the box" characteristics needed for enhancing intercultural communication.

38. Sarah Rossbach, *Feng Shui: The Chinese Art of Placement* (New York: E. P. Dutton, Inc., 1983).

39. *Ibid.*, 2.

40. Dodd, Carley H., *Dynamics of Intercultural Communication*, 3d ed. (Dubuque, IA: Wm. C. Brown Publishers, 1991).

41. Note that my use of "we" has changed. Usually, when I refer to "we" I mean the Americans and me. During this painful and lengthy episode, the "we" usually refers to my Chinese colleagues and me. In this instance, I perceived my role(s) to include maintaining face and hierarchy for me, my college and my work unit.

42. At the time (1988), we could not obtain petrol, salt or sugar in Linfen, except on the black market, one of the hallmarks of Western influence in Chinese culture.

43. There were many who wanted the exchange to work — then Vice President Robert Dillman, Dean Martha Jones, the Art Department and others. The program lasted for 6 years and ended just as we were getting the hang of it.

44. For further explanation, see Chang and Holt: 251–271. See Glossary, this book. Also see Nancy L. Street, *In Search of Red Buddha*, 30.

# 6. GENERAL ELECTRIC AND *SESAME STREET*— A TRUE JOINT VENTURE

1. Alex McNeil, *Total Television: The Comprehensive Guide to Programming from 1948 to the Present*, 4th ed. (New York: Penguin Books, 1996). However, there are disputes about the exact debut date. For example, a *Chicago Tribune* article marked the twentieth anniversary of *Sesame Street* in 1988 with a 13 November article entitled, "Sesame Streetwise the Upstart that Taught Kids— and TV — a Lesson, Turns 20." Accordingly, within the last year, several writers have called attention to the show's 30th anniversary (e.g., Lawrie Mifflin, "But Does Oscar Like It?" *The New York Times* [September 30, 1998], 4; and "30 Years of Sesame Street," *The Gazette* [September 28, 1998], B5.) The confusion usually arises between the exact airdate vs. the season in which it was broadcast.

2. Melanie Proctor, "Take a Live 'Walk on Sesame,'" *New Straits Times* (May 21, 1997), 5. While Ms. Proctor actually claims 17 joint ventures in her 1997 article, several agreements have emerged since then, including China, Russia, Poland and Palestine-Israel.

3. According to GE's web site Fact Sheet, it is the only company that remains from Dow Jones' original index.

4. Mark Clayton, "GE Goes Light-Years Beyond the Light Bulb," *Christian Science Monitor* (March 23, 1987), 18.

5. *Ibid.*

6. Linda Grant, "The Management Model that Jack Built; John Welch has Slashed GE's Torpid Work Force, Toppled Bureaucratic Walls and Now Says His Huge Corporation Must Beat with the Heart of a Small Business," *Los Angeles Times* (May 9, 1993) [database on-line]; available from Lexis-Nexis.

7. *Ibid.*

8. *Ibid.*

9. Robert Kilborn, Judy Nichols and Stephanie Cook, "Etc...." *Christian Science Monitor* (February 14, 2000), 24.

10. This information was taken from the GE Fact Sheet [database on-line]; available from General Electric's web site at www.ge.com.

11. Mark Clayton, "GE Goes Light-Years Beyond the Light Bulb."

12. Michael Maccoby, "Narcissistic Leaders: The Incredible Pros, the Inevitable Cons," *Harvard Business Review* (January/February 2000) [database on-line]; available from Lexis-Nexis.

13. James Blears, "15 Minutes with … Michael Gibbs; Renowned Negotiation and Conflict-Resolution Expert Explains What It Takes to Negotiate with the Best of Them," *Business Mexico* (June 1, 1999) [database on-line]; available from Lexis-Nexis.

14. John S. McClenahen, "Light in the East," *Industry Week* (March 2, 1998) [database on-line]; available from Lexis-Nexis.

15. Jean Louis Barsoux, "Start Slow, End Fast — Jean Louis Barsoux Offers Advice on Working in Multicultural Teams," *Financial Times* (July 8, 1994), 12.

16. Michael Syrett and Klari Kingston, "GE's Hungarian Light Switch," *Management Today* (April 1995), 52.

17. Natalia Wolniansky and Garry P. Leon. "A New Hungarian Spring?" *Management Review* (July 1991) [database on-line]; available from Lexis-Nexis.

18. John S. McClenahen, "Light in the East."

19. *Ibid.*

20. Jane Perlez, "GE Finds Tough Going in Hungary," *New York Times* (July 25, 1994) [database on-line]; available from Lexis-Nexis.

21. Vanessa Houlder, "How GE's Staff Got a Work-Out — Vanessa Houlder Explains the Company's Method of Creating a Boundary-less Organisation," *Financial Times* (September 22, 1995), 9.

22. *Ibid.*

23. Robert Slater, *The GE Way Fieldbook: Jack Welch's Battle Plan for Corporate Revolution* (New York: McGraw-Hill, 2000), 171–172.

24. General Electric web site, www.ge.com.

25. John S. McClenahen, "Bienvenue! Willkommen! Welcome!" *Industry Week* (February 19, 1996), 31.

26. "The Global Company," *Financial Times* (October 10, 1997) [database on-line]; available from Lexis-Nexis.

27. Shari M. Sweeney, "Illuminating Changes," *Inside Business* (September 1997) [database on-line]; available from Lexis-Nexis.

28. *Ibid.*

29. *Ibid.*

30. Carrie Lee, "GEC Gives Top Post to Cheng," *South China Morning Post* (September 2, 1994), 1.

31. Business Wire (June 16, 1998).

32. Ron Grossman, "Sesame Streetwise the Upstart that Taught Kids — and TV — a Lesson, Turns 20," *Chicago Tribune* (November 13, 1988), 1C. Incidentally, Carroll Spinney is more affectionately known these days as "Big Bird."

33. Samuel Ball, Gerry Ann Bogatz, F. Reid Creech, Randolph Ellsworth and Sandra Landes, "The First Year of *Sesame Street*: An Evaluation," a report to the Children's Television Workshop (Princeton, NJ: Educational Testing Service, 1970), 1. The agencies included the Carnegie Corporation, the Ford Foundation, the U.S. Office of Education, the U.S. Office of Economic Opportunity, and the National Institute for Child Health and Human Development.

34. Frank Mankiewicz and Joel Swerdlow, *Remote Control: Television and the Manipulation of American Life* (New York: Ballantine Books, 1978), 229.

35. Ball et al., Appendix A.

36. Grossman, 1C.

37. Mankiewicz and Swerdlow, 229.

38. Greg Joseph, "Sesame Memories," *San Diego Union-Tribune* (April 26, 1989), C1.

39. Scott Moore, "'Sesame Street:' A Monster New Year's Party," *Washington Post* (December 26, 1993), Y6.

40. The title of this show was *Sesame Street Celebrates Around the World*.

41. Moore, Y6.

42. "A Coming Attraction on China's Television: 'Sesame Street' Show," *New York Times* (January 25, 1981), 7.

43. John J. O'Connor, "TV Weekend: 'Big Bird' on Great Wall," *New York Times* (May 27, 1983), 23.

44. *Ibid.*

45. Susannah Patton, "'Sesame Street' Sign Reads in Many Languages," *Phoenix Gazette* (April 12, 1995), E7. In 1980, "SS" created a local Filipino version of its series; but had not gone further into Asia afterwards.

46. Junhao Hong, *The Internationalization of Television in China: The Evolution of Ideology, Society, and Media Since the Reform* (Westport, Conn.: Praeger, 1998), 60.

47. *Ibid.*

48. "Sesame Street Goes to China," *Ottawa Citizen* (February 16, 1998), E2.

49. *Ibid.*

50. Alex Hannaford, "Satellite Plan to Give Rural China a Window on the World," *South China Morning Post* (August 4, 1995), 18.

51. "Curriculum Document: *Zhima Jie*," Children's Television Workshop (December 1996), 1. Used with permission from CTW.

52. *Ibid.*

53. *Ibid.*

54. In Junhao Hong, *The Internationalization of Television in China: The Evolution of Ideology, Society, and Media Since the Reform*, 49. The author quotes Z. Peng's 1987 article in News and Legislation ("Speech at the Forum of Beijing Journalists") when citing these reforms.

55. "'Sesame Street' Extends to Shanghai," *Agence France Presse* (March 12, 1997) [database on-line]; available from Lexis-Nexis.

56. "'Sesame Street' Extends to Shanghai."

57. Jaime A. Florcruz, "'Z' is for 'Zhima Jie:' That's Mandarin for 'Sesame Street' Which is Launching its Learning-is-Fun Show in China," *Time* (January 26, 1998), 54.

58. Elizabeth Guider, "Big Bird Gets Chinese Cousin," *Variety* (January 5–11, 1998), 50.

59. *Ibid.*

60. Florcruz, 54.

61. William Kazer, "CHN: 'Sesame Street' Makes China Debut," AAP Newsfeed (February 16, 1998) [database on-line]; available from Lexis-Nexis.

62. Malcolm Parry, "Sesame Street Set to Travel," *Vancouver Sun* (September 9, 1997), B6.

63. "Biondi to Keynote Global Emmys' Adapted 'Sesame Street' Set for China; New Services to Launch in China; TNT and Cartoon Network Headed for Berlin; Polish TV Picks Up CTW Show Format; Grundy Kids Series Heads to China," *Electronic Media* (November 21, 1994) [database on-line]; available from Lexis-Nexis.

64. "Broadcast GE to Sponsor Chinese 'Sesame Street'; Chinese Voices for Bert, Ernie and Grover," Asia Intelligence Wire (December 15, 1995) [database on-line]; available from Lexis-Nexis.

65. "GE to Sponsor Chinese 'Sesame Street'; Shanghai Television and Children's Television Workshop to Co-Produce 'Zhima Jie' in China," PR Newswire (November 28, 1995) [database on-line]; available from Lexis-Nexis.

66. *Ibid.*

67. *Ibid.* The article also mentions NBC's other, expanded, partnership with CTW, including broadcasts of *3–2–1 Contact* and *Encyclopedia* on its Asian superchannel as well as a tacit agreement to pursue projects similar to *Zhima Jie* in other Asian countries.

68. "Broadcast GE to Sponsor Chinese 'Sesame Street': Chinese Voices for Bert, Ernie and Grover."

69. *Ibid.*

70. *Ibid.*

71. Jocelyn Longworth, "Elmo Meets His Mandarin Cousins," *Kidscreen* (August 1, 1998), 27.

72. "Chinese Co-Production of 'Sesame Street' Takes the Next Step in the Development Process," Business Wire (March 13, 1997) [database on-line]; available from Lexis-Nexis.

73. *Ibid.*

74. "Broadcast GE to Sponsor Chinese 'Sesame Street': Chinese Voices for Bert, Ernie and Grover."

75. Cui Wen and Ralph Wenge, "Sesame Street in China," a segment aired on *CNN World Report* (April 2, 1997).

76. "General Electric and Children's Television Workshop Sign Agreement to Produce and Spin Off Educational Series," Business Wire (April 20, 1999) [database on-line]; available from Lexis-Nexis.

77. Incidentally, this three-year commitment was consistent with GE's other corporate strategies. According to Justin Fox, a journalist for *Fortune*, "That's how GE works. Targets are set, initially at a three-year planning meeting every summer known as 'session one,' and then refined for the coming year at 'session two' in November or December." (In "America's Most Admired Companies: What's So Great About GE?" *Fortune* (March 4, 2002) [database on-line]; available from http://www.fortune.com.

78. General Electric web site,www.ge.com.

79. *Ibid.*

# 7. CASE STUDY: THE HOLIDAY INN NETWORK IN CHINA—MORE IS BETTER

1. Six Continents Hotels, Corporate Information [database on-line]; available from http://www.pressoffice.sixcontinentshotels.com/corporate.cfm.

2. Before its name change, Six Continents Hotels was known as Bass Hotels & Resorts. According to a July 27, 2001, news release, transmitted by Canadian Corporate Newspaper (CCN) Newswire, "The name Bass and the red triangle trademark were sold with the Bass Brewers business in August last year [2000]. A condition of the sale was that Bass cease using that name by August 21, 2002." ("Bass Proposes Name Change to 'Six Continents' Emphasizing the Global Spread of Business" [database on-line]; available from Lexis-Nexis.) Because of its corporate history, however, the names "Bass Hotels" and "Six Continents" are sometimes used interchangeably in this book.

3. According to Six Continents Hotels' Corporate Information web page, this number includes the following brand groups: Inter-Continental (134); Crowne Plaza (152); Holiday Inn (1541); Holiday Inn Express (1173); Staybridge Suites (26); Forum Hotels (14); Parkroyal (30); Centra (19); and Other (25).

4. Kemmons Wilson, "How did Holiday Inn Begin?" [database on-line]; available from http://www.kwilson.com.

5. *Ibid.*

6. "Holiday Inns: Trying the Comeback Trail," *Business Week*, Industrial Edition (July 5, 1976), 64.

7. *Ibid.*

8. *Ibid.*

9. As indicated in an earlier endnote, Bass changed its name to Six Continents after selling Bass Beer.

10. A term used by Mahmoud Masood, General Manager of the Crowne Plaza–Shanghai during a May 2001 interview.

11. Six Continents Hotels, Corporate Information.

12. See endnote #3 for a complete list of Six Continents Hotels' holdings, according its corporate information web page.

13. "Bass Proposes Name Change to 'Six Continents' Emphasizing the Global Spread of Business."

14. "Holiday Inn Leads Way in Mainland Joint-Venture Schemes," *South China Morning Post* (May 29, 1993), 6.

15. The Lido was originally a joint venture between China Travel Service and Cheong Kong (Holdings) Ltd. Holiday Inn received a management contract on the property in 1984. ("What's in a Name?" *Los Angeles Times* [January 8, 1985], 22).

16. "Holiday Inn Leads Way in Mainland Joint-Venture Schemes."

17. *Ibid.*

18. Mr. Masood later moved to Shanghai, where he managed that city's Crowne Plaza hotel for some time. In 2002, he was promoted again at Six Continents, and has since moved to Beijing.

19. "What Regional Hotels Offer," *Asia Today* (December 1994) [database on-line]; available from Lexis-Nexis.

20. *Ibid.*

21. "Holiday Inn Downtown Leads Hotels in Room Occupancy Rate in Beijing," Xinhua News Service (April 15, 2000) [database on-line]; available from Lexis-Nexis.

22. Six Continents Hotels Brand President for the Americas Ravi K. Saligram, interview by authors, 31 October 2001, tape recording, Atlanta, Georgia. In addition to Mr. Saligram (RS), the persons speaking in this interview are Marilyn J. Matelski (MJM); and Nancy Lynch Street (NLS).

23. "China Hospitality Sector Booming in Shanghai's Pudong," CBNET (March 26, 1998) [database on-line]; available from Lexis-Nexis.

24. "Holiday Inn Makes its Bed in Pudong," *Daily China News* (March 18, 1998) [database on-line]; available from Lexis-Nexis.

25. "Holiday Inn Opens New Club," *Daily China News* (March 23, 1998) [database on-line]; available from Lexis-Nexis.

26. *Ibid.*

27. "Bass Hotels & Resorts to Open Third Hotel in Shanghai," *Asia Pulse* (February 2, 1999) [database on-line]; available from Lexis-Nexis.

28. Crowne Plaza-Shanghai General Manager Mahmoud Masood, interview by authors, 30 May 2001, tape recording, Shanghai, PRC. In addition to Mr. Masood, the persons speaking in this interview are Marilyn J. Matelski (MJM); and Nancy Lynch Street (NLS).

29. This refers to the sultry climate of the region — mild in winter, hot and humid during the summer.

30. "Nanjing to Build 200-m High Building," Xinhua General Overseas News Service (April 18, 1993) [database on-line]; available from Lexis-Nexis.

31. Crowne Plaza–Nanjing General Manager Grace Lau, interview by authors, 2 June 2001, tape recording, Shanghai, PRC. In addition to Ms. Lau, the persons speaking in this interview are Marilyn J. Matelski (MJM); and Nancy Lynch Street (NLS).

32. *Ibid.*

33. "Social Responsibility," Six Continents Hotels Press Office [database on-line]; available from http://www.pressoffice.basshotels.com/social.efm.

# 8. CASE STUDY: DAIMLERCHRYSLER— SILENCE IN CHINA AFTER THE "DEAL HEARD 'ROUND THE WORLD"

1. Bill Vlasic and Bradley A. Stertz, "How Daimler Snared an American Icon," *Detroit News and Free Press* (May 21, 2000), 1.

2. "Companies and Finance: Chrysler/Daimler-Benz Merger," *Financial Times* (May 14, 1998) [database on-line]; available from Lexis-Nexis.

3. *Ibid.*

4. "Chrysler, Daimler Talks Were a Cloak-and-Dagger Affair; 'Project Gamma' Talks Began in Detroit in January; Schrempp Made the First Pitch," *St. Louis Post-Dispatch* (May 10, 1998) [database on-line]; available from Lexis-Nexis.

5. Edmund L. Andrews and Laura M. Holson, "Shaping a Global Giant: The Overview; Daimler-Benz Will Acquire Chrysler in $36 Billion Deal that will Reshape Industry," *New York Times* (May 7, 1998) [database on-line]; available from Lexis-Nexis.

6. "Companies and Finance: Chrysler/Daimler-Benz Merger."

7. *Ibid.*

8. "Chrysler, Daimler Talks Were a Cloak-and-Dagger Affair; 'Project Gamma' Talks Began in Detroit in January; Schrempp Made the First Pitch."

9. Bill Vlasic and Bradley A. Stertz, *Taken for a Ride: How Daimler-Benz Drove Off with Chrysler* (New York: William Morrow, 2000), 319–320.

10. Hofstede's work in this area includes: (1) *Culture's Consequences: International Differences in Work-Related Values* (Beverly Hills: Sage, 1980); (2) *Cultures and Organizations: Software of the Mind* (Maidenhead, U.K.: McGraw-Hill, 1991); and (3) *Uncommon Sense About Organizations: Cases, Studies and Field Observations* (Beverly Hills: Sage, 1994).

11. "Difficulties in a Marriage: Culture Potted Theories," *Financial Times* (November 16, 1998), 13.

12. Merethe Gundersen, "Cultural Consequences of International Standard Systems: A Comparison of German and American Enterprise Systems in Norwegian Organizations," an electronic paper presented at the 24 Information Systems Research Seminar in Scandinavia (August 11–14, 2001), 1–11 [database on-line]; available at http://iris24.ifi.uib.no/proceedings/electronic-papers/042-150-Gundersen-electronic.pdf.

13. *Ibid.*

14. Information obtained from a management course at University of British Columbia [database on-line]; available at http://pacific.commerce.ubc.ca/vertinsky/baim502/baim502-3.pdf.

15. Keith Bradsher, "Management By 2 Cultures May Be a Growing Source of Strain for DaimlerChrysler," *New York Times* (March 24, 1999), 2C.

16. Warren Brown, "No Starring Role for Chrysler; Daimler Firmly in Control After Merger of 'Equals,'" *Washington Post* (March 31, 1999), 1E.

17. Susan Carney and Daniel Howes, "With 'Dream Team' Gone, DCX Needs New Blood," *Detroit News and Free Press* (March 18, 2001), 1A. The list included: Robert Eaton, former Chrysler chairman (retired March 2000); Robert Lutz, former Chrysler vice-chairman and president (retired July 1998); Thomas Stallkamp, former Chrysler president (fired September 1999); James Holden, former president of Chrysler Group (fired in 2001 after only a year with the "new" DaimlerChrysler); Theodor Cunningham, former executive vice-president for sales and marketing (fired November 2000); Thomas Gale, former vice-president of design (retired December 2000); Dennis Pawley, former executive vice-president of manufacturing (retired January 1999); Ronald Boltz, former senior vice-president of product strategy (retired October 1999); Thomas Capo, former senior vice-president and treasurer (resigned August 2000); Rex Franson, former president of Chrysler Financial (resigned January 1999); Thomas Gallagher, former senior vice-president of employee relations (retired June 2000); Steven Harris, former senior vice-president for communications (resigned March 1999); John Herlitz, former senior vice-president of design (retired December 2000); Arthur Liebler, former senior vice-president for marketing (retired February 2001); John MacDonald, former senior vice-president of sales and service (retired February 2001); Kathleen Oswald, former senior vice-president of human resources (fired November 2000); E. Thomas Pappert, former vice-president of dealer relations (retired March 1998); Shamel Rushwin, former senior vice-president of international manufacturing (resigned March 1999); and Chris Theodore, former senior vice-president of platform engineering (resigned March 1999).

18. *Ibid.*

19. Jeff Mortimer and Chris Wright, "Do Not Wear Shorts on the Street; Auto Executives Cope with Foreign Languages, Customs and Taboos," Automotive News International (May 2, 2000) [database on-line]; available from Lexis-Nexis.

20. *Ibid.*

21. *Ibid.*

22. Terence Jackson and Mette Bak, "Foreign Companies and Chinese Workers: Employee Motivation in the People's Republic of China," *Journal of Organizational Change Management*, Vol. 11, No. 4 (1998), 282–300. The authors cite Hofstede's work in Hong Kong and Taiwan, but assert that he is "silent when it comes to the People's Republic of China" (p. 285). Their purpose is to expand his model to explain mainland Chinese beliefs, attitudes and values.

23. *Ibid.*, 285–287.

24. Elizabeth Scholz, Human Resourcer (January/February 2001) [database on-line]; available at http://ww.tannedfeet.com/JanFeb2001.pdf.

25. Jim Mann, *Beijing Jeep: A Case Study of Western Business in China* (Boulder, Colo.: Westview Press, 1997), 24.

26. *Ibid.*, 24–25.

27. *Ibid.*, 313.

28. Ted Plafker, "U.S. Firms Lose China Deals; Business Reasons to Blame Not Politics, Says Beijing," *South China Morning Post* (July 13, 1995), 1.

29. *Ibid.*

30. Nathaniel C. Nash, "China Gives Big Van Deal to Mercedes," *New York Times* (July 13, 1995), 1.

31. *Ibid.*

32. James Harding, "Long March to Mass Market: Early Setbacks Aside, Foreign Car Companies Are Keen to Stay in China Because of its Huge Potential," Financial Times (June 25, 1997)[database on-line]; available from Lexis-Nexis.

33. Benz has not been without its problems, however. In 2002, several disenchanted owners held spirited demonstrations over what they perceived to be defective products. On January 11 of that year, *Straits Times Interactive* reported a "disgruntled man" who "had his 700,000 yuan ($89,000 USD) Mercedes SLK 230 model pulled through the streets of Wuhan....The car was later smashed to a wreck with sledgehammers by workers he had hired." (January 11, 2002) [database on-line]; available from http://straitstimes.asia1.com. sg. Four days later, he was joined by four other Mercedes owners—from Beijing, Shenzhen, Ningbo and Zhuhai to protest the quality control of cars sold in China. According to the ChinaOnline report, "All the members have grievances against the German carmaker, ranging from property damage to loss of human life caused, they said, by the defects in the Mercedes they bought....The owners said that they had repeatedly contacted Mercedes-Benz China but received nothing but 'unreasonable refusal' and 'deliberate delay.'...In a statement issued on Jan. 9, the second regarding the car-smashing incident in Wuhan, Mercedes-Benz China called the spectacle 'a publicity stunt' and condemned it as 'irrational and senseless.'" (ChinaOnline, 15 January 2002) [database on-line]; available from Lexis-Nexis.

34. Keith Naughton, "Daimler Thinks Small," *Newsweek* (May 21, 2001), 48.

35. Christopher Tan, "Z-cars to Carry Mitsubishi Marque," *Business Times Singapore* (June 20, 2001), 23.

36. Peter Dron, "What Chinese Drivers Really Want," *Daily Telegraph* (July 21, 2001), 9.

# 9. CASE STUDY: THE FOXBORO COMPANY— INFRASTRUCTURE'S HIDDEN JEWEL

1. The Foxboro Company is currently part of Production Management, a division of

U.K.-based Invensys plc. Invensys Production Management also includes APV, Avantis, Baan, Esscor, Pacific Simulation, Simulation Sciences, Triconex, and Wonderware.

2. From "Foxboro Facts," p. 1. Obtained from Paul Miller, Foxboro Manager, Public Relations.

3. *Ibid*. According to Foxboro Facts, "In February 1999, Siebe and BTR, another leading British diversified engineering company, merged to form Invensys plc, a world class electronics group with global leadership in the high value-added controls and automation industry. Today, Foxboro is a unit of the Invensys Production Management division."

4. Street and Matelski conducted numerous interviews for this case study in both China and the U.S. in May and June 2001. On both sides of the Pacific, Foxboro representatives were very forthcoming, exposing us to not only the culture-communication conundrum so prevalent in intercultural ventures, but also developing the context for their infrastructure.

5. We interviewed more than ten Foxboro Invensys employees in Massachusetts and Shanghai for this case study. We use "SA" to identify the senior administrators whom we interviewed.

6. Shanghai was ready for development and the Chinese government promotes a policy of development in coastal cities. Shanghai was destined to compete with Hong Kong as the "center" of Chinese banking, infrastructure and shipping. Given the history of the Opium Wars and the previous "concessions," Shanghai is seen as the primary "gateway" to the West.

7. In the Bridgewater State negotiations, our administrators dealt primarily with the President of Shanxi Teacher's University and not Party Secretary Guo Pu. When the first delegation came to Bridgewater, MA we had no clue who was in charge. At the time, it was Guo Pu, as we were to find out.

8. Jim Mann, *Beijing Jeep: A Case Study of Western Business in China* (Boulder, Colo.: Westview Press, 1997).

9. This discussion reflects the views of the authors and not necessarily those of Foxboro employees interviewed.

10. Many Americans seemed to hope that the 1989 Tiananmen Square demonstration could or should have ended with the students and their mentors taking power. However, we feel that this would have been a tragic mistake, creating chaos and setting back China's evolution. Further, subsequent investigations demonstrate the truth of the Chinese allegations that outsiders were orchestrating and encouraging the students long past the safety margins. Many do not realize that the demonstrators occupied the Square from April to June. Tiananmen Square in Beijing is akin (for the Chinese and their government) to the Washington Monument in Washington, D.C.

11. For instance, despite the communist-won revolution and theoretical egalitarian views, the Cultural Revolution demonstrated the deep cultural divide amongst the intellectuals and the peasants. Despite the ten years devoted by Mao Zedong to bridging this divide, intellectuals in the '80s and '90s do not demonstrate great regard for the peasants. For this discussion, see Street, Nancy, *In Search of Red Buddha* (New York: Peter Lang Publishers, 1992), 64–89.

12. "China Unveils Huge Welfare Plan," BBC News Asia-Pacific (March 11, 2001) [database on-line]; available from http://news.bbc.co.uk/hi/english/world/asia-pacific/newsid_1213000/1213973.stm.

13. *Ibid*.

14. *Ibid*.

15. This background discussion reflects the views of the authors and not necessarily the views of Foxboro employees.

16. Eric Hoffer, *The True Believer: Thoughts on the Nature of Mass Movements*, reissue edition (New York: HarperCollins), 1989.

17. This section reflects the views of the authors only, not that of Foxboro Company.

18. My father's father, James Lynch, was a farmer during the "dust bowl" era in Arkansas

in the "Great Depression" in the thirties in the United States. James Lynch lost his farm three times in Arkansas. They did not have running water, nor hot water unless boiled. My grandmother (Anna Mae Lynch) did not have indoor plumbing nor a radio until the war began. After three attempts to settle in California and obtain work, my grandfather worked in the "town" (five to six thousand people) of Coalinga as the groundskeeper of the town's park. I was never so happy as a child, as when I could point to my grandfather and proudly proclaim that he was the "boss" of our park. My grandparents had little infrastructure in their house, but moved with the times, being one of the first in our town to have a recording machine to record his and my grandmother's singing of gospel hymns. Today, I have a CD of these recordings.

19. See the beginning of this case study for a brief description of the corporate structure.

20. Bruce A. Henderson and Jorge L. Larco, *Lean Transformation: How to Change Your Business into a Lean Enterprise* (Richmond, Va.: The Oaklea Press, 2000), 94.

21. *Ibid.*, 95–96.

22. *Ibid.*, 187.

23. *Ibid.*, 185–230.

24. Robert Slater, *The GE Way Fieldbook: Jack Welch's Battle Plan for Corporate Revolution* (New York: McGraw-Hill, 2000).

25. Due to the rapidly changing guidelines in China, it is difficult to get a fix on what the nature of the relationship is within the holding company to the government. Making an educated guess, we think the divestiture went something like this: Originally, the government and Shanghai Instrumentation knew they needed Foxboro (or other similar) products to develop needed infrastructure. Back in 1983, Shanghai Instrumentation was probably a state-owned enterprise. If it was like most work units, the company may have had two lines of supervision: the Party line, headed by the Party Secretary; and the production line, headed by the Director or President of the facility.

During that period, there was considerable infighting in work units as to who was to hold power, for obvious reasons, as China was in the early days of its transformation. At first, the two companies were a joint venture, with the Chinese side holding the controlling interest. At first, the Chinese company may have been state owned, later the Party may have sold the state property to people within the company, usually to CCP members. Thus, though we hear that the Chinese government is very worried about free enterprise taking hold in China, in fact, through the CCP membership, they exert influence in the decision-making processes of the joint venture. Surely the move to the holding company was linguistic, with internal ownership remaining with the CCP membership. That is why the Deputy Director of the joint venture is always Chinese (and probably a CCP member). In various interviews, we tried to clarify this situation. If this scenario is even partially correct, it helps explain how foreign companies in China collect information. For how would an outsider know what the government is thinking about doing next? The holding company, the deputy director and the good relationship with the local, provincial, and central government (run by the Chinese Communist Party) insure that their joint ventures know about major contracts coming up for bid around the country. More and more, the Chinese are also providing educated and computer literate workers for joint ventures. But start-up costs and initial technology come from the foreign investors. Thus, from a divided world, we see the *yin-yang* approach of East and West in enterprise.

26. We think that the approach taken in this instance illustrates a more collaborative approach between the Chinese side and the U.S. side than may generally be taken by other multinationals. There seems to be a genuine effort to promote equality within the Shanghai-based enterprise. This is important to note in light of the frequent charges of exploitation of employees in developing countries, as in other parts of Asia, Africa and South America.

27. One senior administrator told us that Foxboro can support 40 languages.

29. See Street, 63–112.

# 10. FINAL THOUGHTS

1. Bruce Cummings, *The Two Koreas* (New York: Headline Series, Foreign Policy Assoc., Inc., 1984), 8.

2. Mao Tsetung (Mao Zedong), "On Practice: On the Relation Between Knowledge and Practice, Between Knowing and Doing (July 1937)," in *Selected Readings from the Works of Mao Tsetung* (Peking: Foreign Languages Press, 1971), 70–71. Though the context is historically different, the principles Mao expressed here are valid and point to the Chinese emphasis on context, participation, process, relationships and trust in the achievement of goals.

3. As we are all aware, not only the desolation of HIV-AIDS but also drought and starvation are appalling issues in Southern Africa.

4. See "Corporate Social Responsibility in China: Practices by U.S. Companies— How U.S. Companies Contribute to the Improvement of Social, Labor, and Environmental Conditions," The Business Roundtable, 3 [database on-line]; available at http://www.brtable. org/pdf/377.pdf.

5. This is "the first in a series of papers exploring corporate social responsibility by U. S. companies around the world.... The goal of this series is to show how U.S. companies can be, and are, constructive and innovative agents of change around the world," 7. N.D.

6. *Ibid.*, 24.

7. From 1985 to 1992, the authors have had direct experience, either in the United States or in the People's Republic of China, with the Chinese hierarchy, with Chinese delegations and with Chinese students from mainland China. Dr. Street was twice the Exchange Professor from Bridgewater State College to Shanxi Teacher's University in Linfen, Shanxi Province, PRC. She also received a Fulbright Grant to study economic development in Taiwan and Korea in 1988, and a second Fulbright Grant to study language and culture in the PRC in 1990. Her book, *In Search of Red Buddha*, was published by Peter Lang in 1992. Dr. Marilyn J. Matelski, author of numerous books on mass communication, including *The Soap Opera Evolution*, is professor of Intercultural and Mass Communication at Boston College. Dr. Matelski has hosted Chinese delegations from the PRC to the U.S. and produced a video documentary entitled *Chinese Opera: Art and Artifact*, based on interviews with Chinese Opera experts sent from Shanxi Province with exhibits from the PRC in 1988. See case study.

8. Roger Fisher and William Ury, *Getting to YES* (New York: Penguin Books, 1983, originally published Boston, MA: Houghton Mifflin Company, 1981). This approach has stirred much controversy. For other works by Ury, see "Reflections on a Wild Idea," *Negotiation Journal* (July 1985); and, Roger Fisher, "The Structure of Negotiation: An Alternate Model," *Negotiation Journal* (July 1986): 234–235. These will lead you to others. We are indebted to former BSC graduate student Diane Metthe for her work in this area in her thesis, "The Win/Win Conflict Resolution Strategy: A Dramatistic Analysis" (unpublished MA thesis, Bridgewater State College, 1988). Talks with her on this analysis led us to consider negotiations, particularly the applicability of "getting to yes" to intercultural negotiations. Throughout this chapter, ideas were generated by Street's graduate students: Shi Jingshun, Yu Shihao (each of whom worked on intercultural themes and analyses, see case study); Philip Patterson and Diane Metthe, who looked at intercultural training and negotiation respectively. Portions of this paper were also part of Street's report following her 1988 Fulbright Study Grant to Taiwan and Korea.

9. See Chapter 1.

10. There are Four Dragons. The Four Dragons are also known as the NICs (Newly Industrialized Countries), the NIE (Newly Industrialized Economies), the Asian Tigers and the countries of the Pacific Rim. From our perspective, the Fifth Dragon, the People's Republic of China (PRC) is the rising Eastern star, thus the designation of "Greater China," which includes Hong Kong, Taiwan and mainland China. Confucian culture originally spread throughout the region from mainland China (in another incarnation). While each

of the Four Dragons has significant indigenous culture, the impact and the traditional dominance of the Four Dragons by the Fifth Dragon (now the PRC) should not be underestimated, nor should the potential for bonding. While Japan was also influenced by Confucian culture, we have not included it here, as that is a complicated discussion beyond the purview of this study.

11. See for example, Donald K. Darnell and Wayne Brockriede, *Persons Communicating* (Englewood Cliffs, NJ: Prentice-Hall, Inc., 1976); Joyce Hocker Frost and William W. Wilmot, *Interpersonal Conflict* (Dubuque, Iowa: Wm. C. Brown Company, 1978): and Brent D. Ruben, "Communication and Conflict: A System Theoretic Perspective," *Quarterly Journal of Speech* 64 (April 1978): 202–213.

12. Diane Metthe, "The Win-Win Conflict Resolution Strategy: A Dramatistic Analysis," unpublished master's thesis, Bridgewater State College, April 1988.

13. Roger Fisher and William Ury, *Getting to YES* (New York: Penguin Books, 1983, originally published Boston, MA: Houghton Mifflin Company, 1981): 1–28.

14. Metthe, 53.

15. In the early days of academic exchanges, the Western side assumed that they were negotiating president-to-president. However, in 1984, unbeknownst to the Western side, the party secretary was the leader of the delegation sent from Linfen, Shanxi Province, not the president of the university. Little attention was paid to this seemingly innocuous member of the delegation. Some of us even discussed the possibility that Guo Pu might be a Communist.

16. On the mainland, the details of life and conducting business can be overwhelming. Unless you are a VIP, you will have to learn to handle many aspects of your life and work. When on a short trip, i.e., from a week to ten days, you will need a very efficient, flexible, patient, good-humored and not easily frustrated person to accomplish this task. To make the negotiations go smoothly, minimize frustration and have a good experience, choose this person carefully. Should you go to Taiwan and South Korea prior to a trip to the PRC, you can be misled by the ease of completing such transactions as an overseas phone call, particularly if you stay in Seoul or Taipei. The major coastal cities of China are also remarkably easy to communicate from. The interior of China is quite another matter. From Shanxi Province, it can take up to three hours to complete a telephone call to Beijing. Be prepared. Patience and humor are indispensable attributes.

17. Edward T. Hall, *The Dance of Life: The Other Dimension of Time* (Garden City, New York: Anchor Books Edition, 1984), 44–58. His chapter on "High and Low Context Messages," 59–77, is also valuable for learning communication strategies in cultures where context is different from the American context (almost everywhere on the planet).

18. The rule in 1997 was no central heating south of the Yangtze (this meant Jiangsu Province) and no central air-conditioning north of the Yangtze (as in Beijing). People could buy individual units if they chose, but would be responsible for the electricity, which is in short supply and quite expensive in China. In this way, larger quarters are not encouraged in cities because they take up too much room in the already overcrowded coastal cities and because of the prohibitive cost. The rule is, of course, based upon reasonable statistics, but one could still expire from the cold in Nanjing in the unheated apartments of friends. Let us be clear. These rules are not arbitrary, nor are they a consequence of communism. The rules exist because they are needed to control resources so that all may have access to these resources.

19. In the eighties, Dr. Street grew used to colleagues, friends and students looking through her papers and other things, simply out of curiosity. One afternoon, while she was taking a bath, a student walked into her house, called out to her, and, being told that she was in the bath, simply replied that he would wait. And after all, why not? Here was a woman living alone in 4 rooms—the only such situation on campus. She could spare some space for visitors.

20. The American Chamber of Commerce in Shanghai can be visited online at www.amcham-shanghai.org.

21. Sydney Chang, *AmChat: Journal of the American Chamber of Commerce in Shanghai*, April 2001 (Shanghai: The American Chamber of Commerce in Shanghai), 3.

22. *Ibid.*, 18. For information on this program, e-mail Shanghai.Offic.Box@ mail.doc.gov

23. *Ibid.*, 13–17.

24. By 2001 standards, 750 RMB would translate into less than $100 dollars.

25. *AmChat*, 8.

26. *Ibid.*, 16

27. *Ibid.*, 11. The AmCham Mission statement reads, "The American Chamber of Commerce in Shanghai is a non-partisan, non-profit organization whose purpose is to promote and support business between American and Chinese enterprises."

28. AmCham's address is: Shanghai-Puxi, 350l CITIC Square, 1168 Nanjing Xi Lu, Shanghai 200041, China. Tel: (8621) 5252 4618 — Fax: (8621) 5252 4616; e-mail: shanghai@executivecenter.com; Web: www.executivecentre.com; or, write to the Portman Ritz-Carlton Hotel, 4 floor, 1376 Nanjing Road West, Shanghai, China, 200040.

29. The American Chamber of Commerce in Shanghai members materials, June 2001. The American Chamber of Commerce is also active in other cities in China, including Beijing.

# APPENDIX A. CHINA PROFILE

1. Information has been obtained from: 1) *China Daily Online* (database on-line) available from http://english.peopledaily.com.cn/china (February 9, 2003); and 2) the BBC News/Country Profiles/Country Profile: China, (March 8, 2002) [database on-line]; available at http://news.bbc.co.uk/hi/english/world/asia-pacific/country_profiles/newsid-1287000/1287798.stm.

# APPENDIX B. TRADITIONAL CHINESE HOLIDAYS AND FESTIVALS

1. Much of the information has been taken from *Lonely Planet: China*, 7th ed. (Victoria, Australia: Lonely Planet Publications, Pty. Ltd., 2000).

# Bibliography

## BOOKS

Altschiller, David. *China at the Crossroads*. New York: H.W. Wilson Co., 1994.

Ball, Samuel, Gerry Ann Bogatz, F. Reid Creech, Randolph Ellsworth and Sandra Landes. "The First Year of Sesame Street: An Evaluation." *A Report to the Children's Television Workshop*. Princeton, NJ: Educational Testing Service, 1970.

Bernstein, Richard. *The Coming Conflict with China*. New York: Alfred A. Knopf, 1997.

Chesneaux, Jean. *Peasant Revolts: 1840-1949*. Translated by C. A. Curwen. London: Thames and Hudson Ltd., 1973.

Child, John. *Management in China During the Age of Reform*. New York: Cambridge University Press, 1996.

Ching, Julia. *Probing China's Soul: Religion, Politics, and Protest in the People's Republic*. San Francisco: Harper & Row, 1990.

*The Communication of Ideas*. Edited by L. Bryson. New York: New York Institute for Religious and Social Studies, 1948.

Cummings, Bruce. *The Two Koreas*. New York: Headline Series, Foreign Policy Assoc., Inc., 1984.

"Curriculum Document: *Zhima Jie*." New York: Children's Television Workshop, December 1996.

Deng Xaoping. *The Selected Works of Deng Xaoping (1975–1982)*. Beijing: Foreign Languages Press, 1987.

Dietrich, Craig. *People's China: A Brief History*. New York: Oxford University Press, 1986.

Dodd, Carley H. *Dynamics of Intercultural Communication*, 5th ed. Boston: McGraw-Hill, 1998.

Evans, Richard. *Deng Xiaoping and the Making of Modern China*. New York: Viking, 1994.

Fairbank, John King. *China: A New History*. Cambridge, Mass.: Harvard University Press, 1992.

Gittings, John. *Real China: From Cannibalism to Karaoke.* New York: Pocket Books, 1997.

Green, Robert. *The 48 Laws of Power.* New York: Viking, 1998.

Gross, Lynne Schafer. *The International World of Electronic Media.* New York: McGraw-Hill, Inc., 1995.

Guo-Ming, Chen, and William J. Starosta. *Foundations of Intercultural Communication.* Needham Heights, Mass.: Allyn & Bacon, 1998.

Hall, David, and Roger T. Ames. *Anticipating China : Thinking Through the Narratives of Chinese and Western Culture.* Albany, New York: State University of New York Press, 1995.

Hall, Edward T. *The Anthropology of Manners.* San Francisco: W.H. Freeman, 1955.

_____. *The Silent Language.* New York: Fawcett, 1959.

_____, and Mildred Reed Hall. *Hidden Differences, Doing Business with the Japanese.* New York: Anchor Books Doubleday, 1987.

Henderson, Bruce A., and Jorge L. Larco. *Lean Transformation: How to Change Your Business into a Lean Enterprise.* Richmond, Va.: The Oaklea Press, 2000.

Hofstede, Geert. *Cultures and Organizations: Software of the Mind.* Maidenhead, UK: McGraw-Hill, 1991.

_____. *Culture's Consequences: International Differences in Work-Related Values.* Beverly Hills: Sage, 1980.

_____. *Uncommon Sense About Organizations: Cases, Studies and Field Observations.* Beverly Hills: Sage, 1994.

Hong, Junhao. *The Internationalization of Television in China: The Evolution of Ideology, Society, and Media Since the Reform.* Westport, Conn.: Praeger, 1998.

Huntington, Samuel P. *The Clash of Civilizations and the Remaking of World Order.* New York: Simon & Schuster, 1997.

Kennedy, George. A. *Comparative Rhetoric: An Historical and Cross-Cultural Introduction.* New York: Oxford University Press, 1997.

Kristof, Nicholas D. *China Wakes: The Struggle for the Soul of a Rising Power.* New York: Times Books, 1994.

Li, Conghua. *China: The Consumer Revolution.* Singapore: John Wiley & Sons [Asia], 1998.

*Lonely Planet: China,* 7th ed. Victoria, Australia: Lonely Planet Publications, Pty. Ltd., 2000.

McNeil, Alex. *Total Television: The Comprehensive Guide to Programming from 1948 to the Present,* 4th ed. New York: Penguin Books, 1996.

Madsen, Richard. *China and the American Dream: A Moral Inquiry.* Berkeley: University of California Press, 1995.

Mankiewicz, Frank, and Joel Swerdlow. *Remote Control: Television and the Manipulation of American Life.* New York: Ballantine Books, 1978.

Mann, Jim. *Beijing Jeep: A Case Study of Western Business in China.* Oxford, UK: Westview Press, 1997.

Mao Tse-tung. *Selected Works of Mao Tse-Tung.* Edited by Bruno Shaw. New York: Harper & Row, Publishers, 1970.

Martin, Judith N., Thomas K. Nakayama, and Lisa A. Flores. *Readings in Cultural Contexts.* Mountain View, Calif.: Mayfield Publishing Company, 1998.

Meyer, Milton Walter. *China: A Concise History.* Lanham, Md.: Rowan & Littlefield Publishers, 1994.

Mosher, Steven W. *China Misperceived: American Illusions and Chinese Reality.* New York: Basic Books, 1990.

Newman, Robert P. *Owen Lattimer and the "Loss" of China.* Berkeley: University of California Press, 1992.

Patten, Christopher. *East and West, China, Power, and the Future of Asia.* New York: Random House, 1998.

Pietrusza, David. *The Chinese Cultural Revolution.* San Diego, Calif.: Lucent Books, 1996.

Quanyu, Huang, Joseph Leonard and Chen Tong. *Business Decision Making in China.* New York: International Business Press, 1997.

Rossbach, Sarah. *Feng Shui: The Chinese Art of Placement*. New York: E.P. Dutton, Inc., 1983.
Scharfstein, Ben-Ami. *The Mind of China*. New York: Basic Books, 1974.
Schell, Orville. *Mandate of Heaven*. New York: Simon & Schuster, 1994.
Schwartz, Benjamin I. *The World of Thought in Ancient China*. Cambridge, Mass.: Harvard Press, 1985.
Seargant, Harriet. *Shanghai: Collision Point of Cultures, 1918-1939*. New York: Crown, 1990.
Slater, Robert. *The GE Way Fieldbook: Jack Welch's Battle Plan for Corporate Revolution*. New York: McGraw-Hill, 2000.
Solomon, Richard H. *Chinese Negotiating Behavior: Pursuing Interests through "Old Friends."* Washington, DC: United States Institute of Peace Press, 1999.
Spence, Jonathan D. *The Search for Modern China*. New York: W.W. Norton, 1990.
Starr, John Bryan. *Understanding China*. New York: Hill and Wang, 1997.
Street, Nancy Lynch. *In Search of Red Buddha*. New York: Peter Lang, 1992.
Stross, Randall E. *Bulls in the China Shop and Other Sino-American Business Encounters*. Honolulu: University of Hawaii Press, 1990.
Tan, Qingshan. *The Making of U.S. China Policy: From Normalization to the Post–Cold War Era*. Boulder and London: Lynne Reinner Publishers, 1992.
Vlasic, Bill, and Bradley A. Stertz. *Taken for a Ride: How Daimler-Benz Drove Off with Chrysler*. New York: William Morrow, 2000.
Welsh, Frank. *A History of Hong Kong*. London: Harper Collins, 1993.
Wong, R. Bin. *China Transformed: Historical Change and the Limits of European Experience*. Ithaca and London: Cornell University Press, 1997.
*The World Almanac and Book of Facts 2000*. Mahwah, New Jersey: World Almanac Books, 2000.
Zha, Jianying. *China Pop: How Soap Operas, Tabloids and Bestsellers Are Transforming a Culture*. New York: The New Press, 1995.

# JOURNALS AND MAGAZINES

Abramowitz, Morton I. "How to Think About China." *Newsweek*, 16 June 1997, 43.
Alter, Jonathan. "On the Road in China." *Newsweek*, 29 June 1998, 29.
_____. "A Time of Long Goodbyes." *Newsweek*, 19 May 1997, 51.
"America's Dose of Sinophobia." *The Economist*, 29 March 1997, 29–30.
Barsoux, Jean Louis. "Start Slow, End Fast — Jean Louis Barsoux Offers Advice on Working in Multicultural Teams," *Financial Times*, 8 July 1994, 12.
Becker, Jasper. "Beyond Mao and Mammon." *World Press Review*, March 1996, 8–10.
_____. "Elderly Accused of Inciting Trouble." *South China Morning Post*, 7 August 7, 1999, 14.
_____. "The Fading Voices of Dissent." *World Press Review*, March 1996, 20–21.
_____. "Good News! You're Fired!" *World Press Review*, February 1998, 31.
Bernstein, Richard. "Chinese Exiles Wonder How Wind Will Blow." *The New York Times*, 21 February 1997, A15.
Bezlova, Antoaneta. "Beijing Views Transfer as a Lesson of History." *USA Today*, 30 June 1997, 6A.
Biskind, Peter. "When Worlds Collide." *The Nation*, April 1999, 11–12.
Bogert, Carroll. "The Freedom Bowl." *Newsweek*, 3 March 1997, 37.
_____. "Pray for China." *Newsweek*, 9 June 1997, 44–45.
_____. "Windows 95, 5 Bucks." *Newsweek*, 26 May 1997, 82.
Boyer, Peter J. "American Guanxi." *The New Yorker*, 14 April 1997, 48–61.
Bradsher, Keith. "Management By 2 Cultures May Be a Growing Source of Strain for DaimlerChrysler." *The New York Times*, 24 March 1999, 2C.
"Britain Delivers 11th-Hour Pleas for Elections, Restraint." *The Detroit News*, 29 June 1997, A10.

Brooke, Peter A. "Where the Currency is Confusion." *The Boston Sunday Globe*, 4 January 1998, E3.

Brown, Warren. "No Starring Role for Chrysler; Daimler Firmly in Control After Merger of 'Equals'." *The Washington Post*, 31 March 1999, 1E.

Brummer, Alex, and John Gittings. "China: The Next Domino?" *The Guardian*, 22 January 1999. In *World Press Review*, April 1999, 37.

Carney, Susan, and Daniel Howes. "With 'Dream Team' Gone, DCX Needs New Blood." *The Detroit News and Free Press*, 18 March 2001, 1A.

Cassy, John. "Capitalism, But Not as We Know It: The WTO Will Admit China But Skyscrapers and Rampant Consumerism Cannot Disguise the Slow Pace of Change." *The Guardian*, 11 September 2001, 24.

Chacon, Richard. "At Harvard, an Ambiguous Welcome." *The Boston Sunday Globe*, 26 October 1997, A19.

Chanda, Nayan, and Kari Huus. "Talking Tough, Waving the Flag." *World Press Review*, March 1996, 12–15.

Chang, Hui-Ching and G. Richard Holt. "More than Relationship: Chinese Interaction and the Principle of *Kuan-Hsi*," *Communication Quarterly*, Summer 1991, 251–271.

Chen, Victoria. "*Mien Tze* at the Chinese Dinner Table: A Study of the Interactional Accomplishment of Face," *Research on Language and Social Interaction*, 1990/1991, 109–140.

"China: Export-Led Growth." *China Economic Review*, 31 December 1999, 21.

"China Issues Commentary on US Human Rights Report." *Beijing Review*, March 23–29, 1998.

"China Makes Nice." *Asiaweek*, 30 October 1998. In *World Press Review*, January 1999, 6–7.

"China Survey." *The Economist*, 8 March 1997, 6–8, 11, 12, 14, 19-22, 25–28, 126–128.

"China to Rush 4,000 Troops into Hong Kong After Shift." *The San Diego Union-Tribune*, 28 June 1997, A-2.

"China's New Tipple." *The Economist*, 5 April 1997, 27, 104–106.

"China, US Improve Relations." *Beijing Review*, 14-20 April 1997, 4–5.

"China's Shipping Industry." *AMChat, Journal of the American Chamber of Commerce in Shanghai*, April 2001, 13–15.

Chote, Robert, and Guy de Jonquiéres. "Doom and Gloom at Davos." *Financial Times*, 29 January 1999. In *World Press Review*, April 1999, 34.

Chua-Eoan, Howard, and James Walsh. "The Last Emperor." *Time*, 3 March 1997, 60–68.

Chu Yu-Lin, David. "Hong Kong: In the Dragon's Jaws?" *World Press Review*, March 1996, 13.

Clayton, Mark. "GE Goes Light-Years Beyond the Light Bulb." *Christian Science Monitor*, 23 March 1987, 18.

"Clinton Salutes House Approval of MFN Status." *China Daily*, 26 June 1997, 1.

Clover, Charles. "Dreams of the Eurasian Heartland." *Foreign Affairs*, March/April 1999, 9.

"Coalition Sets Protest Plans for Chinese President's Visit." *The Boston Globe*, 24 October 1997, A21.

Cohn, Martin Regg. "China Seeks to Build the Great Firewall; Controlled Modernization the Mantra; Censors Patrol Chat Room." *Toronto Star*, 21 July 2001, 1A.

"A Coming Attraction on China's Television: 'Sesame Street' Show." *The New York Times*, 25 January 1981, 7.

"The Communist Dynasty Had Its Run. Now What?" *The New York Times*, 23 February 1997, E1, E5.

Cooper, Matthew and Melinda Liu. "Bright Light." *Newsweek*, 10 February 1997, 22–31.

Cox, James. "Incentives to Lure Industry Stir Debate, Fear in Hong Kong." *USA Today*, 13 June 1997, 4B.

_____. "U.S. Business People in Hong Kong are Bullish." *USA Today*, 13 June 1997, 4B.

_____. "U.S. Criticizes Troop Use in Hong Kong." *USA Today*, 30 June 1997, 1A.

Crowell, Todd. "On Taiwan, 'Showing a Bit of Military Muscle.'" *World Press Review*, March 1996, 15.

Deane, Daniela. "Awaiting the Change: 4 Faces of Hong Kong." *USA Today*, 30 June 1997, 7A.

"Deathbed Documentary." *World Press Review*, March 1997, 24.

"Deng Paved Way for Reunification." *China Daily*, 24 February 1997, 1.

"Deng's China." *The Economist*, 22 February 1997, 19–23, 25–28, 33.

"Difficulties in a Marriage: Culture Potted Theories." *The Financial Times*, 16 November 1998, 13.

Dobson, William J. "US-China Summit: Photo-Op Diplomacy." *Christian Science Monitor*, 30 October 1997, 23.

Dron, Peter. "What Chinese Drivers Really Want." *The Daily Telegraph*, 21 July 2001, 9.

Eckholm, Erik. "Beijing Journal: Delectable Materialism Catching On in China." *The New York Times*, 10 January 1998, 1A.

Economy, Elizabeth. "Painting China Green." *Foreign Affairs*, March/April 1999, 14.

Eliason, Marcus. "China Takes Over." *The Arizona Republic*, 1 July 1997, A1, A6.

Elliott, Dorinda. "Hong Kong's Canary." *Newsweek*, June 1997, 41–42.

_____. "Why the World Watches." *Newsweek*, 19 May 1997, 30–35.

Faison, Seth. "Beijing after Deng: Paramount Indifference." *The New York Times*, 21 February 1997, A1, A8.

_____. "China's Coming, But Stocks are Hot: Hong Kong Market Confounds Experts, Closes with Flourish." *The San Diego Union-Tribune*, 29 June 1997, 11–12.

_____. "Condolence Calls Put Rare Light on Deng's Family." *The New York Times*, 22 February 1997.

Farley, Maggie. "Deng's True Heirs: The Ambitious Young; The Late Leader's Legacy Includes a Sense of Confidence and Entitlement that Worries Many in the Older Generation." *Los Angeles Times*, 24 February 1997, 1A.

_____. "In the Days After Hand-Over, Portents Inundate Hong Kong." *The Fresno Bee*, 6 July 1997, A8.

Fisher, Ian. "A Town's Strange Bedfellows Unite Behind Chinese Refugees." *The New York Times*, 21 February 1997, A1, A32.

Fisher, Roger and William Ury. *Getting to YES*. New York: Penguin Books, 1983.

Fisk, Robert. "Talks With Osama bin Laden." *The Nation*, 21 September 1998, 24–27.

Florcruz, Jaime A. "'Z' is for 'Zhima Jie': That's Mandarin for 'Sesame Street' Which is Launching its Learning-is-Fun Show in China." *Time*, 26 January 1998, 54.

_____. "For Richer or For Poorer." *Newsweek*, 19 May 1997, 40–41.

"Foreigners to be Excluded From Deng's Memorial Service." *The Detroit Free Press*, 21 February 1997, A5.

"A Former Factory Manager is Expected to Carry on for Deng." *The Detroit Free Press*, 20 February 1997, A12.

"From Empire to Empire and Back Again." *Newsweek*, 19 May 1997, 47.

Gargan, Edward A. "In Looking to the Future, Hong Kong and Taiwan Face New Uncertainties." *The New York Times*, 20 February 1997, A11.

Gilley, Bruce. "Vox Populi: No Rebellion, Thanks— We're Getting Rich." *World Press Review*, March 1996, 16.

Gittings, John. "A Great Leap Backwards." *World Press Review*, March 1996, 10–11.

_____. "Hong Kong: Not with a Bang." *World Press Review*, July 1997, 48.

Goldstein, Melvyn C. "The Dalai Lama's Dilemma." *Foreign Affairs*, January/February 1998, 83–97.

Gorbachev, Mikhail. "Our Different Paths." *Newsweek*, 3 March 1997, 34.

Gottliebsen, Robert. "Greenspan's Great Gamble." *Business Review Weekly*, 18 January 1999. In *World Press Review*, April 1999, 35.

Gray, John. "Not for the First Time, World Sours on Free Market." *The Nation*, 19 October 1998, 17–18.

*Great Religions of the World*. Washington, D. C.: National Geographic Society, 1978.

Grossman, Ron. "Sesame Streetwise the Upstart that Taught Kids— and TV —a Lesson, Turns 20." *Chicago Tribune*, 13 November 1988, 1C.

Grunwald, Michael. "Getting Beyond Beijing's Creepiness." *The Boston Sunday Globe*, 26 October 1997, M11–M12.

_____. "New Vs. Old: As Building Soars, What Will Become of the City's Pictorial Past?" *The Boston Sunday Globe*, 26 October 1997, M1, M11.

Guider, Elizabeth. "Big Bird Gets Chinese Cousin." *Variety*, 5–11 January 1998, 50.

Hannaford, Alex. "Satellite Plan to Give Rural China a Window on the World." *South China Morning Post*, 4 August 1995, 18.

Hertsgaard, Mark. "Our Real China Problem." *The Atlantic Monthly*, November 1997, 97–114.

Hoagland, Jim. "Tiananmen Square Matters." *The Arizona Republic*, 2 June 1997, B5.

Holbrooke, Richard. "Much Too Tough to Be Cute." *Time*, 3 March 1997, 68.

"Holiday Inn Leads Way in Mainland Joint-Venture Schemes." *South China Morning Post*, 29 May 1993), 6.

"Holiday Inns: Trying the Comeback Trail." *Business Week*, Industrial Edition, 5 July 1976, 64.

Houlder, Vanessa. "How GE's Staff Got a Work-Out — Vanessa Houlder Explains the Company's Method of Creating a Boundary-less Organisation." *Financial Times*, 22 September 1995, 9.

Hua, Yin. "The Swelling Tide of Information: Beijing Opts to Open Up." Panos Features, 22 October 1998. *In World Press Review*, January 1999, 11.

"Human Rights and Diplomacy." *The Economist*, 12 April 1997, 19–23, 25–28, 52, 110–112.

Huntington, Samuel P. "The Lonely Superpower." *Foreign Affairs*. March/April 1999, 35.

Hutzler, Charles. "A Solemn Memorial." *The Detroit Free Press*, 25 February 1997.

Hwang, Suein L. "Sucked In: How Philip Morris Got Turkey Hooked on American Tobacco." *The Wall Street Journal*, 11 September 1998, A1, A8.

Hwang, Young-Bae and Jacek Kugler. "The Likelihood of Major War in East Asia and the Transition on the Korean Peninsula." *Asian Perspective*, Winter 1997, 41–62.

"Is Hong Kong Ripe for a Bit of Central Planning?" *The Economist*, 12 April 1997, 25–26.

Jackson, Terence and Mette Bak. "Foreign Companies and Chinese Workers: Employee Motivation in the People's Republic of China." *Journal of Organizational Change Management*, Vol. 11, No. 4, 1998, 282-300.

Ji, Tao. "Open Heart, Open Mind: Three Blows to Chinese Prudishness." *China Daily*, 11 September 1998. In *World Press Review*, January 1999, 10–11.

"Joint Efforts Called for Resolving Sino-US Trade Imbalance." *Beijing Review*, 14–20 April 1997, 19–20.

Joseph, Greg. "Sesame Memories." *The San Diego Union-Tribune*, 26 April 1989, C1.

"Joyful Songs Exalt Return of Hong Kong." *China Daily*, 26 May 1997, 1.

Kelley, Jack. "Within Hong Kong, There are Reasons to Fear the Future." *USA Today*, 30 June 1997, 6A.

Kilborn, Robert, Judy Nichols and Stephanie Cook. "Etc...." *The Christian Science Monitor*, 14 February 2000, 24.

Kissinger, Henry A. "No Room for Nostalgia." *Newsweek*, 29 June 1998, 50–52.

_____. "The Philosopher and the Pragmatist." *Newsweek*, 3 March 1997, 42–47.

Klaidman, Daniel. "Cracking a Chinese Code." *Newsweek*, 9 June 1997, 46.

Klein, Joe. "Broken Engagement." *The New Yorker*, 15 June 1998, 4–5.

_____. "Rockets' Red Glare." *The New Yorker*, 15 June 1998, 8–9.

Kornbluh, Peter. "Chile's 'Disappeared' Past." *The Boston Sunday Globe*, 13 September 1998, E2.

Kurtenbach, Elaine. "For Deng's Memorial Service." *The Detroit News*, 23 February 1997, A2.

Kuttner, Robert. "Shock Treatment for Korea is Playing with Fire." *The Boston Sunday Globe*, 4 January 1998, E7.

Kynge, James. "Companies & Finance International: Chinese Book Web Site Set for Launch," *The Financial Times*, 9 December 1999, 33.

Lakshmanan, Indira A. R. "Hong Kong Film Distributors Keep Wary Eye on Beijing." *The Boston Globe*, 24 October 1997, A2.

Lau, Angela. "Immigrants From Colony Mix Trepidation, Apathy." *The San Diego Union-Tribune*, 29 June 1997, A-1, A-18.

Lau, Emily. "After the Handover: New Freedoms Now in Jeopardy." *The San Diego Union-Tribune*, 29 June 1997, G-1, G-6.

Lawrence, Susan V. "A New Critic Tallies the Toll of Corruption: Where Reform Went Wrong." *Far Eastern Economic Review*, 22 October 1998. In *World Press Review*, January 1999, 7–8.

_____. "Edging Toward a Kind of Democracy: China's Official Revolutionary." *Far Eastern Economic Review*, 1 October 1998. In *World Press Review*, January 1999, 9–10.

Lee, Carrie. "GEC Gives Top Post to Cheng," *South China Morning Post*, 2 September 1994, 1.

Lei, Xu. "Old Friends Call for New Order." *China Daily*, 31 May 1997, 1.

Leicester, John. "China's Course Stays True to Deng." *The Detroit Free Press*, 21 February 1997, A5–A6.

Leland, John, and Lynette Clemetson. "Heirs to a Highly Unlikely Future." *Newsweek*, 19 May 1997, 46.

Leonard, Mary. "Faith, Hope, and Policy." *The Boston Sunday Globe*, 26 October 1997, E1, E2.

Leow, A.J. "Holiday Inn Sets Sights on 385 Hotels in Asia." *Business Times*, 20 September 1994, 15.

Levin, Doron. "Leader Brought Greater Economic Freedom." *The Detroit Free Press*, 20 February 1997, A1.

Li, Zijing. "Twelve Nightmares for Beijing." *World Press Review*, March 1996, 19.

Lihong, Shi. "Historians Expose Fake 'Art of War' Discovery." *China Daily*, 24 February 1997, 9.

Lim, Robyn. "The ASEAN Regional Forum: Building on Sand." *Contemporary Southeast Asia*, August 1998, 115–136.

Lin, Jennifer. "China Mourns 'A Great Marxist.'" *The Detroit Free Press*, 20 February 1997, A1, A12.

Liu, Melinda. "Revenge of the Refugees." *Newsweek*, 19 May 1997, 36–39.

Longworth, Jocelyn. "Elmo Meets His Mandarin Cousins." *Kidscreen*. 1 August 1998, 27.

Lynn, Barry. "Unmade in America: The True Cost of a Global Assembly Line," *Harper's Magazine,* June 2002, 34–41.

Ma, Ringo. "The Role of Intermediary in Interpersonal Conflicts in Chinese Culture." *Communication Quarterly,* Summer 1992, 269–278.

McCarthy, Terry. "Is China Next?" *Time*, 21 September 1998, 78.

McElroy, Damien. "International: China's Little Emperors Blamed for Juvenile Crime Wave." *Sunday Telegraph*, London, 7 February 1999, 29.

McGeary, Johanna. "The Big Hand Over." *Time*, 30 June 1997, 36–41.

_____. "Inside China." *Time*, 30 June 1997, 44–56.

_____. "The Next China." *Time*, 3 March 1997, 50–56.

Marcus, David L. "China's Leader Embarks on a Tumultuous Week." *The Boston Sunday Globe*, 26 October 1997, A1, A16-A17.

_____. "From Big Dragon to Big Bird, a Changed Nation: Consumerism Has Taken Hold." *The Boston Globe*, 21 June 1998, A22.

_____. "Tiananmen 'Mistakes' Suggested." *The Boston Sunday Globe*, 2 November 1997, A1, A30.

Mifflin, Lawrie. "But Does Oscar Like It?" *The New York Times*, 30 September 1998: 4.

Miller, Matt. "China's Coming, But Stocks are Hot: Qualcomm a Model of Doing Business." *The San Diego Union-Tribune*, 29 June 1997, 11–12.

_____. "Peaceful Pomp to Accompany Grand Changing of the Guard." *The San Diego Union-Tribune*, 29 June 1997, A1, A18.

_____. "Southeast Asia is More Than Just Hong Kong's Understudy." *The San Diego Union-Tribune*, 29 June 1997, 12.

Mirsky, Jonathan. "China: The Defining Moment." *The New York Review*, 9 January 1997, 33–36.

Mizui, Yoko. "Looking Back on the Historically Inevitable." *The Daily Yomiuri*, 11 December 1997. Database on-line. Available from Lexis-Nexis.

Mohamad, Mahathir. "Call Me Heretic if You Like." *Time*, 21 September 1998, 80.

Moore, Scott. "'Sesame Street': A Monster New Year's Party." *The Washington Post*, 26 December 26, 1993, Y6.

Myers, Steven Lee. "U.S. Sees Few Changes in Chinese Relations." *The New York Times*, 20 February 1997, A1, A11.

Nash, Nathaniel C. "China Gives Big Van Deal to Mercedes." *The New York Times*, 13 July 1995, 1.

Naughton, Keith. "Daimler Thinks Small." *Newsweek*, 21 May 2001, 48.

Nelan, Bruce W. "Can Jiang Hold the Reins of Power?" *Time*, 3 March 1997, 58–59.

Nelson, Jeffery. "Hong Kong Advice: Proceed Carefully." *Arizona Business Gazette*, 19 June 1997, 12.

Nevis, Edwin C. "Using an American Perspective in Understanding Another Culture: Toward a Hierarchy of Needs for the People's Republic of China." In *The Journal of Applied Behavioral Science*, 1983, 249–264.

"The Next Tsar." *New Yorker*, 6 July 1998, 44–53.

"A North-South Struggle Over Human Rights." *Beijing Review*, 14-20 April 1997, 7–10.

O'Connor, John J. "TV Weekend: 'Big Bird' on Great Wall." *The New York Times*, 27 May 1983, 23.

O'Donnell, Lynne. "A Crackdown on 'Splittists.'" *The Australian*, 1 October 1998. In *World Press Review*, January 1999, 8–9.

Oksenberg, Michel. "Deng and His Two Chinas." *The New York Times*, 20 February 1997, Opinion-Editorial Section.

Overholt, William H. "China after Deng." *Foreign Affairs*, May/June 1996, 63–78.

_____. "Twelve Tips for the Markets." *Newsweek*, 19 May 1997, 48, 50.

Pappas, Leslie. "China's New Family Values." *Newsweek*, 24 August 1998, 36.

"Parents Often Feed 'Little Emperors.'" *The Arizona Republic*, 6 December 1998, A22.

Park, Myung-seok and Moon-soo Kim. "Communication Practices in Korea," *Communication Quarterly*, Fall 1992, 398–404.

Parker, Maynard. "Beijing's Toughest Boss." *Newsweek*, 26 May 1997, 41.

Parry, Malcolm. "Sesame Street Set to Travel." *The Vancouver Sun*, 9 September 1997, B6.

Patten, Christopher. "Farewell to My Hong Kong." *Newsweek*, 3 March 1997, 38–39.

_____. "Thinking of China, With Fingers Crossed." *Newsweek*, 14 September 1998, 37–38.

Patton, Susannah. "'Sesame Street' Sign Reads in Many Languages." *The Phoenix Gazette*, 12 April 1995, E7.

Pei, Minxin. "Is China Democratizing?" *Foreign Affairs*, January/February 1998, 68–82.

Plafker, Ted. "US Firms Lose China Deals; Business Reasons to Blame Not Politics, Says Beijing." *South China Morning Post*, 13 July 1995, 1.

Pound, Edward T. "Developer Tied to China Sent Money to Trie Account." *USA Today*, 13 June, 1997, 8A.

Powell, Bill, and Owen Mathews. "An Early Russian Winter." *Newsweek*, 24 August 1998, 40.

_____. "A Fast Drive to Riches." *Newsweek*, 3 March 1997, 32–34.

Proctor, Melanie. "Take a Live 'Walk on Sesame,'" *New Straits Times*, 21 May 1997, 5.

"Regional Reports: China — Constitutional Changes." *World Press Review*, April 1999, 24.

Richburg, Keith B. "Former Judge, Daughter Poles Apart." *The Detroit News*, 29 June 1997, A10.

_____. "New Rules Will Limit Hong Kong Freedoms." *The Arizona Republic*, 15 June 1997, A11.

Ritter, Kera M.C. "A Moment in History: Hong Kong Returns Home." *The Boston Sunday Globe*, 29 June 1997, A26.

Rosenthal, Elisabeth. "Beijing Journal; Buicks, Starbucks and Fried Chicken. Still China?" *The New York Times*, 25 February 2002, 4A.

Ross, Robert S. "An Opportunity for US and China." *The Boston Sunday Globe*, 26 October 1997, E7.

Sachs, Jeffrey. "Global Capitalism." *The Economist*, 12-18 September 1998, 23–25.

Samuelson, Robert J. "Global Capitalism, R.I.P?" *Newsweek*, 14 September 1998, 40–42.

_____. "A World Meltdown?" *Newsweek*, 7 September 1998, 38–39.

Schell, Orville. "The Coming of Mao Zedong Chic." *Newsweek*, 19 May 1997, 42–43.

_____. "Deng's Revolution." *Newsweek*, 3 March 1997, 20–27.

Shenkar, Oded and Simcha Ronen. "The Cultural Context of Negotiations: The Implications of Chinese Interpersonal Norms." *The Journal of Applied Behavioral Sciences*, 1987, 263–275.

Schoof, Renee. "China Calls Family Planning 'No. 1 Difficulty'." *Fresno Bee*, 6 July 1997, A8.

"Sesame Street Goes to China." *The Ottawa Citizen*, 16 February 1998, E2.

Sleeper, Jim. "Toward an End of Blackness." *Harper's Magazine*, May 1997, 35–39, 43.

Sly, Liz. "Party Time in Colony's Final Hours." *The San Diego Union-Tribune*, 30 June 1997, A1, A11.

Soros, George. "Toward a Global Open Society." *The Atlantic Monthly*, January 1998, 20–24, 32.

Spence, Jonathan. "Deng Xiaoping As Past and Prologue." *Time*, 3 March 1997, 69.

Spinelli, John. "Reflections on China." *Union College*, September 1997, 9–12.

Steele, Jonathan. "Nuking the Neighbors." *The Guardian*, 5 January 1999. *In World Press Review*, April 1999, 48.

Stockwin, Harvey. "After the Handover: Will it be China's Joy or Sorrow?" *The San Diego Union-Tribune*, 29 June 1997, G-1, G-6.

Strasser, Steven, and George Wehrfitz. "Out of the Shadows." *Newsweek*, 3 March 1997, 28–29.

Syrett, Michael and Klari Kingston. "GE's Hungarian Light Switch." *Management Today*, April 1995, 52–58.

Talbott, Strobe. "Dealing with the Bomb in South Asia." *Foreign Affairs*, March/April 1999, 110.

Tan, Christopher. "Z-cars to Carry Mitsubishi Marque." *The Business Times Singapore*, 20 June 2001, 23.

Tang, Rose. "Swallowed by Three Gorges." *World Press Review*, February 1998, 40.

Theroux, Paul. "Ghost Stories." *The New Yorker*, 12 May 1997, 54–65.

Thardoor, Shashi. "E Pluribus, India." *Foreign Affairs*, January/February 1998, 128–134.

"30 Years of Sesame Street." *The Gazette*, 28 September 1998, B5.

Tuck, Christopher. "Is the Party Over?" *World Press Review*, March 1996, 16–18.

Turner, Lane. "At the Crossroads." *The Boston Globe Magazine*, 18 January 1998, 16–21, 47–48.

Tyler, Patrick E. "Control of Army is Crucial Issue for China Rulers." *The New York Times*, 23 February 1997, 1.

_____. "Deng Xiaoping, Architect of Modern China, Dies at 92." *The New York Times*, 20 February 1997, A1, A10.

Vatikiotis, Michael. "Growing Anger at Uncle Sam." *World Press Review*, January 1998, 16.

Vlasic, Bill and Bradley A. Stertz. "How Daimler Snared an American Icon." *The Detroit News and Free Press*, 21 May 21, 2000, 1.

Waller, Douglas. "The Secret Missile Deal." *Time*, 30 June 1997, 58.

Walker, Martin. "China Preys on American Minds." *Guardian Weekly*, 6 April, 1997, 6.

Walt, Stephen M. "The Hidden Nature of Systems." *The Atlantic Monthly*, September 1998, 130–134.

Wang, Chen. "Sichuan Feeds 120 Million on Limited Land." *Beijing Review*, 14-20 April 1997, 13–15.

"What's in a Name?" *Los Angeles Times*, 8 January 1985, 22.

Wills, Garry. "Bully of the Free World." *Foreign Affairs*, March/April 1999, 50.

Winchester, Simon. "The Great Skywalk." *World Press Review*, March 1996, 23.

Wo-Lap Lam, Willy, and Frankie Leung. "The Challenges Facing Jiang." *World Press Review*, March 1996, 18–19.

WuDunn, Sheryl. "Can Deng's Heirs Finish the Long March to Capitalism?" *The New York Times*, 21 February 1997, A15.

Yanni, Chen. "HK Countdown in Full Swing." *China Daily*, 21 March 1997, 1–2.

Yanshi, Ren. "A Look at the US Human Rights Record." *Beijing Review*, 17–23 March 1997, 12–19.

Yemma, John. "Thousands Protest, Cheer Jiang in Streets." *The Boston Sunday Globe*, 2 November 1997, A30.

Yong, Deng. "The Asianization Of East Asian Security and The United States' Role." *East Asia: An International Quarterly*, Autumn/Winter 1998, 86–110.

Yong, Wang. "US Adviser: House Should Approve MFN Status." *China Daily Business Weekly*, 22-28 June 1997, 1.

Yum, June Ock. "The Impact of Confucianism on Interpersonal Relationships," *Communication Monographs*, December 1988, 374–388.

Zakaria, Fareed. "Hedging it." *Newsweek*, 3 March 1997, 36–37.

_____. "So Much for Globalization." *Newsweek*, 7 September 1998, 36.

Zarakhovich, Yuri. "A Russian's Lament." *Time*, 21 September 1998, 76.

Zhang, Jiapeng. "Fast-Food Friends." *World Press Review*, March 1996, 10.

Zhao, Quansheng. "Chinese Foreign Policy in the Post-Cold War Era." *World Affairs*, Winter 1997, 114–131.

Zielenziger, Michael. "A Land in Limbo: Two Cultures Head into a World of Questions, Few Answers." *The Detroit Free Press*, 30 June 1997, 1A, 6A–7A.

Zinn, Howard. "Big Government for Whom?" *The Progressive*, April 1999, 17–18.

# ELECTRONIC SOURCES & INTERNET

Andrews, Edmund L., and Laura M. Holson. "Shaping a Global Giant: The Overview; Daimler-Benz Will Acquire Chrysler in $36 Billion Deal that will Reshape Industry." *The New York Times*, 7 May 1998. Database on-line. Available from Lexis-Nexis.

Antononiou, Peter H., and Katherine Whitman. "Understanding Chinese Interpersonal Norms and Effective Management of Sino-Western Joint Ventures." *Multinational Business Review*, Spring 1998. Database on-line. Available from Lexis-Nexis.

"Bass Hotels & Resorts Signs Agreement with inter-touch to Provide Broadband Internet Services at its Properties." PR Newswire, 29 November 2000. Database on-line. Available from Lexis-Nexis.

"Bass Hotels & Resorts to Open Third Hotel in Shanghai." Asia Pulse, 2 February 1999. Database on-line. Available from Lexis-Nexis.

"Bass Proposes Name Change to 'Six Continents' Emphasizing the Global Spread of Business." Database on-line. Available from Lexis-Nexis.

Beach, Sophie. "China's Unseen Unemployed." *Nation* 15 February 1999. Database on-line. Available from Lexis-Nexis.

"Biondi to Keynote Global Emmys' Adapted 'Sesame Street' Set for China; New Services to Launch in China; TNT and Cartoon Network Headed for Berlin; Polish TV Picks Up CTW Show Format; Grundy Kids Series Heads to China." *Electronic Media*, 21 November 1994. Database on-line. Available from Lexis-Nexis.

Blears, James "15 Minutes With ... Michael Gibbs; Renowned Negotiation and Conflict-Resolution Expert Explains What It Takes to Negotiate With the Best of Them." *Business Mexico*, 1 June 1999. Database on-line. Available from Lexis-Nexis.

"Broadcast GE to Sponsor Chinese 'Sesame Street': Chinese Voices for Bert, Ernie and Grover." Asia Intelligence Wire, 15 December 1995. Database on-line. Available from Lexis-Nexis.

The Center for Alternative Development Initiatives. Database on-line. Available from http://www.cadi.ph

"China Bans New Shipbuilding Projects During Remainder of 9th 5-year Plan." AFX News, 5 November 1999. Database on-line. Available from Lexis-Nexis.

"China: China's Rails Gleam with Gold." China Daily, 8 January 2000. Database on-line. Available from Lexis-Nexis.

"China: Companies Flee China Trouble." Electronic Times, 15 June 1989. Database on-line. Available from Lexis-Nexis.

"China: Country Profile," Janet Matthews Information Services; World of Information Country Report, 28 August 2001. Database on-line. Available from Lexis-Nexis.

"China: Economy." Janet Matthews Information Services; World of Information Country Report, 14 September 1999. Database on-line. Available from Lexis-Nexis.

"China Facts & Figures." ABC-CLIO, Inc. (includes information from Europa World Year Book, FAO Production Yearbook and The World Factbook). Database on-line. Available from Lexis-Nexis.

"China: Generation Gap Opens Up in National Fast-Food Fight," China Daily, 16 May 1999. Database on-line. Available from Lexis-Nexis.

"China Hospitality Sector Booming in Shanghai's Pudong." CBNE, 26 March 1998. Database on-line. Available from Lexis-Nexis.

"China Labour Protest Suspended." BBC World News, 22 March 2002. Database on-line. Available from http://news.bbc.co.uk/hi/english/world/asia-pacific/newsid_1886000/1886977.stm.

"China Min: E-Commerce Trade to Hit CNY 10B in 2002 — Report." Wall Street Journal Interactive Edition, 17 February 2000. Database on-line. Available from http://online.wsj. com.

"China: Monetary Policy Committee Weathering Financial Developments." China Business Information Network (CBNET), 20 April 1999. Database on-line. Available from Lexis-Nexis.

"China: Nation Takes on Illiteracy." China Daily, 13 December 1999. Database on-line. Available from Lexis-Nexis.

"China: Public Spending to Bring Hebei to Growth Goal." China Daily, 28 October 1998. Database on-line. Available from Lexis-Nexis.

"Chinese Co-Production of 'Sesame Street' Takes the Next Step in the Development Process." Business Wire, 13 March 1997. Database on-line. Available from Lexis-Nexis.

"Chrysler, Daimler Talks Were a Cloak-and-Dagger Affair; 'Project Gamma' Talks Began in Detroit in January; Schrempp Made the First Pitch." St. Louis Post-Dispatch, 10 May 1998. Database on-line. Available from Lexis-Nexis.

Claire, Sian. "Support for Patten Over Hong Kong Reforms." The Press Association Limited, 13 April 1994. Database on-line. Available from Lexis-Nexis.

Clinton William J. "Interview with Radio Free Asia." Weekly Compilation of Presidential Documents. 29 June 1998, 1207. Database on-line. Available from Lexis-Nexis.

"Companies and Finance: Chrysler/Daimler-Benz Merger." Financial Times, 14 May 1998. Database on-line. Available from Lexis-Nexis.

Courtney, Christine. "Hong Kong Governor Presses Reform Plan, Irks China." Los Angeles Times, 3 December 1993. Database on-line. Available from Lexis-Nexis.

Cox, Chris. "Here's A Bold Agenda for Promoting Freedom in China." Human Events, 11 July 1997, 12. Database on-line. Available from http://www.humaneventsonline.com.

"Doing Business with China: Cultural Aspects." East Asian Executive Reports, 15 January 1991. Database on-line. Available from Lexis-Nexis.

"Eximbank Expands Offerings in China, South Korea." Export Today, November 1998. Database on-line. Available from http://www.tradeport.org/ts/biblio/per. html.

Flanigan, James. "James Flanigan: Where there is No Research the Companies Perish." Los Angeles Times, 25 July 1993. Database on-line. Available from Lexis-Nexis.

Foley, K.P. "China: Visas Of Radio Free Asia Journalists Revoked on Eve Of Clinton Visit." Radio Free Asia, 24 January 1998. Database on-line. Available from Lexis-Nexis.

Forbes, Steve. "Strong Signal." *Forbes*, 13 January 1997, 25. Database on-line. Available from http://www.forbes.com.

Fox, Justin. "America's Most Admired Companies: What's So Great About GE?" *Fortune*, 4 March 2002. Database on-line. Available from http://www.fortune.com.

"GE to Sponsor Chinese 'Sesame Street'; Shanghai Television and Children's Television Workshop to Co-Produce 'Zhima Jie' in China." PR Newswire, 28 November 1995. Database on-line. Available from Lexis-Nexis.

"General Electric and Children's Television Workshop Bring Discovery to Life with New TV Spots for 'Zhima Jie' Viewers in China." Business Wire, 16 June 1998. Database on-line. Available from Lexis-Nexis.

"General Electric and Children's Television Workshop Sign Agreement to Produce and Spin Off Educational Series." Business Wire, 20 April 1999. Database on-line. Available from Lexis-Nexis.

General Electric Homepage. Database on-line. Available from *www.ge.com.*

"The Global Company." *Financial Times*, 10 October 1997. Database on-line. Available from Lexis-Nexis.

Grant, Linda. "The Management Model that Jack Built; John Welch has Slashed GE's Torpid Work Force, Toppled Bureaucratic Walls and Now Says His Huge Corporation Must Beat with the Heart of a Small Business." *Los Angeles Times*, 9 May 1993. Database on-line. Available from Lexis-Nexis.

Gray, Valerie Lynn. "Casting Your Net Abroad." *Black Enterprise*, May 1998. Database on-line. Available from Lexis-Nexis.

Gundersen, Merethe. "Cultural Consequences of International Standard Systems: A Comparison of German and American Enterprise Systems in Norwegian Organizations. Database on-line. Available from http://iris24.ifi.uib.no/proceedings/electronic-papers/ 042-150-Gundersen-electronic.pdf.

Gurdon, Meghan Cox. "China's New Strategy on Hong Kong: Beijing Seeks to Remove Colony from Talks on Democratization." *The San Francisco Chronicle*, 23 February 1993. Database on-line. Available from Lexis-Nexis.

Harding, James. "Long March to Mass Market: Early Setbacks Aside, Foreign Car Companies are Keen to Stay in China Because of its Huge Potential." *Financial Times*, 25 June 1997. Database on-line. Available from Lexis-Nexis.

Hill, Andrew. "Running on a Full Tank: Jack Welch Tells Andrew Hill There is No Place for Gamesmanship and Succession Politics at General Electric." *Financial Times*, 9 November 1999. Database on-line. Available from Lexis-Nexis.

"Holiday Inn Downtown Leads Hotels in Room Occupancy Rate in Beijing." Xinhua News Service, 15 April 15, 2000. Database on-line. Available from Lexis-Nexis.

"Holiday Inn Makes its Bed in Pudong." *Daily China News*, 18 March 1998. Database on-line. Available from Lexis-Nexis.

"Holiday Inn Opens New Club." *Daily China News*, 23 March 1998. Database on-line. Available from Lexis-Nexis.

"Hong Kong: Amnesty International and the Hong Kong Handover." Amnesty International Document, April 1998. Database on-line. Available from http://www.amnesty. org.

"Hong Kong Governor in Australia Speaks on Chinese Reform and Hong Kong's Future." BBC Summary of World Broadcasts, 21 February 1994. Database on-line. Available from Lexis-Nexis.

"Hotel Companies Scale Back China Developments; China: Hotel Mgmt. Companies are Scaling Back Development Projects." *Tour & Travel News*, 9 September 1991. Database on-line. Available from Lexis-Nexis.

"House Passes Final China Bill, Radio Free Asia Funding." *Congressional Quarterly Weekly Report*, 17 November 1997, 2865. Database on-line. Available from Lexis-Nexis.

Hughes, Duncan. "Power to Monitor Pensions Upgraded." *South China Morning Post*, 15 October 1995. Database on-line. Available from Lexis-Nexis.

Hughes John. "Radio Free Asia Deserves a First Birthday Present." *Christian Science Monitor*, 17 September 1997, 19. Database on-line. Available from http://www.csmonitor.com.

"Human Rights and Business As Usual." *The Progressive*, August 1998. Database on-line. Available from http://www.progressive.org.

"In China, The Rich Seek To Become the 'Big Rich.'" *The Washington Post*, 16 March 2002. Database on-line. Available from http://www.washingtonpost. com/ac2/wp-dyn/A38967-2002Mar 16.

"Jiang and Clinton Meet the Press." *Beijing Review*, July 20–26, 1998. Database on-line. Available from http://www.bjreview.com.cn.

"Jiang on Problems Between US and China." *Beijing Review*. July 13–19, 1998. Database on-line. Available from http://www.bjreview.com.cn.

Jiang, Wandi. "Explaining China's Population Policy to the World." *Beijing Review*, 14–20 April 1997, 16–18.

_____. "Fostering Political Democracy from the Bottom Up." *Beijing Review*, 16–22 March 1998. Database on-line. Available from http://www.bjreview.com. cn.

Kampfner, John, and John Ridding, and George Parker. "Major Warns to Uphold Hong Kong Accords." *Financial Times* (London), 5 March 1996. Database on-line. Available from Lexis-Nexis.

Kazer, William. "CHN: 'Sesame Street' Makes China Debut." AAP Newsfeed, 16 February 1998. Database on-line. Available from Lexis-Nexis.

Kemper, Cynthia. "Global Sales Success Depends on Cultural Insight." *World Trade*, May 1998. Database on-line. Available from Lexis-Nexis.

Key, Jeffrey. "Beyond 'Tilting Both Ways': A New Post-Cold War South Asia Policy." *Asian Affairs: An American Review*, Summer 1998, 89. Database on-line. Available from http://www.heldref.org/html/body_aa.html.

Kilborn, Robert and Lance Carden. "The World." *Christian Science Monitor*, 6 July 1998, 2. Database on-line. Available from http://www.csmonitor.com.

Klein, Jill Gabrielle, and Richard Ettenson, and Marlene D. Morris. "The Animosity Model of Foreign Product Purchase: An Empirical Test in the People's Republic of China." *Journal of Marketing*, Winter 1998. Database on-line. Available from Lexis-Nexis.

Kreisler, Nancy H. "Companies Speeding Beijing Exodus." *The New York Times*, 7 June 1989. Database on-line. Available from Lexis-Nexis.

Lau, Vivian. "Anti-Discrimination Legislation in Hong Kong." *International Commercial Litigation*, June 1996. Database on-line. Available from Lexis-Nexis.

Leicester, John. "Gov. Patten and China Vie For Hong Kong's Hearts and Minds." The Associated Press, 26 October 1993. Database on-line. Available from Lexis-Nexis.

Lenckus, Dave. "USA: Adventures in Risk Management Abroad — Communication, Diplomacy Go Long Way in Overseas Joint Adventures." *Business Insurance*, 5 December 1994. Database on-line. Available from Lexis-Nexis.

Li, Haibo. "Harmony Benefits Both Sides." *Beijing Review*, 29 June–5 July 1998. Database on-line. Available from http://www.bjreview.com.cn.

_____. "Pragmatic Sino-US Ties." *Beijing Review*, 20–26 July 1998. Database on-line. Available from http://www.bjreview.com.cn.

_____. "Talking Straight about Tibet." *Beijing Review*, 11–17 May 1998. Database on-line. Available from http://www.bjreview.com.cn.

Li, Jinhui & Zou Sicheng. "Sino-US Relations Urged to Outgrow Their Limits." *Beijing Review*, 29 June–5 July 1998. Database on-line. Available from http://www.bjreview.com. cn.

Li, Ning. "Government Restructuring: A Revolution in New Period." *Beijing Review*, 27 April–3 May 1998. Database on-line. Available from http://www. bjreview.com.cn.

Li, Rongxia. "1 Million Laid-Off Workers Re-employed." *Beijing Review*, 13-19 July 1998. Database on-line. Available from http://www.bjreview.com.cn.

Ling, Connie. "Junk E-Mail Flourishes in China as Fast Growth Bypasses Manners." *The Wall Street Journal Interactive Edition*, 15 February 2000. Database on-line. Available from http://online.wsj.com.

Liu, Hua Qui. "A New Page in the History of Sino-US Relations." *Beijing Review*, 16–22 March 1998. Database on-line. Available from http://www.bjreview.com. cn.

Liu, Melinda, and Watson Russell. "China Kills A Few Chickens." *Newsweek*, 11 January 1999, 40. Database on-line. Available from Lexis-Nexis.

Maccoby, Michael. "Narcissistic Leaders: The Incredible Pros, the Inevitable Cons." *Harvard Business Review*, January/February 2000. Database on-line. Available from Lexis-Nexis.

McClenahen, John S. "Light in the East." *Industry Week*, 2 March 1998. Database on-line. Available from Lexis-Nexis.

"Military Historian Turns In Party Card To Protest Gen. Tran DO's Expulsion." Radio Free Asia, 26 January 1999. Database on-line. Available from http://www. rfa.org.

Mortimer, Jeff, and Chris Wright. "Do Not Wear Shorts on the Street; Auto Executives Cope with Foreign Languages, Customs and Taboos." *Automotive News International*, 2 May 2000. Database on-line. Available from Lexis-Nexis.

Nagy, Barbara A. "State Companies Lured by China's Vast Market; Northeast Meets Far East." *The Hartford Courant*, 8 July 1996. Database on-line. Available from Lexis-Nexis.

"Nanjing to Build 200-m High Building." Xinhua General Overseas News Service, 18 April 1993. Database on-line. Available from Lexis-Nexis.

Ngiam, Desmond. "New Balance Shoes Made in PD Out Next Month." *New Straits Times* (Malaysia), 20 November 1997. Database on-line. Available from Lexis-Nexis.

Ni, Feng. "Recent Development in Sino-US Relations." *Beijing Review*, 29 June–5 July 1998. Database on-line. Available from http://www.bjreview.com.cn.

"Patten Promises to Sweep All Before Him." *South China Morning Post*, 21 June 1992. Database on-line. Available from Lexis-Nexis.

"Patten's Electoral Reform Remains Divisive Issue." *The Nikkei Weekly*, 20 December 1993. Database on-line. Available from Lexis-Nexis.

Perlez, Jane. "GE Finds Tough Going in Hungary." *New York Times*, 25 July 1994. Database on-line. Available from Lexis-Nexis.

Platt, Kevin. "To Head Off A 'Cold War P,' China and Us Try to Warm Up Relations." *Christian Science Monitor*, 28 October 1996. Database on-line. Available from http://www.csmonitor.com.

"A Political Football Called Trade." *Business Week*, 14 April 1997, 118. Database on-line. Available from Lexis-Nexis.

"Qian Talks About International Issues and China's Foreign Policies" *Beijing Review*, 30 March-5 April 1998. Database on-line. Available from http://www. bjreview.com.cn.

"Radio Free Asia Campaign," 13 August 1998. Database on-line. Available from http://www.rfa.org.

Rae, Ian. "Westerners Need Patience to Crack Chinese Puzzle." *Sunday Times*, 9 November 1997. Database on-line. Available from Lexis-Nexis.

"Railway Connecting East China with Europe to Open Soon." BBC Summary of World Broadcasts, 31 December 1999. Database on-line. Available from Lexis-Nexis.

"Reforms Aimed at Beefing up Parliament's Powers." *Hong Kong Standard*, 18 October 1997. Database on-line. Available from http://online.hkstandard.com.

Richter, Richard. " A Message From the President of Radio Free Asia." Radio Free Asia. Database on-line. Available from http://www.rfa.org.

Rosenbaum, Gail. "Long Distance Relationships: Advice for International Dairy-Products Trade." *Cheese Market News*, 27 March 1992. Database on-line. Available from Lexis-Nexis.

Savitt, Scott. "AWSJ: China and the Internet." Dow Jones Newswires, 1 February 2000, *Wall Street Journal Interactive Edition*. Database on-line. Available from http://online.wsj.com.

Schmetzer, Uli. "Democracy Setting on Hong Kong: China Says No Elected Legislature in 1997." *Chicago Tribune*, 1 September 1994. Database on-line. Available from Lexis-Nexis.
_____. "Hong Kong Reformer to Defy China." *Chicago Tribune*, 29 November 1993. Database on-line. Available from Lexis-Nexis.

Scott, Ann. "Search for China's Offshore Oil at Critical Stage; Odds Getting Longer Under Adverse Working Conditions." United Press International, 6 June 1994. Database on-line. Available from Lexis-Nexis.

Selmer, Jan. "The Expatriate Manager in China: A Research Note." *Human Resource Management Journal*, 1998. Database on-line. Available from Lexis-Nexis.

"Shanghai 'Yuppies' Lap Up Luxury." *The Nikkei Weekly*, 12 February 2002. Database on-line. Available from Lexis-Nexis.

Silverman, Dick. "China and Taiwan Look Down the Road." *Footwear News*, 13 February 1984. Database on-line. Available from Lexis-Nexis.

Six Continents Hotels, corporate information. Database on-line. Available from www.sixcontinentshotels.com.

Smith, Craig S. "Private Lessons: In China, Parents Seek to Give their Children an Advantage by Choosing Private Schools." *The Wall Street Journal Interactive Edition*, 20 October 1997. Database on-line. Available from http://online. wsj.com.

Snow, Nancy. "The Smith-Mundt Act of 1948." *Peace Review*, December 1998, 619. Database on-line. Available from http://www.usfca.edu/peacereview/archive. htm.

Snowdown, Sondra. "International Business Protocol." *Chemical Engineering*, 25 November 1985. Database on-line. Available from Lexis-Nexis.

Strasser, Steven, and Melinda Liu. " Skirmish in Beijing." *Newsweek*, 6 July 1998, 26. Database on-line. Available from Lexis-Nexis.

Sweeney, Shari M. "Illuminating Changes," *Inside Business*, September 1997. Database on-line. Available from Lexis-Nexis.

Ta Kung Pao. "China-Owned Paper on Amending Law to Deal With Child Immigrants." BBC Summary of World Broadcasts, 15 July 1997. Database on-line. Available from Lexis-Nexis.

Thomas, Kate. "Chinese Market: A Thing of Beauty; US Skin-Care, Hair-Care Firms Find Few Wrinkles." *Journal of Commerce*, 1 October 1997. Database on-line. Available from Lexis-Nexis.

"Three Men Who Frighten the Party." *Economist*, 2 January 1999, 35. Database on-line. Available from Lexis-Nexis.

Tsang, Eric W. K. "Can *Guanxi* be a Source of Sustained Competitive Advantage for Doing Business in China?" *Academy of Management Executive*, May 1998. Database on-line. Available from Lexis-Nexis.

Tsang Yok-sing. "Old Guard Needs to Learn a New Role." *South China Morning Post*, 10 March 1998. Database on-line. Available from Lexis-Nexis.

"The US." *Christian Science Monitor*, 25 June.1998, 2. Database on-line. Available from http://www.csmonitor.com.

Walker, Gordon R., and Mark A. Fox. "Gobalization: An Analytical Framework," *Indiana Journal of Global Legal Studies*. Spring 1996. Database on-line. Available from http://ijgls.indiana.edu/archive/03/02/walker.shtml.

Wang, Ping. "Opening China's Financial Market In a Planned Way." *Beijing Review*, 23-29 November 1998. Database on-line. Available from http://www. bjreview.com.cn.

"Welcome to Radio Free Asia on the Internet," 11 December 1998. Database on-line. Available from Lexis-Nexis.

Wen, Cui and Ralph Wenge. "Sesame Street in China." CNN World Report, 2 April 1997. Transcript available from Lexis-Nexis.

Wen, Hui. "China, US Should Rethink Relations." *Beijing Review*, 22 September 1997. Database on line. Available from http://www.bjreview.com.cn.

Wen, Sheng. "Chinese Economy Faces Major Adjustment." *Beijing Review*, 23–29 November 1998. Database on-line. Available from http://www.bjreview.com.cn.

"What Regional Hotels Offer." *Asia Today*, December 1994. Database on-line. Available from Lexis-Nexis.

Wilson, Kemmons. "How did Holiday Inn Begin?" Database on-line. Available from http://www.kwilson.com.

Winship, Frederick M. "Evacuation of Americans in China Gains Momentum." UPI, 7 June 1989. Database on-line. Available from Lexis-Nexis.

Wolniansky, Natalia and Garry P. Leon. "A New Hungarian Spring?" *Management Review*, July 1991. Database on-line. Available from Lexis-Nexis.

Wong, Yim Yu, and Thomas E. Maher, and George Lee. "The Strategy of an Ancient Warrior: An Inspiration for International Managers." *Multinational Business Review*, Spring 1998. Database on-line. Available from Lexis-Nexis.

"Xinhua Carries 'Full Text' of Report on Social, Economic Development Plan." BBC Worldwide Monitoring, 17 March 2002. Database on-line. Available from Lexis-Nexis.

Yoko Mizui, "Looking Back on the Historically Inevitable." *The Daily Yomiuri*, 11 December 1997. Database on-line. Available from Lexis-Nexis.

Yuthok, Kunzang. "Dream of Riches Blinds the US to Real China." *The Seattle Times*, 27 May 1994. Database on-line. Available from Lexis-Nexis.

Zhang, Liping. "Chronology in Sino-US Relations." *Beijing Review*, 29 June–5 July 1998. Database on-line. Available from http://www.bjreview.com.cn.

Zhaoxing, Li. "Toward Improved China-US Relations." *China Business Review*, May/June 1998, 32. Database on-line. Available from http://www.chinabusinessreview.com.

"Zhu Asks Officials to Implement Economic Policies Without Fear." *AFX News*, 24 November 1999. Database on-line. Available from Lexis-Nexis.

Zinsmeister, Karl. "Why China Doesn't Scare Me." *The American Enterprise*, July/August 1998. Database on-line. Available from http://www.taemag.com.

# VIDEORECORDINGS

Turner Original Productions, Inc.: CNN Perspectives Presents COLD WAR, 1998, videocassettes.

# UNPUBLISHED MATERIALS

Metthe, Diane. "The Win-Win Conflict Resolution Strategy: A Dramatistic Analysis." Master's Thesis, Bridgewater State College, April 1988.

Shi Hao Yu. "Managing Intercultural Rhetorical Communication: A Case Study of the Delegates from the People's Republic of China in the United States." Master's Thesis, Bridgewater State College, May 1988.

# INTERVIEWS

Carrie, Daniel F. The Foxboro Company. Interview by authors, March 2001. Tape recording. Foxboro, Massachusetts.

Du, Chris. Shanghai-Foxboro Company, Ltd. Interview by authors, May 2001. Tape recording. Shanghai, People's Republic of China.

Frecklington, Shane. The American Chamber of Commerce in Shanghai. Interview by authors. Tape recording. Shanghai, People's Republic of China.

Godek, Michael J. The Foxboro Company. Interview by authors, March 2001. Tape recording. Foxboro, Massachusetts.

Gu, Amy. The American Chamber of Commerce in Shanghai. Interview by authors, June 2001. Tape recording. Shanghai, People's Republic of China.

Lau, Grace. Crowne Plaza Nanjing. Interview by authors, June 2001. Tape recording. Nanjing, People's Republic of China.

Masood, Mahmoud. Shanghai Holiday Inn Crowne Plaza. Interview by authors, May 2001. Tape recording. Shanghai, People's Republic of China.

Miller, Paul. The Foxboro Company. Interview by authors, March 2001. Tape recording. Foxboro, Massachusetts.

Pariseau, Ron. The Foxboro Company. Interview by authors, March 2001. Tape recording. Foxboro, Massachusetts.

Saligram, Ravi. Six Continents' Hotels. Interview by authors, November 2001. Tape recording. Atlanta, Georgia.

Shi, Mingzheng. Council on International Educational Exchange. Interview by authors, June 2001. Tape recording. Shanghai, People's Republic of China.

Sun, John. Foxboro-APV China. Interview by authors, May 2001. Tape recording. Shanghai, People's Republic of China.

Westhaver, Edmund D. The Foxboro Company. Interview by authors, March 2001. Tape recording. Foxboro, Massachusetts.

Yang, Lihong. Council on International Educational Exchange. Interview by authors, June 2001. Tape recording. Shanghai, People's Republic of China.

Yun, Lu. Shanghai-Foxboro Company, Ltd. Interview by authors, May 2001. Tape recording. Shanghai, People's Republic of China.

# Index